Music in the Sky

Music in the Sky

The Life, Art, and Teachings of the 17th Gyalwa Karmapa Ogyen Trinley Dorje

by Michele Martin

Snow Lion Publications
Ithaca, New York ✦ Boulder, Colorado

Snow Lion Publications
P.O. Box 6483
Ithaca, New York 14851
(607) 273-8519
www.snowlionpub.com

Printed in Canada on acid-free recycled paper.

ISBN 1-55939-195-2

Library of Congress Cataloging-in-Publication Data

Martin, Michele, 1942–
  Music in the sky : the life, art, and teachings of the 17th Gyalwa Karmapa
Ogyen Trinley Dorje / by Michele Martin.
     p. cm.
  Includes bibliographical references and index.
  ISBN 1-55939-195-2 (alk. paper)
  1. Ogyen Trinley Dorje, Karma-pa XVII, 1985- 2. Kar-ma-pa lamas—
China—Tibet—Biography. 3. Spiritual life—Kar-ma-pa (Sect) 4. Kar-ma-pa
(Sect)—History—20th century. 5. Kar-ma-pa (Sect)—Doctrines. I. Title.
BQ7682.9.A2O396 2003
294.3'923'092—dc21
                                                          2003005516

Text designed and typeset in Adobe Garamond
by Gopa & Ted2.

To the long life and flourishing activity
of the seventeenth Gyalwa Karmapa Ogyen Trinley Dorje
May all beings find peace, joy, and liberation

Contents

Acknowledgments

Aʟʟ ᴛʜɪɴɢs ᴀʀɪsᴇ in interdependence, a truth most evident in the process of gathering the material for this book. The inspiration for the Karmapa's life story was a version compiled in Tibetan by Tendzin Namgyal, a leading authority on the history of the Karmapas. He incorporated into a short biography sections from a Tibetan text recording the Karmapa's activities. This initial account of twenty pages was a kernel that expanded into the whole section of the Karmapa's life story. It was augmented by numerous conversations and came to include information from the Karmapa himself, from his sister, Ngödrup Pelzom, and from three of the monks who fled with the Karmapa: Lama Tsewang Tashi from Nenang Monastery (Nenang Lama), Lama Tsultrim Gyaltsen from Tsurphu, and Dargye, his driver and now the Karmapa's attendant. The second driver, Tsewang Tashi, also contributed. They were all most generous with their time, patiently explaining the details of their knowledge and experience. Research in other texts, on the Internet, and in films also provided useful information.

Khenchen Thrangu Rinpoche kindly answered many questions about difficult passages in the poetry. Dzogchen Ponlop Rinpoche contributed the life stories of the first sixteen Karmapas. The histories of how the three incarnate lamas were discovered came from those who were directly involved in the process. Tenzin Dorjee, the General Secretary to Jamgön Kongtrul Rinpoche, kindly gave permission to excerpt the main events from the publication *EMA HO! The Reincarnation of The Third Jamgön Kongtrul.* Nenang Lama of Pawo Rinpoche's monastery was also interviewed for the account of Pawo Rinpoche's discovery. Dilyak Drupön Rinpoche and Sangye Trinley provided the narrative of how Dabzang Rinpoche's reincarnation was found. Tashi Gawa was a great help in working with the Karmapa's talks and Khenpo Gawang kindly assisted in deciphering some of the more difficult passages. Valuable editorial suggestions came from Lois DePiesse, Daia Gerson, Peter van Deurzen, Sylvia Warner, and in the end, from Tracy Davis, who worked on the final manuscript. One could not wish for a better editor. Special thanks go to Wangyal Shawa, Head of the Digital Map and Geospatial Information Center at Princeton University, for the wonderful maps and to Naomi Schmidt and Seiji Tsutsumi for their help with the photographs. Conversations with Sidney Piburn of Snow Lion were a wonderful help at all points along the way. His enthusiasm for the book and his sensitive feedback have clearly improved the end result.

Whatever is meritorious here has come from the generous gifts of others. Any faults and infelicities reside with me. May any merit gathered by this text be a cause to bring living beings beyond number into vast and brilliant awakening.

Introduction

THE LIGHT OF ONE CANDLE passing on to the next, and that one passing on to another, and another: this is the traditional image used to illustrate the series of rebirths known in Buddhism as reincarnation. In the case of an enlightened being, these rebirths are taken consciously, motivated by a desire to benefit all living beings and made possible by the depth and clarity of an individual's realization. The first such reincarnation (*tulku*) was recognized in thirteenth-century Tibet. His name was the Gyalwa Karmapa, "The Victorious One of Enlightened Activity." Thereafter, he continued to return, generation after generation, until the present seventeenth Karmapa, who is the subject of this book. The Karmapa is said to embody the activity of all the buddhas of the past, present, and future. Citing ancient texts, traditional histories trace his lives back for eons and continue it forward into the distant future.

Within Tibetan Buddhism, there are four main orders or traditions of transmission, practice, and philosophy. Their differences are mainly evident by whether they emphasize study or practice. These four traditions (Nyingma, Gelukpa, Sakya, and Kagyu) continue to thrive due to the unbroken succession of teachers and students who have kept alive the essential wisdom found in their individual texts and practices. As its leader, His Holiness the Gyalwa Karmapa holds, teaches, and inspires the lineage of the Kagyu order, which is known for its meditative practices, its focus on retreat, and the many realized masters it has produced. The Karmapa is also famous for the Black Crown, a symbol of his wisdom mind, which he wears during a special ceremony. Followers believe that the mere sight of it brings liberation.

Like the Dalai Lama, the Karmapa is regarded as an embodiment of compassion, represented by the deity Chenrezik. The sole purpose of the Karmapa's incarnation is to lead living beings from the suffering of samsara into freedom—the realization of mind's deepest, pure nature. This full awakening, or enlightenment, is possible for every living being who sincerely engages in practice. The stages of this path to liberation are experientially based, giving direct access to another way of being. The Karmapa is said to have traveled this path and fully realized ultimate reality, and this has opened the door to the many unusual events that surround him.

What Westerners might consider magical and impossible Tibetans see as a reflection of the multivalent reality described in the Vajrayana Buddhism that permeates their culture. The Vajrayana tradition emphasizes practices involving visualization and a direct focus on the nature of mind, which reveal increasingly vast dimensions of reality. However great these may be, nothing is excluded; even the smallest detail is not left out. The events of daily life, the alighting of a special bird, the portent of dreams, exceptional weather, unusual sounds—all are constellated in a worldview that imbues them with spiritual significance

The story that unfolds here implies and describes other worlds—cultural, spiritual, and philosophical. It begins with the previous (sixteenth) Karmapa giving his disciple a letter in which he had predicted his next incarnation. Known as the Last Testament, this document is unique to the Karmapas. Before passing away, the Karmapa composes a text, usually in poetic form, that reveals where and when he will be reborn and indicates his new parents' names and other circumstances that might surround his birth. In this way, the Last Testament guides the Karmapa's disciples to discover the new incarnation.

The main events of the seventeenth Karmapa's life depicted in this book come from several sources. Central is the text that the Karmapa brought with him when he escaped from Tibet. Recorded by the administration of Tsurphu Monastery,[1] his main seat in Tibet, it catalogues the events of the Karmapa's life, covering everything from how he was discovered to donors who visit, miracles that he manifested, and his travels to and from the monastery. This was the only book the Karmapa was able to bring out of Tibet when he escaped. Another source was one of the Karmapa's older sisters, Ngödrup Pelzom, who was his main caregiver during his younger years. Now living with the Karmapa in India, she vividly remembered many stories about him and the nomad life they shared. The stories of how he discovered three incarnate lamas (those who consciously take rebirth to benefit others) came from the people who were directly involved. The account of the escape is based on conversations with three of the monks who participated in the planning and execution of his flight from Tibet and accompanied him on the arduous journey to India. Interwoven throughout the life story are my experiences at Tsurphu over the eight years from 1988 to 1996, including the Karmapa's hair-cutting ceremony and his enthronement, plus a number of long visits to his temporary residence at Gyutö Ramoche University in India from 2000 to 2002, where I assisted as a translator for him. All of the translations in the book, both written and oral, are my responsibility unless otherwise noted.

This variety of sources accounts for the differences of style evident in parts of the text. Some sections are relatively bare-bones, reflecting the Tibetan records, and others are more detailed, fleshed out by people who participated in the events. To give some background to the perspective of the text, the story line has been broadened with descriptions of Tibetan culture, both inside and outside of Tibet, plus explanations of Buddhist texts and practices when relevant. My hope is that in the process of reading about the Karmapa's extraordinary life, the reader will also learn something about Buddhism and Tibetan culture.

The original Tibetan text is full of honorifics, but they have been kept to a minimum in the translation. To Tibetan ears, presenting the names of revered teachers without their usual titles and poetic epithets is almost shocking; however, for the Westerner, these lengthy names can hinder the flow of meaning. Hence, instead of His Holiness the Gyalwa Karmapa, the text will simply refer to him as the Karmapa; instead of His Holiness the Dalai Lama, the Dalai Lama, and so forth. (For similar reasons, many of the specific names and places have been placed in footnotes so that the historical record is preserved for those who wish to consult it.) Until a Karmapa is enthroned, he is not yet considered the Karmapa, and therefore, previous to September 1992, he is usually referred to as the young incarnation or, in Tibetan, the *yangsi*.

The focus of the book is on the Karmapa as a religious figure and on the Buddhism of Tibet, assuming that it is the subtle explanations of mind and the practices leading to realization that draw us to the Buddhist teachings and not the politics, which are endemic to any institution. The book is divided into four parts. His life story covers the years from his birth and the unusual events of his young life, through his miraculous escape and years in India. The second section incorporates his teachings, given in northern India from 2000 to 2002 and presented in chronologically ordered sets. It is interesting to note how the subjects of his talks and his concerns as a newly-arrived fourteen-year-old shift as his studies evolve and as he gains more experience. A selection of his poems, each followed by a brief commentary, fills the third section, and the fourth contains historical background: a traditional narrative of the Karmapa's lineage, histories of the Karmapa's sixteen previous incarnations, and the prophetic songs of the sixteenth Karmapa. The Karmapa has a natural gift for brushwork and enjoys making drawings, several of which are reproduced in the color sections. The photographs chronicle significant events in his life or capture an engaging portrait of him; they also include images of people important to him. Finally, an appendix lists and identifies the Tibetan names, and a glossary provides brief definitions of Buddhist and Tibetan terms.

It is my hope that readers will gain a clearer sense of Buddhism, of Tibet, and of who the seventeenth Karmapa is through reading his life story and teachings, enjoying his poetry and art, and looking at the rich history of his lineage.

Part I

The Life Story of the Seventeenth Karmapa

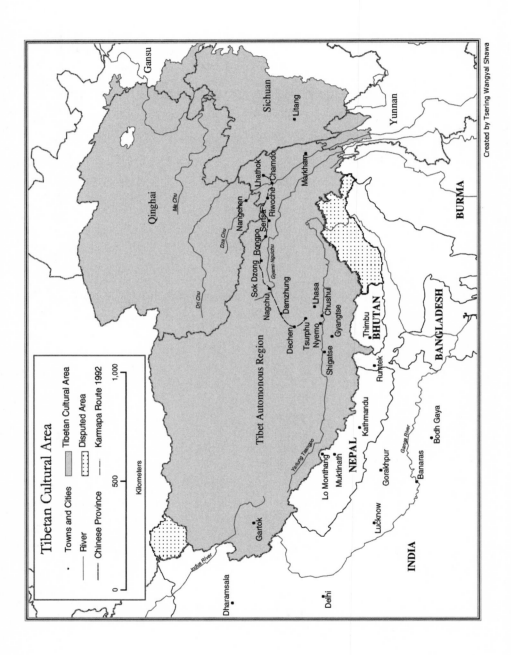

Tibetan Cultural Area

Towns and Cities
River
Chinese Province

Tibetan Cultural Area
Disputed Area
Karmapa Route 1992

Kilometers
0   500   1,000

Created by Tsering Wangyal Shawa

The Discovery

I N LATE 1981, the sixteenth Karmapa, Rangjung Rigpe Dorje, passed away in Zion, Illinois. The years that followed saw much speculation about where he would take rebirth. Tibet was a strong contender. Not long before he died, the Karmapa said to Khenpo Karthar Rinpoche,[2] abbot of the Karmapa's main seat in the West, "My body, these five skandhas, will remain in America, and my consciousness will go to Tibet. Now I can see my father and mother very clearly. Especially, I can see all samsara and nirvana as clearly as if they were in the palm of my hand."[3] After the cremation ceremonies for the Karmapa at his main seat, Rumtek Monastery in Sikkim, India, it was discovered that he had left two footprints in the ashes. They faced north to Tibet.

Before passing away, through the vision of his unobscured wisdom, the Karmapa composed his Last Testament indicating where his reincarnation would be born. In 1981, he wrapped it as a protection amulet and gave it to his close disciple, Situ Rinpoche,[4] who recalled:

> His Holiness was staying in a large suite (No. 177) at the Oberoi Grand in Calcutta and had wanted me to stay with him. We were together for five days, and he gave me the protection amulet (*srung 'khor*) toward the end of our stay. During the day he wanted to go out to buy birds, to see sites such as the Victoria Palace and the museums. He asked me to accompany him, as it had been a long time since we had seen each other. During this time, he gave a lot of advice and told stories from the past. Every evening we talked after dinner. Then once, after I had offered him the fresh orange juice he liked, and not long before we went to bed, he gave me the protection amulet, saying, "This is a very important protection." He did not say, "Open it in the future," or "You will need it." He simply added, "It will be very beneficial for you." I thought it was just a protection amulet. Usually, Tibetan lamas create these out of a piece of paper that has a printed or drawn mandala of a particular deity. It is folded in a special

way to make a square shape, wrapped in colored strings, and enclosed in cloth or leather. This one was enclosed in yellow brocade and I used to wear it around my neck on a gold chain.[5]

Almost ten years later, Situ Rinpoche had the intuition to open the sewn amulet and found an envelope with the words "Open in the Iron Horse Year." On March 19, 1992, a meeting was finally arranged that included the four main tulkus of the Kagyu lineage—Situ Rinpoche, Jamgön Kongtrul Rinpoche, Gyaltsap Rinpoche, and Shamar Rinpoche. They convened in the reception room of the sixteenth Karmapa at Rumtek Monastery to interpret the Last Testament and decide on how they would search for the new incarnation. Situ Rinpoche recalls:

> During the first day, I made a prostration and offered this letter to the Rinpoches. Our late Jamgön Kongtrul Rinpoche and Gyaltsap Rinpoche were very happy, their eyes were full of tears, and I, too, felt that way. Then there was a very long discussion that went on for hours and hours, and finally we decided to interpret the letter. The entire interpretation was written down by the late Jamgön Rinpoche, who made notes for every single interpretation we made.[6]

A few days after the meeting, Jamgön Kongtrul Rinpoche was interviewed on film. When asked about the letter, he replied, "The instructions of the Gyalwa Karmapa are very clear. They are very clear and very precise. That is why we are all very confident about finding His Holiness."[7]

The letter that they were discussing held the following words:

> Emaho. Self-awareness is always bliss;
> The dharmadhatu has no center nor edge.
>
> From here to the north [in] the east of [the Land of] Snow
> Is a country where divine thunder spontaneously blazes.
> [In] a beautiful nomad's place with the sign of a cow,
> The method is Döndrub and the wisdom is Lolaga.
> [Born in] the year of the one used for the earth
> [With] the miraculous, far-reaching sound of the white one:[8]
> [This] is the one known as Karmapa.
>
> He is sustained by Lord Dönyö Drupa;
> Being nonsectarian, he pervades all directions;

Not staying close to some and distant from others,
   he is the protector of all beings:
The sun of the Buddha's Dharma that benefits others always blazes.

After analyzing the text and putting this knowledge together with what they knew of Tibetan geography, the lamas[9] offered their explanations. The letter opens with *Emaho*, which means "How wondrous! Amazing!" Tibetan songs of realization often begin with this word. It opens up the mind to understand what follows. The next two lines express the essence of realization. *Self-awareness* refers to wisdom being aware of its own nature; this is a state of profound and pure *bliss*. *Dharmadhatu* means "the expanse of all phenomena," one of the many synonyms for the ultimate nature of mind. This vast reality is limitless, without beginning or end, without *center* or circumference, beyond time and space.

Having opened out another dimension, the letter's next three lines describe the Karmapa's place of birth. He was born to a nomad family in the northern part of eastern Tibet (the Land of Snow), in the area of Lhathok, which translates as "divine (*lha*) thunder (*thog*)."[10] The name of the remote nomadic community where he was born is Bagor, of which *ba* means "cow."[11] The next line indicates his parents where *method*, the masculine principle, refers to his father, *Döndrub*, and *wisdom*, the feminine principle, to his mother, *Lolaga*. *The one used for the earth* points to an animal that plows, and the Karmapa was born in the Year of the Wood Ox. *The far-reaching sound of the white one* indicates the sound of the conch shell that miraculously resounded in the sky for hours after the *Karmapa's* birth. *Dönyö Drupa* (Amoghasiddhi) is one of the five buddhas in Tibetan Buddhism and could also refer to Situ Rinpoche, who was given the name Pema Dönyö[12] by the sixteenth Karmapa and who was instrumental in finding the reincarnation. The last three lines speak of the Karmapa's special quality or gift, which is his activity—unbiased, all-pervasive, beneficial, and radiant.

As predicted in these verses, the seventeenth Karmapa was born in the eastern region of Kham in a district known as Chamdo Dzong. It contained the area of Lhathok, composed of farming and nomadic lands; of these two, it was the nomadic area of Bagor that was the Karmapa's birthplace. His father was Karma Döndrub Tashi and his mother, Loga (a common form of Lolaga). Amid many special signs, she easily gave birth in the early morning of the eighth day in the fifth Tibetan month belonging to the Year of the Wood Ox (June 26, 1985).

Life in Lhathok _____

At the time of the Karmapa's birth, the family was living in a spacious yak hair tent, high up in the meadowed mountains of eastern Tibet.[13] Nomads spend nine months of the year in these tents, which are famous for not leaking during the summer rains. A family can assemble and stake one out in two hours. Inside, the ground is covered with brightly colored carpets, and the outer rim is encircled with trunks that store all their needs. The fireplace is in the middle, situated beneath an opening in the roof that lets out the smoke and can be closed in bad weather. At the opposite end from the door is the shrine, the central focus of their life, whose butter lamps provide the only source of illumination after sunset.

The Karmapa's family shifted their residence according to a seasonal pattern and the availability of grass for their herds. During the nine months of spring, summer, and fall, they lived in a tent. In the three winter months, they lived in a village made up of four other families where their home was a large, one-room house of stone with a wooden roof. The sheep lived in a barn nearby, and the younger yaks had a lean-to that protected them against the harsh weather.

The family would awaken around four in the morning, well before the sun. The Karmapa's sister, Ngödrup Pelzom, with her shy smile and bright eyes, remembers: "Though it's dark, we are used to the work and can do it even without light. First, we start the fire, and some of us go outside to check on the livestock and bring water in from the stream near our house." In winter, the ice is so thick that an axe must be used to cut through to the water. Around seven everyone gathers for a breakfast that is always the same: tea churned with butter and roasted barley flour (*tsampa*) to which small, red tubers and lots of tea are added to make porridge. The day continues in a natural flow, alternating work with meal breaks at midmorning, lunch at two, tea at five, and dinner at seven. Ngödrup Pelzom recalls, "The people who stay at home have a variety of work to do. They milk the *dri* [female yak] and *dzomo* [a cross between a yak bull and a cow]. The dri and dzomo seem to know who is milking them. If it's someone unknown, the person is likely to be kicked away." The milk is turned into the nomad staples of yogurt, butter, and cheese.

Their food depends on the season; dairy products are plentiful in the summer, and dried meat provides sustenance in the winter. The work is divided among all the household members. The children look after the lambs and calves. The very old tend to stay inside, and if the family is good to them, they circle their *mani* wheels and do their prayers. The women prepare tsampa, spin wool, cook, and share with the men the work of carrying water and looking after the herds. The men also sew and repair their tools, or they may travel on business. Rice, for example, has to be bought at a store that is a day's drive away. About once a month, they ride horses down to the nearest road and catch a ride into town. Their purchases are stored in a communal warehouse that is guarded on a rotating basis by the local families.

Nomad life, however, is not all work. There is time for communal gatherings of meditation practice, stories, and an abundant meal. In the winter, the families take turns preparing the feast and serving as host. For three or four hours, they chant the mantra of Chenrezik (the embodiment of compassion and Tibet's patron deity) or Guru Rinpoche (the Indian siddha whom Tibetans revere as a second buddha) or Tara (the beloved female buddha who protects from danger) and then share a meal together. During part of the summer, the Karmapa's family stayed in a place where more than twenty families gathered. It was an idyllic time, when the fields were emerald green and drifts of flowers added their accents of intense white, red, yellow, and blue. The families are all old friends and here, too, celebrations pass from one home to another. In the freedom, companionship, and simplicity of this world, the Karmapa spent his first seven years. It was life permeated with devotion to Buddhism; four of his eight bothers and sisters are monks or nuns.[14] It is in this environment that the following stories unfold.

The Special Signs

With their long tradition of tulkus, the Tibetans naturally look for special signs around a child's birth and remember them for the future. These are taken seriously as an indication of who the child might be. One of the first questions a search party looking for a tulku will ask is: "Were there any special signs during the pregnancy or birth?"

Before and during the Karmapa's birth, many such special signs occurred. While he was still in his mother's womb, an adult sparrow hawk landed on one of the four guy ropes of the family's tent and gave forth a variety of calls. This was considered very unusual, since this type of hawk rarely comes near a human dwelling. At the time, his mother was returning home with milk and, recognizing the bird as an auspicious sign, offered it some milk with a flick of her ring finger, the traditional way of offering to deities as well. The hawk is considered special because it has resonances within the world of religion and legend as well. Along with the eagle and wolf, the hawk is associated with the *dralhas*, special beings who assist warriors in battle. The hawk also figures in the great epic *Gesar of Ling*, the Tibetan equivalent of the Arthurian legends and still very popular. Here, the hawk is linked to Gesar's minister Denma, who is, in turn, considered an emanation of the Karmapa.[15] Thus, in the figure of the hawk, the natural world conspires with the legendary to indicate the Karmapa.

The cuckoo is also a special bird for Tibetans and, with the crane, considered the best of birds. The cuckoo also heralds the advent of spring when it returns to the colder clime. One day, in their isolated area, a cuckoo landed on top of the family's tent and sang a melodious song, so beautiful and sustained that they all remarked upon it. Since cuckoos are wild birds, it was also unusual that one had come so close to a human dwelling.

Dreams are also thought to be significant indicators of the child carried in the womb, and it is traditional to ask the mother if she had any unusual dreams during her pregnancy. During that time, the Karmapa's mother, Loga, dreamed that three cranes came to her. One carried a bowl of yogurt (a sign of purity and goodness) and another had a letter around its neck. They said to her, "Partake of this yogurt. This letter is the letter of recognition for your son. Until the right time has come, do not speak of it to others." The writing was golden and beautiful. Loga promised to keep it secret and asked the birds who had sent them. The cranes replied, "Guru Rinpoche has sent us." After this, from her heart rainbow lights radiated, and in the space above their tent were rainbow tents containing umbrellas, victory banners, and other auspicious symbols.[16] At that time Loga's husband, Karma Döndrub Tashi, was away on business, and she thought, "I should catch some of these and offer them to him," so she caught one in her hand. When she awoke, the dream was very clear to her—another indication of its importance. As she related it years later, her eyes were alive with the beauty of the images she saw.

Significant dreams are remembered from generation to generation. The Karmapa's maternal grandfather, Trinley Ngödrup, also had a dream related to Guru Rinpoche. Trinley Ngödrup, who belonged to the family lineage of Dargye Tsang, had spent nine years in prison.[17] During that time, he dreamed that he went to his daughter Loga's yak-hair tent. At the juncture of a guy rope and the tent, he saw that the disk holding the knot in place was tied with a *zi* stone— a white and black precious stone, highly valued by Tibetans and thought to give protection. Inside, the tent was brimming with light. Two pillars of gold supported it at the near and far ends. Her father asked, "Where did those come from?" Loga replied, "Guru Rinpoche gave them." The inner resonance of these two dreams, in which Guru Rinpoche sends precious gifts to the mother, would be deemed significant and further indicating a relationship to the Karmapa, who is considered an emanation of Guru Rinpoche.

Another story relates to miraculous events in what we consider to be our ordinary world. While the child was still in her womb, Loga and her son Yeshe Rabsel went into the mountains to check on the livestock. As they walked through the verdant meadows, they came upon a large clump of grass. In its center was a cup filled with milk. Loga said, "Today we have found a wonderful thing." Knowing it was auspicious, she offered some of the milk, flicking it into the air with her thumb and ring finger. The two of them also drank some of it. Marking the spot so they could find it later, mother and son continued up the mountain. On their way back, they searched for the place, but all they could find was a few drops of milk poised on the tips of the grass. Within the Tibetan framework, correspondences would be noted between the cup of milk in the meadow and the bowl of yogurt in Loga's dream, both appearing as related signs, one on the inner and the other on the outer plane.

The birth itself also reverberated in the world of dreams. Around the time of the Karmapa's birth, his elder brother, Yeshe Rabsel, was staying at Kampa Monastery, which belongs to the Drugpa Kagyu lineage, a well-known subschool of the Kagyu. The brother dreamed that he was walking upstream along the rocky bank of a wide river. Coming toward him was Lama Amdo Palden, the head of the monastery where the Karmapa would first be trained. Amdo Palden was walking with a group of lamas who seemed to be looking for something. Yeshe Rabsel asked them, "What are you hunting for?" They replied, "We've lost something and we're searching for it." The lamas continued looking and found many conch shells, but when they blew into them, they gave no sound. (Used as ritual instruments, conch shells should be resonant and powerful, as they represent the proclamation of the Buddhist teachings.) Yeshe Rabsel continued walking up the riverbank where he came upon a right-turning conch shell that had come halfway out of the ground. He picked it up, and when he blew into it, the conch gave off a large, vibrant tone. The lamas said, "This is what we were looking for. Please give it to us," so Yeshe Rabsel offered it to them. Then Amdo Palden said, "Your mother has given birth to a fine child." When he looked around again, everyone had disappeared.

A dream like this would be considered significant, since it was replete with religious symbols and featured a well-known, respected lama. Such dreams are shared, and Yeshe Rabsel told people at the monastery, "I had an unusual dream. Please perform the ritual of the protector Mahakala." This was to help ensure positive results. Afterward, a person from the monastery went to the family's home and told of Yeshe Rabsel's dream. It had coincided perfectly with the birth of the Karmapa on June 26, 1985.

When the Karmapa was born, a cuckoo appeared again, landing on top of the tent and singing for a long time. Three days afterward, echoing the line of the Last Testament of the sixteenth Karmapa, referring to "the miraculous, far-reaching sound of the white one," the people of the surrounding area heard the sound of the conch for a long time, which was followed by the music of low- and high-sounding cymbals and reed horns known as *gyaling*. Another auspicious sign was a rainbow that encircled the sun. All the people of the area heard and saw these events.

Ngödrup Pelzom recalls first hearing the conch sound inside the tent. "In the early morning as the sun was slowly rising, we heard what we thought was the sound of a thermos, which sometimes can vibrate and hum from the pressure inside. So we looked for it inside, but then the sound seemed to come from the outside, and when we looked outside, the sound seemed to come from the inside. We could not find it. Then it seemed to come from near Mother's bed, and we thought it was a bumblebee, but nothing was there. As time went by, the sound became louder and louder, and the whole family heard it clearly. Then as it increased even further, it filled the sky with the reverberations of the conch shell. Everyone in the area heard it for a long while."

Three days after his birth, in a loud and loud clear voice, the yangsi said to his mother, "Ama" ("Mother"). On this same day, toward evening, his father sent Ngödrup Pelzom to fetch water, and on the way back she saw a cuckoo land on the roof of the tent. It perched there, dipping its tail up and down and giving beautiful calls. She called to her father, "Come quickly!" He came out of the tent just in time to see the cuckoo, the divine bird. These seemingly minor events are given deeper significance from their context: an isolated mountain area where life is simple and the unusual stands out, and an environment that is permeated with a religious and symbolic sensibility.

The Karmapa's Early Years

The Karmapa's family would work throughout the day until after sunset. His mother was often outside feeding the herds while the young boy slept inside. They had no electricity, and at night the only light was from butter lamps. Often, when his mother came into the darkened tent, the only light was from the young boy's face, which seemed to be illuminated from within. This was especially clear when he was three months old.

Unusual phenomena of light continued to appear in connection with the child. From the time of his birth until he went to the monastery at the age of four, a globe of light would often move inside the tent. His mother saw it many times, and sometimes everyone saw this light in the still darkness of the tent at night. It came suddenly out of nowhere and disappeared in the same way. This light also seemed to appear outside their tent. One night a dri staked near the tent had pulled her rope and escaped. Ngödrup Pelzom and Trinley Wangmo, two of the Karmapa's older sisters, went to look for her. They caught the dri and while they were bringing her back, near the tent, a beam of light about eight inches in diameter shone ahead of them. They thought it was their brother coming with a flashlight, but no one was there.

There were other unusual phenomena. Sometimes outside the tent, they heard the sound of footsteps when no one was there. The family was so concerned about the strange noises that they went to see a lama at their nearby monastery. He said that it was probably the sound of the protectors moving about and taking care of them. These protectors belonged to a pantheon of protective deities in Tibet, which is manifold, ranging from enlightened beings—whose essential nature is compassion and whose form is wrathful—to local deities who must be propitiated.

As the yangsi grew older, his next-oldest sister, Mönlam, give him the affectionate name Apo Gaga (The One Who Makes Us Very Happy). She also called him Gurphuk Dorje (The Vajra Cave of Guru Rinpoche). One day when he was about four years old, his father Karma Döndrup had to leave on business during a big snowstorm that had already caused accidents. Inside the tent, the child was playing with Mönlam and suddenly said, "Oh, look! Father's fallen down." Not wanting him to bring bad luck, his sister said, "Don't make bad omens." Then he said quite naturally, as if actually seeing it, "Now it's OK. Nothing happened." When his father returned, he told how the vehicle he was riding on had slipped off the road and its load of wood had fallen on top of him, but all he had to show for it was a small cut on his finger.

In the Tibetan tradition, all the unusual signs that appeared in relation to the Karmapa indicated that a special being had been born. Since they had experienced some or all of these signs and heard the miraculous stories, the people of the area believed that the child was extraordinary. Lamas, too, felt that he was special. His sister Ngödrup Pelzom recalls that in his young years, the Karmapa tended to be more quiet and concentrated; he did not scatter his energy as other children did. And his games were different from other children's as well. He would build monasteries out of stones and earth, saying to his playmates, "This is a monastery, and you are lamas. I am a lama, too." Then he would hold ceremonies and chant, playing happily for hours. Often he would say, "I am a monk," and when his sisters teased him, saying, "You should grow your hair long and become one of the boys"—men from eastern Tibet are proud of their long hair braided with red threads—he would get angry.

The Karmapa was also naturally kind-hearted and compassionate. When he played, he was very gentle and did not harm animals or kill insects. In nomad life, it is necessary from time to time to butcher animals, and if the young boy saw this, he would cry. On those days, his parents would arrange for someone to take him for a walk far away.

Sometimes he would sit on a stone throne and clap two stones together as if they were cymbals, while chanting the famous Seven-Line Prayer to Guru Rinpoche over and over:

> In the northwest border of the land of Ogyen,
> On the pistil of a lotus flower with its stem
> You attained wondrous, supreme siddhis.[18]
> Renowned as the Lotus-Born,
> You are surrounded by myriad dakinis.
> I practice following your example.
> Please come and grant your blessings.

Since the Karmapa is understood to be an emanation of Guru Rinpoche, this close connection is accepted as natural. Later, in response to a question about his connection at a young age to Guru Rinpoche, the Karmapa recalled, "We nomads who live in tents had to change our location several times a year, and before such moves, we went out to find a good place. At these times people gathered to search together, and when my father was leaving to join them, he would say to me, 'You stay at home and chant the Seven-Line Prayer. We have to find good land. It's very important.'" The Karmapa then added, "I have a special feeling for Guru Rinpoche. With him, even if I don't formally practice and just recite the Seven-Line Prayer, a positive experience swiftly appears."[19]

His father Karma Döndrub remembered this close connection with the Seven-Line Prayer. While the yangsi was living at home, he taught him to write the alphabet in the *ume* or cursive script. Sometimes he knew the letters fluently and could spell aloud without hesitating and repeat three or four stanzas of a prayer. Sometimes it was as if he knew no letters at all. The Seven-Line Prayer to Guru Rinpoche, however, he always knew.

From the age of four, the yangsi also studied at nearby Karlek Monastery, where he would spend a week to ten days. Founded by a disciple of the ninth Karmapa, Karlek was the personal monastery of the previous king of Lhathok. The current head was the master Amdo Palden,[20] who, before the yangsi was born, had asked the Karmapa's parents to send their future son to his monastery. He was also important as the first monk to teach the Karmapa, providing him with a guiding influence during his early years. Amdo Palden was born in an area of Lhathok about two days' ride from the monastery, and until the age of sixteen, he studied intensively and spent periods of time in retreat. As a disciple of Khamtrul Rinpoche, a great Drugpa Kagyu lama whom the Karmapa's mother greatly respected, he followed the tradition of a *thogden*, or yogic practitioner who does not cut his hair. He spent four years in uninterrupted retreat and continued to practice extensively until 1959 when Karlek Monastery was destroyed along with its statues and texts. When it was again possible to practice openly, he traveled around to villages offering *puja*s (rituals) to benefit the people.[21] Slowly the monastery was rebuilt, thanks to the great respect the local people had for Amdo Palden.

In the Buddhism of Tibet, it is customary to make offerings to nuns and monks and ask them to make prayers for you. Both parties are believed to benefit in the process. Ngödrup Pelzom recalled that someone who had made an offering to Amdo Palden would think all day, "Now Amdo Palden is doing the prayers I requested," and feel very good about it. Through his years of service, the surrounding community had come to have great confidence and faith in him.[22]

Faith is the link that creates bonds throughout the Buddhist community. Amdo Palden himself had great faith in the Karmapa: "He is the master whom

I always place above my head and whom I always keep in my heart." He recalled his early connection with the seventeenth Karmapa:

> When he turned four, many monasteries requested that the boy come to be a monk at their place, but Karma Döndrub replied that he had already agreed that the boy would go to Karlek. At this time, I talked with his father about bringing him to the monastery. In the shrine hall, we made a small throne and did a simple ceremony. When he was six, his parents thought he should really learn how to read and study. When he likes learning, he learns very fast. Other times, he likes to play. When he likes to study, his mind is very sharp.[23]

Knowing that he was special, the monks at Karlek Monastery honored the young incarnation and set up a small throne for him next to the high lama, though no one knew yet his true identity. After short stays at Karlek, the yangsi would return to his parents, who felt he was too young to live at the monsatery for a longer time. At home, he often played with his next oldest sister, Mönlam, his younger brother Tsewang, and his favorite goat, a female with a white face, black body, and no horns, born a few months before he was. He spent hours with his goat, riding it up into the mountains and leading it everywhere. After the yangsi left for Tsurphu, the goat became a local celebrity.

The yangsi also spent time inside their home with his mother, to whom he was close. One day she had churned some milk into butter and took the first part of it to offer at the shrine. In the Tibetan belief system, the first part of anything, often food, is considered the best and is offered to a deity. Walking to the far end of the room, she stopped before the altar where there were pictures of the previous Karmapa, Rangjung Rigpe Dorje, and the previous Khamtrul Rinpoche. When she placed the butter on the protector's offering stand, her young son pointed to the two pictures and asked, "Who are you offering the butter to?" She replied, "I'm offering it to the deities." "Which deity are you offering it to?" "To all the deities." The boy then pointed to the picture of the sixteenth Karmapa and said, "If you're offering it to him, that's me and I'll have it." His mother replied, "Oh, you really shouldn't say such things."

The two pictures of the famous teachers on the shrine reflected the two religious traditions within the family. Loga and her family had a close connection to Khamtrul Rinpoche, and Karma Döndrub had great faith in the sixteenth Karmapa, who had given him his name, Karma Döndrub Tashi. (All the names given in the Karmapa's tradition begin with Karma.) One day, his mother went to fetch water accompanied by the young incarnation and his younger brother, Tsewang Rigdzin.[24] Playfully testing his mother's affiliation, the young incarnation asked her, "In the whole world, which lama do you have the most faith in?" She replied, "In all the lamas." "Do you have more faith in the Karmapa or in Khamtrul Rinpoche?" She answered, "It's the same." "Well, I'm just making this up, but say I'm the Karmapa and my little brother Tsewang is Khamtrul Rinpoche. In whom would you have more faith?" Again she said, "They are alike," and so he ended their dialogue with "That's fine." His mother had wisely refused to take sides, keeping to the deeper reality that the wisdom mind of one lama is not different from the wisdom mind of another.

The young boy passed the years from four to seven moving back and forth between his home and Karlek Monastery, studying with Amdo Palden. Now the time of his predicted discovery was approaching, and in 1992, when the young incarnation was seven years old, he urged his family insistently to move their tent a month earlier than usual. Knowing that their child was special and that his persistent request was unusual and probably significant, his parents shifted their residence and livestock to the area of Bagor. This change allowed an important connection to be made: Not long after the move, when the party searching for the Karmapa came from Tsurphu Monastery, they met the Karmapa in Bagor as predicted in the sixteenth Karmapa's Last Testament. Many felt that this confirmed his connection: he knew what he had written in a previous life and was aware of what was happening in this life as well.

The Search

While the yangsi was making his plans to meet the search party, plans were being made in India to find him. Situ Rinpoche and Gyaltsap Rinpoche[25] had sent the Last Testament of the sixteenth Karmapa as soon as possible to the Karmapa's main seat of Tsurphu in Tibet, located about twenty miles west of Lhasa. Khenpo Tsenam of the Tibetan Medical Clinic and Lama Tsewang Tashi from Nenang Monastery (Nenang Lama) delivered it along with a directive from the two rinpoches. This instructed Drupön Dechen Rinpoche,[26] who had the main responsibility for the search in Tibet, along with the Tsurphu administration and monks, to look for the reincarnation. Drupön Dechen was a special lama, for among all those inside and outside Tibet, he was the one whom the sixteenth Karmapa saw had the right karmic connection and powerful aspiration to rebuild Tsurphu Monastery, devastated during the Cultural Revolution. In the early eighties, Drupön Dechen had arrived at Tsurphu to undertake this task and to nurture connections with the surrounding community, reestablishing relationships that went back for centuries. He was the natural choice to guide the search process, which involved working with the government in Tibet as well.

On May 5, 1992, the government of the Tibetan Autonomous Region (TAR) was informed of Tsurphu Monastery's plans and shown the Last Testament. Subsequently, it gave permission to invite the Karmapa to Tsurphu and also helped in various ways, such as providing cars. This was indeed historic: it was the first time that the government of the TAR had allowed a tulku to be recognized. There was great hope that this would inaugurate an era of increased religious freedom for all Tibetans.

The Tsurphu search party consisted of three monk administrators—Domola, the head officer; Lodrö, the secretary; and Döndrub, a former head officer—as well as the monk Titi, who was to be the Karmapa's companion in his younger years, and two drivers. On May 12, 1992, they left Lhasa and headed east through the towns of Biru Shaggyu, Khyungpo Trido, Riwo Chejong, Chamdo, and Beri Ngalhang Zhungsang. Since they had to keep the path of their search secret, when they came in range of their destination, they left the cars and rented eight horses to ride and carry their things. Their route lay over a high mountain pass considered the residence of many local deities. The whole area was covered with snow so deep they sank in it up to their knees. The large snowfall was considered a good omen, a sign that the local deities were happy. Finally arriving in Khampa Gar, they met the head of the monastery, Nyendrak Lak, who asked the usual questions: "Where's your home? And what's your business here?" Fabricating a classic cover story, they replied, "We're from Lhasa. We came here on pilgrimage and to meet some relatives in the area." Nyendrak Lak was not easily fooled: "You're not pilgrims. I suspect you people have another purpose."

On May 18, 1992, the search party went to Karlek Monastery in Lhathok, where the Karmapa had been spending short periods of time since the age of four. Meeting its steward, Yeshe Dorje, they asked him, "Where is the area called Bagor?" and he replied, "What business do you have there?" They answered, "We want to meet our relative Loga."[27] The steward said, "Oh yes, Loga, the one who is Karma Döndrub's wife. A son from that family is here now," and he sent for Yeshe Rabsel. Filled with happiness that the names matched the prediction, the search party thought, "Without great difficulty, our work has been accomplished."

When Yeshe Rabsel arrived, the search party spoke more openly, telling him that they were looking for a tulku. They could now say: "Your family's son is a tulku from our monastery." They did not mention the Karmapa but made plans to visit his home: "The day after tomorrow we'll come to your place." On May 19, after giving some explanation to those responsible for Karlek Monastery, they traveled to nearby Dzodzi Monastery to say prayers that their mission be free of obstacles. As ostensible pilgrims, it was natural for the search team to visit the different monasteries in the area, where they gathered blessings for the final stages of their journey.

Having received the wonderful news that Apo Gaga had been recognized as a tulku, Yeshe Rabsel left quickly for his parents' home to tell them that the search party was coming. When his brother arrived in the afternoon, the eight-year-old yangsi was out playing in the hills as he often was, and came running down to meet him. Yeshe Rabsel said, "Apo Gaga, some Tsurphu Monastery monks are coming, and they're looking for the reincarnation of a tulku." Hearing this, the young boy started to laugh and dance with joy. That very morning, before his brother came, the young incarnation had packed his clothes and loaded them onto his favorite goat and said to his mother, "Now it's time for me to go to my monastery. If Karlek Monastery gives me a present, that would be good." His mother asked, "Where is your monastery?" He did not reply in words but gestured toward the west and central Tibet. In anticipation of the search party's arrival, the parents put up a small tent and laid out some sheepskins to offer the guests a place to stay.

Once the search party had gathered their information about the area of Bagor and received the good news that Loga and Döndrub were to be found there, they rented horses and mules for the journey. They arrived in Bagor on May 21, but it was not the best day astrologically, so they did not speak with the parents for long that day. Such an important occasion would have to wait for the planets and stars to constellate favorably. May 22 turned out to be a good day: a Friday that fell in the constellation of Uttarashada on a day of double earth elements and the conjunction of Great Joy. As the sun rose on that morning, the search party entered the tent that was the simple residence of the young incarnation. To create an auspicious connection, they were offered tea and *droma*, a small, red and sweet tuber that is prepared on special occasions.

Refreshed and settled comfortably, the search party asked the parents to tell the story of their son. Karma Döndrub related that they had long wanted to have another son. In 1978, they had traveled all the way to Lhasa to pray for one at the Jokhang before its famous image of the Buddha, the Jowo. They had also gone to see the great master Karnam Rinpoche and made a request: "Please give your blessing that we may have a son." The master responded, "The mother should recite the refuge prayer one hundred thousand times. Pray to the Three Jewels.[28] Be generous to the poor. Also give to the birds and the fishes. Through your accomplishing all of this, the compassion of the Three Jewels will bring you the gift of a son."

The parents had also asked for a similar blessing from Amdo Palden of nearby Karlek Monastery, who was to have a special relationship with the young incarnation. In reply to Karma Döndrub's request for a blessing, Amdo Palden had said, "You should do as the great master has said. If you supplicate the Buddhas of the ten directions and make aspiration prayers as best you can, a son will come. I will also pray." Then he asked, "Would you agree to my taking care of the child as a monk in my monastery?" "That would be fine," they answered. (Karma Döndrub added here, "This is a reason the yangsi later became a monk at Karlek Monastery.") Karma Döndrub and Loga devoted themselves as best they could to accomplishing what the lamas had counseled, and this eventually brought them the son they had wished for.

Quite assured that they had found the long-sought reincarnation of the Karmapa, the members of the search party showed the letter of the Last Testament to Karma Döndrub. While he was reading the text, the search party's leader, Domola, took a photograph. When it was developed, they could see a white light encircling the entire body of the father. At this time as well, the sweet sound of the cuckoo's song was heard.

Karma Döndrub related that after the child was born, he dreamed the following: "In a broad and open place, different types of Tibetan and Chinese people had gathered. In their midst was an ancient stupa in slight disrepair and nearby, a massive heap of discarded statues. At the same time, from within a crowd of unknown people, a very old lama with a flat head and a large bald spot appeared. He said to me, 'Without letting others see you, carry a statue to that mountain on the other side of the river.' I took a bronze statue of Chenrezik plus another bronze statue and placed them in the pouch of my chuba [Tibetan coat]. When I arrived at the mountain on the river's far side, my mind became very happy." After the Cultural Revolution in Tibet (1966–77), there were many such heaps of discarded statues, and the places of worship that had not been destroyed were in disrepair. From among all the possible statues, Karma Döndrub's choice of Chenrezik highlights his connection to the Karmapa, who is considered an emanation of Chenrezik.

In accordance with the age-old custom of making an auspicious connection, the search party made an offering to the parents of *khata*s (long white scarves) and some money. These gifts were on a smaller scale and appropriate to the occasion, a prelude to the official recognition. On May 24, the party left Bagor to return to Tsurphu with their good news. As they journeyed to Karlek Monastery, in a vast blue sky, three smaller suns appeared around the sun itself. Everyone in the area saw them clearly, and some fifty miles away in Chamdo, people saw them as well. All over the world, such meteorological phenomena—rainbows are a common example—are often associated with spiritual events. Tibetans are particularly sensitive to these occasions, giving them significance and holding them in memory.

Afterward, as they traveled homeward, the members of the search party met Akong Rinpoche, the representative of Situ Rinpoche, and Sherab Tarchin, the representative of Gyaltsap Rinpoche, who were delayed in Kathmandu by a time-consuming visa application. They were on their way from India to Bagor and had been sent to Tibet with a dual purpose. One was to request at several monasteries the traditional forty-nine days of prayers for Jamgön Kongtrul Rinpoche, who had tragically passed away at the end of April. Their second purpose was to act as the representatives of Situ Rinpoche and Gyaltsap Rinpoche in supporting the search for the incarnation of the seventeenth Karmapa. When they met the young reincarnation, Akong Rinpoche and Sherab Tarchin were told by the parents about his birth and informed in great detail about how the search party had investigated and found him.

After several long days of travel, the search party arrived in Lhasa on May 27. The next day, the members met with the relevant officials in the government of the TAR and apprised them of what had happened. The officials supported the search, saying, "This is excellent." Finally, that afternoon, the search party returned to Tsurphu. Drupön Dechen, who held responsibility for the search from Tsurphu, and the officers of the monastery asked to hear all the details of how the sixteenth Karmapa's Last Testament had led the party to find his reincarnation. On the following day, the news was made public with the announcement: "The reincarnation of the glorious Karmapa has been born." From the top of the temple, flags and victory banners were raised, long *radung* horns and conch shells resounded from the valley walls, and the auspicious ninefold cycle of music for the reed horn pierced the air. A special meal was offered to all the monks. The joyful news traveled quickly throughout Tibet and the world, drawing people from all parts and all traditions to Tsurphu.

Situ Rinpoche and Gyaltsap Rinpoche also received the news that without any doubt the search party had found the yangsi in the Bagor area of Lhathok, as the letter had predicted. Following previous tradition with care, both rinpoches went to Dharamsala in northern India to offer all the information to the Dalai Lama. Traveling from Delhi to Dharamsala on June 6, they arrived at a time when the Dalai Lama was in Brazil attending a conference, but his Private Office forwarded the news to him and the Dalai Lama replied. Previously, in the flawless vision of his deep wisdom, he had seen the signs of the reincarnation's birthplace. He speaks of the event:

> I do not rely on one or two texts, but proceed with a method regarding the choosing of a reincarnation, and when the indication is positive, I decide that it's good. [In the case of the Karmapa,] I had a kind of dream of the location, the area where the present reincarnation was born. There are stones and meadows. It looked like a high altitude and faced south with beautiful streams. That is the main picture. Then someone, some source without form, was telling me, "This is the place where the Karmapa is born."[29]

On another occasion he added that there were no trees, animals, or people and that two rivers flowed down on the right and left.[30] Based on this and the evidence of the search party, the Dalai Lama made a provisional statement confirming the identity of the Gyalwa Karmapa. On June 12, Situ Rinpoche and Gyaltsap Rinpoche returned to Rumtek and officially announced the discovery of the Karmapa. In June as well, both the head of the Sakya lineage, Sakya Trizin, and the head of the Nyingma lineage, Mindroling Trichen, confirmed the recognition and composed long-life prayers for the Karmapa.

One Kagyu lama, Shamar Rinpoche, had doubts about the identity of the Karmapa, even though he signed a letter affirming his support.[31] The Dalai Lama met with Shamar Rinpoche separately on June 29 and later that same day met with Situ Rinpoche and Gyaltsap Rinpoche. On the following day, June 30, the Dalai Lama issued the letter known as the Buktham Rinpoche, in which he clearly confirms the recognition of the Karmapa's reincarnation:

> In accordance with the Last Testament, the boy born to the father Karma Döndrub and the mother Loga in the Year of the Wood Ox is definitely recognized as the reincarnation of the sixteenth Karmapa. With prayers for his well-being and for the success of his sacred activities,
>
> The Dalai Lama.
> The thirtieth day of the fourth Tibetan month
> in the Water Monkey Year, June 30, 1992.
> Translated by Kalön Tashi Wangdi

Along with the confirmation, the Dalai Lama offered his advice to Situ Rinpoche and Gyaltsap Rinpoche:

> In Tibetan, there is a proverb that says where there is great Dharma, there is immense Mara [or, where there is great truth, there is great negativity], and so there has been a little disharmony and some difficult situations, but these do not have great importance. What is important is the focus on what has real and profound significance. Until now, you have worked, keeping in mind what is most important and essential, and you should continue to focus on what is vital, what is crucial.[32]

Now the process of the search was complete: it had moved from the discovery of the Last Testament through to the final confirmation by the Dalai Lama. With good fortune, the timing of everything had worked out, and all the events had fallen into place.

Return to Tsurphu

NOW WAS THE TIME for preparations. In Barkhor, the yangsi was preparing to depart and wished to leave a gift for his family. Near their winter house was a spring they had used, but it had been dry for several years. Along with his younger brother, who was three-years-old at the time, the yangsi went to the barren spring and planted a juniper tree nearby. Being very young, he did not know how to chant rituals, so he repeated the Seven-Line Prayer to Guru Rinpoche many times. After some months, the spring came back to life again.

In central Tibet, Tsurphu Monastery was preparing to receive him. With Drupön Dechen Rinpoche as their leader, a party of monks from the monastery went to Lhasa on May 29 to make an application to the Religious Affairs Bureau of the TAR.[33] They asked that the young reincarnation be enthroned and further requested that people be allowed to come to Tsurphu for the occasion from all over Tibet and other countries, and that all the supporters of the previous Karmapa be permitted to attend as well. Their request was granted and on June 1 they finished their preparations for the journey to invite the yangsi to Tsurphu. In a convoy of five vehicles, twenty-three monks and lay people, headed by the General Secretary Domo, rode out the main gate of Tsurphu with white scarves trailing in the air. On June 2, they arrived in Lhasa and then continued along their route to eastern Tibet until June 8, when they reached Lhathok and Karlek Monastery. This time they were expected, and they themselves had made careful preparations for this important event.

On June 9 at Karlek Monastery, the young incarnation put on new robes[34] and was offered a mandala (symbolizing the whole universe) and the three supports of body (a statue), speech (a text), and mind (a stupa). This was followed by an offering of tea and special saffron rice. Everything was done to create an auspicious occasion in the traditional style, which called for generous gifts to the family and the monastery. The head monk, Amdo Palden, and all the other monks were offered gifts of tea and money. The parents and their children were given livestock, brocades, clothes, and many fine objects. Appropriate gifts were presented to all the relatives of the parents as well. From nearby Karma Gön, a monastery founded by the first Karmapa, Dusum Khyenpa, in the twelfth century, monks and lay people came to pay their respects, meeting with the yangsi and receiving blessing cords. On the morning of June 10, the party left Karlek Monastery and headed toward Tsurphu. Included were the yangsi's parents, his older brother Yeshe Rabsel, and his two closest companions, his youngest sister Monlam and younger brother Tsewang Rigdzin. The usual journey would take one day by horse and five by car.

On June 14, they were met by a welcoming party at the foot of a famous mountain, Nyenchen Thanglha, about thirty miles due north of Tsurphu. Striking parts of the Tibetan landscape, such as lakes and mountains, are thought to be inhabited by a variety of deities, and this special peak is considered the residence of an eighth-level bodhisattva who has protected numerous incarnations of the Karmapa and shown great kindness to him.[35] The lamas and monks who came to receive the yangsi at this sacred site were led by Drupön Dechen Rinpoche. The welcoming party invited the young incarnation to sit on his Dharma throne, which was set in a spacious tent. Following the tradition of "opening the gates to an auspicious connection," he was offered a mandala and the traditional statue, text, and stupa, along with tea and rice. This connection was further affirmed by an auspicious sign: At the exact moment the young incarnation set foot inside the tent, triple claps of thunder—signifying to Tibetans fame that reverberates everywhere—came one after the other, and a light rain, considered a blessing, fell.

The next day, June 15, the party turned off the northern Lhasa-Shigatse highway,[36] and crossed over a wide wooden plank bridge to enter the Tölung Valley, home to Tsurphu. They followed a gravel road up the north side of the valley, while on their left the river flowed down through a quilt work of fields with brilliant yellow flowers. In front of them, clouds of juniper smoke billowed their welcome from white cairns and heaps of branches set along the roadside. Riding past welcoming parties waiting along the road, they arrived at Nenang Monastery, the seat of Pawo Rinpoche, just down the valley from Tsurphu. Here, close to his new home, the young incarnation participated in all the traditional rituals of welcome, receiving khatas from everyone who had gathered to meet him and giving them his blessing.

The long caravan continued up the curves of the valley while horseback riders dressed in their best chubas and hats galloped alongside the vehicles. The yangsi rode in the front passenger seat of a new white jeep, which was soon covered with khatas. In a short while, for the first time in this life, he would glimpse his old monastery settled against the mountainside.

Slowly the yangsi's cavalcade passed through the crowds of his followers, who were lined up in deep rows holding incense and long white scarves while making supplications, offering prayers, and chanting *Karmapa khyenno* ("Karmapa, think of me," the Karmapa's mantra). Closer to the monastery, a procession of monks led the way in full regalia with their brocade hats and long yellow silk shawls. There were two monks carrying long bundles of incense, followed by others holding tall banners of multi-colored brocade, and many playing musical instruments—conch shells, long radung horns, reed horns, cymbals, and the large green circles of drums, edged in red and gold and held high on their long handles. The monks were accompanied by costumed figures wearing large masks of Indra (king of the gods), the monk Hashang and two children, the protectors Mahakala, Mahakali, and Dorje Legpa (Damchen), plus the ones who especially invoke good fortune: Old Man of Long Life, the Musician, the Juggler, and the Snow Lion.

At a place called Kunga Delek (All Happiness and Goodness), not far beyond the Lower Park, the young incarnation mounted a brightly caparisoned white horse and rode to the main temple. He wore a gold brocade robe trimmed in red and the traditional golden domed riding hat of lamas on a journey. Masked dancers came out to meet him and, along with the crowd, tossed flowers along his path.

The young incarnation proceeded to the main courtyard, where he paused to sit and receive the traditional offerings of khatas, the dances of four snow lions, and a cup of their milk. Carried up the wide stone stairway, he changed his hat to the Crown of Activity (*las zhwa*) with its golden diamond and entered the main temple hall. At the end of the central aisle stood the high, brocade-covered throne. Taking his seat at the head of rows of monks, he was presented with a mandala and the three offerings to body, speech, and mind. Making the occasion festive, the monks' tables were piled high with stacks of *kapse* (large fried biscuits in different forms), fruit, sweets, and nuts. Tea and saffron rice were offered to everyone. All the monks and lay people passed in front of his throne to receive his blessing.

Outside, entertainment was provided in the form of a Tibetan opera telling the history of the generations of Tibet's rulers and special songs for the occasion, interwoven with expressions of good luck and prosperity. To celebrate, many joined in traditional folk dancing with its circling and rhythmic song. After a very full day, the young reincarnation retired to his new residence on the top floor.

On June 27, a delegation of forty government officials came to meet the yangsi and acknowledge him as the true reincarnation of the sixteenth Karmapa. This event took place in the shrine hall where the government officials were seated in chairs arranged on one side and the monks sat in their ceremonial places on the other while one official stood in the middle and read the government's document. Afterward, in a gesture of respect, they came to the yangsi's quarters to offer him long khatas. The first officers greeted him with a khata and then took his hand and shook it; the yangsi quickly caught on to this new custom, extending his hand to the rest who followed. The parents were also in the room and received khatas as well.

On June 29, along with thousands of followers, the yangsi watched the lama dances, featuring Mahakala, the protector of Tsurphu Monastery, and based on a vision of the sixth Karmapa, Thongwa Dönden. The large wrathful masks, long brocade robes, and intense, stylized gestures must have evoked a deep response, for afterward the yangsi was often seen to spontaneously imitate their movements.

A new routine at the monastery was being structured around the yangsi. Official positions were created to take care of his daily life, and personal attendants were appointed: a chamberlain, a butler, an appointment secretary, a correspondence secretary, a shrine master, and a special guard for his general audiences. Soon after the yangsi arrived at Tsurphu, Situ Rinpoche and Gyaltsap Rinpoche met the young incarnation on July 13. Those present said that it felt like a close family reunion.

On July 3, 1992, soon after the yangsi's arrival at Tsurphu, *umdze* (chant master) Thubten Zangpo became his tutor for reading; their sessions were from nine to eleven in the morning and from three to six in the afternoon. Umdze-la sat next to his young student and indicated the letters with a wooden pointer as they read together the long rectangle-shaped pages.

Close to the previous Karmapa, Umdze Thubten had spent years at the sixteenth Karmapa's Rumtek Monastery, Sikkim, India, and often traveled abroad to assist lamas on their tours. His long white beard and friendly smile were familiar to many Western disciples. As older Tibetans sometimes do, Umdze Thubten had returned to his home to spend the latter years of his life in Tibet. Before the yangsi's arrival, he had come back to his family's home set near the road running up the valley to Tsurphu. Reflecting the architecture of the area, their house was constructed of wood and gray stone, and brightened by flower boxes with generous red and pink blossoms. Tibetans love to grow flowers, and tin cans often double as flowerpots for cosmos and geraniums. Umdze Thubten's return to Tibet was timely and he served the Karmapa until passing away in 1997.

From July 5, the Tsurphu secretary, Lodrö, began to teach the yangsi calligraphy as it had been taught in Tibet for centuries, by writing on a wooden board with chalk or ink that can be wiped away. The letters are written and erased over and over. With a framed model in front of him, the young student bent over his board and wrote with great concentration. Having an elegant handwriting is important in Tibetan society, to the point that advancement in administrative positions could depend upon it. The yangsi's teachers were pleased with his progress, telling others that to be the Karmapa, one needs to be someone like this.

Though he quickly adjusted to life in the monastery, the yangsi did not forget his nomad home. About a month after arriving at Tsurphu, he called into his room Lama Tendzin Gyurme, who had also grown up as a nomad and was now an attendant of Gyaltsap Rinpoche. The young incarnation asked everyone else to leave and locked the door. For a while he talked to the lama about nomad life and what it was like to roam the mountains and live in a tent.

All of a sudden, he shifted the subject: "Last night, I saw Rumtek clearly."[37] And he proceeded to describe the layout of Rumtek Monastery in Sikkim, which was built by the previous Karmapa, and to point out the rooms where the important tulkus had stayed. He commented, "It's strange. The building lower down on the hillside is empty, but in the big building up on the hill, many monks are staying." Lama Tendzin Gyurme explained to him that at the time, the monks' quarters in the lower monastery were being rebuilt, and therefore the monks were temporarily housed in a big building located on the hillside above the monastery (the Nalanda Institute for Higher Buddhist Studies).[38] It is interesting to note that this type of higher perception or clairvoyance appears to him as a natural part of his reality, just as when he was younger he "saw" his father's accident.

The Hair-Cutting Ceremony

The hair-cutting ceremony for great lamas signifies their entering the gate of Dharma and follows the tradition of Shakyamuni Buddha, who cut his hair on the banks of the Nairanjana River, near Bodh Gaya, India. The day chosen for the ceremony was August 2, the anniversary of Shakyamuni Buddha's first teachings in the Deer Park of Sarnath, India. The day before, the party traveled to Lhasa. The yangsi with his apple-red cheeks was full of curiosity about all that he saw.

The hair-cutting ceremony for the seventeenth Karmapa would be performed at the Jokhang Temple in Lhasa, in front of Jowo Rinpoche, the most sacred statue of the Buddha in all of Tibet and its patron deity. The thirteenth Karmapa, Dudul Dorje, had also received the hair-cutting ceremony in the Jokhang—a privilege usually accorded only to the Dalai Lama and the Panchen Lama.

On August 2, through the darkness of the early morning, the headlights of the jeeps, carrying the yangsi, Situ Rinpoche, Gyaltsap Rinpoche, and all the main lamas and officers of Tsurphu, found their way into a cobblestone courtyard of the Jokhang. The Barkhor is a broad walkway around the temple, usually filled with circumambulating pilgrims and locals from Lhasa, monks and nuns doing pujas, beggars, small stalls selling a variety of Dharma articles and other goods, and the smoke of juniper offerings. Now it was completely silent. The party made its way through the main courtyard, open to the distant stars, and down the hall leading to the temple. At the threshold, they paused as pilgrims usually do, to pay their respect to the temple and its statues and to make prayers, for it is said that prayers made right here will be realized. They turned to the left and passed rows of butter lamps lending their glow to the gold of Guru Rinpoche's statue with its wide-awake eyes. The yangsi, followed by Situ Rinpoche, Gyalt-sap Rinpoche, Khenpo Karthar, Lama Norlha, and a group of monks, walked down the left aisle to the temple's far end where the Jowo is enshrined in a small, intimate room. The iron chains that guard the statue after visiting hours were pulled aside to give a full view of the brilliant, golden Buddha, jeweled with pearls, turquoise, coral, and diamonds. Amid all the splendor, his face is a still pool, his eyes gazing from time beyond time. After three prostrations, the yangsi sat on a throne facing the Buddha.

On this special occasion, great offerings were made, including gold leaf to cover the face of the Jowo and objects made of gold such as butter lamps, plus the five ritual offerings of flowers, incense, butter lamps, perfumed water, and food. The yangsi descended to make prostrations again to the Buddha and then remained in front of the statue. Situ Rinpoche and Gyaltsap Rinpoche cut a few strands of his hair to signify his first step in becoming fully ordained and offered him his new name, which they read aloud from elegant letters brushed onto a rectangle of gold silk: Pal Khyabdak Ogyen Gyalwe Nyugu Drodul Trinley Dorje Tsal Chokle Nampar Gyalwe De (Glorious Master Ogyen, the Emerging Victorious One, the One Whose Activity Tames Beings, the Vajra's Creative Play, Victorious in All Directions). Included within this name is "Ogyen Trinley" (Enlightened Activity of the One from Oddiyana), found in the predictions of Chokgyur Lingpa,[39] underscoring the Karmapa's close connection with Guru Rinpoche, the One from Oddiyana. The two rinpoches conveyed to the young incarnation the gifts they had brought from the Dalai Lama: a blessing cord, his personal meditation beads, and a long white scarf.[40] The Karmapa then resumed his place on the throne, and everyone there offered scarves and received his blessing. The ceremony complete, the yangsi and the lamas visited the Potala (residence of the Dalai Lamas) and other important places in Lhasa. They made extensive offerings of prayers and butter lamps, which are considered very auspicious, for they symbolize eliminating the darkness of ignorance and the flourishing of wisdom.

Enthronement

The hair-cutting ceremony was attended by a small group of lamas, Tibetans, and a few Western disciples. By contrast, the ceremony of enthronement, which would be the final affirmation of the young incarnation as the Karmapa, was a very well attended and public occasion. Over 20,000 people, both ordained and lay, gathered from all across Tibet and abroad. Situ Rinpoche explains that enthronement or consecration "means something like putting a flag on the top of a castle and blowing trumpets, really announcing the event. By empowering the Karmapa, he then becomes what he is, on the relative level as well as on the ultimate level; ultimately he is always the Karmapa, but relatively, he's not enthroned yet."[41]

On September 27, 1992, the morning was brisk and cold. It had snowed the previous night, and the mountain to the west of Tsurphu Monastery rose like an undulating pyramid, freshly covered in soft white. The mountain was said to be the residence of a protector deity, brought to Tsurphu by the Karmapa. Its white mantle was considered an auspicious sign that the deity was pleased and was blessing this day. In front of the mountain and flowing down the valley were the many smaller peaks of cream-colored tents, some with indigo blue borders and traditional designs, set five and six across along the curves of the Tölung River.

On this special day, the yangsi entered the shrine hall led by Situ Rinpoche and Gyaltsap Rinpoche who were carrying fragrant incense. The ceremony itself was divided into two parts. In the first one, the government officials participated. Present for the ceremony were the head of the Religious Affairs Bureau from the central government, Mr. Ren Wuzhi, the higher-level officers, and other officials from the government of the Tibetan Autonomous Region. The second part was the traditional religious ceremony, which began at noon, a time of positive constellations and signs.[42] In addition to some 210 representatives from the branch monasteries of Tsurphu, representatives from all the various schools of Tibetan Buddhism[43] and many famous incarnate lamas[44] were present. Led by Situ Rinpoche, Gyaltsap Rinpoche, Thrangu Rinpoche, and retreat master Bokar Rinpoche, more than 400 lamas from Dharma centers abroad representing twenty-seven countries came to participate in the enthronement ceremony.

Inside the main temple, the two-story tall pillars were covered with deep blue, green, yellow and red brocade interwoven with gold, while the lower parts were wrapped in a black yak skin, offered by the local nomads. Down the center of the hall in a path leading to the high throne, glowing with color, were long rows of offerings: silver and gold vases, ritual cups, offering bowls of varying sizes stacked four tiers high, tall tea servers, Tibetan rugs, long stacks of brick tea, bright red and blue bags filled with barley, wheat, rice, and other foods the Tibetans enjoy, and musical instruments—reed horns, shorter horns of silver, radungs, silver-adorned conch shells, and rows of cymbals of all sizes and shapes, their concentric circles punctuating the rich colors and shapes. Behind these flowed the broad stripes of multicolored brocades. The gifts were placed as symbols of the offerings that devoted followers would be making during the day—a sign of their devotion and a way to affirm their connection with the Karmapa in a concrete way.

Between the offerings and the throne was a long row of brocade-covered tables and carpeted high cushions; the row stretching to the left was occupied by the religious hierarchy, starting at the middle aisle with the Karmapa, Situ Rinpoche, Gyaltsap Rinpoche, and others down a long line of rinpoches who had come from afar. Also present was Amdo Palden, the head of Karlek Monastery, where the Karmapa had often stayed as a young monk. On the right side of the aisle were the Chinese government officials.

As the first part of the ceremony began, Mr. Ren Wuzhi from the Religious Affairs Bureau of the central government read a document stating that the Gyalwa Karmapa was the first reincarnation to be recognized by the Communist government since its inception. He offered the Karmapa an official letter, encased in red brocade, acknowledging him as a "living buddha" (a term the Chinese use for a incarnate lama). The government delegation also made offerings of many fine gifts.

After a half-hour break, the traditional religious ceremony began. The young incarnation stepped onto the high throne, supported by golden lions, which are symbols of fearlessness, and the monks recited the traditional prayers of refuge, *bodhichitta*, and consecration. He was offered copies of the sixteenth Karmapa's Last Testament and the Dalai's Lama's letter known as the Buktham Rinpoche.[45] As they chanted the relevant sections of the ritual, Situ Rinpoche offered the young incarnation the eight auspicious substances,[46] and brightly colored representations of the eight auspicious symbols,[47] the seven royal articles,[48] and so forth. Each one of these has a symbolic meaning. For example, the sense faculties are empowered by the auspicious symbols: the eyes are consecrated by offering the auspicious fish; the tongue, by the auspicious lotus, and so forth. A short long-life empowerment concluded this central part of the ceremony, which made official the young incarnation's status as the Gyalwa (Victorious) Karmapa.

Then, to recall the profundity of the Dharma and its connection with the Karmapa, the ceremony continued with talks by four masters of the teachings. Khenpo Zhonu Nyima from Palpung Monastery (the seat of Situ Rinpoche in eastern Tibet) explained the condensed meaning of the *Abhisamayalamkara*, a text elucidating stages of realization. From Nangchen, also in eastern Tibet, the accomplished Drugpa Kagyu master Ade Rinpoche gave a talk about enlightened body, speech, mind, qualities, and activities, and Khenpo Lodrö Dönyö from Bokar Monastery explained the meaning of "The Praise to Manjushri," the embodiment of wisdom. Gyaltsap Rinpoche spoke of the Five Perfections (of the teacher, time, place, teaching, and retinue) and gave an extensive explanation of the mandala offering, which he then performed.

According to their standing, the incarnate lamas, monks, nuns, and lay people made their offerings to the new Karmapa. For hours, they came in lines that extended into and beyond the crowded courtyard, and gradually, everyone was able to meet him. The Office of Tsurphu then offered plates heaped with kapse, fruit, and sweets, which were followed by tea and saffron rice. As the ceremony in the main shrine hall drew to a close, dances and a Tibetan opera composed by the previous Karmapa began outside on a broad, stone-paved courtyard that was filled to overflowing with his followers, dressed in their best outfits and jewels, a sea of color with glints of brocade and silver and, woven into the women's black hair, the intricate patterns of turquoise and coral.

The next day, at Gyaltsap Rinpoche's monastery, located in the area behind Tsurphu's main shrine hall, Situ Rinpoche, Gyaltsap Rinpoche, and Drupön Dechen Rinpoche presided over an extensive feast offering to consecrate the foundation for a statue known as Changchub Chenmo (Great Enlightenment), a large statue of the Buddha in the earth-touching mudra. On this day as well, the Karmapa along with Situ Rinpoche and Gyaltsap Rinpoche gave blessings to a large crowd of Tibetans, Chinese, and Westerners. On the following day, sitting in a balcony above the crowded courtyard and wearing the curved red hat of the pandita, the Karmapa bestowed his first empowerment, the standing red Chenrezik.

On the fourth day, the pilgrims began to fold up their tents, pack up the shops that had provided everything from reliquary boxes and silver jewelry to biscuits and sunflower seeds, and make the long journey home, where they would tell the stories of their travel and how the seventeenth Gyalwa Karmapa had come once again to bring the Dharma into the world for the benefit of all beings.

Soon after the enthronement ceremony, Situ Rinpoche and Gyaltsap Rinpoche had an important meeting with the local officials and the lamas of Tsurphu to stress the necessity of the Karmapa's earliest possible visit to his monastery in Rumtek, Sikkim, India. The local officials had talked to the Tsurphu administration and they had stated that when the appropriate time came in the near future, the Karmapa could visit India. This, however, never happened.[49]

Life at Tsurphu

Beginning on December 5, 1992, the Karmapa chanted in his quarters every day without fail the rituals for the protector Mahakala, Dukkar (The White Umbrella), a ritual to remove obstacles, and the protector Senge Dongma (the Lion-Faced One). As time passed, he also began to perform, along with ten monks, the rituals related to special days of the Tibetan lunar calendar (the tenth, fifteenth, and so forth) and recited the prayers requested by his followers. Every month without exception he engaged in practices to benefit those who had passed away, including Chenrezik Who Overturns the Basis of Samsara and the ceremony of leading those who have passed away onto a higher level. He also recited special dedication and aspiration prayers that people had requested. These are all practices that he will continue throughout his life.

As the months passed, the Karmapa's study and practice schedule continued to shape his days. Between sessions, on the flat roof top outside his room, he played with his remote-controlled jeep or a wind up helicopter that sometimes disappeared over the balcony's edge. His monks were challenged to figure out every new electronic toy, many of which were recycled soon after their arrival. He also liked small toy cars and at times six or seven of them were traveling in different directions all over his room. The young reincarnation went for walks along the river valley where he could relax away from monastery. Yaks were often gazing on the slopes beneath an infinite azure sky.

Daily audiences with the yangsi began around one o'clock when long lines of disciples, or those simply wishing to meet him, walked up the steep stairs to the second floor of the temple, where the Karmapa sat on a throne in a sunlit room. Wearing his thick meditation cloak, he blessed each person as she or he passed by, and if special lamas or groups of disciples arrived, he would meet with them in his own room. Lively and responsive, he answered questions, posed for photos, and, borrowing a camera, often took some pictures himself. Visitors to the Karmapa often included his parents who had found a house in Lhasa and came to see their son.

~

In August 1993, traveling from the United States, Dzogchen Ponlop Rinpoche,[50] Bardor Tulku Rinpoche,[51] Tenzin Chonyi[52] and a small group of disciples paid a long visit to Tsurphu to spend time with the Karmapa. One day, the three of them walked far up the river valley past the wall of mani stones to the sky-burial site, where they made the traditional prayers for those who have passed away. On the way back, they passed by the Upper Park and noticed that delicious mushrooms had come up in the meadows. They picked some to offer to the Karmapa, and Tenzin-la carried them back in his hands. Later, when they were sharing a meal with the Karmapa, Bardor Rinpoche said, "We picked these mushrooms yesterday and hope you like them." The Karmapa replied, "I saw that. You all went to the sky-burial site and as you came back, Tenzin-la had a handful of mushrooms. But I never looked at you. While I was reading a text, I sat like this"—he put his hands in the meditation mudra and sat up straight—"and I saw it all." In the Tibetan tradition, it is said that great masters see the past, present, and future clearly, as if looking at the palm of their hand.[53] This fluidity of time is opened up through meditation practice; for a master like the Karmapa, it seems to be something simple and natural, a given of his experience.

On September 16, 1994, the nine-year-old Karmapa traveled to major monasteries in central Tibet: Tashi Lhunpo in Shigatse (the seat of the Panchen Lama), Sera, Drepung, and Ganden (the three main Gelukpa monasteries), and Nyethang Drölma Lhakhang, founded by the eleventh-century master Atisha, whose texts the Karmapa has now studied. Ten days later, he flew from the airport in south central Tibet to the Chengdu airport in China. Over the next month, he visited famous places in China, including Beijing, Nanjing, Chamdo, Shanghai, (where he was taken shopping and showered with toys), and finally Langchen Gyingri, the pilgrimage site where the Buddha's regent, the arhat Kashyapa, passed away. The people from these areas and the monasteries were generous in their welcome while the press gave good coverage of the main events.[54]

In Beijing, the Karmapa appeared as a guest of honor at the National Day celebrations on October 1. He met with numerous government officials and again made requests to be able to study in India with his teachers Situ Rinpoche and Gyaltsap Rinpoche or be allowed to invite them to Tibet. He was formally introduced to President Jiang Zemin and Chairman Li Peng. The Karmapa later commented that he had heard so much about China's leader, but when they met, he experienced Jiang Zemin as a simple human being.

At one event commemorating the forty-fifth anniversary of the founding of the People's Republic of China, Jiang Zemin told the gathering that the Karmapa was studying in earnest and growing up in good health. He noted that after applying himself with effort and becoming a tulku for whom his country is important and for whom the Dharma is important—the sequence here is significant—the Karmapa should contribute to the development of Tibet. Years later, at a press conference on April 27, 2001, the Karmapa recalled this tour of China. He had heard, he said, that "the Government of China was planning to make use of me. I was certainly treated as someone very special. For example, when I was taken on tour in China and Beijing, I was well-treated." The Karmapa added, however, that he had come to suspect that "there might be a plan to use me to separate the people within Tibet from His Holiness the Dalai Lama."[55]

After the political leaders had made their speeches at the celebration in Beijing, the religious leaders came forth. The vice president of the Buddhist Association of China, Mr. Dao Shuren, introduced the Karmapa and told an astonishing story, not only in its content but particularly in light of the context. The day before the Karmapa was to visit the stupa that sheltered a relic of the Buddha, five-colored rainbow lights appeared around the stupa. Dao Shuren considered this a wondrous and most auspicious sign—the Buddha's prophecy of the Karmapa's arrival. Also in Beijing, there was an unusual sign on the morning of that very day: a clear rainbow appeared above the palace of the previous emperors, and photographs were taken of it. The rainbow was regarded by those with faith as a sign that the Karmapa and the previous rulers of China had the relationship of priest (the Karmapa) and patron (the emperor).

Following in China the footsteps of the third Karmapa, Rangjung Dorje, who had given teachings there over 650 years ago, the Karmapa made a pilgrimage to Wutai Shan (in Tibetan, Ri bo rtse lnga, the Five Peaks). Situated a good day's journey from Beijing, the mountains are considered sacred to Manjushri and home to many temples where realized masters have visited for centuries. The trip to China also gave the nine-year-old Karmapa many new kinds of experience. He saw an ocean and fireworks for the first time, and in the urban areas, he encountered the technology of the modern world that had not yet spread in Tibet.

After this guided tour of China, the Karmapa returned to Tsurphu and continued his studies. His petitions to the Chinese officials about meeting with his teachers, Situ Rinpoche and Gyaltsap Rinpoche, were not successful. In 1995, Tenzin Chönyi travel to Beijing to meet with government officials and request that the Karmapa be able to travel and that his teachers come to visit, but this mission also bore no fruit.

∼

February 25, 1995 was a Saturday, considered the auspicious day of the week for all those like the Karmapa who were born in the Wood Ox Year. In Tibetan, it is called *laza*[56] or "soul day," a favorable time to initiate projects and pursue important themes in one's life. On this special day, when he was only nine years old, the Karmapa finished memorizing perfectly over two hundred pages of prayers and supplications. He also knew by heart all the main tantras (ritual practice texts) of the lineage, which are hundreds of pages long and include the major deities of Chakrasamvara, Vajrayogini, and Gyalwa Gyamtso. It took him from June 15, 1992, when he first came to Tsurphu Monastery, until this day in 1995— a little over two and a half years—to complete a task that usually takes seven years or, for a very gifted monk, five years.

To mark this occasion and to make an auspicious connection, the Karmapa acted as the chant leader for the extensive ceremonies the monks performed in the main temple. This meant that he had to know all the verses by heart, as well as the melodies for chanting, the timings and tunes of the musical instruments, and the many complex offerings to be made. It was a festive occasion when everyone rejoiced in his accomplishment. The Tsurphu administration offered the assembled monks and incarnate lamas tea, soup, an extensive midday meal, and money. Numerous disciples[57] came to create an auspicious connection, and representatives from Lhasa's Religious Affair Bureau came to offer their respects.

During the years he was at Tsurphu, unless an important person had come who needed to meet with him, the Karmapa's teachers and tutors carried out their responsibilities, teaching him on a regular basis. The Karmapa himself was very assiduous in keeping to his studies, which came to include the study of Chinese as well. Khenpo Loya[58] and Lama Nyima, who had trained at Sera Monastery and completed a three-year retreat at Tsurphu, taught him the classic texts covering the different Tibetan scripts, grammar, poetics, and synonyms, which are learned for the appreciation and writing of poetry and other compositions.[59] Following Tibetan custom, the Karmapa memorized all of their root texts and studied the commentaries in detail. His teachers remarked that his knowledge of these traditional sciences came to him with great ease. His study of these texts also became a catalyst, inspiring him to write his own poetry.

Beginning at the age of eleven, the Karmapa studied traditional dialectics and debate. As the years passed, he continued to memorize the root verses and study the commentaries of major treatises dealing with practice and philosophy. It is said that in this way, each incarnation is reintroduced to the heart of his rich intellectual and meditative tradition. The Karmapa's early years were spent working with these texts, which would become a major focus of his life and the basis for his future teaching.

One of the first treatises he studied was *A Guide to the Bodhisattva Path* (*Bodhicharyavatara*). The Karmapa had such mastery of the text that he would sometimes give explanations of it to others.[60] For all Tibetan traditions, this text is the template for learning how to lead a life of wisdom and compassion, exemplified by a bodhisattva. One of its most famous verses states:

> For as long as beings are sick,
> Until all disease is cured,
> May I be their physician,
> Their medicine, and their nurse.[61]

Another important text *The Lamp of Certainty*, was composed by the great nineteenth-century scholar Ju Mipham. It treats knotty philosophical issues under seven topics posed as questions, such as, "What is the common object of disparate perceptions? Which of the two realities is more important?"[62] *The Gateway to Knowledge,* also by Ju Mipham, is a compendium of the major topics of Buddhist philosophy.[63] *The Supreme Continuum* is one of the five texts of Maitreya through Asanga, which are particularly important for the Kagyu lineage.[64] The text emphasizes the radiant and cognizant nature of mind and thereby forms a bridge between Mahayana philosophy with its emphasis on emptiness and Vajrayana practice with its visualizations of deities. *The Supreme Continuum* is also a major source for teachings on buddha nature—the innate goodness or ultimate nature of mind—present in every living being. A series of nine examples illustrate how this pure nature or potential is hidden from us by flaws, which can be removed through practice:

> Just like a precious statue covered by clay,
> This potential is present within all living beings,
> Yet veiled by the flaws of temporary afflictions.[65]

Composed by the third Karmapa, Rangjung Dorje, *The Profound Inner Nature* is another treatise the Karmapa studied, and it deals with the intricacies of the subtle body and the theories that pertain to it. This is a key text for those undertaking the long three-year retreat.

In his free time between study sessions, the Karmapa often read the biographies of spiritual masters from the different religious traditions in Tibet. This gave him the firm conviction that all these traditions are worthy of faith and respect. Within his own tradition, the Karmapa mentioned that he felt a special affinity for the collected works of the fifteenth Karmapa, Khakhyab Dorje, and read them extensively.

The Karmapa also studied the range of practices that constitute the major rituals of the Kagyu tradition.[66] It is said that his skill in these meditations arises through his direct and unhindered wisdom. The Karmapa was expert in the detailed and complex tasks of the shrine master (*vajracharya*) which demand unwavering concentration and an impeccable memory. In particular, he knew the key points of the meditation practices belonging to the generation stage, which focuses on the precise visualization of a deity and mantra recitation, and of the completion stage, which involves the dissolution of everything back into emptiness. The Karmapa was also adept in the rituals for constructing mandalas, in the creation of *torma*s (sculpted ritual offerings), in arranging the shrine, in the tones and melodies of the rituals, and in the musical accompaniments of the reed horns, cymbals, and so forth. In lama dancing (*'chams*, a meditative practice in motion), he knew all the gestures and movements with a natural precision.

~

While residing at Tsurphu, the Karmapa presided over the great ceremonies of the protector Mahakala that precede the Tibetan New Year and, further, the extended Guru Rinpoche practice that takes place for eight days in the fourth Tibetan month. During the summer months, a large blue and white tent with a long courtyard was raised in the Upper Park and offering ceremonies were performed. The Karmapa's presence at Tsurphu served as a magnet for the Tibetans and led to the revival of traditional celebrations. From Tö Ngari (western Tibet) and U-tsang (central Tibet), from north and south as well as Kham (eastern Tibet), the faithful came to Tsurphu for the festive ceremonies. They enjoyed lama dancing, received initiations, and offered scarves to the huge (60 x 100 feet) appliqué *thangka*[67] of the Buddha, laid out on steps running up the mountainside opposite the monastery. The story of the thangka's creation encapsulates the renaissance of Tsurphu's traditions and buildings that was inspired by the Karmapa.

The great thangka was displayed for the first time in May 1994 on the date of the Buddha's full awakening and *parinirvana*. Two years in the making at a tent factory in Lhasa, where similar techniques of stitching had been in use, it was sewn from brocades, silks, and satins of seventy different shades. Its spacious style was one developed by artists associated with the Karma Kagyu lineage in the 1500; known as the Karma Gadri style ("style of the Karmapa encampment"), it was so named because the Karmapas of that time lived in great tent towns that moved from place to place.[68] Drupön Dechen Rinpoche remembered the previous great thangka, destroyed in the Cultural Revolution, so the new one followed its pattern closely, with two exceptions: of the figures surrounding Shakyamuni Buddha, the two below him were the sixteenth Karmapa, Rigpe Dorje, and his devoted disciple, the third Jamgön Kongtrul Rinpoche. This change in design is also typical of how a tradition will evolve: charismatic and beloved teachers not only mould the way teachings are given, but they also influence the art, shaping what is depicted and the style as well.

The background surrounding the deities and masters in the thangkas is not so bound by rules and therefore is more open to change. Here in the great thangka, around all the figures, "clouds and rainbows illuminate the sky above; peacocks and gazelles graze peacefully before the lamas below; particularly, the endangered species of Tibet's wildlife are featured: yaks, asses, white-lipped deer, antelopes and the blue-horned sheep all have a place in the image for special protection. Tibetan cranes and various other birds are also present, even if sometimes hidden in the foliage."[69] On the first day, the great thangka was displayed during four hours while monks performed ceremonies and the devoted offered scarves. This was to be come an annual festival on the twelfth day of the fourth Tibetan month. Subsequently, a large thangka of Mahakala was created and displayed during the celebrations previous to the New Year (Losar) when Mahakala pujas were performed.

On such occasions, to the nearly ten thousand people who usually came, the Karmapa gave audiences, empowerments, the transmission of Chenrezik and Guru Rinpoche's mantras, plus the Karmapa's own guru mantra, *Karmapa khyenno* (Karmapa, think of me). Whatever people needed, he gave in such a way that their faith grew.

During the years that the Karmapa was studying and fulfilling his activities, he also demonstrated other extraordinary accomplishments, some of which were recorded in the text kept by the Tsurphu Monastery's administration. While the Serdung Temple at Tsurphu was being rebuilt, he laid his hand on a stone and left a clear print. This was later incorporated into the wall so that pilgrims circumambulating the main shrine complex could see it. The print became clearer and deeper over time. On February 4, 1996, from the side of the mountain behind Tsurphu, he took from the earth a large cache of Dharma articles, including cymbals of different sizes.

As before, his natural connection to what is unseen could surface unexpectedly. Once he told his secretary Lodrö to write a response to his friend saying that he was glad to hear from him and know that he was well. The friend's letter had not mentioned that his father had passed away, but the Karmapa simply added, "Your father who passed away has been reborn in the realm of the gods. I will make supplications and prayers for him." This kind of knowledge, another aspect of clairvoyance, was not unusual for the Karmapas. Through the centuries, important lamas would ask them to discover where someone special to them had been reborn.

The lunar calendar regulates the activities in Tibetan monasteries, and a special awareness keeps a focus on what day it is, if it commemorates an event in the Buddha's life, or if it relates to a deity or teacher special to their lineage. The first fifteen days of the first Tibetan month coincide with the time when the Buddha demonstrated miracles. When the Karmapa was ten years old, he chose this time to demonstrate what transcends our ordinary world.

In 1996 on the thirteenth day of this month (March 3), the Karmapa left the monastery complex and walked up the valley, following the curves of the river to the meadows of the Upper Park and then farther to the stone mandala of the sky-burial site. Soon he turned up the steeply rising, rocky hill that forms the first part of the middle pilgrimage circuit. The walk through its sparse vegetation leads to the meditation caves of the previous Karmapas found on the middle pilgrimage route called Circumambulating the Mountain.[70] First appears the cave of the ninth Karmapa, Wangchuk Dorje, set high off the trail, then the cave of the tenth Karmapa, Chöying Dorje, with its abundant spring and miniature sacred mountain to circumambulate, and finally, the famous cave of the second Karmapa, Karma Pakshi, (and the third Karmapa, Rangjung Dorje). A two-story building has been constructed in front of the cave so that meditators can practice close-by. The modest shrine room has a small opening to the actual cave and a footprint in stone of Karma Pakshi; in the square space in the middle, between four pillars, *dakinis* are said to appear.

On this day, the Karmapa passed by this middle route and climbed farther up following a path to the barren area of jagged rock called Circumambulating the Peaks[71] to a place known as Damchen. Here, on a rock facing west, the Karmapa left a very clear handprint. Noticing the impression, Lodrö mentioned it to the Karmapa, who replied, "It's the radiance of Guru Rinpoche's smile." Continuing along the trail to a place above the Lhamo Shrine, the Karmapa left another handprint in a rock close to Snow Tortoise Spring,[72] named after the nearby cave of a famous practitioner called Gyalwa Gang Bel. This handprint was seen by the retreat master, Lama Panam, but when he mentioned it to the Karmapa, he replied, "Don't tell others about it."

That afternoon the Karmapa and the monks came to the Tsurphu retreat house, located next to the Karma Pakshi cave and sitting on a large rock promontory far above the monastery. Its white stone walls seem to grow directly out of the rock as it overlooks the long, narrow valley. At an altitude of over fourteen thousand six hundred feet, with no trees and rough weather, the location of Tsurphu is said to produce excellent masters of meditation. On a footpath to the northeast of the retreat house, an immense boulder sits next to the trail. The Karmapa stroked it with his *zen* (monk's shawl) and his mantra, *Karmapa khyenno*, appeared clearly on the rock face in dark red letters.

The following day (March 4, 1996), the Karmapa again walked up to the peaks behind Tsurphu and once more stopped at Damchen to take a rest. While there, he laid both his hands on a rock and left a double imprint in the stone. All the monks who had accompanied him on the outing saw these clearly.

On the next and final day (the fifteenth day of the Tibetan month, March 5, 1996), the Karmapa said to Lama Panam, "In the area of Damchen there are very precious objects that are to be found by you." He knew that Lama Panam had this special karma and that he would not need a map or other indications. Lama Panam took nine monks with him to the high peaks, and after searching Damchen, they unearthed a beautiful jade cup with a white metal stand and cover, plus many old coins.[73] They also found two wooden cups, one with a wide lip for use in the summer[74] and one with a narrower opening and tucked at the waist for use in the winter.[75] The custom of using these different cups was a part of the monastic regulations at Tsurphu. All the objects he found Lama Panam offered to the Karmapa.

~

Later, when residing in India, the Karmapa was asked if he had supernatural powers and he replied:

You can call it supernatural powers. I believe that whatever power is there is the power of the Dharma. It is due to this that all my predecessors did many unusual things such as leaving hand- or footprints in stone. People say there are many things I can do. But for anyone who practices the teachings, these things might happen.[76]

It is said that the Karmapa kept a pure vision of his root teachers, the lamas who taught him the Dharma, and the *khenpo*s (abbots with a deep knowledge of texts and, with some, of meditation) who taught him the great treatises. He paid them homage, gave offerings, and showed great respect. In this way, he displayed what are considered the signs of a genuine and noble being.

In Tibet, an especially eloquent language is used to praise a great master. It employs descriptions of the sharpest intelligence and highest states of realization found in Buddhist philosophy and practice. General Secretary Tendzin Namgyal, a master of this style, has praised the Karmapa in the following way. "The brilliance of the Karmapa's mind allows him to comprehend the meaning of something by merely looking at it. He knew the nature of his mind the instant it was pointed out, and this increased his intellect's ability to clearly distinguish phenomena. He sees apparent existence as a mandala of infinite purity. Not merely relying on an analytical mind, he directly understands phenomena that are hidden from ordinary view and masters them without hindrance. When he recognizes incarnate lamas, who are known as the life tree of the teachings, he sees everything clearly in the mirror of his mind. As his predictions about them proved to be true, they cleared away any doubt about their identity."[77]

Visions and Rainbows

T HE TRADITION of recognizing tulkus began with the Karmapa's lineage in thirteenth-century Tibet and then spread to other traditions. Not only was the Karmapa a tulku himself, he was also renowned for his remarkable ability to recognize other tulkus. For centuries, the Karmapas were called upon to discover the location of reincarnations who were the precious holders of different lineages. Similar to the sixteenth Karmapa, who was about ten when he first recognized a tulku,[78] the seventeenth Karmapa began to identify tulkus at a young age. By the time he was sixteen, he had identified more than forty tulkus, including the fourth incarnation of Jamgön Kongtrul Rinpoche, the eleventh incarnation of Pawo Rinpoche, the seventh incarnation of Dabzang Rinpoche of Dilyak Monastery, and the fifth incarnation of Riba Selche Rinpoche.[79] All of these are important tulkus for the Kagyu lineage, who, through their mastery of practice and knowledge of texts, were able to inspire disciples and make the teachings widely available. These masters also were the central focus of their monasteries, which benefited greatly from their presence.

The process of recognizing a tulku usually begins soon after the passing of a lama. (The recognition of the Karmapa is a different process since he leaves his own letter to identify his next reincarnation.) The administration of a particular tulku's monastery will approach the Karmapa; usually, requests are made at least three times, after which the Karmapa gives a letter indicating various signs related to the location of the reincarnation. Traditionally, it is said that the recognition of tulkus comes through the direct and unobscured knowledge of the three times that belongs to the Karmapa's primordial wisdom, which allows him to see what is deeply hidden. Subsequently, it is the responsibility of the monastery's administration to send out a search party and find the tulku. Once they feel they have found the right one, they report back to the Karmapa, who will then give his confirmation (or maybe not). The search party then returns to the home of the tulku to ask the parents if they would allow their child to become a monk and live at the monastery. The parents most often agree since it is considered a great honor to have this special child born into their family. The tulku is given a ceremonial bath and new robes to signify his future life. He will also come to visit the Karmapa to receive his blessing and, if possible, the hair-cutting ceremony. A tulku who is very young will be left with his or her parents until old enough to live at the monastery or perhaps the child will alternate visits to the monastery with family life.

In 2002, the Karmapa spoke about this process: "When recognizing tulkus, my mind feels rather normal, not overly sad or overly happy. In that state, the recognitions come. It's not like being possessed by a deity. I do not rely on divinations, calculations, or deities. Mainly, you have to look directly at your own mind—the natural, uncontrived mind—and thereby a great certainty can arise.

"Usually, the recognitions come through with the names of the parents and the name of the year in which the child was born, and so forth. For all the tulkus I have recognized, the information has come through in this way. Sometimes people send letters that request the recognition of a child as a reincarnation and describe special signs and events. For the most part, these indications mean that this child has a good accumulation of merit, which is the source of the positive signs. One can't rule out that the child could be a tulku, but one cannot identify them definitely as a tulku either. Therefore I don't particularly make decisions based on these requests.

"The recognition of Jamgön Rinpoche was a special occasion, since it was the only one to appear while I was in meditation. Previously, people from his administration made many requests asking me to find his incarnation, and I kept those in mind. Then one day when I was resting in meditation, I remembered Jamgön Rinpoche, and at that time, I saw it; the recognition came into my mind."[80]

What follows are the stories of the Karmapa's recognition of three major tulkus when he was ten and eleven years old. Each one begins with a brief history of the tulku's previous incarnations, tracing their importance for the Karma Kagyu lineage and for the Karmapa himself, as two of them, Jamgön Kongtrul Rinpoche and Pawo Rinpoche, were his personal teachers in previous lives.

Discovering the Reincarnation
of the Third Jamgön Kongtrul Rinpoche _____

The first Jamgön Kongtrul was a great scholar and meditation master of the non-sectarian movement in nineteenth-century Tibet.[81] His many works, including the famous Five Treasuries, preserved the core Tibetan Buddhist teachings and practices. The second incarnation was the son of the fifteenth Karmapa and a great practitioner. The third Jamgön Kongtrul was a devoted disciple of the sixteenth Karmapa and a beloved teacher to many disciples in the East and West. In Rumtek Monastery, Sikkim, he took care of the sangha and the lay community and fulfilled the Karmapa's main wish there, by building the Karma Shri Nalanda Institute for Higher Buddhist Studies. He also traveled the world and established many centers and guided many beings, benefiting Buddhism in general and the Karma Kagyu lineage in particular. The third Jamgön Kongtrul also founded charitable projects and activities for social benefit, especially for the poor and needy.

Two years after the passing of the third Jamgön Kongtrul in 1992, Tenzin Dorjee, the general secretary of his administration, began a series of requests to the Karmapa, entreating him to recognize the reincarnation. The first three times, the Karmapa replied that it was not yet time and advised Tenzin Dorjee to perform offering rituals and supplications for Jamgön Kongtrul's swift return. The fourth time, in August 1995, the Karmapa answered that in the following year he would have good news.

In April 1996, Drupön Dechen Rinpoche sent a letter from Tsurphu encouraging Tenzin Dorjee to visit. A month later, he and Sönam Chöpel, a monk of the previous Jamgön Kongtrul, met the Karmapa at Tsurphu Monastery. It was the last day of a long ritual practice when a beautiful thangka was being displayed on the mountain opposite the monastery. The Karmapa, who was eleven years old at the time,[82] said, "Now I will let you know the good news, but come to me this afternoon." It was then that he gave directly to Tenzin Dorjee the letter describing the signs. Tenzin Dorjee recalled, "At that very moment, a single thunder clap roared in the skies. Sönam Chöpel and I were together with His Holiness. When we left the room, heading to see the late Drupön Dechen Rinpoche, I noticed a very light rainfall with sunshine which we Tibetans call rain of flowers.[83] In our tradition, it is believed to be an auspicious sign."

The Karmapa had written:

From here, in the direction to the south, the place is a distance of seven days on a good steed.

A son was born in the Year of the Pig to a father whose name includes *ga* or *ma*[84] and to a mother whose name includes *tha* or *kha*.[85] There are eight in their family. As for the place, in front there is a great black mountain, its view partially obscured by the mountains to its right and left. Between a mighty river rushes forth. The house is two stories and well built; its door faces east. This vision of his birthplace has appeared to me. As for the pujas to be performed, if one hundred thousand *tsok*-offering pujas of the Protector and as many pujas of Gyalwa Gyamtso as possible are done, his activity as the glorious protector of beings and the doctrine will be ensured.

I, therefore, grant this letter describing the signs of Jamgön Rinpoche.

Karmapa Ogyen Trinley Dorje
April 11, 1996

Since the letter did not exactly indicate where the incarnation could be found, Tenzin Dorjee and Sönam Chöpel returned to seek the Karmapa's instructions on how to proceed with the search. They met the Karmapa outside his chambers. He said that he had witnessed some very auspicious signs that day, the thunder and rain the two monks had seen and also a rainbow above the southern mountain in front of the monastery.

Once inside his rooms, the Karmapa described the place of Jamgön Kongtrul's birth. Turning to a blank page in his exercise book, the Karmapa drew a mountain, rainbows above it on the left, and the family's home on the upper right of the page. He also wrote some Tibetan letters. The Karmapa explained that the mountain was the one in front of Tsurphu and the house was to the south of it. Turning to a fresh page, he mapped out the family's home with an enclosure and the surrounding houses. He said that in front of the home rises a black mountain, flanked on both sides by mountains that partially hide it. He sketched what looked like a spring or a river coming from the mountain and casually remarked, "There is water." Pointing to the drawing, he said that the house has two stories and that the entrance faces due east.

The Karmapa then drew a third image on the back cover of his exercise book. Tenzin Dorjee requested him to be more precise about the location, and he replied that the place is around Chushur Dzong (or county) to the south of Lhasa, about thirty miles from Tsurphu. Written on the sketch were three names: Chushur, Nyemo county, and Nyethang, the latter two being on the western and eastern borders of Chushur Dzong.

Following the Karmapa's advice, the search for the incarnation was begun on July 31, 1996. On that occasion, Tenzin Dorjee asked the Karmapa about the time of year when the tulku was born. He replied, "Not in the beginning, neither at the end, nor in the middle, but between the middle and the end, nearer the end." The Karmapa also helped their search by sending his personal tutor, Lama Nyima, with an attendant and his own car with a driver. On July 30 and 31, Tenzin Dorjee and Sönam Chöpel visited the central shrine of Tibet, the Jokhang in Lhasa, to make prayers for the success of their search. They also offered new robes for the Jowo, the sacred statue of the Buddha, plus grain and butter lamps.

The Karmapa told them that during the past year, he had had frequent visions of rainbows above the mountain in front of Tsurphu. Within the rainbows, he could see the third Jamgön Kongtrul, luminous with radiating lights. The rainbows, the vision of Jamgön Kongtrul, and the lights then dissolved into each other and disappeared behind the mountain. He had also had a vision of Tibetan letters indicating the names of the parents.

After many false starts and further instructions from the Karmapa, the lamas finally met a young girl, who turned out to be the reincarnation's aunt. She told them that she knew of a baby born in the Pig Year and bade them follow her. They walked about fifty yards and came to a house. Just as they approached, a middle-aged lady with a baby bound on her back came out the main gate. Tenzin Dorjee noticed that the baby was dressed in the colors of a monk, wearing a yellow shirt and a maroon chuba, with a bracelet of light green beads around his wrist. He asked the lady if the baby was her own. She replied that he was not her son but her grandson. Lama Nyima asked how many there were in her family, and she replied that there were eight. When asked for the parents' name, she said, "His father's name is Gonpo and his mother's is Yangkyi." The signs were matching up.

Tenzin Dorjee recalled:

The baby kept looking at me, and he was smiling in a very special way. Even though we were strangers, he was not afraid. It seemed that we were familiar. At that moment, I wondered about the black mountain, the river, and the family's home, all of which seemed to match the signs in the Karmapa's letter. A feeling of sadness, yearning, and joy all mixed together came over me. I have never experienced such a feeling before, and I was very close to tears. Lama Nyima reminded me to be strong and not cause any suspicion in the lady.

The black mountain was exactly as the Karmapa had described. It turned out to be Karak Khyung Tsun, a mountain sacred to Guru Rinpoche. On its right and left were two mountains that partially obscured its view. In front were the village and the parents' house, which had two stories and a gateway facing east. A spring emerged on the left between the mountains, and a big river, the Yarlung Tsangpo (Brahmaputra), separated the family home from the mountain. They also found out that the baby was born in the previous Year of the Pig on the fourth day of the tenth Tibetan month (November 26, 1995), just as the prediction had stated that his birth date would be "between the middle and the end, near the end" of the year. All was just as the Karmapa had described.

Everyone in the search party felt good about the events of the day. They were quite confident that they had located the reincarnation and that the Karmapa would most likely agree and decide on this child. They returned to Lhasa and celebrated with Yönten Phuntsok, the general secretary of the second Jamgön

Kongtrul, who had been responsible for finding the third incarnation in the mid-1950s. In 1992, when the third Jamgön Rinpoche tragically passed away, Yönten Phuntsok told a distraught Tenzin Dorjee not to worry: he would find the reincarnation whom he would recognize from the very special feeling he would have when meeting him for the first time.

~

The search party returned to Tsurphu on August 5 and related all the events to the Karmapa. He was calm and looked carefully at their photographs. When they described the family's home, he showed them a house he had constructed out of his Lego toys and asked them, "Does it look like this?" Indeed, it did. As it was getting late, the Karmapa told them to take a rest and return to see him the next morning.

The following day when they were alone, the Karmapa asked Tenzin Dorjee if he felt happy with the baby he had met the day before. He replied that he was happy, since everything had matched the Karmapa's letter. He was depending on the Karmapa, so his personal impressions and feelings regarding the child did not matter. The Karmapa replied that the reincarnation was very important for all of Buddhism and in particular for the Karma Kagyu lineage, because Jamgön Rinpoche was a lineage holder.[86] A mistake about him would mean that he would not be able to carry out his activity of benefiting the teachings and living beings. As the Karmapa spoke, Tenzin Dorjee could not help feeling very impressed with him. Although the Karmapa was only eleven years old, he was extremely clear about what he was doing and about his responsibility as the supreme head of the lineage. His prophecy and instructions had been very precise.

On August 12, the Karmapa bestowed on Tenzin Dorjee the letter of recognition saying, "Now this is the letter of recognition of the fourth Jamgön Rinpoche. Your administration should be happy. You have all worked very hard." The letter stated:

> In Chushur county in Sehmed township, a boy was born in the Year of the Pig to a father named Gonpo and a mother named Yangkyi. This boy and the circumstances of his birth have been carefully examined in accordance with the letter describing the signs. Since I am now certain that this boy is undoubtedly the reincarnation of the third Jamgön, I hereby offer my recognition of him as the fourth Jamgön. I pray that his life be long and that his activity flourish.
>
> Karmapa Ogyen Trinley Dorje
> The Seventeenth Rabjung, Year of the Rat,
> sixth lunar month, twenty-seventh day.

The Karmapa then offered a golden silk scarf and a red blessing cord to be presented to the new incarnation.

On August 16, a small group that included Yönten Phuntsok, Tenzin Dorjee, and Sönam Chöpel[87] visited the family of the reincarnation at their home. Calling all their members together, Tenzin Dorjee formally announced that their eight-and-a-half-month old baby had been recognized by the Karmapa as the reincarnation of the third Jamgön Kongtrul Rinpoche. On behalf of his administration, he requested them to accept the Karmapa's recognition. In reply, the grandfather Lodrö told the visitors that two months earlier, his grandson had become very restless. He cried continuously and could not sleep at night. The family had consulted a doctor, but he could find nothing wrong. Not knowing what else to do, they brought him to see an uncle who was a monk. He performed a divination and told them that their grandson was disturbed because the family owned something that belonged to a monastery. The grandfather said that at the time, he could not understand what this had meant, since his family owned nothing that belonged to a monastery. Now, however, it was clear that it was the child himself who belonged to the monastery of Jamgön Kongtrul. Speaking for his entire family, the grandfather said that they accepted the Karmapa's recognition of his grandson as the fourth Jamgön Kongtrul. They were happy that at least one member of their family would be of great benefit to beings. The child was then given the traditional ceremonial bathing, a new set of robes, and the golden silk scarf and blessing cord from the Karmapa.

On September 1, 1996, the fourth Jamgön Kongtrul made his first visit to Tsurphu Monastery to pay homage to the Gyalwa Karmapa. That day a spell of bad weather had cleared into a bright sky, which Drupön Dechen Rinpoche interpreted as the *maras* (negative spirits) being dispelled into space. The following day was a very auspicious one in the Buddhist calendar, as it marked the time when the Buddha descended from the god realm where his mother had been reborn. He had taught her there for three months to repay her kindness and liberate her. At the break of dawn on this special day, the Karmapa performed the traditional hair-cutting ceremony for Jamgön Kongtrul and gave him a new name.[88] At Tsurphu on April 22, 1997, the Karmapa gave Jamgön Kongtrul Rinpoche the oral transmission of mantras, rituals, and prayers, including the transmission of writing, and clothed him in monastic robes for the first time.

~

On November 17, 1997, a beautiful day of brilliant sunshine, Jamgön Rinpoche arrived in Nepal. Joyous crowds greeted him at the airport and festive gates to welcome him arched over the route he would take back to his main seat at Pullahari. The road to the monsatery, located on a hilltop outside Kathmandu, was filled with a long procession of thousands of monks and nuns who came to escort him home and receive his blessing. When Jamgön Rinpoche emerged from his car, a huge rainbow appeared around the sun. Numerous other unusual rainbows and colored lights appeared in the skies. Not yet two years old, the young incarnation remained alert and attentive throughout the three-hour ceremony welcoming him back to Pullahari.

Rainbows signal auspicious events in many cultures and they have appeared on numerous occasions in connection with this young tulku. In the beginning of the search, the Karmapa told the party that he had seen visions of the third Jamgön Kongtrul appearing within rainbows. When he gave Tenzin Dorjee the letter to find the tulku, the Karmapa mentioned that he had seen a rainbow above the mountain in front of Tsurphu. After the formal recognition of Jamgön Rinpoche, several families in his village recalled that they had seen a special rainbow near the time of his birth, which appeared to come from a sacred spring in the mountain before their village and to end at his family's house. Rainbows also appeared when he returned to his monasteries in India and Nepal and during the celebration of his second birthday. When he visited Karma Lekshey Ling Monastery on the other side of the Kathmandu Valley, a huge rainbow appeared around the sun. All these events were witnessed by many people, and they began to refer to Jamgön Kongtrul as Ja lama, "the Rainbow Lama." His tutor, Drupön Khenpo Lodrö Namgyal, explained that the appearance of rainbows "is a sign that His Eminence's incarnation is authentic and that his activity will be colorful and pure like the rainbow."[89]

The fourth Jamgön Rinpoche now lives at Pullahari, his main seat in Nepal, and also spends time in Kalimpong, India, and visits his monastery at nearby Lava. He is accompanied by another young tulku, discovered by the Karmapa in Nepal, Shelri Dölpo Rinpoche, whose previous incarnation was a close disciple of the second Jamgön Kongtrul and who had offered his monastery in Dölpo to the third Jamgön Rinpoche. The two tulkus are studying English and learning to read and write Tibetan while learning basic Dharma texts.

The Discovery of Pawo Rinpoche

A few miles down the valley from Tsurphu, Nenang Monastery is home to Pawo Rinpoche, one of the heart sons of the Karmapa.[90] In the Kagyu lineage, Pawo Rinpoche is considered an emanation of Manjushri, who embodies the wisdom of all the buddhas. Holding a text and the sword of wisdom, Manjushri is the special deity of scholars, and some of Pawo Rinpoche's incarnations were particularly noted for their scholarship and their nonsectarian approach, which respected the variety of philosophical systems found in Tibet.

His name, Palden (Glorious) Pawo (Hero) Tsuglak (Scholar), has a special history. The first Pawo Rinpoche, Chöwang Lhundrub,[91] was a disciple of the seventh Karmapa, Chödrak Gyatso, and, following in the steps of his teacher, he, too, was a great scholar and master of meditation. It is said that he displayed many signs of accomplishment, including raising his body's temperature, walking through walls or on water, and leaving footprints in stone. The people of the area praised him as the very embodiment of a hero, and so he acquired the name Pawo. All the incarnations of Pawo Rinpoche also have as part of their name Tsuglak, which usually means "the sciences" or "sacred literature" and here has the meaning of a "powerful scholar" or "an expert in the Buddhist sciences." The second Pawo Rinpoche, Palden Pawo Tsuglak Trengwa,[92] was a famous scholar and the disciple of a very great scholar, the eighth Karmapa, Mikyö Dorje. The tenth Pawo Rinpoche, after living a long time in France, had spent his final years in Nepal, where he passed away in 1991.

After completing a three-year retreat at nearby Tsurphu, Lama Tsewang Tashi became the one responsible for Pawo Rinpoche's Nenang Monastery and soon became known as Nenang Lama. With expressive eyes and a small moustache, he has an outgoing personality that allows him to connect with people easily. Nenang Lama was the main force behind the reconstruction of the monastery and also started schools for the local people. His charge further included finding and enthroning the reincarnation of the last Pawo Rinpoche. After his passing in 1991, Nenang Lama requested the Karmapa to recognize Pawo Rinpoche's reincarnation. The Karmapa was a natural choice, for in addition to his known abilities, he and Pawo Rinpoche had shared the relationship of teacher and disciple for many incarnations. In June 1995, Nenang Lama went up the valley to Tsurphu to ask the ten-year-old Karmapa for the definitive letter that would allow the tulku to be found.

The Karmapa replied that Pawo Rinpoche had taken rebirth and that prayers were necessary before he could be identified. He counseled Nenang Lama to perform rituals to dispel obstacles—one hundred thousand repetitions of the concise ritual of the protector Mahakala and a recitation of the Kangyur and Tengyur—the whole corpus of Buddhist texts, numbering over 350 volumes. The Mahakala practice was completed at Nenang Monastery, and the reading of the Buddhist canon was divided among other monasteries. The reading of these texts can be quite lively occasions. Texts are brought down from the shrine where they are usually stored, and distributed to the monks. Then all the monks simultaneously begin to read aloud the text they have received. This continues until all the volumes have been recited. In less than a month, the task was accomplished, and Nenang Lama went back to visit his root lama, Drupön Dechen Rinpoche, at Tsurphu. Learning that the ceremonies had been completed, Drupön Dechen counseled him to ask the Tsurphu administration for another meeting with the Karmapa, and this was granted.

Appearing before the Karmapa, Nenang Lama offered prostrations and informed him that all the rituals had been completed. He placed his request before the Karmapa, asking him to let them know how to find the incarnation. The Karmapa rested in meditation, and then said, "When you find him, you should bring him to the monastery right away as there are obstacles." Then the eleven-year-old Karmapa took paper and pen from the table in front of him and a letter flowed forth. "Now it's been written," he said.

The letter contained the following explanation:

This is the fruition of having been supplicated three times concerning the precious reincarnation of Palden Pawo Tsuglak Mawe Wangchuk. To the northeast of the temple of Tsurphu there lies the town of Nagchu, and nearby on its north side, there is a family from Kham where the father's ancestral family has a good name.[93] Their house faces north and there are ten family members, but it's not certain that all of them are there. As a sign for locating the house, you will see that in front of it there is a big build-ing, red in color like a shrine for the spirit *tsen*.[94] Near the house are stacked mani stones or boulders. The mother's name has the prefix *d* and the father's name has the syllable *lha*. Of the twelve-year cycle of animals, the child is either a Dog or a Pig. This one with good signs is Pawo's unmis-taken reincarnation. If he is recognized, he will definitely bring benefit to the teachings and to living beings.[95]

Nenang Lama took the letter to Drupön Dechen Rinpoche, who said, "Now you have to search. But if you yourself go, many people will know that you are from Nenang and will say, 'They are looking for the reincarnation of Pawo Rin-poche,' so you must send other people."

Following Drupön Rinpoche's advice, Lama Nyima (the Kamarpa's tutor) and another monk from Tsurphu went on the search disguised as traders. Arriv-ing in Nagchu, about 170 miles north of Tsurphu, they went to the north of the town and found a house facing north with mani stones stacked nearby. In front of the house was a red monastery. When they asked the name, they were told it was "the Monastery of [the Shrine to] the Spirit Tsen."[96] It was all as the letter had predicted. The monastery belonged to the Nyingma tradition and yogis practiced there. On their way to the house, they had met one carrying a skull cup full of nectar, which they considered an auspicious sign.

When they came to the house, an old woman was coming out the front door. The two Tsurphu traders asked her, "How many people live here in this family?" She replied, "There are ten family members, but two have gone away, one on pil-grimage and another to school in China." This too matched the letter exactly.

They thought, "This must be the place." They asked about the children and their birth dates; one was born in the Dog Year. With all these queries, the old woman was beginning to have suspicions. "You're not traders. You're looking for a tulku," she said. Lama Nyima replied, "That's true. We're from eastern Tibet and are searching for a minor tulku." They then asked for the names of the parents. "The father is called Lhagpa and the mother Yangchen." This matched exactly the recognition letter which stated that the father's name contained the syllable *Lha* and the mother's name had a *d* prefix (Yangchen is spelled dyangs chen in Tibetan).

Having found the house with all the right signs, the two delighted monks returned to Tsurphu without saying anything directly to the family, as they needed to confirm the results of the search with the Karmapa. They called Nenang Lama asking him to come from Lhasa to Tsurphu, and together they all went to see Drupön Dechen. Following the well-worn path, they came to Drupön Dechen's quarters: a small courtyard of flowers and one wall of windows that gave onto his room. He sat next to the windows for most of the day, dispensing to all who came advice, stories, and answers to questions about life and practice. The monks told him the story of their search, and he was delighted. The tulkus were coming back to take birth again. Afterward, the monks offered the details of the search to the young Karmapa, who confirmed their conclusions: "He is definitely the one. There's no mistake. Settle on him."

Soon after, Nenang Lama and Wangdu, the former steward of Pawo Rinpoche's monastery and one of its main benefactors, went by car to Nagchu, bringing offerings and new robes for the reincarnation. Arriving at the house on July 19, 1995, they told the family that their child was Pawo Rinpoche and explained to them the contents of the letter and its signs, relating how everything had matched perfectly. Knowing how important Pawo Rinpoche was, the parents were completely surprised. Nenang Lama asked them: "Since your child is clearly Pawo Rinpoche's reincarnation, will you give him into the care of Nenang Monastery?" They replied, "It is the Gyalwa Karmapa who has confirmed that he is Pawo Rinpoche's yangsi, and so we believe that it is true and without error. If it will benefit the teachings, we will give him to his monastery." Nenang Lama gave the young incarnation the traditional ritual cleansing. Together with the steward Wangdu, he offered new robes to the young tulku and, having placed him on a Dharma throne, offered the yangsi a mandala.

Many years before, the steward Wangdu had gone to France and met the previous Pawo Rinpoche, who was then staying in his Dharma center in the south. This had created a connection between them, and now that they were together again, the very young tulku made a ball of his saffron rice, prepared for special occasions, and put it into the steward's mouth, touching foreheads with him in a warm and traditional greeting, which brought tears to Wangdu's eyes.

The parents recounted that there were no unusual signs at the tulku's birth, but he did seem to be a special child. He walked at the age of six months and was stronger than other children. When he was found at the age of about fourteen months, he looked much older. Unlike most babies, who like to move around a lot and cannot sit still, he liked to sit up straight and remain quiet as if in meditation. He also showed great faith in the Dharma and would prostrate the moment he came into a shrine room. Then he would walk around bowing to the various deities and clean off the monks' low puja tables.

~

Headed by Lama Panam (the three-year retreat master who represented Drupön Dechen Rinpoche) and Nenang Lama, a group of eighteen monks and lamas from Tsurphu and Nenang went to Nagchu to officially invite the young incarnation to his monastery on July 7, 1995. In accord with the government's request, this was done without the usual publicity and pageantry.

The next day the journey began, and they traveled a good part of the day. That night they all pitched tents, staying below Nyenchen Thanglha, the mountain whose deity is considered the protector of all virtuous activity, where the Karmapa was received when he first came to Tsurphu. If they had continued that same day to the monastery, they would have arrived late at night, which is considered inauspicious—better to arrive in the morning with the rising sun. Usually, it rains a lot during the summer season, but there had been no rain for a long time and the fields were dry and scorched. The farmers were worried about their crops. On this evening, rain began to fall and continued softly throughout the night, filling the people with gratitude and faith.

The next day, as they came down the Tölung Valley, though the sky was clear and the sun was shining, a gentle rain fell. Another auspicious sign. Not too far from Nenang Monastery is Nampar, where a spreading meadow was filled with summer blossoms. Monks from Tsurphu Monastery, Gyaltsap Rinpoche's monastery, and Nenang Monastery waited there for the incarnation to arrive. Following the custom of coming ahead to meet an important person, Drupön Dechen Rinpoche had come down the valley from Tsurphu. When he welcomed Pawo Rinpoche, it seemed as if they already knew each other. Exchanging khatas, they touched their foreheads together. Pawo Rinpoche then sat on a throne while Drupön Dechen Rinpoche sat on a lower seat beside him. The young incarnation felt so close to Drupön Dechen that he jumped off his throne toward him. Drupön Rinpoche deftly caught him and, touching their foreheads, lifted him gently back onto his seat.

The ceremony completed, the whole group then moved up the valley to Nenang Monastery, where all the monks from Tsurphu and Gyaltsap Rinpoche's monastery waited to greet the tulku with banners, flags, and the traditional music of drums, cymbals, long horns, reed horns, and conch shells. The young incarnation was placed on his throne and gave blessings to the three thousand people who had gathered to welcome him home. Afterward, on September 13, 1995, the young incarnation went to Lhasa, where his parents, who work for the government, have a private house. While he was staying there, he went with his attendants and family to the Jokhang and offered gold for the covering of the face of the Buddha and many other fine objects.

The family returned to Nenang Monastery on October 11. Accompanied by the monks and staff of his monastery, Pawo Rinpoche went to see the Karmapa for the first time on a day that had been chosen for its positive astrological signs. When they arrived near the Lower Park of Tsurphu, Pawo Rinpoche, about a year and a half old now, was asleep, but he woke up and joining his palms together, said *Karmapa khyenno* in a voice so loud and clear that everyone in the jeep heard it.

Pawo Rinpoche was first welcomed at Tsurphu's Lower Park in the second story of the summer house, where a throne had been prepared. After saffron rice and tea, the party then continued up to the main monastery of Tsurphu, and the young tulku was taken to a room near the Karmapa's quarters. Seated on his throne there, he recited *Karmapa khyenno* distinctly and clearly for the second time.

In the morning of October 11,[97] he went to meet the Karmapa in his private rooms. The child was too small to make real prostrations, yet he placed his palms together and bent forward to put his head on the floor. Standing again, he went up to the Karmapa to offer a khata and touch foreheads with him. The Karmapa looked delighted.

Afterward, they descended to the main shrine hall, where the Karmapa performed the hair-cutting ceremony as it had been performed for him and gave the young incarnation the new name, Palden Pawo Tsuglak Mawe Drayang (Glorious Hero and Scholar, Melodious Sound of Speech). Then they went to the Upper Park, whose gentle knolls, meandering stream, and green meadows are a favorite place for the monks to relax and play. During this visit, the Karmapa also transferred to Pawo Rinpoche the possessions belonging to the previous tenth Pawo Rinpoche. He was following the tradition of keeping safely, until the reincarnation is discovered, the key possessions of a great lama who has passed away. After this visit, Pawo Rinpoche returned to Nenang, and for the next years of his young life, he spent part of the time at his own monastery, part at Tsurphu, and part with his parents in Lhasa.

∼

In August 1998, when he was not yet five years old, Pawo Rinpoche and one of his attendants went with a few monks to the southeast of Nenang where a river flowed beneath a soft meadowed mountain. As the monks were washing their clothes in the stream, Pawo Rinpoche began to climb up the mountain all by himself. The monk Urgyen noticed him leaving and thought, "It's not good for him to go alone up the mountain," and so he followed after him. They had walked up quite far, when Pawo Rinpoche asked him, "Do you need a zi stone?" Urgyen responded, "Yes, I do need one. Where can I find it?" "If you need a zi, it's here under the ground," Pawo Rinpoche replied. "Really?" "Yes, really. If you don't believe me, then dig and you'll see." Breaking off a small branch from a nearby bush, they marked the spot and went back down the mountain.

When they returned to the river, Pawo Rinpoche said to his attendant, "On that mountain there is a zi stone. If you go there, you'll see the place we've marked." The attendant was doubtful. "Rinpoche, you are an important lama, and if you say that there is something there when there isn't, you'll be ashamed." "It's really there," Pawo Rinpoche affirmed. "If you don't believe me, then go and dig."

So all the monks went up to the place and dug down about three feet without finding anything. Their enthusiasm seemed to flag, but Pawo Rinpoche encouraged them to dig a little bit more, and soon they found a flat black stone that had the shape of a bird and the size of an open hand, an oval black stone, and a small conch shell. Pawo Rinpoche commented, "That's exactly right. The zi will not come out today. These three are enough for this time. We can go back now. If we come back the day after tomorrow, the zi stone will come out."

The party returned to the monastery and spent the next day there. Early the following morning, they went back to the special place. On the way there, Pawo Rinpoche said, "This dawn two zi stones have come out. The protector [of Nenang Monastery, Gongtsen] dug them out last night." When they arrived, there was a zi stone protruding from the earth at the bottom of the hole they had dug. Digging farther, they found another zi stone, plus coral, turquoise, silver, and gold—in all, about two handfuls of semi-precious stones in many different shapes. Pawo Rinpoche said, "That's enough. Now carry them down to the monastery." Once there, he layered five silk cloths of different colors—white, blue, yellow, red, and green—and then he put the precious stones inside, folded the silk up, and tied and sealed them. This packet was placed in the glass cabinet containing a statue of the protector Bernachen, and the cabinet was then sealed as well.

The three objects that came from the ground on the first day were placed in the shrine hall for everyone to see. Pawo Rinpoche explained that the black bird-shaped stone was the emanation of the Buddha, the oval stone symbolized the Buddha, and the conch shell was the symbol of Guru Rinpoche. When Nenang Lama returned from Lhasa, he asked Pawo Rinpoche, "Who buried these objects?" He replied, "The one who buried them is the eighth Pawo Tsuglak Chögyal."

Later, when Bokar Rinpoche was asked about the story, he said that Pawo Rinpoche is a very precious lama, and that about two hundred years have passed since the objects were buried by the eighth Pawo Rinpoche, who thought they would be beneficial in the future when his incarnation would find them. Bokar Rinpoche continues:

> In the Buddhist tradition, there are past and future lives. Especially in the case of a tulku, there is a clear continuum of mind between the past and the future. The truth of that continuum is revealed by signs and unusual events. In the case of Pawo Rinpoche, he revealed treasures that had been hidden by his previous incarnation. The young Pawo Rinpoche has a memory of deeds from his previous life and this shows that he is a true reincarnation. The body disappears, but the essential nature of the mind remains the same.
>
> Due to our ignorance, we have doubts about karma and past and future lives. Such a wondrous event will help to eliminate these doubts and wrong views, showing that past and future lives do indeed exist. His discovery of the hidden objects also indicates that this is the true reincarnation of Pawo Rinpoche.[98]

From a young age, Pawo Rinpoche displayed the temperament of a meditative monk. Unlike other children, he liked to remain quiet without a lot of commotion around him. Around the age of four, he especially liked to stay in the retreat center, which he preferred to the monastery. In retreat, the monks kept to a schedule of meditation sessions, and following this example, Pawo Rinpoche would sit straight and meditate for twenty minutes or so.

On October 31, 1999—an auspicious day called Lhabab Duchen[99]—Pawo Rinpoche went to Tsurphu. To make an auspicious connection, in the afternoon the Karmapa first taught him the alphabet. Until 2001, Pawo Rinpoche resided at his monastery and then the government made him move to Lhasa, where he lives with his parents and attends school.[100]

The Discovery of Dilyak Dabzang Rinpoche

Dabzang Rinpoche is known as a great practitioner and scholar of the Kagyu lineage, and he is also considered an emanation of Gampopa, the twelfth-century master who wrote *The Ornament of Precious Liberation*, which remains to this day the practice manual for the Kagyu tradition. In a long-life prayer for Dabzang Rinpoche, the previous sixteenth Karmapa wrote:

You, who guide the chariot of the teachings
Of the glorious Karmapa, heart of the practice lineage,
You, who are the miraculous vajra dance of great Gampopa,
Intentionally appearing as a perfect form body,[101] may your life
    be long.

In 1959, Dabzang Rinpoche traveled with the sixteenth Karmapa and passed through Bhutan. He eventually settled in Baudhanath, Nepal, where he built two monasteries, one of which is situated next to the great stupa. Dabzang Rinpoche was beloved by other lamas and known for his generosity, precise divinations, and deadpan humor. During his second visit to Tibet in 1990, Dabzang Rinpoche brought with him numerous Dharma texts, statues, shrine implements, brocades, robes for lama dancing, and many other objects. He made a tremendous effort to bring so many articles into Tibet, and finally arrived at Dilyak Monastery, the residence of his previous incarnations, where he offered everything he had brought and stayed for a while. When he was about to leave, the monks and senior government officials of the area requested him to come back soon. Dabzang Rinpoche replied: "This time I had many things to bring and travel was difficult. Now I will go to Nepal, where I have some work. Then, through Hong Kong, I will return here alone not carrying anything at all." Within a year of this visit, he passed away in Hong Kong on April 2, 1992. His followers in Tibet then understood his parting words, "I will return alone and not carrying anything at all," to mean that Dabzang Rinpoche would take rebirth as a child in Tibet.

~

When a great lama passes away, it is customary to perform forty-nine days of ceremonies. During these long rituals for Dabzang Rinpoche, Dilyak Drupön Rinpoche (his regent in Nepal) and representatives from Dilyak Monastery in Tibet petitioned Situ Rinpoche to find the reincarnation. Soon after, however, the seventeenth Karmapa returned to Tsurphu, and Situ Rinpoche requested him to find the reincarnation. Traditionally these requests are made at least three times, and so the monks from Dabzang Rinpoche's monastery asked Drupön Dechen Rinpoche at Tsurphu to remind the Karmapa about the letter of recognition. This he did several times, but the Karmapa always replied, "He has not been born yet." The Karmapa's letter of recognition finally came through in June 1996, not even a month after Dabzang Rinpoche's birth on May 20, 1996. It is quite unusual for a recognition to be made so quickly after a tulku's birth.

In a short time, the letter was brought to Nepal by Kunchok Dorje, the retired general secretary of Dilyak Monastery, who lived in Nepal and had a business in Lhasa, which gave him reason to travel back and forth between the two countries.

The letter of recognition was placed inside the shrine in the private quarters of the previous Dabzang Rinpoche while they waited for an auspicious day to open it. Soon after the letter arrived, that day came; the letter was taken out of the shrine, and placed on a special altar, and khatas were offered to it by Sangye Tulku, the regent of Dabzang Rinpoche in Tibet, Drupön Rinpoche, the regent in Nepal, and a few senior officers. When the letter was opened by the two rinpoches, they learned that the reincarnation was indeed reborn in Tibet. The letter read:

Om swasti.
Brilliant with the major and minor marks of an incarnation,
    unmistaken and supreme,
May your profound illumination extend throughout the world.

To the northwest of Dilyak Monastery, in the mountain range of Drida Zalmo Gang, there is a child born in the Mouse Year to a father named Karma and a mother named Drölma. Here with this recognition,

This lotus of the Practice Lineage and teachings will bloom
And surely attract the bees who long for liberation.

Written in the Fire Mouse Year, on the sixth day of the fifth month, by Ogyen Trinley Dorje, who holds the name of Buddha Karmapa, on the sixth day of the fifth month of the Fire Mouse Year (June 22, 1996).

Over saffron rice and Tibetan tea, they discussed how to pursue the search. It was unusual that the letter of prediction clearly indicated the names of the father, Karma, and the mother, Drölma, as normally only one letter or syllable of each name is given. The location of their home was said to be northwest of Dilyak Monastery in Nangchen, a province of Kham (eastern Tibet), famous for its numerous monasteries and realized practitioners. In that direction lay two large districts, Dzatö[102] and Dritö,[103] which would have been difficult to search; therefore, Sangye Trinley, a personal attendant of the previous Dabzang Rinpoche, was sent from Nepal to Tibet to request further information from the Karmapa. When asked which district to search, the ten-year-old Karmapa immediately replied, "Dzatö."

Sangye Trinley traveled to Dilyak Monastery and gave the news exclusively to the few individuals involved in the search. Thinking they could find the parents through an official register, the monks asked a helpful government official to see if there was a male child born in the Year of the Mouse to parents named Karma and Drölma. Among the more than three hundred children born in the Mouse Year, not one was found whose parents had these names.

Sangye Trinley returned to Tsurphu and once again climbed the stairs to the top floor of the main temple to meet with the Karmapa, who stated firmly, "The parents are definitely there. You must search for them." When asked how to conduct the search, the Karmapa replied, "The best way is to search on foot disguised as simple pilgrims. The monks should make their own investigation of the area and find the names of all families with male children born in the Year of the Mouse. Once they have finished, bring all the names to me and I will make a decision."

Sangye Trinley returned to Nepal, where he reported to Drupön Rinpoche of Nepal and Sangye Tulku of Tibet, who was visiting Baudhanath and about to return to Dilyak Monastery in Tibet. With this new information, it was clear that Sangye Tulku should take responsibility for finding the reincarnation, and soon after returning home to Tibet, he sent out four search parties dressed as simple pilgrims. As instructed, they gathered all the names and then traveled to Tsurphu to offer the Karmapa the results of their quest. On their list, was one family with parents named Karma and Drölma, just as the letter had predicted. Their names had not yet been written into the official registry, because they were itinerant workers and had come to Dzatö from Surmang only two years before. All of this the Karmapa had clearly seen, and he chose the child of Karma and Drölma right away as the true reincarnation.

Joyful that their search had been successful, Sangye Tulku and senior monks from Dilyak Monastery, accompanied by the head officer of the Dzatö county government, went to visit the parents and let them know that their son was the reincarnation of Dabzang Rinpoche. At the time of this meeting, a clear, vibrant rainbow appeared over Dilyak Monastery in Nepal. Asked if they would give the boy to the monastery, the parents willingly agreed, and the young reincarnation was given the traditional ritual cleansing and his first set of monk's robes. According to custom, the monastery offered many gifts to the parents, including a horse and livestock for the father, brocades for the mother, and a house for the entire family.

During the festivities, the parents told of the unusual events surrounding the child. While the reincarnation was still in her womb, rays of white light appeared to his mother and dissolved into her heart. In the winter, there were loud claps of thunder. This was extremely unusual, as thunder is a summertime phenomenon. Simultaneously, they saw a wondrous tent of light surrounding their house. All the people of the area noticed it and thought it quite amazing.

When the child was born, the inside of the house was filled with an appearance of light, and the place where the child slept was encircled by white light. The family had a small shrine with seven offering bowls lined up across the front, and on the day of their son's birth, the father saw a white rainbow circle in one of them. On that day as well, the spring that provided the family's drinking water turned a milky white. Considering this auspicious, they drank the water, which tasted like milk. Later, an old monk who seemed to appear out of nowhere offered an image of Gampopa to the child,[104] and then the monk disappeared as mysteriously as he had come.

When they occurred, these various signs had seemed significant but isolated events. The recognition of their son as a tulku shaped them into a pattern that then continued to unfold. When the young incarnation was leaving his home and coming to Dilyak Monastery for the first time, the sounds of conch shell horns, cymbals, and reed horns were heard by people in the area, who thought that monks had come to receive him, but no one was playing music.

~

In the beginning of the next year, a letter was written to the Karmapa requesting him to perform the hair-cutting ceremony on August 7, 1997, the anniversary of the Buddha's first teachings. Four months later, about a year after the tulku's birth, monks were sent to invite the young incarnation to Tsurphu for the hair-cutting ceremony, at which he would also be given a new name.

On August 6, the young incarnation traveled to Tsurphu and was welcomed by its monks, who played reed horns and offered fragrant incense. When informed of his arrival, the Karmapa asked the tulku to come and meet him that afternoon at three. When they met, the young tulku could not yet speak, but he was all smiles. The Karmapa blessed him and gave him blessing pills, which he spontaneously bowed to receive.

At dawn the next day, August 7, the monks gathered in the main shrine hall of Tsurphu to perform the ceremonies. After an offering of tea and saffron rice, the young tulku was carried to the Karmapa's throne, and he cut the remaining strands of hair and read out the yangsi's new name, written on a piece of white silk: Karma Ngedön Tenpe Nyima Trinley Tsungma Mepe De[105] (Karma, Definitive Meaning, Sun of the Teachings, Unequaled Enlightened Activity). Afterward, the Karmapa placed a golden khata and a blessing cord around Dabzang Rinpoche's neck and offerings were made. Only one year and three months old, he sat on the throne for hours and blessed all who had come.

After a celebration in the Upper Park, Dabzang Rinpoche spent one more night at Tsurphu and then took the long eastbound journey back to Nangchen. He has begun to study, but since he is still quite young, he spends part of the time in the monastery and part with his family, journeying a day by horseback from the monastery to the new house built for his parents.

"It's Now or Never"

URING HIS STAY at Tsurphu, the Karmapa was fully involved in rebuilding his monastery. Gathering all the resources he could find, he restored the temples, shrines, stupas, and residences that had been destroyed. Following his great interest in texts and study, he also built a *shedra*, or an institute for higher Buddhist studies, which started in late 1998 and was officially opened in May 1999.[106] With the shedra constructed, the rebuilt Tsurphu was complete in all its main aspects: there were places for long-term meditation retreats, for the practice of complex rituals of the daily ceremonies in the main temple, and, finally, for examining and debating the profound philosophical treatises of the Buddhist tradition.

Tsurphu seemed to be flourishing and yet there was a shadow side as well. In the summer of 1998, an attempt was made on the Karmapa's life. Two unidentified Chinese men with knives were found hiding under a blanket in the library, which had a door leading to the Karmapa's quarters. At the time, the Karmapa was away at a picnic; his intuition of danger kept him unwilling to return even though it had started to rain. The two men admitted that someone in Lhasa had given them money and promised more if they were successful. It is said that despite the great concern of the monks at Tsurphu, local officials did not pursue the case, nor did they increase security at the monastery.[107]

The Karmapa continued his studies and practice, yet the time came when he needed uniquely qualified teachers who were not available In Tibet. He had not yet received the full range of empowerments and reading transmissions found in the precious Golden Garland of the Kagyu lineage.[108] Without these, he would have the name Karmapa but would not be able to perform his many activities to their full extent. His two root lamas, Situ Rinpoche and Gyaltsap Rinpoche, resided in India; the Karmapa had repeatedly asked the government for permission to travel there to receive the Dharma teachings and transmissions he needed, but his requests had not been granted. He also appealed for permission to invite the two rinpoches to Tibet and this as well never received a positive response.

Over the years, he had made these appeals earnestly and repeatedly, but neither one was ever granted.

The Karmapa's knowledge of his situation inside Tibet included many factors. He recalled, "One Chinese government official gave me a hint: 'In the future when you are eighteen, they will take a great interest in you.' This gave me doubts." When he reached the age of majority, the Chinese government could tighten the circumstances around him and require him to function as an adjunct of government policy. Pressure was already being put on him; for example, he had to attend the hair-cutting ceremony of the Panchen Lama chosen by the Chinese.[109]

Another impetus for the escape probably came from the Karmapa's second visit to China in early 1999. In Beijing, he met with Chinese leaders[110] at official gatherings, visited temples, gave blessings, and spoke with the press. He was also forced to attend ceremonies with the Chinese-selected Panchen Lama, who gave a speech that was obviously memorized, talking to the Karmapa about "you and me working together so that the country will develop and that Dharma will develop," rehearsing the same lines that Jiang Zemin had put forward years before. When asked by the official press about the Chinese Panchen Lama, the thirteen-year-old Karmapa skillfully replied without making any direct comment about the candidate: "If the Panchen Lama is an emanation of Amitabha, then he should be a good incarnate lama. And, by the way, a incarnate lama is one who has the three qualities of knowledge, diligence, and correct conduct. He has also attained the positive qualities that come from listening, reflecting, and meditating on the Dharma. Further, a tulku has great enthusiasm for the Buddha's teachings and great joy in seeing the sangha flourish."[111]

In a similar indirect way, the Karmapa stood up for the Tibetans, saying to the press, "One's own people is priceless." The Karmapa's tutor, Lama Nyima, accompanied him on the trip, and this whole visit must have been difficult for both of them, foreboding a difficult future.

The Chinese also tried to enlist the Karmapa's support for the Communist Party. When asked to read a speech written by a local official, the Karmapa queried: "'Do you wish me to say that I am giving this speech on your behalf?' The startled party representative explained that the speech was to be delivered as though it were his own. 'In that case,' said the Karmapa, 'I have no need of this text.' No speech was given."[112]

The pattern of pressure and reluctance was certainly there, but the overwhelming reason that compelled the Karmapa to leave was the impossibility of meeting with his teachers. For years he had made requests, and for years they had been refused. The Karmapa explained the importance of studying with his root teachers: "In our Karma Kagyu tradition, from Vajradhara to Tilopa, Naropa, Marpa, and down through the lineage, for each different tradition of Dharma there is a different lineage, which one lama gives to another, who then passes it on to the next. The previous Karmapa gave our lineage to Situ Rinpoche and Gyaltsap Rinpoche. He did give this lineage to other lamas, but these two rinpoches are outstanding lamas, and they also have a special connection to the Karmapas in that they have been his close spiritual sons for generations. The responsibility to give the initiations to the next incarnation of the Karmapa falls to these spiritual sons."[113]

Situ Rinpoche has also underlined the importance of lineage:

Within the Tibetan tradition, the definition of Buddhism is lineage. If there is no lineage, there is no Buddhism. Lord Buddha was enlightened, and he manifested the teaching to disciples, who practiced, upheld, and cherished it. The teachings then continued to the next disciple, who upheld, cherished, and practiced it. In this way, the lineages of teaching come down to us today.

There is a lineage for every aspect of the teachings—for meditation, prayer, initiations, rituals, philosophy, and for each one of the vows— Tantric, Mahayana, Theravadin. Any aspect of the Buddha's teaching is valid if it has a living lineage, which means that it has continued unbroken, and it is not real Buddhism if there is no living lineage. So first I must receive the lineage and then I must maintain it. For example, if I receive a teaching from my master and do not uphold it, cherish it, or respect both the teaching and the teacher from whom I received it, then the pledge or samaya is broken and that teaching has no value. It's just information. It is the same with a vow. The end of Buddhism will mean that all the lineages are discontinued. Buddhism is alive as long as the lineage continues.[114]

Finally, to maintain his lineage and fulfill his role as its leader, the Karmapa had no choice but to leave: all avenues of approach had been exhausted, and his goal still remained out of reach. Slowly, he began to make clandestine plans to escape. Months before he left, the Karmapa had hinted at his plans, telling one Western disciple in September 1999 that he would meet him outside of Tibet the next time. He also told Southeast Asian disciples that he would be coming to Taiwan in the not too distant future.

Situ Rinpoche recalls:

Through the years, we made requests to both the Chinese and Indian governments asking that His Holiness the Karmapa be permitted to come to his Seat in Rumtek and to other places, but we were unsuccessful. Finally,

His Holiness the Karmapa thought that he should go to India, and he communicated his plans to me several times in letters and messages. As soon as possible, I conveyed this information to His Holiness the Dalai Lama and he kindly gave his advice, which I cherished. As best as I could, I tried to identify the risks involved and remain sensitive to the situation as a whole. I conveyed to Gyalwa Karmapa key points to consider and all the dangers and problems involved. He advised me, however, that for many reasons, including his situation and the time, he had no other choice but to travel to India. In this way, just as his previous incarnation, the Karmapa by himself alone decided to come to India as a refugee. Given the place, time, and situation, there was very little I could do to help him, but I did my best. For example, I arranged for the Gyalwa Karmapa to travel directly to meet His Holiness the Dalai Lama in India.[115]

In the late fall of 1999, about two months before he left Tibet, the Karmapa presided over a *drubchen* (extended practice) of fifteen days for the deity Serö Ngadra. He had made a new arrangement of this practice and its instructions, and it was performed at this time in this largest-known ceremony for the deity. Each day, the Karmapa gave two long talks to the assembled monks, emphasizing that the very basis of the teachings is the sangha and that it was vital that they study well and maintain their vows. He encouraged them to study the texts of the seventh Karmapa, Chödrak Gyatso, and the eighth Karmapa, Mikyö Dorje, who were great scholars, and the ninth Karmapa, Wangchuk Dorje, who wrote the main practice texts on mahamudra, describing the nature of the mind and how to realize it. He spoke about how to rely on a teacher,[116] about taking refuge[117] and generating bodhichitta, the awakened mind.[118] He reminded them of the Four Reflections: the preciousness of human birth, the impermanence of all phenomena, karma as the infallible working of cause and effect, and all the defects of samsaric existence.

He especially emphasized impermanence: "Everything compounded is impermanent. You may be looking at me now and thinking, 'He is young and we will often meet,' but given that all is impermanent, maybe I won't be around for so long. Even if impermanence gives you problems, you should always study and maintain your discipline. In the future, we will have the chance to meet again." Hearing this, none of the monks thought that he would be leaving Tibet, but rather that he was referring to the traditional contemplation of impermanence and death. Having explained the practice of meditation and spoken of how their experience and realization would grow, the Karmapa asked the monks to keep his instructions deep in their hearts.

At that time, the Karmapa also made extensive offerings: each monk at Tsurphu received a new note of one hundred yuan; Gyaltsap Rinpoche's monastery was presented with forty pieces of gold, and money was donated to his monks as well. The monks who had come out of three-year retreat were given an elaborate meal. In addition to benefiting the monks, these offerings also served to eliminate obstacles for the escape, which, of course, was not mentioned.

Gathering Companions for the Road

About the time of the extended practice for Serö Ngadra, the Karmapa confided in his tutor, Lama Nyima, that he wanted to escape and asked for his help. The Karmapa recalls that Lama Nyima responded, "Please consider the future carefully. It might be difficult for you. Things could go badly." Despite his worries for the Karmapa's sake, Lama Nyima agreed to help in any way he could.

The personal stories of the individuals who helped the Karmapa to escape reveal much about life in Tibet where tradition continues alongside the modernizing world. In particular, they illustrate the role a great master plays in people's lives and, further, how Tsurphu Monastery is linked to the world around it.

Lama Nyima was well prepared to be the tutor of the Karmapa. He had studied the major Buddhist treatises at Sera Monastery, where he was famous as the best among the students of his tutor. He was skilled in dialectics, debate, and textual understanding, especially the writings of one of Tibet's great scholars, Je Tsongkhapa, whose difficult major work[119] Lama Nyima had memorized in two months, further increasing his fame. Wishing to broaden his experience and focus on practice, Lama Nyima came to Tsurphu in 1989 and talked to Drupön Dechen. As a result of their conversations, Lama Nyima entered the traditional three-year retreat the following year at the age of twenty-five. It is rare for someone with such a great knowledge of texts to undertake this long retreat of continual meditation, and his wisdom was invaluable for the other participants. When the three years were finished, Drupön Dechen sent him to Lhasa to study the subtleties of language, poetics, and advanced grammar with the well-known teachers Khenpo Tsenam and Tashi Palden. He was an excellent student, and when he finished, Drupön Dechen appointed him to be the Karmapa's tutor. Umdze Thubten Zangpo had taught the Karmapa how to read and study in the Tsurphu tradition, and Lama Nyima took responsibility for his advanced learning. He also helped in other important matters, such as finding the reincarnations of Jamgön Kongtrul and Pawo Rinpoche. Now aged thirty-seven, he was ready to risk his life for the Karmapa.

In the months before the escape, the only other person in Tibet who knew about the evolving plans was the Karmapa's older attendant, Tsimpön Drubngak. Born in 1938 in the village next to Tsurphu, he became a monk at the age of seven during the time of the previous Karmapa, remaining at Tsurphu Monastery until it was destroyed. Having no place to stay, he moved to a nomad settlement at the end of the valley and remained there until 1984 when the restrictions on religious practice were relaxed and, according to one's wish, one was allowed to engage or not in religious practice. At that time, Drubngak chose to return to Tsurphu and live as a monk again. He worked for years hauling earth and stones to rebuild the monastery, and then became manager of the construction workers. He also participated in the practices in the main shrine hall, and sometimes in the Protector shrine room, he would chant the rituals of the protector Mahakala. When the Karmapa returned to Tsurphu in 1992, Drubngak became his attendant. He would also take flight with the Karmapa years later.

Knowing that more help was needed for the escape, Lama Nyima thought of his close and trusted friend Nenang Lama[120] from Pawo Rinpoche's Monastery. He was born three kilometers from Tsurphu, and his family had been closely connected to the Karmapa for generations. His great-grandmother was a sister of the fourteenth Karmapa, Thekchok Dorje, and she married the older brother of the eighth Pawo Rinpoche. The family went to Tsurphu for all important events—New Year's celebrations, the blessing of their children, the days of intensive practice and lama dancing—and many of his family members had become monks there. Nenang Lama went to the village school from age six to fifteen and then worked on his family's land. After studying at the Institute of Buddhist Studies at Nechung,[121] at the age of twenty-two, Nenang Lama entered the first three-year retreat at Tsurphu. During this time, the previous Pawo Rinpoche sent many letters asking him to stay at his seat of Nenang Monastery. There was no lama and the monks were poor and needed help. Nenang Lama replied that he had no special qualities and was not very capable; others in retreat were more qualified and it would be good to ask Drupön Dechen to send one of them. Pawo Rinpoche then wrote to Drupön Dechen and requested that he send Nenang Lama. Finishing retreat in 1990 when he was twenty-four, he finally went to Nenang Monastery and began to rebuild it, in preparation for the arrival of Pawo Rinpoche's reincarnation, whom he was instrumental in finding. Nenang Lama also started an orphanage and a school of 120 students in grades one through five. His stores and travel business in Lhasa helped to support many humanitarian projects. Lama Nyima knew that with his devotion, experience, and connections Nenang Lama, who was now thirty-six, would make a perfect companion. Further, his frequent travels to and from Lhasa on monastery business meant that all his activity in preparation for the escape would not be suspect.

Telling the administration that he was sick and had to go for an extensive checkup and possible medical treatment, Lama Nyima went to Lhasa to meet with Nenang Lama and tell him of the Karmapa's wish to leave for India. Lama Nyima repeated the Karmapa's words, which he had spoken with intensity and great courage: "If I stay here, it will be difficult to benefit the teachings and living beings in an extensive way. If I leave, it will be possible." Deeply concerned, Nenang Lama went to Tsurphu and spoke with the Karmapa: "I've heard that you are planning to leave for India. Please consider it carefully. It is so dangerous, and if they catch you, we don't know what might happen."

Subsequently, Nenang Lama and Lama Nyima met in Lhasa for a second talk, traveling outside of the city to a remote place where they could not be overheard. This became their custom in the weeks that followed. Walking together, they spoke for a long while. Nenang Lama said, "We don't have much time to make plans. It might be better if the Karmapa doesn't go this year but waits for two or three years." Lama Nyima replied with the Karmapa's words: "If we don't go this year, the opportunity to escape will not come again." Aware of the great danger they faced, Nenang Lama replied, "But this is not a movie. It's for real—and very difficult to pull off successfully. We're not so important, but if the Karmapa falls into Chinese hands, that could be very serious." Lama Nyima answered, "The Karmapa has precognition. He knows what will happen and has said that it's time to go. He must leave this year. It's now or never. And he's certain that we'll make it to India.

"We're having a difficult time finding reliable people to help with the escape," he continued. "We had wanted to ask you before, but hesitated because you have so much work and so many responsibilities. You have Pawo Rinpoche to look after, and his monastery, his education, the school, and so on."

As he listened to his friend, Nenang Lama was thinking, "I am a disciple of the Karmapa and have complete faith and trust in him. It's for the benefit of the teachings and all beings that he is taking the huge risk of going to India. If I help, it will be an activity full of merit." Nenang Lama also had a pure connection and trust in his friend Lama Nyima, so he replied, "If you want me to, I'll go with you. The work I do at Nenang Monastery is small compared to the vast activity of the Karmapa. For the time being, I'll give up this work to help." Lama Nyima was overjoyed.

But more help was needed. "We must find one more person," they agreed and thought of another monk from Tsurphu, Lama Tsultrim Gyaltsen, who was just turning thirty. With his moon-shaped face and large brown eyes, he had a more quiet character. Lama Tsultrim had participated in the same three-year retreat as Lama Nyima and was also a close friend of Nenang Lama. Lama Tsultrim was born about seventy-five kilometers south from Tsurphu in Nyemo, where farmers lived in a valley encircled by snow mountains. For many generations, his relatives, as many from this area, have had a close bond with Tsurphu. About two thousand households in Nyemo's district of Zuri estate are connected to Tsurphu, and Lama Tsultrim's father worked for the monastery there. From age nine to eighteen, Lama Tsultrim attended the local schools and then went to work planting crops in the fields, looking after the family's sheep, and doing carpentry. One day his mother said to him, "For generations our root lama has been the Karmapa. Our religious tradition has been Kagyu, and we have had a close bond with Tsurphu. The world of samsara has no real worth, and it would be excellent if you became a monk." With these words, his mother expressed his own wish: he wanted to practice the Dharma and be near the Karmapa. So he went to see Drupön Dechen Rinpoche at Tsurphu and said, "My family has an old connection with Tsurphu. I am from Zuri estate and my mother said 'Maybe it would be good if you, my son, became a monk.'" Not raising any objection, Drupön Dechen responded, "That is fine," and immediately cut his hair, making him a novice monk.

For the next four years, Lama Tsultrim studied texts in the morning and evening and did carpentry around the monastery in the afternoon. By the time he was twenty-three, he had memorized all the texts for the main practices at Tsurphu, and then asked Drupön Rinpoche if he could participate in the three-year retreat. "We'll see" was the reply. There were only eighteen places and, as usual, many more monks than that had applied. When the heads of the monastery met to decide who would be accepted, Drupön Rinpoche spoke up for Lama Tsultrim, saying, "If he does retreat, it will benefit the monastery."

After completing three years of retreat, Lama Tsultrim served as the personal shrine master for the Karmapa. Soon, Drupön Dechen asked him to take on a new job. The large courtyard in front of the monastery where lama dancing was performed needed new pavement. The project also included constructing a complex drainage system underground so that the stones remained level and in place. For over three years, Lama Tsultrim worked on this project. First he had to raise the funds, and so he traveled to Kham in the east, Amdo in the north, Nari in the west, and other places to perform rituals and consecrations, give empowerments, and teach the Dharma. The actual work began a year later and came to include a new floor for the shrine hall and the administrative offices as well. At the age of thirty, he completed this undertaking, and friends playfully called him the Stone Lama. Lama Tsultrim now spent part of his time at the monastery, part in Lhasa, and part traveling to give teachings and empowerments.

One day in late October, while on a visit to Tsurphu, Lama Nyima told Lama Tsultrim of their plans. Wanting to think over this turning point in his life, Lama Tsultrim did not answer right away, but pondered the two possibilities: freedom to practice in India or possible imprisonment if caught. About two weeks later, while Lama Tsultrim was staying in Lhasa on monastery business, the Karmapa called him to his quarters in Tsurphu and told him in complete secrecy, "I'm escaping to India. Please talk to Lama Nyima and Nenang Lama and see what is best to do." Lama Tsultrim responded, "This is not a small matter. It's critical." The Karmapa replied, "I've thought it through completely and have made my decision." And so Lama Tsultrim said, "I'll offer all the help I can." The Karmapa told him, "You three must now decide how the escape should happen."

Lama Tsultrim returned to Lhasa to meet Lama Nyima and Nenang Lama. He called them on his cell phone—as did many in Tibet, all three monks had cell phones—from an isolated place near the Kyichu River, flowing to the south of the city and a favorite spot for picnics in the summer. Lama Tsultrim phoned, "This is a delightful place," he said, "Why don't you join me for a relaxing stroll?" and the two monks soon arrived. That day, the three made a commitment among themselves that even if it meant losing their lives, they would work with their whole heart to help the Karmapa and would not tell anyone else of their plans.

They also realized that they had to take into their confidence the Karmapa's cook, Thubten, a monk in his late twenties. He often visited the Karmapa and brought him his meals; he would certainly know if the Karmapa was not there. The Karmapa was very fond of Thubten, who in turn, had great faith in the Karmapa and would do anything for him. Later, when Nenang Lama came to Tsurphu, there were always too many people around to be able to speak with Thubten in private. Thubten, however, came up to him, took his hand firmly, and winked, saying, "No problem. Don't worry." All during the preparations, Thubten helped Lama Nyima when he was at Tsurphu.

Which Route?

Lama Nyima, Nenang Lama, and Lama Tsultrim discussed in detail what the Karmapa had said and how to divide the tasks involved in helping the precious head of their lineage escape. They decided that Lama Nyima would be responsible for the Karmapa's safe exit from the monastery building itself. From the time he entered the car all the way down to the Indian border, the responsibility would fall to Nenang Lama and Lama Tsultrim. Under the Karmapa's direction, they were to lay out the plans, but it was the Karmapa who would decide when and where to go and what to do along their escape route.

The next major decision was the route itself. They mulled over the possibilities: Should they go through Kongpo to the south? Through the west passing near Mount Kailash? Through nearby Dram where many go? Not able to make a decision, they decided to meet again in three days. During this time, Lama Tsultrim casually asked around to gather information about the different routes. How long does it take to reach Mount Kailash? What are the roads like to Kongpo? What's the best way to get to Nepal? Are the roads good to Mustang? Where are the police checkpoints? Are there villages close to the road? What about the army camps? They had to know every possible danger.

After three days, they all met in an isolated place to compare the information they had gathered. It was decided that while Lama Nyima would stay in Lhasa, Nenang Lama and Lama Tsultrim would investigate an escape route through western Tibet to Mustang, an ancient kingdom belonging to the Tibetan cultural realm and now part of Nepal. This seemed the best way since few travelers used this road and the check points were not so strictly guarded. Though barely a trail, the road also went all the way over a pass into Nepal. They would need a good car for this journey and later for the escape itself, so Nenang Lama, who had funds from his various projects, bought a white Toyota jeep and resold it at a low price to Lama Tsultrim. With the jeep in his name, Lama Tsultrim now had a vehicle at Tsurphu and could establish a pattern of traveling in and out on monastery business. They also made sure that the jeep was thoroughly checked and repaired.

~

Meanwhile, in India, word of the Karmapa's plan was conveyed to Lama Tenam, Situ Rinpoche's trusted attendant, known for his openness and ready smile. In 1959, Lama Tenam left Tibet with his parents and become a monk in Nepal while quite young. After many years at a monastery, he attended the Tibetan Institute of Higher Studies in Sarnath and finally moved to Sherab Ling Monastery to serve Situ Rinpoche. He taught the young monks there and studied English as much as he could. Eventually, he began to travel abroad, accompanying Situ Rinpoche on all his journeys.

In 1992, Lama Tenam meet the Karmapa in Tsurphu and had returned there with Situ Rinpoche in addition to coming twice on his own. These visits had established a close and warm relationship with the young Karmapa. Lama Tenam recalls: "We knew ahead of time that His Holiness was considering leaving Tibet, but we didn't know when or how he would come." Staying in Delhi, Lama Tenam was the one who made the connection with Situ Rinpoche: "Whatever news I received, I communicated to Situ Rinpoche. He then went to His Holiness the Dalai Lama and let him know that there was a hope that the Gyalwa Karmapa would come."[122]

~

Back in Tibet, the two monks needed reasons for making this long trip to the west of Tibet, so they came up with projects they needed to do. Previously, they had met a man from Saga county, not far from the Nepali border, who had given an interesting piece of information: from his place, he had seen people escaping over a mountain into Nepal. It also happened that a sponsor had asked Lama Tsultrim to come to Saga, as he had done before, to conduct ceremonies and give Dharma teaching. This gave Lama Tsultrim a reason to take a leave of absence from the monastery. He told the officials that his sponsors had said,

"You haven't come for two or three years and we were worried about you. We're delighted that you will be visiting us." The administration gave him a special letter of introduction, stating that he was a monk from Tsurphu and traveling on monastery business. This permitted him to travel in this sensitive border area, which was usually closed off. For his part, Nenang Lama said he had to go to Nari in the west to look after a building project for Bokar Rinpoche, a great Kagyu retreat master who lives in India.

About a month before the actual escape, the two lamas left for western Tibet together with Lama Tsultrim's driver, Dargye, who did not know about their plans. A monk in his late twenties, Dargye came from Tashi Gang, a village near Nenang Monastery. His family, who farmed in Tsurphu's Tölung Valley, had had a connection with the Karmapas for many generations. As a child, Dargye looked after the family's cattle and sheep and then attended four years of the government school. Afterward he studied carpentry and worked on building the main temple at Tsurphu. During this time he became a monk and studied texts in addition to working at the monastery. Lama Tsultrim first made a connection with him when he asked Dargye to come and help raise funds for his project of paving the courtyard, and this began years of traveling and working together. While Lama Tsultrim went to Hong Kong to raise funds, Dargye learned to drive the monastery's Tata truck. Now he would drive the two monks on the scouting trip in the white Toyota jeep that Lama Tsultrim had bought from Nenang Lama.

All three men, Nenang Lama, Lama Tsultrim, and Dargye, were dressed in fur-lined brocade chubas and fur hats, looking just like traders. Actually, when not at the monastery or directly performing monastic duties, it was not unusual for the monks to dress in lay clothes, which were warmer and permitted easier movement. Since Lama Tsultrim had the official papers, Nenang Lama was his assistant for this journey. Lamas rarely travel alone, so it was natural for him to have a companion.

Their first destination was Saga county, where they met with Lama Tsultrim's delighted sponsors. Changing into monk's robes for a day, he conducted prayers and gave an empowerment. The brief visit went smoothly. Their second destination, still in Tibet, was Khuyug Monastery, which is a branch of Tsurphu.[123] Between these two places flows the Yarlung Tsangpo (Brahmaputra), a major river in Asia, but there is no bridge, as the government sees no need to facilitate travel to the other side and beyond into Nepal and India. The broad and powerful river has to be traversed in a boat or else in a car when the ice is thick enough to hold its weight. Leaving their jeep with a sponsor, they rode horses over the frozen edges of the river. At the center, the river's powerful current had kept ice from forming, forcing them to swim on the backs of their horses across the churning waters. Recalling stories of people who had been swept away downstream, from their hearts they repeated *Karmapa khyenno* for protection.

Safely on the other side, they rode to Khuyug Monastery. The monk in charge, Lama Pema, was a good friend of Lama Tsultrim and also knew Nenang Lama. So that Lama Pema would not be implicated in their plans, the true purpose of their visit was kept secret. Nenang Lama explained to him: "As the one responsible for Pawo Rinpoche, I'm going to monasteries and requesting ceremonies to clear away obstacles. The yangsi is to be enthroned soon, but there are some difficulties." It is not uncommon for ceremonies to be performed to remove obstacles and free the way to an important event. Lama Pema was delighted to help, as Pawo Rinpoche is a very high lama in the Kagyu lineage and had been recognized by the Karmapa.

After the first night of their stay, Nenang Lama discussed with Lama Pema his plans to visit relatives in Mustang. This was not unusual; along with pilgrimage and business, visiting relatives is a major reason for Tibetans to travel. Further, one of Nenang Lama's relatives was a tulku of Lama Pema's Khuyug Monastery. He had been recognized by the previous Karmapa, so naturally Lama Pema knew about him. This tulku and his brother lived in Lo Monthang (the capital of Mustang) and would play a role in the escape, though nothing of this was mentioned now. Nenang Lama also explained to Lama Pema that they were looking for a incarnate lama. He had not mentioned this earlier at Tsurphu since the route into Mustang lay over a very sensitive border area and may have aroused suspicion. Lama Pema would understand the general need for secrecy, and since lamas often went in disguise on such searches, the fact that they were dressed in lay clothes would not surprise him.

One day while still at Khuyug, the three monks from Tsurphu went up to the top of a nearby hill, and Nenang Lama said playfully to Dargye, "Lama Tsultrim and I are escaping to India. Want to come along? If things don't go well for us, it'll be the same for you. If they do go well for us, you'll be lucky, too." Dargye answered, "No. Definitely not. I don't want to escape. I can't make those words come out of my mouth. I'm worried that the Chinese would catch us. There's no point in even trying. If you want to go, fine, but I'm staying. I won't drive for you on that trip." They replied, "We were just joking. We're not escaping. But we do need to go to Nepal this year." "Why?" Dargye asked. "We have relatives to visit. And His Holiness has recognized a tulku who lives in Mustang. We need to go and examine him. Take a good look at this landscape. We might pass by here again." The two monks were not behaving like normal lamas on a Dharma trip. Dargye wondered about this. "Would His Holiness be escaping? No, it couldn't be that. It must be Pawo Rinpoche they are taking to India." [124] Doubts lingered in his mind.

From a friend of Lama Pema, the monks traveling as traders hired a car. Lama Pema took them to the nearby military encampment of Dranggo to obtain a special pass for their party of four—Nenang Lama, Lama Tsultrim, Lama Pema, and the driver Dargye. Well-known in the area, Lama Pema offered to stand security for the three lamas if they did not return. On the basis of this, the army officer gave them a letter stating that they were traders and would return in two or three days. They spent the night near the army camp. After a four-to-five hour drive, they arrived at the second army camp close to the Nepali border, and here, they showed their letter. The officers checked their car and said, "Make sure you return."

Observing their surroundings carefully as they went, the four drove in the jeep across the Tibet-Nepal border to Nechung. The primitive road had been made by traders going back and forth to Tibet. From Nechung, the monks rode horses to the house of Nenang Lama's relatives further south. As they traveled, they had much to keep in mind. Outwardly, they were dressed as traders, but the lamas were also looking for a young incarnation named Nenang Wangdu[125] whom the Karmapa had identified. He was a tulku from Pawo Rinpoche's monastery and therefore finding and taking care of him was Nenang Lama's responsibility. So their journey actually had three levels: they were outwardly traders; inwardly, monks looking for a tulku; and secretly, seekers of a route for the Karmapa's flight to India.

They did find the tulku, identified in the Karmapa's recognition letter, and Nenang Lama explained to the child's parents that if the political situation was good in Tibet, they would bring him back there, and if not, they would bring him to a place in Nepal. Nenang Lama asked, "There's a problem, however, as the pass I had allowing me to exit through Dram"—the usual path for those leaving Tibet—"has expired, so I can't go that way. In the future, if we get permission again as we did this time, could you help us? I might need to go to central Nepal on business for Nenang Monastery. I would drive here and then leave the car. If this happens, could you help me to go down into central Nepal and back to Tibet?" The parents were happy to help and had no suspicions of any other purpose, since in Kathmandu there was a monastery belonging to Pawo Rinpoche and it would be natural for Nenang Lama to visit there.

Having received an affirmative response to his first request, Nenang Lama added, "When I go back to Tsurphu, I will inform the Karmapa about the young tulku, and if he confirms the recognition, then I might have to bring him to Kathmandu. If that turns out to be the case, I could be coming with quite a few people. That won't be a problem for you?" "Not at all," they replied. The parents were very happy to know that their son was possibly a tulku and said, "We will help in every way we can." So Nenang Lama made his final point: "We'll probably be returning in about a month with six or seven people. Please have horses ready for us and someone to bring them back."

Continuing their research, the lamas asked many questions about the roads and left some money to cover future expenses. The four reported in at the army camp near the border and said that business had gone well. The guards were glad to see them back in the three days as promised. They inspected the jeep and the goods they had brought back—blankets and clothes—and let them pass.

As they drove along the route, the monks took note of what they were passing by and also took photographs along the way. After a good night's sleep at Khuyug Monastery, Nenang Lama and Lama Tsultrim bade good-bye to Lama Pema and returned to Lhasa, with Dargye driving them back the same way they had come. All in all, their first scouting tour had taken around sixteen days.

～

Back in Lhasa, Nenang Lama called Lama Nyima on his cell phone, speaking in the language of commerce that they often used: "Business went well on this trip. I'd like to tell you about it." They met in a safe place to talk about the escape and decided to ask Lama Tsultrim's driver, Dargye, to come on the escape as well. They would talk to him later. The timing of the escape had been discussed previously, and they thought that since the Karmapa had the custom of going on retreat every winter, his entering retreat again this year would raise no suspicions. Lama Nyima would continue staying in the Karmapa's room as he usually did, playing the bell and drum and eating the meals to make it seem that the Karmapa was still there. Nenang Lama told Lama Nyima, "If you can maintain the guise of the retreat for three days, we'll be across the border. After that, you should look out for yourself and see how you can escape."

Around this time, Nenang Lama contacted someone he knew in Nepal. "I'm bringing a high lama to Lo Monthang. Would it be difficult for you to help out?" The man replied, "I usually don't do this kind of work, but you I cannot refuse. I know the area of Mustang a little, and if you wish, I will help. When are you coming?" "When we decide on a time, I'll call you."

The car had performed well on the trip down to the border but had some problems on the way back, so it was brought in for repair again. Lama Tsultrim stayed one day in Lhasa to develop the photographs and brought them to Tsurphu the following day to show the Karmapa. He offered the young Karmapa a description of the land, the roads, the checkpoints, the distance and driving time from one place to the next, and so forth. Having explained different routes, he then left it all up to the Karmapa: "We are simple human beings and do not know everything. Please, you decide."

The Karmapa listened very carefully but did not make a decision right away. He recalls that in making decisions about the escape, "I mainly relied on my own mind and sense of the situation. Once, however, I wrote on two pieces of paper, 'To go' and 'Not to go' and put them in a little box. When I shook it, the paper with 'To go' came out." He used a similar method concerning which route would be best: Dram, the usual route escaping Tibetans take, Mount Kailash to the far west, or Mustang, the route they had investigated.

Two days passed while the three lamas waited in suspense. Finally, the Karmapa phoned Nenang Lama and asked him to come to Tsurphu. He questioned him in detail about the route, "Can we go this way through Mustang?" Nenang Lama responded, "I've examined the route and it's about 95 percent good." After offering all he knew, Nenang Lama said to the Karmapa, "The decision to escape is yours. Your judgment is what counts. Please take everything carefully into consideration. Whatever you decide and whatever happens, whether we are successful or not, we have pledged our lives to you." The Karmapa was only fourteen years old, yet serious and calm; with great self-assurance he replied, "All right. Since this is the situation, I'll go. The decision is made. You must make all the preparations. I'm going into retreat." It was a terribly difficult decision: the young Karmapa had made up his mind to leave his homeland, monastery, sangha, parents, brothers and sisters, and Tibetan followers. No one asked him to come and no one told him to leave. He had shouldered the great responsibility he carried as the leader of a major lineage and with his own judgment determined the course of his life.

Nenang Lama returned quickly to Lhasa and phoned Lama Nyima: "If we don't close this deal right away, we're going to lose the merchandise." The three met in Lhasa, and Nenang Lama reported that the Karmapa wanted to travel along the route they had investigated. To fulfill his part of the original plan, Lama Nyima returned to Tsurphu, while Lama Tsultrim and Nenang Lama stayed behind in Lhasa to prepare for the trip. Nenang Lama then called his contact in Nepal who would be their guide and let him know approximately when they would be arriving in Lo Monthang. About two weeks before they left, one of them called and spoke with a person who lived near their escape route. In the course of conversation, he casually inquired about the weather. "It's quite mild for this time of year," they responded.

The jeep was given a full checkup and renovated with new parts for the motor, new tires, and a new interior. A roof rack was installed to hold the three fifty-liter gas tanks that they would need in remote areas. The windows were tinted brown to block the view from the outside.

During this time, the Karmapa performed purification offerings,[126] offered paper mandalas that the winds carried aloft, and hung lengths of brightly colored prayer flags through the mountains. These were to eliminate obstacles to his forthcoming journey, though this purpose was not told to others.

Funds were needed for the trip, so Nenang Lama made the rounds of the many people he knew, using his connections to borrow a little bit here and a little bit there. He gave six months of provisions to the monks at Pawo Rinpoche's Nenang Monastery, and salaries to the teachers at his school, and he saved the rest to cover the expenses they would have on their way to India. For provisions on the road, they purchased tsampa, butter, dried meat, tea, and a good thermos. For the Karmapa, they bought the best quality of what he would need: warm bedding, a down jacket in red and dark gray, gray pants, a hat, a scarf, gloves, and sunglasses.

Lama Tsultrim went to the Jokhang, the central temple in Lhasa, and also traveled to the large monasteries near Lhasa, Sera, and Drepung, and farther away to Ganden and Samye. Everywhere, he made silent prayers that their voyage would be free of trouble. He prayed, "Buddhas and bodhisattvas, we are leaving for the sake of the Buddha's teachings and all living beings. Please eliminate all obstacles and negative conditions along the way to India."

Lama Tsultrim wished to bid good-bye to friends and relatives in his village of Nyemo. He told his seventy-five-year-old mother, who was staying at Tsurphu, that he wanted to return home for the New Year. (Nyemo has a special custom of celebrating one month earlier than other places in Tibet.) New Year is a special time when families gather to enjoy each other's company and also attend the religious ceremonies. Mother and son drove to Nyemo together, where Lama Tsultrim met with his family and friends for the last time before leaving. After two days, an urgent phone call came from Lama Nyima, now at Tsurphu. "You must come quickly to get permission to leave." All distant travel required official consent from the monastery. Lama Nyima did not want Lama Tsultrim to wait until the last minute in case the administration caused problems. Lama Tsultrim left the next day and took the jeep in for a thorough checkup. With Nenang Lama, he went to inspect the roads and the place at the end of the valley where the Tsurphu road joins the northern highway to Shigatse. It was here that Nenang Lama would wait for the group escaping from the monastery.

Escape from Tsurphu

CHAPTER FIVE

O N DECEMBER 26, Nenang Lama called the fourteen-year-old Karmapa and
asked, "Have you made your decision about lending money to that friend?
Will you lend it to him?" The Karmapa responded, "Don't worry. All the money
is collected, wrapped up in a cloth, and ready to be carried away." Nenang Lama
understood: everything was set for the departure.

The Karmapa announced to everyone that he was going on a strict twenty-
one-day retreat, which he began on December 27. Lama Tsultrim took the jeep
back to Tsurphu and explained that the families of Tsurphu sponsors in western
Tibet had requested more prayers and he needed to return. Nenang Lama told
all the people with whom he worked that he had found a sponsor in China who
wanted to see him. Through his travel agency in Lhasa, he had connections with
many people in Tibet, China, and abroad. It was common knowledge that sponsors were needed to sustain the monasteries, and therefore everyone naturally
accepted that this was an important trip.

According to their plan, the cook, Thubten, would continue to go in and out
of the Karmapa's room as if he were still there. Lama Nyima usually stayed in the
room with the Karmapa at night and served him during the day, so there was
nothing odd about him staying there. Lama Nyima would play the bell and
damaru (small hand drum) at various times as if the Karmapa were present. In
retreat, there are also times when one does not play instruments but simply rests
in meditation, and therefore silence would not raise suspicion. Lama Nyima
would be brought blessing cords and thangkas to consecrate, be given requests
for prayers, and so forth, just as if the Karmapa were there. The cook and the
teacher were good friends and usually worked closely together.

Very early on the morning of the 28th, during one of the coldest times of
year, an arctic chill froze the land. The surrounding mountains were covered in
white, the river was iced over, and bitter winds blew. It was before sunrise and
Lama Tsultrim was returning to Tsurphu. Taking the narrow road up the winter
valley, the jeep got stuck in ice and he had to call the monastery for help. The

vehicle that came brought good news as well as assistance. It carried Phurphu, the head of the security guards. As the jeep was being pulled out, Phurphu mentioned that he would be leaving for three days on vacation to Yangpachen—perfect timing for the escape.

Arriving at the monastery around 9:00 A.M., Lama Tsultrim took out the carefully wrapped clothes they had bought for the Karmapa and told one of his attendants, "These are Lama Nyima's. Please bring them to him." In this way, the Karmapa's change of clothes arrived safely in his room. Then Lama Tsultrim went to talk to the administration about leaving. In line with his former paving project, he said, "We need a courtyard in front of the new temple of the Tsurphu Lhachen. I want to go and raise funds for it in Nagchu." He was easily given permission to leave and returned to his room, where he lived alone. He was too worried to eat. Thinking that he was leaving on a long trip, his friends came to visit with him. They offered to take his things to the car, but he replied, "I'm not sure if I'm leaving tonight or tomorrow morning, so let's wait on that." Bidding him good-bye and good luck, they left.

～

This same day, Lama Nyima telephoned from Tsurphu to Nenang Lama in Lhasa. In the course of their conversation, he mentioned: "This evening at 10:30 the Chinese are showing a special program on TV. Why don't you take a look at it?" Nenang Lama responded, "I'd like to see it." This way he knew that the guards would be watching TV at 10:30 and the Karmapa could escape then.

That afternoon, Lama Nyima and Thubten said to the driver, Dargye, "Bring around the car and let's go for a little drive." They went to the Lower Park, a beautiful place with a summer residence for the Karmapa and the home of a special deer. They left the car on the road and walked up into the park. "Let's sit down here. Have a seat," they said to Dargye. "We had a special purpose in inviting you here. His Holiness is leaving for India and thought that you would be the best person to drive. You're an experienced driver and know the car so well. If you don't want to go, that's all right. We're not forcing you in any way. Everything depends on your mind and inclination. Can you make up your mind to leave your parents and relatives? Think it over carefully. If you decide to go, we leave tonight at 10:30. If you come, it's a great decision. If you choose not to go, it's all right, but you must not tell anyone else." Dargye reflected: "I have many relatives and friends in Tibet, but one day I will die and have to part from each one of them. His Holiness is a great master of Tibet and has been for so many generations. My broader responsibility is to him." He replied: "I will go with you. Don't worry."

Around five o'clock that afternoon, Lama Nyima came to visit Lama Tsultrim in his room to confirm that they would be leaving at 10:30. He gave him a necklace of coral and zi stones for the Karmapa saying, "When he arrives at Rumtek, it would be beneficial to wear it during lama dancing." He advised Lama Tsultrim to be extremely careful on the road, taking good care of the Karmapa so that the police would not capture him and they could arrive safely in India. He said, "If His Holiness can escape to India and meet Situ Rinpoche, Gyaltsap Rinpoche, and Jamgön Rinpoche and finally go to Rumtek, I will have no regrets even if I lose my life."

~

During the day, Nenang Lama called from Lhasa to check on the situation: "Are the preparations for the show going well? Will it start soon?" He too was making preparations, packing bags with provisions for the long trip and arranging for a vehicle to take him to their meeting point, the junction of the northern highway to Shigatse and the road up the Tölung Valley to Tsurphu.

In the evening, he told his driver, Tsewang Tashi, who was in his late twenties and a former monk at Nenang Monastery, "I have some business to take care of. You should come along." Giving Tsewang Tashi a false destination, Nenang Lama hired a taxi, and the two of them arrived at the junction about 10 P.M. At the side of the road, they unloaded the supplies for the long trip and sent the taxi back. While they waited at the roadside, Nenang Lama told Tsewang Tashi: "Listen well. You have been very fortunate to attain a precious human rebirth. You should make it meaningful when you have the chance. Tonight His Holiness is escaping to India and will need help. Think hard about this. It's a major decision. If you don't feel you can go and serve him, that's OK. It's up to you. You must make up your own mind. However, if you decide not to go, do not tell anyone else of these plans." Tsewang Tashi was astounded but readily agreed to go. He thought, "Such an opportunity to help His Holiness is a rare thing in this world." His great concern for the Karmapa diminished his worry about his mother and four brothers and sisters, whom he had to leave behind without even a farewell. Tsewang Tashi recalled that it was with a happy frame of mind that he decided to help His Holiness, whom he had met so many times at Tsurphu. Now they had a second driver.

~

Back at Tsurphu, the driver Dargye went to see Lama Tsultrim and reported that of the six monks who functioned as guards, the two on duty that day were known to Lama Tsultrim. This would make it easier to relate to them in case they had to be distracted. Two or three of these monk guards made the rounds of the monastery at unpredictable intervals, sometimes after one hour, sometimes after five. Lama Tsultrim said, "We have to trick the guards. You park the car behind the protector shrines and hide. I will go up to the guard behind the temple and tell him that I'm looking for you and ask him to find you, because I have to leave right away. He will leave and then His Holiness can enter the car." Their plan settled, Dargye left Lama Tsultrim with one bag and loaded everything else into the jeep, including a thermos of fresh tea and three nested wooden bowls, which the Karmapa enjoyed using for meals. They also placed in the jeep the only text the Karmapa brought out with him—the official account of his life written by the administration at Tsurphu.

Thubten the cook also visited Lama Tsultrim, telling him, "If the Chinese don't catch me, that would be the best. Then I'll come to India. If they do catch me, it could be very terrible. These are the two possibilities. Please ask the Karmapa to pray for me." Tears welled in Lama Tsultrim's eyes.

Near eight o'clock, Lama Tsultrim made the rounds of the five protector shrine rooms: Mahakala, Yönten Gönkhang, Sangtik Phurba, Dorje Drolö, and Tseringma. In each one he made prayers for their trip, offering butter lamps and khatas and asking for pujas to be done. Silently, Lama Tsultrim prayed, "Deities, protectors, and guardians. With whatever powers you have, now is the time for you to help. His Holiness is escaping this evening. Please give all your support."

As the evening progressed, three kung fu action videos rented by Lama Nyima were playing on the rented TV in a warm and cozy kitchen. Thubten had prepared rich tea and hot soup to bring the guards in from the bitter cold night. Among the five monks in the kitchen, three attendants were regarded by others as Chinese sympathizers; of the two cooks, only Thubten knew about the escape. The rest of the monks were studying in their rooms, lit by electricity from a small hydroelectric turbine in the river nearby. With their boss on vacation, the guards were taking it easy. The late hour and the intense cold kept anyone else from wandering outside.

Dargye came back to Lama Tsultrim's room around 9:00 P.M., having left the car behind the row of rooms that formed the protectors' shrines. Leaving it there was not unusual since he had gone in and out many times and parked the car in various places. At 10:20 P.M. they left Lama Tsultrim's room, walking together through the narrow alleys that ran between the earth and stone walls of the monks' quarters, finally coming onto the path used to circumambulate the center of the monastic complex. At the far outside corner of the main shrine hall, they separated. Lama Tsultrim went to the jeep, and Dargye walked farther to a temple known as the Tsurphu Lhachen, which used to enshrine a famous statue of the Buddha. Here he waited with his back flat against a side wall, out of sight of any guard who might be on patrol.

Meanwhile, the young Karmapa completed his preparations. He had written a letter to leave behind giving his reasons for departing. The Karmapa recalls, "In the letter, I stated that I was leaving so that I could receive the Dharma from my root teachers. I had made many applications so that we could meet, and they all had been refused. I affirmed that I was not turning against the country, nor was I leaving because I did not like the Chinese. I also said that I would be returning to Tibet." The Karmapa did not write in the letter that he was going to Rumtek to retrieve the Black Crown that he wears during a special ceremony,[127] or the Dharma treasures, including unique statues and ritual implements that have been passed down through generations of Karmapas. He stated, "The first time I wrote the letter, I considered saying that I was leaving to get the Black Hat and Dharma treasures. Then when I thought about it, it seemed too small a reason and I threw the letter away. This was not the main purpose. The main reasons were to receive the necessary teachings and benefit the Dharma and, further, to return to Rumtek and meet with my many disciples abroad."[128]

Together with his letter, the Karmapa placed a letter from the Dalai Lama on the table in his room. He recalled, "Several years before, I had offered a letter to His Holiness the Dalai Lama, and this letter was his answer. He wrote that he was happy to receive my letter and asked me to study well and serve the teachings in Tibet. I thought it would be good to leave this letter along with mine."[129]

Finally, the time to leave came. Softly closing the door behind them, the Karmapa, Lama Nyima, and the attendant Drubngak slipped out of the Karmapa's room on the top floor into the darkness and came down the steps to the second floor of the main building. Moving quietly, they walked past the audience room where the Karmapa had blessed so many and around the windows of the clerestory that looked down into the darkness of the large shrine hall. There below, butter lamps gleamed and gold light shimmered from the statue of the sixteenth Karmapa, Rangjung Rigpe Dorje. Then, passing into a storage room, next door to the kitchen where the videos played on, they climbed out a window onto the roof of the Tseringma shrine.

On the ground below, Lama Tsultrim was walking around checking the temple buildings where the guards usually made their rounds. The two guards posted behind the main hall and the protector shrines were not there. He knew that one of them was in his room watching a video. Thinking the coast was clear, he motioned Dargye to the jeep. Picking up a little stone, Lama Tsultrim threw it up on the roof, and Lama Nyima whispered "You've arrived?" "Yes, I have." At that moment, a flashlight came around the corner of the building. Lama Tsultrim instantly turned and walked toward the monk coming on guard duty, while

Dargye ducked behind the car and then slowly slipped inside. But it was too late. The guard had seen Dargye. Not knowing that the guard had spied his driver, Lama Tsultrim asked the guard, "Where is Dargye? It's time for us to leave." The guard replied, "But he's right here behind the car," and shone his flashlight into the car. "Oh, he's here!" said Lama Tsultrim, faking surprise, while Dargye pretended to be asleep. They were caught in the middle of their game. The ruse had failed.

Right then, the cook Thubten appeared. Seeing the problem, he had come up the other side of the main complex and joined them. He greeted the guard in a very friendly way and said, "I must borrow that video from you tonight. I've got to watch a movie now," and asked for a video he knew the guard had. The guard replied, "I'm on duty now. I can't lend it to you right away. There's no one else here, so I'm not going to leave." Thubten coaxed him very amiably, "Oh, please, I really need it now. You can leave for just a few moments. It won't take long. I just have to have it. I've been waiting so long to see it." The guard was firm: "I can't leave. There's no one else here." Thubten replied, "Lama Tsultrim and Dargye are here, so we can go." At that, the guard slowly walked away with Thubten who guided him down the pilgrimage path and out of sight.

Those waiting hidden on the roof had seen the light coming and waited in suspense. Lama Tsultrim paused a short while and then went to see how far away Thubten and the guard had gone. They had receded into the night, so he threw another stone. The Karmapa descended from the low roof of Tseringma's shrine, his agile body landing easily near the car. With this leap, he left everything behind. He was wearing lay clothes for the first time since he was seven years old. Next came Drubngak, who was helped down by Lama Nyima holding him from above and Lama Tsultrim and Dargye catching him from below.

They left instantly, avoiding the main gate by taking a side road. This exit had been made for vehicles involved in the recent construction projects at Zuri Monastery, located on the far side of the main Tsurphu complex. The road passed below the front walls of the monastery compound. The guards stationed there, if they had looked, would only have seen the roof of the jeep and part of the darkened windows. But they had no reason to be suspicious of the jeep, as they had already been informed that Lama Tsultrim and Dargye were leaving around 10:30. In the quiet of that night, Lama Tsultrim dared not look back for fear that they were being followed. Soon, they crossed the familiar bridge over the Tölung River and passed the rock face covered with a painting of the fierce protector Bernachen.

As they drove down the valley, Nenang Lama, concerned about the delay, contacted them via cell phone: "Come quickly! I'm waiting." Soon after, from the Karmapa's quarters in the monastery, Lama Nyima called Nenang Lama on his cell phone: "Our purpose has been accomplished." The jeep stopped for gas at the county town of Tölung, which was set next to the narrow valley road. Like all gas stations in Tibet, this one was open twenty-four hours and run by the Chinese. Busy with their job, the attendants focused on Lama Tsultrim, whom they knew. He was seated in the front on the passenger's side and paid them. Half an hour after leaving Tsurphu, the Karmapa arrived at the end of the valley, where Nenang Lama waited at the junction of the northern Shigatse road. He and Tsewang Tashi quickly loaded the provisions from Lhasa, and they were gone.

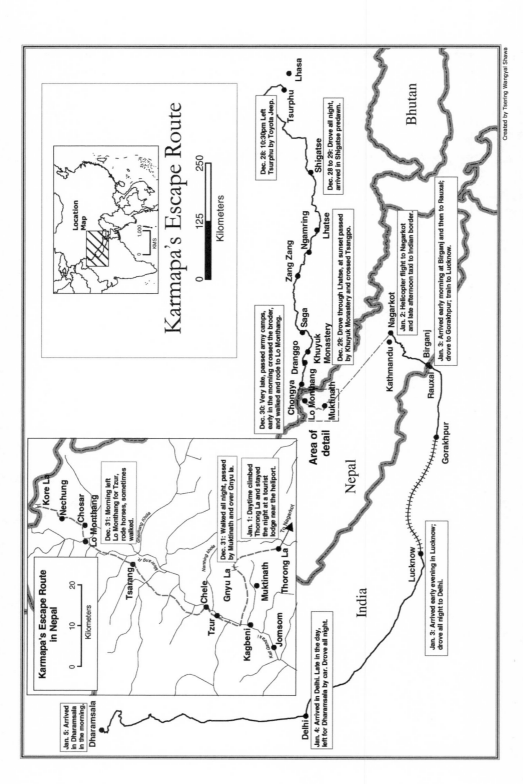

Karmapa's Escape Route

Location Map

Kilometers
0   125   250

1,000 KMS

Dec. 28: 10:30pm Left
Tsurphu by Toyota Jeep.

Lhasa
Tsurphu

Shigatse
Dec. 28 to 29: Drove all night,
arrived in Shigatse predawn.

Ngamring
Zang Zang
Lhatse

Dec. 29: Drove through Lhatse, at sunset passed
by Khuyuk Monastery and crossed Tsangpo.

Draggo
Saga
Khuyuk
Monastery

Dec. 30: Very late, passed army camps,
early in the morning crossed the broder,
and walked and rode to Lo Monthang.

Chongya
Lo Monthang
Muktinath

Area of
detail

Bhutan

Nagarkot

Kathmandu

Jan. 2: Helicopter flight to Nagarkot
and late afternoon taxi to Indian border.

Birganj

Rauxal

Jan. 3: Arrived early morning at Birgani; and then to Rauxal;
drove to Gorakhpur; train to Lucknow.

Nepal

Gorakhpur

India

Lucknow

Jan. 3: Arrived early evening in Lucknow;
drove all night to Delhi.

Karmapa's Escape Route
in Nepal

Kilometers
0   10   20

Kore La
Nechung
Chosar
Lo-Monthang

Dec. 31: Morning left
Lo Monthang for Tzur,
rode horses, sometimes
walked.

Tsarang

Jan. 1: Daytime climbed
Thorong La and stayed
the night at a tourist
lodge near the heliport.

Dec. 31: Walked all night,
passed by Muktinath and over Gnyu la.

Tzur
Chele
Gnyu La
Muktinath
Thorong La

Kagbeni
Jomsom

Jan. 4: Arrived in Delhi. Late in the day,
left for Dharamsala by car. Drove all night.

Delhi

Jan. 5: Arrived
in Dharamsala
in the morning.

Dharamsala

Over the Highest Mountains

T HE KARMAPA sat in the back seat of the jeep between Drubngak and Nenang Lama. In the front with Dargye, who drove until dawn, were Tsewang Tashi and Lama Tsultrim. The very back was filled with their provisions: hot tea and hot water, rounds of bread, dried meat, roasted barley flour, bed sheets, and blankets. The road they were now traveling was a main artery of Tibet, so even at this late hour, trucks and jeeps plied the busy lanes. Watching the headlights pass as they drove through the night, they were glad to be inside, warmed by the jeep's heater. Their fear that the Chinese were in pursuit kept them from being the least bit drowsy. Their first talk was about what had just happened and how they almost did not make it out of the monastery. It was thanks to the quick thinking of Thubten that they had been successful at all. Yet they were still worried, not knowing whether the guard really suspected something or was just walking away slowly. Perhaps he would be telling the Chinese officials that something fishy had happened behind the protector shrine hall. But Dargye felt that it was not a problem, since His Holiness was officially in retreat and no one saw him leave. As they drove away from their homes, families and friends, Dargye felt that they would be able to escape; his persistent thought was the hope that they would be able to return one day to Tibet.

As they traveled, they chanted *Karmapa khyenno,* and when it seemed they might be coming to a difficult place they tossed into the air some rice that had been blessed by the Karmapa. Usually colored with saffron, this rice is believed to have special properties of protection and was carried by the monks whenever they traveled. Sometimes in the past when an important prisoner had escaped, checkpoints would be set up on the road and cars were stopped and inspected, but thanks to the rice, they were always able to pass through. It would serve them well on this trip too.

It was still dark when they reached the important city of Shigatse, an ancient trading center and the home of the Panchen Lama's monastery, Tashi Lhunpo. During the day, the city is filled with people going about their business, cars passing in the streets, and police checking on activity. Now it was very late, and the weather was freezing cold; the streets were empty and silent. After stopping to fill the car and the three tanks on the roof rack with gas, they were able to drive straight through to the far side of Shigatse, where the road forks: one side leads to Dram, the shorter route most people take to Nepal, and the other to western Tibet, the route they were taking. This is one of the major intersections in Tibet, usually tightly guarded by police, who man the two barriers across the road and stop everyone to see if both the passengers and the vehicle have proper passes. The party was blessed and very lucky: the police were gone and, though the long pole of the barrier was down closing off the road to Nepal, it was up in the air for the route to western Tibet, giving them easy passage to the next stage of their journey.

From Shigatse, they traveled the predawn hours of December 29 to Lhatse where the rising sun lit the edge of the night sky. They stopped briefly so that Tsewang Tashi could take over the driving from Dargye. From there on the two drivers took turns, changing every hour or so. They went on to Ngamring, and in a desolate place before Zangzang, for the first time, they stopped a while to get out of the jeep and have a quick picnic under a wide blue sky. In this remote area, the villages were scattered and distant from the road. Even if they came closer, the nomads would not have recognized the Karmapa in lay clothes and sunglasses with a scarf around his face. No one would bother them. As they continued through to Saga,[130] the weather stayed clear and bright. In the late afternoon as they drove toward the sun, rays of rainbow-colored light bathed the windshield of the jeep for ten minutes, giving them a strong sense of being blessed on their journey.

Worried about Lama Nyima, they stopped at the next village and tried to call him, but the phone was not working. Feeling thirsty, Lama Tsultrim went to buy a Coke, and on the way to the store, happened to meet someone he knew. "We're on our way to Lhasa," he said, giving the opposite direction. The acquaintance passed near their car but did not try to look through the darkened windows. It was a close call. About thirty miles beyond the village, they stopped to fill the jeep with gas from the three tanks on the roof and left the cylinders concealed some distance from the road. Here they decided to wait for an hour until the sun set to give them the cover of darkness. They had to pass beneath Khuyug Monastery, and people could have recognized the jeep from the previous trip.

The next hurdle was crossing the Brahmaputra, the broad river that runs nearly the whole length of southern Tibet. Earlier, on their first scouting trip, the monks were forced to ride horses through the middle part of this surging river. For a long time, they searched in the frozen, white landscape for a safe passage across, someplace where the ice was strong enough to hold the jeep. On the earlier trip, they had looked during the day, but now it was the dark of night and everything looked different. Unable to find a path they could trust, they decided to ask a local person to show them the way across. As a cover story, they would give out that they were returning staff from the government office in Dranggo county on the far side of the river. Unfortunately, the residents in the nearest house knew Nenang Lama and Lama Tsultrim from their previous trips, so to avoid discovery, the two of them left the jeep and set out to cross the river on foot.

It was a difficult and dangerous passage, as the surface could give way at any moment. Nenang Lama decided to cross straight over to the other side, and Lama Tsultrim stayed back to take a different route, watching as the jeep drove off toward the house. He was worried, since in its path lay another river, a tributary of the Brahmaputra, that had to be crossed. At it drove away, the jeep became smaller and smaller and then did not seem to move at all. Lama Tsultrim feared that it was stuck in the icy river. He waited and then walked half a mile toward it to see what was happening. On his way, he crossed several streams, and what looked solid and safe was often not; he sank to his knees in cold water that turned to ice as he walked. Ahead of him, he could see the Karmapa's jeep that now seemed to inch across the frozen river. Following at a safe distance, he met up with the vehicle and Nenang Lama on the far side.

It turned out that the jeep had stopped at a house near the river to ask for directions. The escaping monks asked the family to send their child to show them the way, but the family suggested that an older, more experienced person would be better. So the head of the household came and found a path for them. They could not drive along the bank of the river to look for a passage but had to make a long detour away from the river and come back. Once they found it, the way was quite clear, with the tracks of the many trucks and jeeps that had preceded them. For around two months in the winter, the river here is solid enough to hold even a heavy truck bearing a load of stone. The group was grateful to be back on the right road. They gave their guide some money and a flashlight to see his way home.

The reunited group continued on what was hardly a road—a path rarely traveled and easy to lose. A buffeting wind blew over the plain and drove sand particles into their skin whenever they stopped to find their way. They had to inquire at two houses before they came onto the road to Dranggo Army Camp.

Around 10:30 on the evening of December 29, they arrived at this first army encampment about two miles before the town of Dranggo[131] and not far from the Nepali border. From the previous trip, Nenang Lama knew that the guards did not go to bed until 1:30 A.M. and that the people of the village stayed up late as well. Afraid that the noise of their motor might be heard, they turned it off as well as the headlights and waited some distance away. Earlier, they had broken the jeep's taillights so they would not be detected from behind.

Looking at the camp ahead of them, they could not see any of the guards, who usually stood right by the road. On this night, when skin would stick to metal, they were sitting in their huts a short distance away, sheltering themselves from the cold. Nevertheless, worry and anxiety conjured up terrifying images. Dargye recalled: "Sitting in the car, I would look out the front into the pitch dark and a figure would seem to appear. It must be the police. When I got out to check, no one was there. A sound rattled behind the car, and when I went around to look, there was nothing. I'd get back in the car and it was impossible to sleep. His Holiness said, 'There's nothing to be afraid of. They are human beings and we are human beings. Nothing to fear.' Even though those were the words of His Holiness, my anxiety would not stop. Fear held us tight."[132]

Around 1:30 in the morning, all the lights ahead were out and everyone seemed to be asleep. In the pitch darkness, they began to creep toward the camp while one person walked ahead to indicate the road. When they were a quarter of a mile away, a flashlight gleamed in the night. "The police!" Dargye gasped. They were certain they had been discovered.

On the spot, the Karmapa, Drubngak, and Dargye left the jeep and headed for a nearby mountain. Nenang Lama stayed behind for a few moments to discuss plans with Lama Tsultrim and the driver Tsewang Tashi. They decided that the latter two would drive very slowly through the camp, while the other four would climb what appeared to be an easy route over the nearby mountain and meet them on the other side of the encampment. If the car was stopped by the Chinese, they would say nothing about the other passengers. Since Lama Tsultrim had passed through the camp before, they would know him and not make problems. If they did, then Nenang Lama would walk with the Karmapa across the border into Nepal. There was no other option in these isolated areas, for even if they decided to take the risk, there were few trucks or cars to stop and ask for a ride. Their discussion finished, Nenang Lama left quickly to join the Karmapa and the others.

Without a moon, it was difficult to see where they were climbing. The way up the mountain turned out to be very steep, with loose sand and stones underfoot, so as they made their way up they kept sliding back down. Prickly bushes were often their only handholds, and the Karmapa's hands were covered with stings. It took them three grueling hours to weave their way back and forth up the mountain. All the time, they were filled with concern that Lama Tsultrim and Tsewang Tashi had been caught at the army camp.

Meanwhile, down below, the two in the jeep navigated their way through the camp. Since they thought they had been discovered, they turned on their headlights and prepared a story about going down the road to Kyirong. Generally, when stopped by a guard, if the driver gave a destination, that would suffice. Lama Tsultrim and Tsewang Tashi had decided that if the guards asked for details, they would reply, "We're traveling on business," or "We're going to see a relative," or "We have to pick up a friend," whatever seemed right at the moment. For official documents, they had a driver's license and the identity card that all Tibetans carry. Along with a black and white photograph, it shows their name, date of birth, and where they were born. The minutes edged by, but no one stopped them, and they drove safely past the camp wreathed in sleep.

On the far side, they continued up over the pass near the mountain that the Karmapa and the fleeing monks were climbing. At a place where the houses were far from the road, they turned off the car lights and waited and waited. Their anxiety growing as the time passed, they feared that the Karmapa had been caught by the Chinese, perhaps by the person carrying the flashlight, or perhaps there had been an accident on the climb. In the moonless night, they got out of the car and walked back along the road to try to find the others but could see nothing. For two and a half hours, they were held in suspense.

Once the Karmapa's party reached the top of the mountain, they were in an area that could not be seen from the army camp. Since Dargye was young and strong, they asked him to take an easier path straight down the mountain to see if the car was still there, or if there were people going back and forth, and then report back. Dargye remembered where the car had been left, but when he came in sight of that place, it was bare. The car had new tires that left very clear tracks in the dusty road. He followed the trail past a few houses and up the small pass, all of which were behind a round hill that formed the backside of the army camp, so he could not be seen by anyone from there.

Meanwhile, for the two in the jeep, time seemed endless. The moon came up over the mountain to outline the landscape with its distant light. At last Dargye found them. "They didn't catch you!" "No." "Where's His Holiness?" "He's coming." The Karmapa and the two others had stayed hidden in case the Chinese had captured the vehicle and were using it as a decoy. If they had, the four would have had to disappear immediately and find their way to Nepal on foot. But after coming closer, Dargye saw just the two familiar heads in the car.

With the help of the moonlight, the two drivers, Dargye and Tsewang Tashi, went back along the trail to find the Karmapa and the two monks, while Lama Tsultrim stayed with the car. But when they came to the place where they had agreed to wait, no one was there. Thinking it was not safe, the Karmapa, Drubngak, and Nenang Lama had moved away to another place. For an agonizing half hour, they searched, not so much worried that they had been caught as concerned that the sun would soon come up and they would be visible again. They needed to find the Karmapa quickly.

Finally, from afar, the Karmapa blinked his flashlight and Lama Tsultrim in response immediately turned on the jeep's headlights, a beacon to guide them. Soon, out of the pale indigo, the figures of the Karmapa, Drubngak, and Nenang Lama appeared. It was an incredible relief to be together again. (The Karmapa later recalled that this was one of the two most difficult times during the escape.)

Around four in the morning, everyone was back in the warmth and relative safety of the jeep. They left immediately, for once the sun was up, the army sentries would be patrolling the mountain pass near the camp and certainly see the escaping jeep just on the other side. (Later, Dargye surmised that the flashlight they had seen was not a soldier's but belonged to an inhabitant of one of the houses near the road.)

Benefiting from the moonlight, they continued straight on their way and soon came to another fork in the road at Chöngya.[133] One road led to Mount Kailash, the sacred mountain in the far west of Tibet, and the other led to their destination of Mustang. Two hundred yards from this fork, down the road to Kailash, was another army camp, holding forty to fifty soldiers whose job was to guard the border, just a short drive away. The escaping monks feared that the local people near the first camp might have alerted the army or the government, letting them know that a strange car had waited down by the road in the early hours of the day. But it was very late, and the weather was so wretchedly cold that the whole army camp was inside, warm and asleep. Since it was the dead of night and the camp was some distance away with only a small village nearby (quite a different situation from the first camp), they decided to make a run for it and drove the jeep at high speed down the fork leading south away from the camp and into Nepal. They passed undetected and another major obstacle was behind them.

This area of Tibet is desolate and uninhabited. The actual border crossing was marked only by a solitary stone with CHINA written on one side and NEPAL on the other. But arriving in another country gave them no sense of relief, for at any time the Chinese could come after them. It was also possible that the Nepali government had been notified and warned their border guards, who often returned escaping Tibetans.

About two miles beyond the border into Mustang, the road became very difficult; they had to make their way across a barren landscape with its arid vistas of eroded and yellowed stone. Descending from the high pass of Kore, they drove over what seemed to be solid ice, but it gave way, and the wheel of their jeep lodged in an icy hole. They pushed and rocked the jeep but could not free it. There was no choice but to pack some food and belongings and continue on foot—an added burden after the long, strenuous trip when everyone was bone tired. In one place, where his old attendant Drubngak slipped off the path, the fourteen-year-old Karmapa quickly caught him and brought him safely back up.

Passing by the first hamlet of Nechung, after about an hour and a half they arrived at Chosar, where relatives of Nenang Lama lived. It was very early in the morning of December 30 and Nenang Lama had to shake his relative awake: "We need horses right away!" The relative rushed around and rented them from his friends, and the group of escaping Tibetans could ride on to his older brother's house in Lo Monthang, the capital of Mustang. After a while on the road, they decided that it was best to go back and retrieve the jeep, so the relative and the two drivers went back to pull it out. By this time of day the sun had melted the ice, so it was easily done. They left the jeep with a family in the area along with some money and food. "Please keep it safely. We're going on pilgrimage and will need it on our way back," they said. People might have been suspicious if the jeep was just abandoned.

With the jeep safely stored, the three came back to join the Karmapa and the others, who had all arrived at the relative's house in Lo Monthang. The travelers were happy to be with friends, to have good food and a place to sleep for the night. As they settled in for the evening, the relatives and friends talked about the exceptionally mild weather. "Last year, the snowfall was huge and so deep you couldn't move through it. The winds were incredible. Little children had to be tied down with a rope or get blown away." The relatives also asked the usual questions about Nenang Lama's companions, who were all dressed in ordinary clothes. "Where do they come from? What do they do?" They knew Lama Tsultrim was a Tsurphu monk, and the two drivers were easy to explain. Drubngak was described as the steward of Nenang, whose job it was to look after the goods of the monastery. Nenang Lama played the role of the most important monk, since the relatives all knew that he was the main person responsible for Nenang Monastery and young Pawo Rinpoche. The Karmapa was passed off as one of Nenang Lama's young monks, who had been studying at a Chinese school (not unusual for young Tibetans). During vacation, the story went, he had come to visit Nenang Lama and decided to become a monk; learning that Nenang Lama was going to Nepal, the new monk had asked if he could come along and was given permission. The Karmapa played the role of a young attendant quite well, serving tea and carrying the lama's possessions with due respect. When not so engaged, he kept his head wrapped with a scarf to partially hide his face. Nenang Lama explained that the strenuous hiking and the changing weather had given him a cold and he needed to stay warm. Both the Karmapa and Nenang Lama knew Chinese and used it when they needed to communicate in secret. The disguise worked well. The photos of the Karmapa that people would have seen were now out of date, for he had grown and changed considerably. (The lore about tulkus states that they mature much more rapidly than other children.) Further, they did not recognize him because the Karmapa was not in robes, which completely changed his appearance. Finally, they never dreamed that he could or would be escaping.

Word that important lamas had arrived spread through the village, and many people came to visit. Knowing that Nenang Lama had a close relationship to Tsurphu, they asked, "How are things at Tsurphu? We really want to meet the Karmapa one day. When we come to Tsurphu, will you help us make a connection?" He replied, "Don't worry. You'll meet him, no doubt about it."

While they passed time in the capital, Lo Monthang, a friend arranged in utmost secrecy for the party to have tea with the king of Mustang.[134] From here, they also phoned Lama Tenam in India, who would help them once they had crossed that border. Lo Monthang was an important meeting place for another reason, too. According to their plans, a guide for Nepal was to meet them there, but he had not arrived and there was no way to contact him. The escaping party went to sleep for the night thinking they might have to continue without him. There was, however, a backup plan: Nenang Lama's two relatives had agreed to take them down to the small airport at Jomsom, and they would fly from there. In addition to the guides, they also discussed the trail for the next day and where they would have their meals.

Early on December 31, in the deep cold of the morning, Nenang Lama and a guide left Lo Monthang ahead of the others to arrange for lunch and dinner for everyone farther down the trail. Meanwhile, the old horses were sent back to Nechung and new ones rented by relatives in Lo Monthang. Riding these, the rest of the group would come later, with a relative acting as the guide. Their number was enlarged by the owners of the horses, which were typically small but sure-footed.

Moving south, they passed through Marang and Tsarang and continued to follow a precipitous trail that zigzagged along the waist of the mountains. It was a frightening, steep path with areas where the horses had trouble going and the Karmapa had to dismount and walk. In a few places where there was no room for a trail, some logs were stretched out over space. Without handholds, they had to balance their way across and dared not look down. The trail covered many passes and valleys, sometimes crossing a river, sometimes following along it. Before coming to Chele, set on the edge of a spectacular narrow gorge, they stopped to have lunch in a remote house, its whitewashed walls made of stone and earth beneath a grayed, wooden roof. In the mountains, it is the custom for families to offer meals to travelers in return for a small fee. The party was shown into the shrine room on the second story, which served as a guest room, and given steaming hot *momo*s (dumplings). Grateful for the pause and the warm food, they continued their arduous climb. The Karmapa's horse became tired, and Lama Tsultrim offered his mount.

~

As he moved down the wintry valley, Nenang Lama kept his eyes open for the guide—perhaps he was held up and would be coming late along the trail. The evening meal was planned for a small restaurant in Tzug, and when Nenang Lama walked in the door, there was the guide seated at a table and waiting for him. Delayed along his route, he had guessed that they would have to come down this main trail. In a quiet corner, the two discussed possible plans for the next stage of the journey. Around eleven at night, the rest of the group arrived tired and hungry. The guide was overwhelmed to see the Karmapa and offered his respects with a full heart. Over a late night meal of noodle soup, they discussed their next step.

The group was faced with a crucial decision. From Tzug, it was around three hours to the well-known town of Dzong Sarpa, locally named Jomsom,[135] with its small airport. It would be so much easier to fly, but if the Nepali police saw a group of Tibetans trying to buy plane tickets, they would suspect that they were escaping and arrest them. There were also many Tibetans in Jomsom, and the Karmapa might be recognized. Further, the flight from Jomsom landed at Pokara, a popular tourist resort with a view of the Annapurna range reflected in its famous lake. Many Tibetans lived there and the Karmapa could also be recognized. If the fleeing monks went through Manang,[136] the route was much longer and grueling, but the danger of being caught was less. On the other side of the pass was a small airport where they could call in a helicopter, as tourists often did.

After they had discussed the situation with the guide for a while, the Karmapa finally decided that they should divide into two groups and take the longer route despite the formidable hardship. Since the helicopter would be small, the relative and the two drivers, who were no longer needed, would form another group. Taking enough funds for the road, these three planned to go to Kathmandu. From there, the two drivers could leave Nepal and eventually join the Karmapa in Dharamsala.

Bidding good-bye to their companions, the small group of the Karmapa, Drubngak, Nenang Lama, Lama Tsultrim, their guide, and a caretaker for their new set of horses started out for Manang. With little food and no sleep, they would traverse mountains and valleys hiking all night long into the new millennium and all day long on January 1. Packing some dried meat and water, they began their journey through what would be the longest night of their escape. Soon they had to cross the Kali Gandaki River, which is swollen in the summer but much smaller in the winter, so they could pass over on the ice. They walked in the direction of Muktinath, a pilgrimage site for both Buddhists and Hindus, renowned for its springs with an "eternal flame" fed by natural gas. This coincidence of fire and water has drawn pilgrims for centuries. It was here that Guru Rinpoche and his consort Mandarava perfected the practice of long-life. The escaping party and their fourteen-year-old leader passed not far from it but dared not stop. Afterward they turned back up another valley to start the long ascent of their first high pass, the Gnyula at 13,563 feet.[137]

The guide led them down the mountain valley over a trail that wound back and forth along the slopes, past precipitous dropoffs and over narrow passages. Sometimes it was possible to ride and sometimes it was so steep they had to lead the horses. As they started the trail up to Gnyula, they had had no sleep and the night was dark. Lama Tsultrim was carrying a long flashlight with four large batteries that had to be replaced twice. For about two hours, they rode down a long valley and finally came to the base of the mountain. The trail up to the high pass was too steep and uncertain to ride so they led the horses until the trail disappeared into a forest of boulders. Trying to find a way through, the guide lost his way several times and they had to backtrack for half a mile.

Since some of the horses walked faster than others, the group had become a bit spread out. At one point, Drubngak called out, "Tsultrim Gyamtso, where is Döndrub? " For the journey, the Karmapa had taken his father's name, Döndrub, which means "The One Who Accomplishes His Goal" or "The One Who Accomplishes Benefits." Lama Tsultrim answered, "Döndrub's here with me. Please be careful as you walk." Giving each other support as they moved through the darkness, they took two hours to arrive at the far side of the boulders. By now the trail had become so tortuous that they could not ride the horses and had to lead them for the rest of the climb.

As they climbed the heights for four hours, the stars became more brilliant in the late night sky, a panorama of cool, glittering lights. For the Karmapa, however, the climb was extremely painful as he suffered from altitude sickness; the pain in his kidneys and his stomach was so severe he could barely walk. When asked about difficult times on journey, the Karmapa replied, "There were no difficult times." Then he smiled and said, "Well, there have to be difficulties. The first one was the first army camp and having to climb over that mountain. The bushes had something like thorns on them and they pricked your skin. The second time was when we reached the top of the first pass on the way to Manang. I was quite sick then." Nenang Lama was also ill; he had a chronic stomach problem that gave him difficulty throughout the night, while his knees ached and were close to giving out. Yet they had no choice but to continue, and they still had to negotiate a much higher pass.

Hiking southeast, they finally came to the head of the trail up Thorongla Pass sitting at an altitude well over 17,768 feet. It is the highest point on the route circling the Annapurna Range, impossible to cross when covered with snow and known as a place where snowstorms can spell danger. Guidebooks warn of a tough ascent and the risk of frostbite if one stands around too long. For the high altitudes, they recommend resting one day at the base of the peak to acclimatize, but the fleeing Tibetans did not have this luxury.

That morning, they could find only simple food at a small house by the trail. Exhausted and facing the most difficult climb of their escape, the group began their ascent. The trail was steep and demanding and they often had to lead the horses when it became too narrow or sheer. Used to the mountains, the horses knew how to move up the sharp inclines and over the slippery places, but these were times when the party of escaping monks often had to crawl. Sometimes the trail disappeared completely, forcing them to make their own way.

The times when they could ride were not easy either. In need of sleep, they still had to remain completely alert; drowsing off could have meant slipping over the edge of a precipice. The high altitude and the lack of food and drink brought additional hardship. The Karmapa was not well and continued to suffer from an upset stomach. Normally, when symptoms of altitude sickness appear, one would immediately descend to a lower level, but this was not possible. Despite all his problems, the fourteen-year-old showed tremendous determination to reach his goal of freedom. Once when he was leading the party, he looked back at Nenang Lama, who was feeling totally depleted, and said, "Right now we're escaping. We must take big strides. This is not an easy time. We must be courageous." The rest of the group, in addition to physical hardship, also had to bear their concern for the Karmapa's health and safety. They worried about what might happen if the Chinese had discovered their departure and were trying to catch them. What sustained them was their faith and trust in the Karmapa.

After six hours of climbing, the horses were too tired to go any farther, so they led them and continued by foot, arriving around six in the evening at the top of the pass. Here, they found stupas and piles of stones carried by previous hikers to mark their offerings and prayers. The group had expected to come upon a small lodge on the far side where they could rest and have something to eat, but a desolate landscape shattered this hope of repose. There was nothing but a trail and more hiking. Depleted and hungry, they faced the descent down the back side, even more difficult than the ascent, since their legs were worn out and their knees hurt. The Karmapa, Nenang Lama, and Lama Tsultrim set out first, and Drubngak, much older in years, came along more slowly with the help of the guide. In some two hours, about halfway down the far side of the mountain, they came to a small restaurant that served hot tea. Another hour of a rough trail brought them to the heliport, a forty-foot circle on the ground marked with a big white H. In another half-hour, still leading the horses, they saw the roofs of the trekker's lodge and then the large main building with its two wings of rooms.

Inside, it seemed they had arrived in a paradise of luxury. They had a warm good meal and spent the night in comfortable beds. In the dead of winter, there were no other guests, just the staff members. They made a phone call to order a helicopter for the following day, which was nothing unusual and required no special permission or papers,[138] and telephoned Lama Tenam in Delhi to discuss plans. They also called back to the Karmapa's room at Tsurphu to find out if Lama Nyima was still there: "Whaay! (Hello!) Who are you?" At Tsurphu, the voice replied, "Who are you?" It was not Lama Nyima. An unknown voice in the background urged, "Say it's Lama Norbu"—an attendant of the Karmapa.[139] They hung up instantly, realizing that their escape had been discovered. They would have to be even more careful now, as the Chinese would surely let other authorities know that the Karmapa had fled.

Indeed, according to reports from inside China, the ruse of the retreat was discovered sometime on December 30. On the main roads leading south from Lhasa to the Nepali border, check points were set up, reportedly manned by the People's Liberation Army and Public Security Bureau personnel, to inspect everyone traveling to the border area and to check their travel documents. "All monks at Tsurphu were interrogated; after some days the monastery was closed off to all visitors on the grounds that the road was impassable."[140] But all these measures had come too late.

The next morning, January 2, everyone rose early to catch the helicopter, but it did not arrive on time. Nenang Lama went to see the Karmapa, who was standing outside looking at the landscape. He said, "From the lower valley, two ravens flew straight into the sky above, circled around overhead, and immediately flew away. Now the plane is about to arrive. There's no doubt." Nenang Lama thought, "Wherever the Karmapa goes, wherever he stays, the deities and guardians are certainly protecting him." (Ravens in particular are connected with the Karmapa's special protector.) Soon, around 9 A.M., the helicopter did arrive, but it was very small, with seats for only three people, and had to make two trips. The first flight carried the Karmapa, Drubngak, and Nenang Lama's friend. They landed in Nagarkot, a tourist resort in the hills outside Kathmandu with a stunning view of the snow-capped Himalayan range.

Nenang Lama and Lama Tsultrim were left behind on the mountain with a promise from the pilot to return soon. The two monks packed up their things and walked to the airport, where they waited for hours with no sign of the helicopter. Worry mounted as they feared that the Chinese government had contacted Nepali officials and the Karmapa had been arrested. To complicate matters, the two monks had no money, since all of it had been given to Nenang Lama's Nepali relative. There was always a danger for Tibetans that anything valuable they had could be taken from them if they were stopped by Nepali police. Turning to his circle of prayer beads, Nenang Lama made a divination about the situation; it came out very well, so they continued to wait. About 3 o'clock a small speck on the horizon turned into the helicopter, which descended and lifted them away.

The helicopter was late because plans had changed while the first group was in the air: instead of landing at a nearer location, they had decided to go all the way to Nagarkot, on the far side of Kathmandu. Now, half an hour into this second flight, the pilot unexpectedly landed to get gas, which was depleted from the previous trip, and here, their worst nightmare came true. At the landing site was a solemn-looking Nepali officer in a dark blue uniform and cap. The two lamas were positive they had been discovered: the Karmapa had been found out, and this officer was coming to arrest them as well. Filled with concern about the Karmapa and certain that they were going to die, they split between them Lama Tsultrim's four relics[141] from the bodies of the previous Karmapas and four black pills[142] from the Karmapa, all of which were considered to have a very great blessing.

The black pills along with the Black Crown are special to the Karmapa. It is said that taking a black pill will spare one the suffering of the lower realms. The black pills are made of special substances that come from previous incarnations of the Karmapas, as well as other precious, sometimes legendary substances, such as water that has turned into snow lion milk in the skull cup of the protectress Tseringma. Usually, blessed pills are made by monks during a period of intensive practice, but the black pills the Karmapa makes with his own hands, blending in many substances along with his own blessing during one or two weeks of practice. Among the black pills, there is a special one called a mother pill, which in response to deep faith produces small black pills.

The relics in Lama Tsultrim's possession came from the body of the ninth Karmapa, Wangchuk Dorje, who composed major texts on mahamudra, or the nature of mind, that are still used today. His body was not cremated but preserved in a stupa after his death. During the Cultural Revolution, the body was removed from the stupa and burned near the location of the towering flagstaff called Darchok near the main courtyard of Tsurphu. The burning of the Karmapa's body produced shiny black and opalescent white relics that were found near the site for years afterward. In this way, with the most special substances they knew, the two lamas were preparing for their death.

The fueling completed, the Nepali officer got into the helicopter with them and never said a word. When they landed at Nagarkot, he simply walked away on his business. With joy and the relief of those who have been given back their lives, the two lamas were reunited with the Karmapa and Drubngak. During the day, they all rested at the resort, enjoying a good meal and a view of the Himalayas from the another side and now at a welcome distance.

The next stage of their journey would take them into India. This part of the escape had been planned for a while, thanks to cell phones in India and public phones in Nepal. Earlier, Nenang Lama had contacted Lama Tenam in Delhi, after arriving in Lo Monthang and once more from the lodge on the far side of Thorongla's high pass. In the last call from Nepal, the conversation was more specific. Lama Tenam recalls: "I received a phone call in Delhi and learned the number of the train from Gorakhpur to Lucknow and what time it would arrive. I let them know the name of the hotel where I would be staying."[143] Early that evening in Nepal, two taxis were ordered for the long drive to India and the last stages of the young Karmapa's journey to freedom.

Following the winding road as it descended through the Himalayan foothills to the flatlands of the Nepali Terai, they drove all night and arrived at Birganj on the southern border of Nepal in the early morning of January 3, 2000. The Indian border was their next barrier with its dusty town of Rauxal some 230 miles north of Bodh Gaya, the sacred site where the Buddha attained enlightenment. Worried about being caught, they decided to offer the officials the bribe that often allowed refugees to pass into India. Via taxi, they continued to the train station in Gorakhpur, where they boarded a train for Lucknow about six hours away.

In the meantime, Lama Tenam had flown from Delhi to Lucknow and settled into his hotel. At the appointed time, he arrived at the train station to wait for the Karmapa and his party. He stood with eyes straining to see that one familiar face, not really able to believe that the Karmapa was coming until he actually saw him. Concerned about his safety, he wondered if the Chinese had informed the Indian government of the Karmapa's absence.

Lama Tenam waited and watched, but the Karmapa did not appear at the designated time. For a stretch of two hours, his fears mounted as he scanned the night crowds moving in and out of the shadows. No one he knew appeared. Finally, having no other choice, he returned to his hotel. There the desk clerk told him that some people had come and were waiting in his room. Hurrying up the stairs, he opened the door to see the Karmapa and all who had fled with him. They had arrived around eight, and not seeing Lama Tenam, had come directly to the hotel. Lama Tenam remembers: "I was very happy to see him and also a bit sad. Usually, the Karmapa is wearing the elegant robes of a monk, and now he was in simple lay clothes, looking quite tired and thin after his ordeal. This made me a little downhearted, so I knew both joy and sadness together."[144]

Lama Tenam suggested that if they were not too tired, it would be better to leave that evening for Delhi. The sooner they were in the safety of the Dalai Lama's presence, the better. The Karmapa reflected for a moment and then agreed. Two cars were rented at once, and they drove the whole night to Delhi, arriving the next morning on January 4. Not stopping to rest, they rented two Ambassadors, India's most famous and durable vehicle, and set out for Dharamsala. In the first car, the Karmapa and Tenam-la rode in the back, with Nenang Lama and Drubngak in front with the driver. On their way north, they stopped in Chandigarh at a tourist restaurant for a meal and a brief rest. Back on the night road, some slept as they moved through the thick fog outside.

In the second taxi, Lama Tsultrim was sitting relaxed in a cross-legged position with his shoes on the floor, enjoying the comfort of motorized travel. Suddenly, he saw the Karmapa's car veer off the road and land angled against a tree. He leaped out the door and ran barefoot to the Karmapa, arriving in time to see him emerge unscathed. The area was flat and the car had been moving slowly, so no one was injured. But the car was disabled, and they had to wait at the edge of the road until another vehicle emerged from the fog.

They flagged the car down and it brought one of the party to a larger town. There a Sumo jeep was rented and they were soon on the road again. The Karmapa, along with Drubngak and Tenam-la, went in the Ambassador as it had a smoother ride on the bumpy roads. In the Sumo were Lama Tsultrim and Nenang Lama plus two friends of Lama Tenam. They were coming close to their goal of meeting the Dalai Lama in Dharamsala, but not yet able to give that final sigh of relief. "I was worried all the way to Dharamsala," recalled Lama Tenam. "We knew that the Chinese were aware of the escape." Anything could still happen.

~

Known as "the Little Lhasa," the village of upper Dharamsala is settled along the ridge of a Himalayan foothill. Two narrow, at times precarious, roads wind from the lower village to the upper one, which is home to the Dalai Lama and the Tibetan Government-in-Exile. Here, along the two main streets, in stores or on tables set outside, one can find everything an ordained or lay Tibetan might need: statues, ritual implements, incense, khatas, monks' robes, silk blouses, and chubas, all ready-made or ready to be made by a nearby tailor. There are Buddhist books in Tibetan and English, juniper branches for fire offerings, dried cheese, roasted barley flour, sweaters, stoles, travel agents, bakeries, and cyber-cafés. The vendors of these goods and services often sit out in the street or keep their doors wide open, ready to join in conversation with passers-by. The pace is leisurely as people stop to share the latest news and watch others come and go. If you want to find out what is happening in the village or know who is doing what where and when, a stroll down the main street will add to your store of knowledge. The traditional Tibetan greeting, "Gaphar thega?"—"Where are you going?"—leads into a mine of information that is retained for future use.

The Karmapa's older sister, Ngödrup Pelzom, had come to Dharamsala to see the Dalai Lama. For years in Tibet she had dreamed of going on pilgrimage to India, but for a long time she was not able to obtain a passport. In 1996, she went on pilgrimage with her mother Loga and monks from the Karmapa's Tsurphu Monastery to Mount Kailash. After returning to Lhasa to look after her family's home there, she applied for a passport in 1997, but was refused. She remembers: "In 1999, I wanted to try for a passport again, so I asked His Holiness, 'If I get a passport, should I go to India?' He replied, 'It would be good to go, but do not tell others.' So I applied once more, and this time the Chinese gave me a five-year passport, which allowed me to go to Nepal for three months each year. They never give longer than that." From Nepal, it is then possible to travel to India.

"Before I left, I called my parents in Kham: 'They gave me a passport, and I'll be leaving for India. Please come to Lhasa for a visit before I go.' So they came to our place in Lhasa, which is very near the Barkhor and just a few minutes from the Jokhang. We stayed together for four days. I told my parents, 'I'll return to you in three months.' My father was especially sad at my going. He said, 'Please come back quickly. I will miss you very much. You must come back as soon as possible.' And he shed tears. I replied, 'I'll be back within three months.'"[145]

On November 22, she left on a plane for Nepal with a friend. After a short stay in Baudhanath near the famous stupa, Ngödrup Pelzom was able to travel to India with friends and continue her pilgrimage. Wishing to meet with the Dalai Lama, she went to Dharamsala, where, small village that it is, she soon met two monks sent by Situ Rinpoche to help the Karmapa. They told her that the Karmapa would be arriving the next day and that they had come to rent a room for him at the Bhagsu Hotel. It was the best possible news.

$\sim$

Situ Rinpoche had known of the escape for quite a while. He recounts: "The Karmapa had sent me some messages, and on several occasions I also conveyed them to His Holiness the Dalai Lama. I personally felt that it would be very dangerous for the Karmapa to take the step of escaping and sent a message back to Tibet saying so. Finally, he made his decision. When I heard this, I could just pray and hope that everything would go well. It was a miracle that he managed to escape without any major problem. It was very frightening. His Holiness the Dalai Lama was extremely concerned about his safety and worried: 'If he escapes, what might happen?' But the Karmapa decided himself to flee and his decision was right. It happened.

"At Sherab Ling, I came to know he had escaped when he was already out of Tibet. I was very happy. Nothing bad had happened, and he was already well over the danger. If I had heard beforehand, I would not be able to sleep. He saved me that by letting me know only after he had completed the most difficult parts of the trip. That was a relief, otherwise, it would be terrifying."[146]

$\sim$

Braced against the damp cold, the two monks and Ngödrup Pelzom went up the road at the far end of the village, past the large tourist hotels to the Bhagsu. Rooms were available on the second floor, and so they began a long wait. Ngödrup Pelzom remembers: "The two monks went outside to see what was happening and I stayed back, waiting and waiting. Finally, around 3 A.M. I feel asleep. While it was still pitch dark, the phone woke me up. It was Nenang Lama: 'His Holiness will be coming soon.' I went downstairs and found the two monks sent by Situ Rinpoche with Nenang Lama and Lama Tsultrim who had arrived first."[147] Using cell phones, they were in contact with Lama Tenam who was riding with the Karmapa.

For about twenty minutes, they stood outside in the cool predawn. Then Ngödrup Pelzom heard a car and soon saw a group of Tibetans in ordinary clothes coming up the path into the hotel: "When I saw His Holiness, I became so sad and cried. His face looked drained, and he was thinner. I could see that he had been through great hardship. Somehow I had thought that he would be able to come to India without so many difficulties. To see him so exhausted was overwhelming. And then, since 1992, when he was recognized, this was the first time I had seen him wearing anything but monks' robes. For some reason, this also made me very sad.

"We invited His Holiness up to the room we had reserved for him, where he could bathe and put on the robes that Situ Rinpoche had sent from Sherab Ling." Ngödrup Pelzom had cared for the Karmapa when he was a child in Lhathok and now she noticed, "On his hands, he had so many marks from tiny thorns. These were bothering him so I tried to ease his discomfort. I washed them and put on medicine. But I was so sad. I was thinking, 'He's young. He's carrying the name of Karmapa. He's a great lama. Why did he have to go through such trials?' His Holiness said, 'It's nothing. There's no need to be upset.'"[148]

Lama Tenam had arrived in the car with the Karmapa and as soon as possible telephoned Khedrup-la, the main secretary of the Department of Religion and Culture in the Tibetan Government-in-Exile. Since Lama Tenam knew him, he could bypass the usual formalities and say directly: "You should come immediately to the Bhagsu Hotel. I have extremely important news." Khedrup-la arrived within an hour, at about 10 A.M. Lama Tenam met him in the hallway outside the Karmapa's room: "The Gyalwa Karmapa has come. Please let His Holiness the Dalai Lama know as soon as possible. If you would like to meet His Holiness, he is waiting inside." Khedrup-la was stunned. "I can't go," he said at first. Lama Tenam thought, "Perhaps he doesn't believe me," and finally persuaded him to go in. As he entered the room, he made the traditional three prostrations, and the Karmapa blessed him with his hand. Khedrup-la asked, "Was it not very difficult for you?" But they did not talk much.

Once again outside in the hallway, he said to Lama Tenam: "It's strange that you didn't tell me before. I should be wearing a chuba and carrying a khata." Tenam then understood his hesitation, and replied that the situation was delicate

—if he had said everything on the phone, Khedrup-la might have become excited and exclaimed "Karmapa!" so everyone in the room with him would have known. Khedrup-la went directly to the Private Office of the Dalai Lama and soon returned wearing a chuba and carrying a khata: "Please come right now to see His Holiness the Dalai Lama." The Karmapa and his party left immediately for a meeting that would culminate the long arc of their journey, the months of planning, all the hardships and dangers, and the joy of arrival.

The Dalai Lama had closely held his knowledge of the Karmapa's wish to escape. After the Dalai Lama had returned from a visit to Bodh Gaya, Situ Rinpoche had driven two and a half hours from his monastery, Sherab Ling, to Dharamsala to speak with him. Situ Rinpoche remembers, "On the fourth of January, the day before the Karmapa arrived, I came to tell the news to His Holiness the Dalai Lama in Dharamsala. He was very relieved that the Karmapa had come out safely. On January fifth, it was only the Dalai Lama who was expecting him. It was too dangerous to let everybody know. In that situation, the safety of His Holiness the Karmapa was more important than anything else."[149]

With no one suspecting who was inside, the cars carrying the Karmapa and his party passed up the long driveway and through the ornamental iron gates that guard the Dalai Lama's compound. Descending from his car, the Karmapa was welcomed by the Dalai Lama, who had walked out of his house to come and greet him. They touched foreheads in a traditional greeting, and, holding the Karmapa's hand, the Dalai Lama led him inside. Several times he looked at him from head to foot, saying how happy and amazed he was. He praised the Karmapa for his courage and thanked him for facing so many difficulties to reach India. Ngödrup Pelzom recalls, "The Dalai Lama said, 'When I heard that you were coming, I thought, "How could he come? All the roads to India are under such close observation. I was very worried.'"

The Dalai Lama said that while the Karmapa was living in Tibet, he had heard about him and his special attributes, and that the signs of being the incarnation of the Karmapa had naturally arisen. He was indeed the one able to follow in the footsteps of the previous Karmapa. With great love and affection, the Dalai Lama received the young monk who had risked his life for the sake of the Buddhist teachings. About this special meeting with the Dalai Lama, the Karmapa said, "I came to Dharamsala because His Holiness the Dalai Lama was there. I had trusted and believed in him for so many years. In this first time seeing him, my joy knew no bounds."

The Dalai Lama counseled the young Karmapa to rest in Dharamsala for several days, and then go to Situ Rinpoche's monastery, Sherab Ling. Eventually, he would be able to return to Rumtek Monastery, his main seat in Sikkim, India. It was an ideal plan.

Times of Uncertainty

IN THE EARLY DAYS of the millennium, television, radio, newspapers maga-zines, and Internet sites were humming with the news of the Karmapa's escape from Tibet. Word also arrived at the Karmapa's main seat in Rumtek, Sikkim. The monastery's buildings climb up a steep green mountainside and overlook a deep valley, its slopes ribboned with rice paddies. Following the traditional Tibetan style, the expanse of its white walls is interrupted with brightly ornamented win-dows and roofs. The complex contains shrine halls, monks' quarters, the Nalanda Institute for Higher Buddhist Studies, and a three-year retreat center. As the res-idence of the previous sixteenth Karmapa, Rangjung Rigpe Dorje, his followers believe Rumtek Monastery to hold the blessing of his presence. The main build-ing also enshrines the precious objects he brought out of Tibet when in 1959, he too was forced to escape.

A golden Buddha presides over the central shrine hall where blue-green walls are painted with murals depicting the Buddha, Kagyu masters, and the main deities of the lineage. Here, in the winter of 2000, Gyaltsap Rinpoche was giv-ing an extensive series of empowerments known as *The Treasury of Oral Instruc-tions*. The ceremonies were drawing to a close and Gyaltsap Rinpoche was bestowing a long-life blessing to the large crowd that filled the shrine hall, its veranda, and the broad courtyard. Suddenly, a young monk came running down the central aisle past the long, low rows of painted tables. Everyone watched in astonishment. This was against all protocol, and Gyaltsap Rinpoche's eyes grew large. A little scared, the young monk offered up the envelope in his hand. Know-ing it was important, Gyaltsap Rinpoche stopped his ritual reading of the text and opened the letter. Tears welled in his eyes and he paused to gaze at the letter and then up into space. Then he rose from his throne and walked straight out the cen-tral aisle. Ripples of whispers rustled in his wake. "What could it be? What's the news?"

Ten minutes later Gyaltsap Rinpoche returned and spoke quietly to the tulkus and lamas near his seat; from them the news spread like a wave through the shrine hall and out into the courtyard. "The Karmapa has escaped to India!" Everyone was amazed and ecstatic; older Tibetans were in tears. Days of joyous celebration followed.[150] Later, Gyaltsap Rinpoche recalled, "When I heard news of His Holiness's arrival, I thought I was dreaming. I couldn't believe it. When I understood it was true, I was overflowing with happiness."[151]

This joy was felt by the Karmapa's followers all over the world, and reporters flocked to Dharamsala to cover the story, waiting for hour after hour, camped outside Chonor House where the Karmapa was staying in seclusion with Situ Rinpoche, who had arrived on the afternoon of the fifth. The Indian government was uncertain about the reasons for the Karmapa's escape—Did he come of his own accord? Was he sent by the Chinese? Was he drawn in by Tibetans?—and sent intelligence officers to interview the Karmapa and those who escaped with him. With all this attention, it was soon obvious that the party could not stay much longer at the Chonor Guest House: given the sensitivity of his situation, the Karmapa needed protection and also a more appropriate place to stay that would be safe and more spacious. Under the direction of the Dalai Lama, the Department of Religion and Culture found a temporary residence for the Karmapa, his attendants, and his administration at Gyütö Ramoche University about twenty minutes drive from Dharamsala. Five days after his arrival in India, the Karmapa was escorted to his new residence in the protection of the early morning hours.

From the perspective of the escaping monks, to arrive in India—known for its generosity to Tibetans—was the overriding goal. There was a sense that once they were safely in Dharamsala, with the escape behind them, everything else would go easily; the Karmapa would be given the papers he needed and be able to travel. But soon another obstacle loomed to cast its persistent shadow: the Karmapa's legal status in India was to remain ambiguous for over a year. Questions abounded. Would he have to leave India for another country? Would he be given political asylum? Or the refugee status accorded most escaping Tibetans? What was being discussed between the Indian and Chinese governments? A pervasive sense of uncertainty was mixed into the relief at their successful escape to a democratic nation, known to Tibetans as the "noble country," the place of the Buddha's enlightenment and teaching.

Except for visits to the Dalai Lama and the doctor, and a few public occasions, the fourteen-year-old Karmapa would be confined to Gyütö for thirteen months. Set on a plain with spectacular views of the Himalayas rising behind, Gyütö's main building had been completed, but the residences for the monks were still under construction. Approached from the ground level, the central building of Gyütö rises above double flights of wide red stairs that lead to the main shrine hall on the second floor. The ground floor, with its high ceilings for a cooler summer, is entered from the right side, where the door gives onto a hallway, guard post, and reception room. Down the central corridor and along the far side of the building are special rooms for visiting high lamas, such as Situ Rinpoche, Gyaltsap Rinpoche, or Thrangu Rinpoche, who would come to give teachings and empowerments. There are also simple living quarters for the monks, the general secretary and his staff; an office for Gyutö Ramoche itself (whose monks have been very accommodating); rooms for the Indian security officers living at the monastery; the general kitchen, and large room for dining. The second floor has residential rooms and the provisional office of the Karmapa's *labrang* (administration). Monks' quarters fill the third floor and the fourth is home to the Karmapa's sister, the nun Ngödrup Pelzom, as well as the resident khenpo, and some of the Karmapa's attendants. The general feeling here is one of spareness, a temporary situation that might end at any time and yet somehow goes on.

The Karmapa was given the top floor, which houses his sleeping quarters, accommodations for his attendants, a kitchen, and a long-windowed reception room carpeted in maroon. A veranda encircles the top story and offers views of the lush Kangra Valley in front, rice paddies and meadows on the sides, and the formidable wall of Himalayas behind, often coated with fresh snow. Day and night, through cold weather and hot, the Karmapa's monks circle around this open balcony on guard duty, shifting every two hours. The reception room opens onto a large, flat roof overlooking the front of Gyutö, where the Karmapa can take walks. In the early days after his arrival, he would stand here above the temple's facade, so that his followers who were not permitted inside could at least catch a glimpse of him. He could not leave the building without permission from Indian authorities, and access to him was very limited, especially in the early days. Outside the building, stationed around it, and at the main entrances were the everpresent guards from diverse organizations: the secret service of the government of India, the Dharamsala local and secret police, and the Tibetan Government-in-Exile.

For a while, the Karmapa had some difficulties with his health. Not long after his arrival, he spoke of chest pains and stomach problems. It seems that he was experiencing some trouble in adapting to the new environment, which was quite different from the high, dry climate of Tibet, and to the new food, which was quite different from the simpler provisions of Tibet. Over the following months, the Karmapa saw several doctors, and it was finally Tibetan medicine that helped him adjust to his new surroundings.

~

Beyond the circle of Gyutö, the leading Kagyu teachers and the Karmapa's disciples were greatly concerned about his situation and decided to call a meeting in India. Word was sent out to all the major and minor Kagyu lamas and to the officers of the Karmapa's administration in Rumtek, requesting that they come to a conference. On January 28 and 29, 2000, they gathered at Norbulingka, an institute established to preserve Tibetan art and culture, situated fifteen minutes' drive from Gyutö. Amid its peaceful gardens and flowing waters, they discussed plans for the Karmapa's future. With Situ Rinpoche and Gyaltsap Rinpoche presiding, they talked of where the Karmapa, his sister, and the monks would stay, the question of his legal status and documents, his travel, the complex situation at his monastery in Rumtek, and what his future activities might include.

One day during the meetings, the main teachers of the Karmapa's lineage who live outside Tibet—Situ Rinpoche, Gyaltsap Rinpoche, Thrangu Rinpoche, Bokar Rinpoche, Tenga Rinpoche, and Ponlop Rinpoche—went to see the Dalai Lama to confirm who would be the Karmapa's tutor. This was a major decision, and especially poignant since the Karmapa had taken such risks to pursue his education. As a great scholar and meditation master, Thrangu Rinpoche was considered the perfect candidate. Born in 1933 in eastern Tibet, he was recognized as a tulku at the age of four. He spent his young years in study and practice, receiving empowerments, reading transmissions, and commentaries from many great lamas, but among all of them, the main teacher who introduced him to the depth of mind's true nature was the sixteenth Karmapa. It was he who gave him the title Khenchen (great scholar and master) and who asked him to be abbot of Rumtek Monastery and the tutor of the four main Kagyu tulkus living there. In 1976, the sixteenth Karmapa asked him to travel abroad and teach, which he continues to do in Asia, Europe, and North America, where he is renowned for his clear presentation of difficult texts and his magnificent smile. Thrangu Rinpoche's special interest in education has led him to found several educational institutions, ranging from primary schools in Nepal to his Vajra Vidya Institute in Sarnath, India, where the most complex philosophical studies are pursued. The choice of the Karmapa's tutor was obvious. Despite Thrangu Rinpoche's humble protests, the Dalai Lama encircled a khata around his neck and the decision was confirmed.

~

During the months following the escape, it seems that thoughts of freedom were on the Karmapa's mind, for he mentioned it in his public talks at Gyutö Ramoche University and also spoke of it on February 19, the occasion of the sixtieth anniversary of the Dalai Lama's enthronement:

> In some regions and places, due to the lack of freedom to enjoy the right to individual freedoms and the lack of knowledge and understanding, conflicts occur. To take the case of Tibet, the Land of Snows, it used to be a land where the sacred [Buddhist] faith and all aspects of intellectual and

literary culture flourished. Over the last twenty to thirty years, Tibet suffered a great loss whereby Tibetan religious traditions and culture are now facing the risk of total extinction.[152]

This concern for preservation of a rich cultural heritage was also present in a poem, "A Joyful Aspiration," that the Karmapa wrote while escaping:

> The most excellent virtue is the brilliant, calm flow of culture:
> Those with fine minds play in a clear lotus lake;
> Through this excellent path, a songline sweet like the pollen's honey,
> May they sip the fragrant dew of splendid knowledge.

The complete song was set to music by the Tibetan Institute of Performing Arts (TIPA) in Dharamsala and performed for the Kagyu lamas at the end of the two days of meetings in January.[153]

The Kagyu lineage is known for these songs of realization, especially those of Milarepa (1040-1123), the cotton-clad master, whose verses are beloved by all Tibetans. On March 7, 2000, three months after the Karmapa's escape, TIPA presented the life story of Milarepa, "The Laughing Vajra, Lord of Yogins." This was an event the Karmapa could attend and the Dalai Lama spoke warmly of him:

There were two heart disciples of Milarepa, the Incomparable Physician from Dagpo (Gampopa) and Lama Rechungpa. From a heart disciple of Gampopa came the first Karmapa, Dusum Khyenpa (Knower of the Three Times). The lineage of the Karmapas descends until the seventeenth reincarnation, who happens to be able to be here with all of us at this gathering today. I think it's quite unexpected and surprising, as it clearly is for everyone. From a young age, Karmapa has displayed the maturing and manifesting of latent qualities that were inherited from his previous lives. And now, regardless of obvious dangers, he has arrived here in good health.

Previously, when I first heard about Karmapa Rinpoche's intentions to escape from Tibet and come here, I became very worried, thinking, "How could he possibly manage to do so?"[154] However, later, when I returned from Bodh Gaya, the very day of my arrival in Dharamsala, I learned that Rinpoche had managed to escape successfully and that he was in India. It was truly amazing. Later, when I met with Rinpoche, we first talked about his intention and his reasons for escaping. He came here with the hope and aspiration to be able to benefit and serve the cause of Tibetan Buddhism and people. He said that it was impossible for him to accomplish this while staying in Tibet. Motivated by such thoughts, he came. That is what he told me. And it pleased me greatly. I replied, "It is very good."

Since the Karmapa is young now, on the very first occasion when we met, we discussed what would be the most important things for him to do. For the coming ten years, he will be studying scriptures, receiving initiations, oral transmissions, and instructions from teachers, retreats, recitations, and other practices. It is very important for him to actualize his latent tendencies from previous lives and bring them forth into this one. Therefore, receiving teachings, contemplating, studying, and meditation practices are of great benefit for him. He fully agreed. His intentions were identical with mine. Now that many of us have gathered here, I thought it a great opportunity to meet the Karmapa so that we can know each other better. I encourage you to direct your aspiration prayers that all the plans and wishes of Karmapa Rinpoche be fulfilled effortlessly, without any hindrances or obstacles.[155]

The generous support of the Dalai Lama, personally and politically, was a stable point amid all the unknowns. Another stable point was the structure of the Karmapa's daily life. Gradually settling into Gyutö, the Karmapa arranged a schedule that he has followed for the length of his stay. The morning begins with his daily meditation practice, and after breakfast, from 9:00 to 11:00 A.M., he studies a major Buddhist text with Thrangu Rinpoche or another teacher. As the restrictions around him relaxed a little, he was allowed to give private audiences to his disciples from 11:00 A.M. to noon in his reception room on the top floor. From noon to 1:00 P.M., he has lunch and then time for study, painting, or poetry. At 2:30 P.M., he gives a public audience in the main shrine hall of Gyutö. As people pass in front of him to offer khatas, he gives each one a blessing cord, and often a special blessing to a newborn child or a sick person. Once the audience is settled on the wide rust-colored rug, he gives a reading transmission for the practice of the deity Chenrezik, embodiment of compassion.

Within the oral tradition of Tibet, reciting a text aloud is said to sustain the flow of the transmission from the one who has heard to the one who is listening, the resonant words bringing the blessing of the practice and a connection with the masters of the past. Reading transmissions are also given for practice manuals and philosophical texts. After reciting the practice text, the Karmapa often gives a Dharma talk before dedicating the merit for the benefit of all living beings. From 3:30 P.M. onward, he receives initiations and reading transmissions from his teachers or discusses a text with them. This is followed by the ritual practice of the protector Mahakala, which he has performed daily since December 1992, when he was seven years old. Later in the day, or between his practice and study sessions, the Karmapa will stop by to chat with his sister or walk through the building, taking the stairs down from the top floor to meet with his teachers or talk with his administration and the monks. His unexpected appearance seems to instantly energize everyone and bring the room alive. His curiosity about the people and world around him is intense and boundless.

~

During this uncertain year, the Karmapa continued to recognize tulkus. Dzogchen Ponlop Rinpoche described one occasion:

> One evening, we were doing the Mahakala puja, and His Holiness the Karmapa asked me to bring the computer. I was very uncomfortable bringing the computer to the Mahakala puja, but it was a command, so I brought his laptop to the puja. Then he said to write down what he would dictate, and so in between the chanting, I was writing his words down. He would say one word and then play the music with the damaru and bell, and then he would say another word. At first, I could not tell what he was dictating, and then at the end of the Mahakala puja, I realized he had composed a recognition letter for a young tulku. It just comes like that. There is the name of a place, the father's name, the mother's name, and the year in which the child is born. Amazing! I have heard of these things before but never experienced them directly.[156]

Following his original motivation to escape, the Karmapa continued to review, supplement, and expand the studies and practices he had started in Tibet. Thrangu Rinpoche first gave him the reading transmission and commentary for *The Seven-Point Mind Training* by Atisha, a fundamental text on developing bodhichitta through sending all one's happiness to others and taking on all their suffering. The text also teaches mindfulness through the use of pithy phrases that are contemplated throughout the day and blended together with one's mind:

> Consider all phenomena to be dreams.
> Be grateful to everyone.
> Don't be swayed by outer circumstances.
> Don't brood over the faults of others.
> Explore the nature of unborn awareness.
> At all times, simply rely on a joyful mind.
> Don't expect a standing ovation.[157]

Thrangu Rinpoche also taught the more philosophical text of *The Treasury of the Higher Teachings*[158] with a commentary by the eighth Karmapa, Mikyö Dorje.[159] (All the teachings the Karmapa receives are considered to be reviving for him what he knew in former lives, and therefore commentaries by previous Karmapas are often selected.) This fundamental text interweaves metaphysics and theories of perception to form a rich psychology. The treatise gives a map of mental functioning and defines the sets of concepts that are the basic building blocks of Buddhist philosophy; for example, the five aggregates constitute our psychophysical makeup and include the mind and mental factors detailing the variety of mental states we pass through. In actual meditation practice, these categories of analysis are used to observe how the mind functions.

In time, teachers from other Kagyu institutes of higher learning came to Gyutö to share their knowledge with the Karmapa. Khenpo Tsultrim Namdak and Khenpo Tashi Gyaltsen arrived from Situ Rinpoche's monastery, and Khenpo Garwang from Rumtek Monastery, whence came other monks who served as debate partners for the Karmapa. It is customary for important tulkus to have debating partners who receive the same teachings as they do and then unlock the arguments of the text in the lively atmosphere of debate. It is said that engaging in an animated debate is the best way to put the Dharma in your bones.

The Karmapa also began to receive the empowerments and transmissions for which he had risked everything in coming to India. These transmissions are considered a central current in an individual's spiritual history and mark major events. In particular, the oral instructions are known as the lifeblood of the lineage, which must be received directly from a teacher who has mastered the practice. A careful record is kept of each one including the specific names of the text and its author, the teacher who bestowed it, plus the time and place. The records of these occasions provide the outline of a unique spiritual career, detailing influences that would shape the realization and teachings of a particular lama, and also form the treasury of the inheritance that is passed along to the next generation.

Now at last in India, the Karmapa was able to meet with Situ Rinpoche and Gyaltsap Rinpoche, who visited often to give him these transmissions. Situ Rinpoche offered the Karmapa the unbroken lineage for the empowerments, reading transmissions, and oral instructions of *Knowing One Liberates All,* a large compendium of practices related to peaceful and wrathful deities[160] and also *The Treasury of Kagyu Mantras,* an uninterrupted lineage of deity practices and mandalas central to the Kagyu tradition.[161] Beyond his own lineage, the Karmapa also received *The Treasury of Spiritual Instructions,* "a systematic presentation of the most important instructions of all the Buddhist sects. The *gdams ngag* [oral instruction] is the guru's practical instruction to the disciple. Its essence is a record of the insights of an experienced master."[162] Situ Rinpoche has also offered the Karmapa all aspects of practice for the protector Mahakala, and all the essential texts on mahamudra, the core Kagyu teaching on the essential nature of mind.

Over the years, Gyaltsap Rinpoche has offered the Karmapa the empowerments from *The Treasury of Precious Terma,* a collection (usually of sixty volumes) that gathers the most important discovered texts (*terma*) that its compiler, Jamgön Kongtrul, considered authentic. These volumes contain ritual texts for empowerments and practices that had come to Tibetan masters while in a special state of mind. Appearing for over one thousand years, terma have allowed Buddhism in Tibet to stay vivid and responsive to change over time. They provided an acceptable (though not undisputed) avenue for the expression of a master's genius when a new text might not have been accepted by the more orthodox religious culture.

A core tenet shared by all Buddhist traditions is the lack of a self, the fact that a permanent, inherently existing entity cannot be found. In the Tibetan tradition, the central locus of this philosophical study is the sixth chapter on wisdom from Chandrakirti's *Entering the Middle Way* (*Madhyamakavatara*), which demonstrates the impossibility of finding a lasting, autonomous entity in an individual or a phenomenon.[163] With Khenpo Tashi Gyaltsen from Sherab Ling, the Karmapa studied this philosophy of emptiness, following traditional methods in memorizing the root text and examining the commentary.[164]

Since their meeting in India, the Dalai Lama has given special attention to the Karmapa's studies and continually asked about them. Further, in all that concerned the Karmapa's stay in India, the Dalai Lama has taken responsibility, speaking directly with the Indian government and writing official letters when needed. During this first year, the immediate concern was the Karmapa's legal status and obtaining official permission to stay in India. Until these questions could be resolved, the Karmapa would not be allowed to travel or even move from Gyutö. The Karmapa was also seeking permission to return to his Rumtek Monastery in Sikkim. This was a complex subject due to an old court case and to Sikkim's location on a Tibetan border not yet recognized by the mainland government of China. On all these issues, the Dalai Lama supported the Karmapa in whatever way he could. On a personal level as well, he was unwavering in his kindness and consideration. Whenever the Karmapa wished to meet him, he found time for a relaxed meeting, no matter how busy he was, even if he was on retreat, and gave the Karmapa advice as if he were a member of his own family.

~

The fifteenth birthday of the Karmapa was approaching and although there was still no confirmation of his legal status, his birthday would provide the change of a festive occasion. The celebration of the Karmapa's birthday, which began in India with the first one on June 26, 2000, has been repeated each year of his stay at Gyutö. Planning starts weeks ahead, and on the day itself, crowds come early to secure a good place to see the Karmapa and the dances. The schedule includes a morning in the shrine hall with prayers and mandalas offered for the Karmapa's long-life; then as the lines pass in front of him, he gives his blessing to each person. The shrine is hung with large thangkas for the occasion, and a table with tiers of elaborately decorated cakes adds a Western note. For the Karmapa's fifteenth birthday celebration, a lunch was provided for everyone after the morning ceremonies. During the afternoon, Tibetan dance groups from TIPA, local schools, and cultural groups performed, representing the diversity of Tibetan culture in song, dance, and costume. This is one of the many ways Tibetan culture is being preserved in the diaspora community. With Situ Rinpoche and Gyaltsap Rinpoche on either side, the Karmapa watched the performances from the shrine hall veranda above, perhaps remembering the times he had seen such dances from his balcony at Tsurphu.

Though unable to travel abroad, the Karmapa continued to be international news, appearing on the cover of *Time's* Asian edition for July 17, 2000. His legal status, however, was still not settled, and Rumtek remained a distant goal. There were quiet indications that he would be permitted to stay in India, but no formal travel documents were granted. Finally, a meeting was convened to work toward a solution of these issues, to invite the Karmapa to teach in his centers all over the world, and to thank the Indian government and the Dalai Lama for their support. Starting on August 18, 2000, and lasting for three days, over four hundred monks, nuns, and lay representatives from India, Nepal, the United States, and Asia—some thirty countries in all—gathered at Gyütö for the Third International Karma Kagyu Conference. Most participants had not yet met the Karmapa, so it was a special and moving occasion for them.

The discussions, in which the Sikkimese participants played an important part, led to a resolution that was offered to the Indian government, expressing gratitude for taking care of the Karmapa and requesting assistance for his plans to return to his main seat in Rumtek and to pursue his activity of offering teachings and benefiting people.[165] On the last day of the meeting, everyone traveled to upper Dharamsala and the Dalai Lama's Namgyal Monastery. In the warm gold of its shrine room, the Dalai Lama addressed the gathering, touching on the concerns of the day: "Together with the Indian government, we have started discussions on the issues of resolving the Karmapa's residence status in India. I told the Indian government that the original seat of the Karmapa is in Tsurphu in Tibet, and the second seat is in Rumtek, Sikkim. It is logical that the seventeenth Karmapa after his arrival from Tibet should go directly to Rumtek and will naturally regain the second seat of his predecessor."[166]

The Dalai Lama also added a personal note:

When I met the Karmapa, I told him that the present generation is getting old and I am already sixty-five years old. We have always prayed for the long-life of teachers, but in reality, everyone has to leave sooner or later, and there is no second choice, not even for Shakyamuni Buddha. I became a refugee forty-one years ago and [we are still] struggling for Tibet's freedom.... In the near future, something like ten to twenty years away, the new lineage holders of the Sakyapas, Gelukpas, Kagyupas, and Nyingmapas will be very important. During that time, it will depend entirely on the younger generations of lineage holders. At present, the generation between fifteen to twenty years of age is very important; for example, the son of His Holiness the Sakya Trizin and the present seventeenth Karmapa, Ogyen Trinley Dorje.[167]

Buoyed by this visit with the Dalai Lama and reminded of a long-term perspective, everyone returned to Gyütö for a final blessing from the Karmapa and his talk. He thanked everyone for coming and for all the invitations to visit their monasteries and centers. He encouraged the practice of bodhichitta, so that all living beings might be free of suffering and brought into liberation. Closing with the aspiration that all may attain wisdom and work to benefit others, he prayed that all conflicts in the world would come to an end.

Throughout the fall and long winter months, discussions were conducted with Indian authorities to settle the Karmapa's legal status and obtain permission for him to leave Gyütö and travel. It was a difficult time, the tenor of which was captured in this report:

Confined in a small, previously uninhabited monastery, the Karmapa is guarded closely by armed Indian soldiers and is unable even to walk the monastery grounds without permission. The young boy is said to be growing increasingly restive and suffering from ill-health. Tibetan refugees in India are normally free to travel wherever they wish. But... the Karmapa has been allowed to make only occasional excursions to Dharamsala to attend religious functions and to visit the Dalai Lama....

He told one recent visitor: "My main reason for coming out [of Tibet] was to fulfill the wishes of my disciples throughout the world, and to preserve and propagate the pure lineage of Buddha's teachings to benefit everyone. But for the moment, I am unable to do this. . . ." [T]he cramped conditions at Gyütö, and the restrictions on his movements have had a marked effect on his spirits and his health.[168]

Reflecting on his situation, the Karmapa told one reporter, "I sometimes wondered who had taken my freedom away."[169]

Throughout these times, the Karmapa's petitions were supported by the Tibetan Government-in-Exile and, in particular, by Kalön (Minister) Tashi

Wangdi of the Department of Religion and Culture. A skilled diplomat with years of experience, he acted as the main liaison with the Government of India. With a seventeen-year-old son of his own, he knew from his own experience how difficult for a young teenager a confinement like the Karmapa's would be.[170] Tall and lanky with an easy smile, Tashi Wangdi also interfaced with the media when the Karmapa was not allowed to meet the press directly. At important junctures, he underlined his government's support for the Karmapa's desire to return to Rumtek: "It was but natural and rightful for him to go to [Rumtek], as the seat of the Kagyu sect set up by the sixteenth Karmapa, whose reincarnation the Karmapa is. Any other arrangement for the Karmapa, be it at Gyutö Monastery or at [Situ Rinpoche's] Sherabling monastery at Bhattu near Baijnath, would merely be his temporary abode."[171] When problems continued to arise about the Karmapa's legal status, Tashi Wangdi relied on a deeper perspective: "It is his being that will make him the Karmapa, not a piece of paper."[172]

Finally, in the middle of winter, the clouds began to disperse. After the constant efforts of the Karmapa's administration (led by General Secretary Tendzin Namgyal) and the assistance of the Tibetan Government-in-Exile, more than a year of uncertainty came to an end. On February 3, 2001, Kalön Tashi Wangdi announced at a press conference: "Today, I am very happy to inform you that the Government of India has formally communicated to us that the 17th Gyalwa Karmapa Ogyen Trinley Dorje has been granted refugee status in India."[173] He had been given a home at last. This also meant that he would be allowed to travel, inside India at first, and to meet with the press. The doors were slowly opening.

Emerging As a Leader

THE KARMAPA used his new freedom to fulfill one of his long-held wishes. In February 2001, the Karmapa went on pilgrimage in India, traveling through the northern states of Uttar Pradesh and Bihar to visit major Buddhist sites. It is said that in one lifetime, every Buddhist should visit the four places that mark the central events of the Buddha's life: in Nepal, his birthplace at Lumbini; and in India, Bodh Gaya, the place of his enlightenment; Sarnath, where he first taught; and Kushinagara, where he passed into parinirvana.

The Karmapa's initial destination was Sarnath, where his tutor, Thrangu Rinpoche, had established the Vajra Vidya Institute for Higher Buddhist Studies. It is a few minutes' walk from the Deer Park, known in ancient times as "the place where the sages gather." It was here that the Buddha first turned the wheel of Dharma. Varanasi, neighboring Sarnath, is sometimes called the Cambridge of India, and is home to well-known universities that perpetuate the ancient interest in knowledge.

The Karmapa's visit coincided with the Tibetan New Year (Losar), which usually falls in February or March. A central event in the Tibetan lunar calendar, Losar is preceded by days of the protector Mahakala's ceremonies in the monasteries to purify the negativity of the preceding year and prepare for the coming one, while in the homes of lay practitioners, everything is cleaned and food is prepared for the days of visiting and relaxing that follow. New Year's Day itself is spent visiting one's teachers and the surrounding monasteries to make an auspicious connection for the year to come. In the main shrine hall of Vajra Vidya Institute, visitors from afar celebrated the New Year with the Karmapa on February 24 and chanted a long-life prayer for him written by the Dalai Lama, which reads in part:

> Your virtuous activities for the Dharma are images of light;
> The succession of the Karmapa's lives, a string of pearls.

Skilled in perfectly sustaining complete liberation,
Resplendent protector of beings, may your life be long.[174]

Long lines of devotees passed in front of the Karmapa's throne to receive his blessings. Afterward, he prayed for peace in the world, and especially in his homeland of Tibet.

For the ten days of his stay, the Karmapa resided in the top floors of the Institute, which contain his personal shrine room, reception room, and study and, on the very top, a spacious shrine room where his monks perform ceremonies. On the balcony outside, the Karmapa took walks and enjoyed the view that looks over the monastery courtyard with its pool and gardens across a vista of trees to the dome and spire of the Deer Park.

In Sarnath, the Karmapa bestowed a long-life empowerment, visited a children's school, gave a talk at the Institute for Higher Tibetan Studies, and offered a garland of bright orange marigolds at the Ganges River. One day he traveled north to Koshambi, still marked by an Ashokan pillar, where the Buddha is said to have spent a summer retreat.

The Karmapa toured the Deer Park with Thrangu Rinpoche, who explained the history of its monasteries, stupas, and temples, the ruins of which give evidence of a flourishing Buddhist community. When the great Buddhist king Ashoka (third century B.C.E.) was building monuments to mark important sites in India, he placed an especially beautiful pillar in Sarnath. The image of its regal lions facing in four directions has become the national emblem of India, appearing in the center of the national flag and on its currency.

After circumambulating the Dhamekh Stupa, the Karmapa took his seat on a throne set in the gardens nearby. With lines of maroon-clad monks beside him and rows of butter lamps offered in front, he performed ceremonies and made prayers for world peace. On another day, he returned to pay his respects to the relics of the Buddha kept in the Mulagandhakuti Temple. For this special occasion, the monks opened the stupa containing the relics so that he could directly receive their blessing.

Leaving Sarnath, the Karmapa traveled half a day southeast to Bodh Gaya, the primary Buddhist pilgrimage site in India. It was here that the prince Gautama arranged a seat of durva grass underneath a pipal tree and sat in meditation, resolving that he would not rise until he had attained full awakening. He meditated through the night, conquering aggression and the seductions of desire; at dawn he realized the utterly pure and vast nature of his mind, becoming the Buddha, the enlightened one. This *vajrasana* (diamond seat) is still shaded by the generous limbs of the bodhi tree, said to descend from the original, whose heart-shaped leaves are carried home by disciples. Right behind it is the elaborately carved temple, the slopes of its sides and the bell of its spire visible from afar. The

The fourteen-year-old Karmapa in 1999 at Tsurphu Monastery, Tibet.

Photographer unknown

His Holiness the sixteenth Gyalwa Karmapa Rangjung Rigpe Dorje, who passed away in 1981.

Photo: Blair Hansen

The seventeenth Karmapa in 1992 at the age of seven,
when the search party found him in Lhathok.

Photographer unknown

The birthplace of the Karmapa. Its meadowed mountains and streams were reflected
in the Dalai Lama's dream of the location.

Photographer unknown

The Karmapa's parents, Loga and Karma Döndrub Tashi, at Tsurphu in 1992.
Photo: Michele Martin

The Karmapa's family and their yak hair tent in Lhathok.
Photo: courtesy of Ngödrup Pelzom

The Dowo Valley leading up to Tsurphu Monastery, with the river on the right.

Photo: Kate White

The whole complex of Tsurphu Monastery and the Dowo River, viewed from the opposite mountain side.

Photo: Ward Holmes

Wearing the riding hat of a lama, the Karmapa arrives at Tsurphu Monastery on June 15, 1992.

Photo: Ward Holmes

The courtyard in front of the main shrine hall at Tsurphu in 1992, where disciples wait to receive the first empowerment given by the Karmapa.

Photo: Michele Martin

In his quarters at Tsurphu, the Karmapa and his teacher Umdze Thupten, who taught him reading and basic texts.

Photo: Ward Holmes

The Karmapa and his tutor Lama Nyima, a scholar and master of meditation.

Photo: courtesy of Dalha Yeshi

The Karmapa and one of his root lamas, Situ Rinpoche, during a picnic in the Upper Park of Tsurphu, July 1992.

Photo: Michele Martin

Bottom: Drupön Dechen Rinpoche, responsible for rebuilding Tsurphu and for the search in Tibet to find the seventeenth Karmapa.

Photographer unknown

In the summer of 1992, the seven-year-old Karmapa on the roof outside his quarters.
Photo: Michele Martin

At Tsurphu in July 1992, the Karmapa wears the hat known as the Crown of Activity.

Photo: Michele Martin

Situ Rinpoche makes an offering to the Karmapa during the enthronement ceremony, September 27, 1992.

Photo: Ward Holmes

In 1992 at Tsurphu, in the back row from the right: Lama Tenam, Situ Rinpoche, Gyaltsap Rinpoche, and Tendzin Gyurme. Seated in front: Akong Rinpoche and Sherab Tarchin.

Photo: Michele Martin

Amdo Palden came from his Karlek Monastery to Tsurphu for the Karmapa's enthronement. He was the Karmapa's first teacher and an advisor to his parents.

Photo: Michele Martin

The Karmapa and Dzogchen Pönlop Rinpoche pause during a walk up the Dowo Valley.

Photo: Rudi Findeisen

The Karmapa in May 1996 taking a walk on the rooftop near his quarters.
Photo: Michele Martin

Jamgön Kongtrul Rinpoche, identified by the Karmapa in April of 1996, visits him at Gyutö Ramoche University.

Photo: courtesy of Tashi Gawa

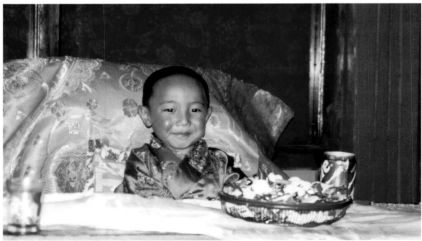

Identified by the Karmapa in 1996, Pawo Rinpoche at his Nenang Monastery near Tsurphu in 1998.

Photographer unknown

Dabzang Rinpoche, identified by the Karmapa in 1995

Photo: Courtesy of Bardor Tulku Rinpoche

On the left, Karma Mönlam Rabsay at Gyutö Ramoche University for a celebration in June 2002. A reincarnation identified by the Karmapa, he was found in Mustang, Nepal.

Photo: Michele Martin

The Karmapa wears the Gampopa hat to give empowerments at Tsurphu in 1999.

Photographer unknown

The Karmapa in brocade robes and ceremonial crown descends the stairs from his quarters to participate in Lama dancing.

Photo: courtesy of Bardor Tulku Rinpoche

The Karmapa participating in Lama dancing.

Photo: Palmo Arzt-Januschke

The Karmapa descending the stairs from his rooftop quarters, the same path he will take on the night of his escape.

Photo: courtesy of Bardor Tulku Rinpoche

peace and magnetic presence of this sacred place draw pilgrims from all over the world. In 2001, many came to be with the Karmapa.

Bodh Gaya is also a multinational home to monasteries of the many traditions and forms that Buddhism took as it spread throughout the world. After making his offerings to the vajrasana and performing ceremonies in the central shrine, the Karmapa visited the temples belonging to the traditions of Bhutan, Burma, Japan, Thailand, Taiwan, and Vietnam. At the Gelukpa monastery (of the Dalai Lama's tradition), the Karmapa gave a long-life empowerment and a short talk. Throughout his busy schedule, he also found time to give interviews to disciples.

Within a day's drive of Bodh Gaya are many places of Buddhist pilgrimage. The Karmapa journeyed to Vulture Peak in Rajgir, where the Buddha taught the Perfection of Wisdom sutras that comprise his second cycle of teachings. These are collectively known as the Mahayana, or great vehicle; both its philosophy and its meditation practice focus on compassion and the expanse of mind's empty nature. Not far from Rajgir are the ruins of the great center of Buddhist learning, Nalanda University. Its library was an important repository for Buddhist texts from the earliest traditions and especially for the Mahayana. Within its spacious grounds, scholarship flourished; it was home to renowned panditas, among them Nagarjuna and his disciple Aryadeva, Asanga and his brother Vasubhandu, Chandrakirti and Maitripa.[175] The writings of these masters, and others, were preserved in Tibet and presently form the core of the Karmapa's academic education.

After a last circumambulation of the main stupa, the Karmapa left Bodh Gaya for Delhi. Here in the capital city, the security forces protecting the Karmapa were quite apparent. When the Karmapa traveled by car, he was escorted by a motorcade including some seven vehicles; wherever he went or stayed, four government security guards accompanied him. While he stayed in the capital, special meetings were organized around the Karmapa, in particular by the citizens of Ladakh, situated in the west of India, and Sikkim in the east, where the Karmapa's main seat of Rumtek is located and people feel a close connection to him. The prime minister of Sikkim, Pawan Kumar Chamling, plus other ministers and members of the Sikkimese government, met with the Karmapa. Reaffirming their previous connection with him, the government of Sikkim and its people offered him their support and a petition outlining the preparations that had been made for his return to Rumtek. These meetings also gave the Karmapa an opportunity to express his gratitude to the Dalai Lama and to the government of India for their generous assistance to him and, further, to all the Tibetans who have come to India. The Karmapa also met with interdenominational religious groups and paid his respects at a Hindu temple and Sikh gudwara. When requested, he signed the guest register with a spontaneous poem.

On another day, the Karmapa visited the expansive park of the Gandhi

Memorial, where he offered flowers and prayers. Many Tibetans feel a special connection to Gandhi and consider him a true bodhisattva, a model for activity that benefits others. The Karmapa also went to the Buddha Jayanti Park, built to commemorate the 2,500th anniversary of the Buddha's birth. Interestingly, the celebration in 1956 had drawn Buddhist masters from all over the world, including the sixteenth Karmapa. This time in 2001, the seventeenth Karmapa gave to monk and lay disciples the long-life empowerment called *The Queen of Practice*, to which he seems to have a special connection, giving it in several places. The text was composed by the realized yogini Machik Labdrön, one of the most famous female masters of Tibet. Her lineage of Chö practice, which directly cuts through ego-fixation, is said to be the only teaching lineage to have traveled from Tibet back to India.

His visit over, the Karmapa returned north via the main route through Chandigarh. Bypassing Gyutö, he drove straight through Dharamsala up to Dahl Lake near the Tibetan Children's Village, a boarding school supported by the Tibetan Government-in-Exile. No rain had fallen in this area for a long while; the farmers were having a very difficult time and had requested the Karmapa to come and help. After performing a special ceremony, he advised them, "In the future, you should keep this lake very pure." That evening and throughout the night, rains fell and drenched the fields.

During March the Dalai Lama gave in Dharamsala a series of talks on Lam-rim Chenmo, the teachings on the gradual path of his Gelukpa tradition. On the 22nd, as a sign of his respect for and gratitude to the Dalai Lama, the Karmapa went to take teachings from him and to make offerings of food and one hundred rupees each to the fourteen hundred monks and nuns assembled there. This distribution of offerings is one way that Tibetans support the ordained community. Donors make direct offerings to the sangha, usually of money accompanied by a khata, or they sponsor a meal. The practice works in several ways: it benefits the ordained sangha, creates a dharmic connection between them and the donor, and accumulates merit.

Soon after, the Karmapa departed on pilgrimage, this time to Rewalsar Lake (also called Tso Pema, the Lotus Lake), a sacred site favored by Tibetan Buddhists for its connection to the life of Guru Rinpoche. It is said that Guru Rinpoche and his consort, Mandarava, had returned to her kingdom after engaging in a long-life practice at Maratika Cave. (When fleeing Tibet, the Karmapa passed near this cave in Nepal.) Mandarava's father, the king of Zahor, was furious at them and attempted to burn Guru Rinpoche with large quantities of oil. The fire blazed for days, but when the king came to inspect the site, Guru Rinpoche was found cool and fresh in the middle of a lotus-covered lake.[176]

While the Karmapa was visiting Tso Pema, many followed him as he walked for hours around the lake, stopping at one place to feed the fish, who seem to know when food is coming and set the surface quivering as they swim back and forth for popcorn, bread, and grains. At the Nyingma monastery,[177] he participated in a special feast offering of the second Karmapa, Karma Pakshi, and also performed a purification offering[178] related to Serö Ngadrak, the deity whose practice he had revived at Tsurphu. Afterward, the Kyirong people from India's northern Himalayan region performed their dances and songs, dressed in costumes whose style and rich colors had not changed for centuries. Here, as with all the monasteries the Karmapa visited, he offered food and money and they responded with generous hospitality.

The next day, a wood pavilion set in a grove of trees bordering the lake was decorated for the empowerment. The monks in yellow sleeveless shirts covered the platform and pillars in brilliant silks and brocades, set up a throne, and cordoned off seating areas for the various groups who would come. Many had camped overnight in another area of the park. When the time came for the empowerment, more than eight thousand people had gathered on the banks of the lake. Amid the grove of trees fluttering with multicolored prayer flags, hung with blessing cords, and basking in the lambent light of the sun, the Karmapa gave a blessing empowerment of Karma Pakshi that was especially based on his own practice. He also gave a short talk on the value of giving up negative actions and performing positive ones.

The following day, the Karmapa went to visit the famous meditation caves located along the mountaintop overlooking the lake. He chanted prayers in the Guru Rinpoche cave and was offered lunch at a small temple there. Before leaving Tso Pema, the Karmapa walked once again around the lake to visit a Hindu temple and a Sikh gudwara. The days with the community in Rewalsar were sunny and relaxed. According to ancient tradition, the clusters of reeds in the lake (known as *pedong,* or lotus stems) move around it when a special master is nearby, but they had not moved for a long time. During the Karmapa's visit, many people noticed that two of the clusters had made a complete circle around the lake.

Returning to Gyutö on March 28, the Karmapa stopped at the nearby Suja Tibetan Children's Village, home to seventeen hundred students, almost all of whom come from Tibet; many are teenagers close in age to the Karmapa. In a open plaza before a stage where the Karmapa sat, the students of the Suja Dance Troupe presented traditional Tibetan dances and songs. During the performance, blue-gray clouds gathered above him and took the shape of the elongated, clear eyes of the Buddha found on statues and stupas. They remained for a long time while photographs were taken and the dances came to a close, just as large raindrops began to fall.

~

Since permission had been given for the Karmapa to meet with the media, his first press conference was set for April 27, 2001. Preparations, not always easy in the more remote areas of India, started weeks ahead. E-mail announcements had to go out to the world via a tiny cyber-café whose proprietor's absences were frequent when the village fairs were open; the only available fax machine was a twenty-minute drive away and not always functioning. Material for a press kit had to be gathered, furniture rented, and food ordered. The Karmapa was keenly interested in the whole process and also kept his sense of humor. When practicing the short speech he wanted to give in English, he was having trouble with the *th* in "thanks," as all Tibetans do, since the sound does not exist in their language. After several attempts, he turned to Lama Tenam, whom he affectionately calls Ashang-la (Uncle), and said, "All right. Ashang-la, when I get to this part of the talk, you stand up and say, 'Thanks.'"

Some had expected only a few reporters to make the long and uncomfortable journey overnight from Delhi—if twenty-five showed up, that would be lucky. As it turned out, one hundred journalists from India and abroad came to Gyutö. The back of the shrine hall was lined with TV cameras, their lenses aimed past the curving rows of tables set up for the journalists, and beyond the photographers who filled the well in front, to focus on the Karmapa himself, seated in a brocaded chair with a garden of mikes before him. During the preparations, one of the main issues under discussion was whether to open the floor to questions or to protect the fifteen-year-old Karmapa, who had never experienced a press conference, by asking for written queries that could be vetted ahead of time. At the last minute, it was decided to trust his wisdom and open the floor. An old India hand was amazed: "You're throwing him to the sharks," he said. Yet Karmapa fielded questions with such self-assurance and skill that even seasoned reporters were impressed.

In his statement to the press, the Karmapa explained in brief how he had left Tsurphu and the difficulties they had all undergone in coming to India. He stated again that his motivation to leave was his wish to obtain the empowerments, reading transmissions, and oral instructions of his Karma Kagyu tradition, which he was now receiving in India. He underlined the reasons he should travel to his main seat in Rumtek and stated, "From my point of view, going to Rumtek Monastery would be like returning home to continue the activity of my predecessor."[179] The Karmapa thanked the Indian government and the Dalai Lama for their assistance and concern. He also stated that the previous Karmapas had not engaged in politics and therefore there was no precedent for him to do so either. Concerning Tibet, the Karmapa said that he rejoiced in the activities of His Holiness the Dalai Lama and would follow his lead in these matters.

During the question and answer session, the young Karmapa responded clearly and without hesitation. His humor also came through.

Q: Your Holiness, since you have come to India, the government of China has asserted that you did not come to take up residence in this country, but only to reclaim the Black Hat and other possessions of your predecessor.

A: It is true that I left a letter behind me, but as I wrote the letter myself, I'm perfectly aware of what was in it and what wasn't. I said in the letter that I left because, although I had for a long time, persistently and repeatedly, requested permission to travel internationally, I had never received it and so I had to leave. I did not in the letter mention the Black Crown. Why would I want to retrieve that from India and bring it back to China anyway? The only thing that would be served or accomplished by doing so would be to place the Hat on Jiang Zemin's head.

Q: Are the Chinese waiting for the Dalai Lama to pass away in the hopes that this will be the end of the Tibetan independence movement and that they will thereafter be able to fully absorb Tibetan culture within Han Chinese culture?

A: His Holiness the Dalai Lama is not that old and is in very good health. In addition, I constantly pray for his longevity and I am confident that his passing will not occur for a long time. It is quite possible that before then, the political situation in China will change considerably. In addition, the power of His Holiness the Dalai Lama's aspirations and compassion is inconceivable. With regard to the youth of Tibet, I think the most important thing is for them to concentrate on the preservation of the spiritual and cultural traditions of Tibet. And His Holiness the Dalai Lama regularly gives them the same advice.

Q: What future would you like to see for Tibet?

A: Since the foundation of the spiritual tradition of Tibet is nonviolence and peace, my greatest aspiration is that Tibet abide in the future in a state of nonviolence, peace, and tranquillity.[180]

The media people left enchanted with their visit ("I've never seen my colleagues behave so well," commented one), and some stayed behind for private interviews on the weekend, which took place in the Karmapa's reception room. Behind the yellow-curtained door, at far end of the room, the Karmapa stood to receive them. For the interviews, he sat in an armchair before brocaded thangkas of the Buddha flanked by images of two Indian masters. On the right, was a simple shrine. During the interviews, he leaned slightly forward, attentive to the many questions. One reporter described her impression: "It is his eyes that seal his status. Beautiful, dark and hypnotic like horizontal teardrops that hold secrets of the past 1,000 years. Cloaked in flowing maroon and saffron, his copper skin shining with adolescence, Ogyen Trinley Dorje exudes a spiritual opulence that belies his relatively modest surroundings."[181]

After the press conference, worldwide coverage on TV and radio and in the newspapers and magazines was universally positive. In an article entitled "The Most Powerful Teenager in the World Breaks His Long Silence," one reporter noted, "What we saw yesterday was not merely the incarnation of an august lama but an impressively intelligent and self-assured young man."[182] Another stated, "The 15-year old Karmapa produced an impressive mixture of acumen and dexterity during the press conference, dealing with a range of sensitive diplomatic, political and religious issues concerning his homeland."[183] There was humor, too, as reflected in the title of one article: "Daunting Audience with a 900-Year Old Teenager."[184]

~

In a corner room on the fourth floor of Gyütö monastery, the thankga painter Shedrup Yongdu from Kathmandu and his two Nepali assistants had been working since the fall of 2000 on a large canvas portraying the Karmapa's dreams and visions. Laced to a wooden frame, the canvas was so tall that to reach the upper area, the painters had to sit on a raised platform with a wide basket full of paint jars beside them. The central figure in the thangka was the golden Serö Ngadrak, who embodies the activity of all the buddhas. He was the focus of the long ceremony that the Karmapa had performed at Tsurphu before he escaped. Instead of the traditional landscape of mountains, rivers, and trees, the space surrounding Serö Ngadrak was filled with images the Karmapa had described from his visions and dreams.

The Karmapa commented: "Everyone dreams. As a human being, I, too, dream. And not every dream is significant. But sometimes in my dreams, some significant things emerge. In fact, many of my predecessors also dreamt of significant happenings and had premonitions of future events through dreams. Because of their inherent importance, these dreams were painted. I try to follow the same tradition.... If there is any element of truth in what I have dreamt, then there are certain things in my dreams related to the future of Tibet, and the future of the world."[185] Conversing about different states of mind, the Karmapa said, "Once I had a dream of the Buddha Bhagavat.[186] It was indeed a dream, but afterward, I had a special feeling, as if he were close, like a relative. Whether it was good or bad, I don't know, yet even now there is a feeling of joy in this connection."[187] At the very top of his new thangka, in the center, stands the Buddha in flowing saffron robes, surrounded by rainbows of light. Perhaps this was the dream that he had described to the artist.

In mid-May, the retreat master Bokar Rinpoche came to stay at Gyütö and offered daily teachings to the Karmapa on *The Ornament of Precious Liberation* by Gampopa, a fundamental text for the Kagyu tradition, discussing meditation practice and the philosophy behind it.[188] The text begins with an explanation of buddha nature, the ultimate reality of mind or basic goodness within every living being, and then explains the preciousness of human life and the value of a spiritual friend to give guidance along the path. Its focus is on practice, which begins with taking refuge and developing bodhichitta (the awakened mind), and then moves to developing the six perfections: generosity, discipline, patience, diligence, stable contemplation, and a deeper knowing. The final stages involve traversing the progressive levels of realization that lead to full awakening. With this comprehensive focus, the text is a complete manual and reference work for those who are serious about meditation practice.

Gyaltsap Rinpoche returned in June for three months to continue offering the empowerments from *The Treasury of Precious Terma*. Every morning, Khenpo Garwang from Nalanda Institute in Rumtek offered teachings that covered the difficult points in the eighth Karmapa, Mikyö Dorje's, commentary on *Entering the Middle Way*.[189] In fulfillment of his wishes, the Karmapa received a continuous stream of teaching and empowerments throughout the summer.

In early September, he traveled to Ladakh, whose lunar landscape and stark peaks have been home to the Buddhism of Tibet since the eighth century. Elements of Ladakhi architecture, dress, and language would be familiar to the Karmapa. Numerous monasteries are secluded in its mountains and others are set close to the villages, forming the focus of their daily life. In the capital of Leh, a major stopping point on the old silk road, he was greeted by crowds of Ladakhis who lined the streets, holding out their bright flowers and traditional welcoming vases. During the days of his visit, the Karmapa traveled to monasteries throughout Ladakh, gave empowerments to thousands, consecrated a stupa, temple, and monastery, attended official dinners, and gave the transmission of Chenrezik's mantra to the lay people in the villages along the way.

The Karmapa returned to Delhi the day after September 11. As he had prayed for the victims of the Gujarat earthquake earlier in the year, the Karmapa offered his prayers for those who perished in the World Trade Center: "The United States has had to face a terrible tragedy at this time. Since September 11, it has been my prayer that this sort of event, in which so many lives are lost and people injured, not happen again in the future anywhere in the world. My wish is that every human being live in peace. And whatever conflict there may be between countries might be resolved to the benefit of all, without war."[190] The Karmapa also requested the monks at his main seat in Rumtek and at other Kagyu monasteries to make prayers for peace by performing one hundred thousand special ceremonies and offerings.

In November, Khenpo Tsultrim Gyamtso came to offer teachings to the Karmapa. Born in eastern Tibet in 1934, Khenpo Tsultrim followed the tradition of many famous masters and traveled through Tibet as a wandering yogi. While at Tsurphu, he received profound instructions on the nature of the mind from the sixteenth Karmapa and further clarifications from Tsurphu's retreat master, Dilyak Drupön. After escaping to India, Khenpo Tsultrim spent nine years at the nonsectarian institute of higher Buddhist studies in Baxa, home to many who were forced to leave Tibet in 1959. The sixteenth Karmapa gave him the title of Khenpo and invited him to teach the new generation of Kagyu tulkus and scholars in Rumtek. Khenpo Tsultrim also founded Marpa Institute for Translators in Nepal, whose graduates now translate all over the world. He is known for his skill in debate, his spontaneous songs, and his ability to present complex ideas with great clarity. He offered the Karmapa teachings on the subtleties of Middle Way philosophy and on Milarepa's songs of realization.

～

In early December, the Karmapa, Gyaltsap Rinpoche, and their monks engaged in ten days of practice focused on Vajrakilaya, a protector deity with a special connection to the Karmapa. Soon after, he left for Bodh Gaya and the Kagyu Mönlam, a week-long prayer festival that draws thousands of the ordained and lay sangha every year to meditate at the seat of the Buddha's full awakening and to pray for world peace. The Karmapa led the ceremonies and gave daily teachings on *The Ornament of Precious Liberation* by Gampopa. He also found time to give teachings in the evenings to disciples from abroad.[191]

During the festival, the Karmapa offered to all the participants a book that he had published, composed of texts important to the Kagyu tradition. He commented: "I have old texts, and from these I selected the most valuable and useful, the important ones from various traditions. To serve the Kagyu tradition in general, I thought it would be good to present the teachings of all the previous Kagyu teachers."[192] The first of two volumes included praises of Shakyamuni Buddha and the female buddha Tara, practices composed by previous Karmapas, texts on meditation by Gampopa, and other instructions on how to work with buried faults or take joy in what is positive. The contents were rounded out with aspiration prayers and a dedication of merit. Seven months later, the Karmapa would publish a second volume with rare texts from various Kagyu traditions, some in danger of dying out.

The Karmapa's tutor, Thrangu Rinpoche, notes that the Karmapa loves books. He has books about everything from everywhere, and one of the best gifts for him is an old and rare text.[193] Thrangu Rinpoche recalls:

The sixteenth Karmapa benefited sentient beings greatly, and he had a special interest in birds. It is said that when some of his birds died, they stayed in what looked like meditation. The special interest of the seventeenth Karmapa is books and, in particular, the rare and old texts of the previous Kagyu masters. No matter what the difficulty in obtaining these books from far away Tibet or India, no matter what the cost, he seeks them out or has copies made. For a seventeen-year-old, he has an extraordinary interest in esoteric, old books, as most teenagers would be occupied with music, dancing, and other entertainments. I was wondering why he had such a liking for texts and remembered that when the sixteenth Karmapa had to suddenly leave Tibet for India, he could not bring many texts with him. When it came time to build monasteries and institutions of learning, he had to work very hard to find books. So I think his interest in texts is an awakening of habitual patterns from his previous incarnation.[194]

When asked about the previous Karmapa's fondness for birds and his own fondness for books, the Karmapa replied, "I do like books and I like birds, too. But I have a strange thought. If you catch a bird and bring it here far away from its environment, it will remember its home and long to be there. It will be quite sad. If we didn't own them, the birds would be free. And also, we do not know their thoughts and cannot take care of them so well. For all these reasons, I do not keep them now."[195]

After the Kagyu Mönlam, the Karmapa returned in early January for a second visit to his tutor's Vajra Vidya Institute in Sarnath. He had another plan he wanted to carry out in meeting with the main teachers of his tradition, for not only was the Karmapa interested in publishing books, he also recognized the importance of practicing the meditations they describe. Within the Kagyu lineage, an important master was Marpa the Translator (1012-1097), who undertook several journeys to India at great risk in order to receive teachings and transmissions of tantric practices (*sadhanas*). When codified, these became known as the thirteen tantras of the Marpa Kagyu tradition. In addition to specific visualizations, mantras, and mudras, the practices include making sand mandalas and tormas, the music of drum and wind instruments, and lama dancing. At this young age of sixteen, the Karmapa was looking to the future with an intention to revive these practices. He stated:

Previously, the thirteen tantras of Marpa Kagyu were kept alive through practice, but these days there are not many ten-day intensive retreats for each one of them. For example, in one monastery, the monks will only practice three main sadhanas (usually, Gyalwa Gyamtso, Dorje Pagmo, and Khorlo Demchok). If this does not change, then all the great efforts that the previous Kagyu masters have made will be lost.

When I was first considering this, I thought that each monastery should practice all thirteen sadhanas. However, in the beginning it's difficult to perform them all, so we started with each monastery taking on one or two of the practices. In the future, however, I have the hope that each monastery will be able to practice all thirteen classes of tantra stemming from Marpa, and beyond these, many other practices belonging to the four classes of tantras.[196]

Previously at Tsurphu, one hundred tantras were practiced. All the other Kagyu traditions, such as the Drugpa, Drikung, and Barom, have their own specific lineages of practice, many of which have almost disappeared. So now we will try to revive them and maintain this precious resource so that in the future, these practices can spread and bring all their benefits.[197]

The rinpoches, lamas, and officials all agreed with the Karmapa's project, and the thirteen practices were divided among the Karma Kagyu monasteries in India, Nepal, and Bhutan, with the larger places receiving more than one.

In January 2002, the Dalai Lama also came to Sarnath. In the Deer Park, the Karmapa sat beside him under a golden canopy, its pillars studded with bright marigolds, as they offered a day of prayers for world peace. The Karmapa also went farther afield to Kushinagara, the place where the Buddha passed into parinirvana. The village of Kushinagara is only thirty-five miles east of Gorakhpur, where the escaping Karmapa had boarded a train to Lucknow on his way Delhi and Dharamsala two years before. Now he had time to visit and be a pilgrim. At Kushinagara, King Ashoka had also built stupas and pillars. They mark the sala grove where the Buddha gave his last advice to the assembled sangha before his parinirvana: "Everything created is impermanent. Accomplish your practice with diligence." Surrounded by stately trees, a temple now enshrines a large statue of the Buddha lying on his right side, his head to the north. Another stupa set in a grassy park marks the cremation ground. As all pilgrims do, the Karmapa circumambulated these sites and made offerings of flowers and light.

On January 24, Karmapa returned to Bodh Gaya, where the Dalai Lama was to give the Kalachakra empowerment but he had become ill. The next day, the Karmapa and Ganden Tri Rinpoche led tens of thousands of monks in ceremonies and prayers at the Bodhi tree for the return of the Dalai Lama's health and his long life. Afterward, the Karmapa returned to Gyutö to welcome the Year of the Water Horse with traditional ceremonies. It had been hoped that this New Year would be celebrated at Rumtek or Sherab Ling, but permission was not forthcoming. Again in March and April, petitions from the Dalai Lama and the Tibetan Government-in-Exile for the Karmapa's return to Rumtek were strongly put forward, but success still eluded them.

~

Meanwhile, the Karmapa continued to be the focus of international attention. The cover story for *Time's* April 22, 2002 Asian edition— "Time salutes the individuals who inspire us"—featured the Karmapa, who had been chosen as one of the twenty-five Asian heroes. The article about him was written by a Tibetan, born and brought up in India, and reflects the influence the Karmapa is having on the younger generation:

> [N]ews of his escape came like a reviving gust of fresh air that blew away the cloud of confusion and inertia. . . . Despite . . . efforts at brainwashing him and despite his youth, the Karmapa grew up with a strong sense of his own convictions. . . . When the contradictions between his beliefs and the public role he was expected to perform—especially when it came to denouncing the Dalai Lama—became irreconcilable, he decided to flee. . . . The Karmapa's escape was a loud wake-up call to those of us who have spent a lifetime in exile.[198]

In a more meditative mode, a veteran Indian journalist interviewed the Karmapa. She learned that he enjoys composing tunes on the flute and noted, "This young man's spirit shines through. To me, he seems quite his own person, with his own views. His response [to my questions] makes me think that perhaps what incarnates, in the case of realized beings, is their wisdom, and not the personal characteristics of a particular birth. . . . [T]here emanates from him what I can only describe as a profound stillness. He seems to be simply observing all that's happening around him. The disturbances, no more than ripples on water, arise and gently taper away."[199]

The Karmapa's main tutor, Thrangu Rinpoche, returned to Gyutö in April and May to complete his explanation of *The Treasury of Higher Teaching.* During this time, he also offered the Karmapa a new set of books. Tibetan texts are long rectangles of unbound, hand-printed sheets held between two boards and wrapped in cloth. Thrangu Rinpoche told of an experience related to these texts: "I am a bit of a skeptic when it comes to miracles. I usually do not pay much attention to them, but this was an unusual event that I experienced myself. This year, I had the temporary use of a rare collection of six volumes, so I made a photocopy for the Karmapa. These pages, however, were not numbered, and not only was the photocopy out of order, so was the original. Each of the six volumes contained numerous smaller texts, and three of us had to work for days putting all the loose pages back in order again. Finally, there was just one short text of three pages left, but one page was missing. We had looked everywhere and could not find it. His Holiness the Karmapa would sometimes come downstairs to talk and this time he asked, 'How is the arrangement of the text going?' And I replied, 'There is one page missing.' The Karmapa reached forward and pulled one leaf out of the text I was holding. It was the missing page."[200]

~

At the end of May, the Karmapa was the guest of honor at the Shotön (Yogurt) Festival, during which Tibetan opera was played every day, all day for a week. Tibetans from Dharamsala brought picnics and camped out on the ground around the players. Sung in a recitative punctuated with long-held notes, the tales are traditional ones, resembling in many ways the morality plays of medieval Europe but featuring Buddhist values and Tibetan legends. The costumes are brilliant and the movements stylized. The story lines are enlivened with contemporary references: when the beautiful goddess rewards the fisherman for his faithful service, she bestows upon him a visa and plane ticket to the dreamland of America. The Nepali emissary presents the King and Queen with heaps of Wai Wai noodles, the best-selling brand in Kathmandu. Tibetan foibles are pilloried; perseverance and faith, rewarded. In his talk at the end of the festival, the Karmapa emphasized, as he had so often in the past, the importance of maintaining Tibetan traditions while allowing them to interact with contemporary culture. With this openness and a sensitivity to tradition, all the arts can maintain their roots while evolving and staying relevant.

~

In June, Gyaltsap Rinpoche once again offered the empowerments from *The Treasury of Precious Terma*. Each morning, he engaged in the preparation ceremonies, and each afternoon, the Karmapa received the empowerments. Khenpo Tsultrim also returned to continue teaching the Middle Way philosophy. This time, he focused on the most famous treatise on emptiness, *The Root Verses on Wisdom* by Nagarjuna. In twenty-seven chapters, the great Indian scholar examines major topics, such as motion, time, suffering, agent and action, becoming and destruction. Meticulously demonstrating that not one of these has a concrete, permanent existence, Nagarjuna analyzes each one into its empty nature. His arguments are summarized in the key statement: All phenomena arise in dependence one upon the other and are therefore empty. It is said that if one realizes the meaning of the first lines in the text—often taken as an object of meditation in themselves—there is no need to read the rest:

> Whatever arises in dependence
> Has no cessation and no arising,
> No extinction and no permanence,
> No coming and no going,
> And is neither different nor the same:
> Mental constructs completely stilled,
> It is taught to be peace.[201]

June also brought the third celebration of the Karmapa's birthday at Gyutö. Along with many lamas and government officials, also in attendance was the newly elected head of the Tibetan Government-in-Exile, Samdhong Rinpoche, who gave the keynote speech. In Rumtek as well, the day was celebrated with the young Jamgön Kongtrul Rinpoche, who had come to preside over the festivities. Victory banners in brocade, long radung horns, plumes of incense, and the floating signatures of white scarves lined the road all the way to the Rumtek Monastery gate, welcoming the young tulku, who had spent most of his previous life in this very monastery.

In this same month of June, the Karmapa received from the Dalai Lama the empowerment of Guhyasamaja, one of the thirteen tantras of Marpa that the Karmapa hopes to revive. In July, the Dalai Lama, assisted by Gyaltsap Rinpoche, bestowed on the Karmapa the novice vows of a monk. Thrangu Rinpoche explains:

The Karmapa's hair-cutting ceremony at the Jokhang in 1992 was similar to taking refuge vows, the first sign that we have entered the gate of the Dharma. After the novice vows, which the Karmapa has just received, the next set of vows are those of full ordination, or *gelong* vows. Traditionally, these are not taken until someone is twenty years old, the age when it is thought that they can decide for themselves.

Within the Vinaya (Buddhist monastic rules), the novice vows are considered the preliminaries for taking the full vows. Although the Karmapa does not need to enter the Dharma in stages like this, to illustrate his compliance with the Vinaya, he went through the hair-cutting ceremony and then received the novice vows from the Dalai Lama, who is considered the spiritual leader for the Buddhism of Tibet. In particular, during this time of the seventeenth Karmapa, the two have a very close connection, and the Dalai Lama has given special care and attention to the young Karmapa. Previous Karmapas have also received these vows from the Dalai Lamas.[202]

The monsoon rains continued through the month of August and brought the sad news that the Chinese had detained Lama Nyima, the Karmapa's tutor at Tsurphu, and Thubten, his cook. Until this report arrived, there was great hope that they, too, would be able to escape to India. The Tsurphu retreat master Lama Panam had also been arrested. Radio Free Asia reported: "Lama Panam was detained in March in Tibet's Kham Prefecture, while Lama Thubten was arrested in January while trying to flee to India, sources said. Lama Nyima was arrested in June, in Kongpo. . . and has staged a hunger strike in prison."[203] The Karmapa has urged the Chinese to release them:

I appeal to the Chinese government and the Tibetan Autonomous Region government that those arrested may be released quickly, and that they may be spared harsh treatment while in prison. I am greatly disappointed and also worried. I escaped to pursue my religious studies, not to achieve political goals. . . . Lama Nyima had been my teacher and I am very grateful. Whatever I learned is from his teaching and guidance. Thubten was my cook and he was extremely devoted.[204]

Following the Karmapa's lead, concerned individuals are now gathering support from international organizations and governments to encourage the Chinese to set these monks free.

~

The Karmapa was again permitted to travel in September when he was invited to Kolkata[205] as the guest of honor at the 138th anniversary celebration of Anagarika Dharmapala, who in 1891 founded the Maha Bodhi Society of India, now perhaps the most influential Buddhist society in India, with the motivation to revive the practice of Buddhism in India and restore its places of pilgrimage. In 1893, after attending the World Parliament of Religions in Chicago, Anagarika Dharmapala became an international figure and made several trips abroad. His main work, however, was in India itself, where the Maha Bodhi Society has constructed schools, libraries, residences for monks, and, in 1931, the famous Mulagandhakuti Vihara in Sarnath that enshrines a sacred relic of the Buddha and where the Karmapa and the Dalai Lama conducted ceremonies for world peace in 2001.

On his first day in Kolkata, the Karmapa held his second press conference, speaking again of the three monks who were imprisoned. Displaying a mature grasp of the political situation in which he finds himself, the Karmapa also spoke of a return to his monastery in Rumtek, Sikkim: "Certain preparations need to be done before I can go back there. An immediate return is not possible, firstly, because of Sikkim's border with China and, secondly, my presence there will be a very important occasion, historically and spiritually. The timing of my arrival has to be fixed after all these [preparations] are made. . . . Whatever be the hurdles, they will be cleared soon. Though there is no timetable fixed, I believe I will be there within two years. The people of Sikkim, which is an integral part of India, want me to be there."[206]

Looking toward travel outside of India, the Karmapa has applied for an identity card, the document that allows Tibetan refugees in India to travel abroad, and plans are in the making for the Karmapa's first world tour. He has been waiting a long time for this voyage. In 1992, soon after he had returned to Tsurphu, there was a photo session in his residence. Its long room was lined with windows on the south side, looking onto the graveled top of the shrine hall, over the Dharma wheel flanked by deer to the mountains beyond. The Karmapa stood on a throne in the far back corner of the room, and above him was a large photograph of the sixteenth Karmapa seated in meditation. Someone had given the seven-year-old incarnation a blue, green, and white globe. As he held it firmly and gently in the spread of his hands, it stood out, almost glowed, among the darker tones surrounding him. The only object brighter was the oval of his face. He smiled and then grew serious, his almond eyes ancient and young at once, looking straight into the world.

Part II

The Teachings of the
Seventeenth Karmapa

Introduction
to the Teachings

S OON AFTER ARRIVING at Gyutö Ramoche University, the Karmapa began to give public audiences in its bright and airy shrine hall, two stories high and painted a soft yellow. Windows ring three sides of the room, and the raised shrine in the front holds an immense golden statue of the Buddha, flanked by smaller images of the lineage figures and rows of butter lamps, and in the middle, a throne for the Dalai Lama. The floor is covered with rust-colored rugs on which people sit in random rows. Around 2:30 from Friday to Monday, people of all ages from nearby Dharamsala, other areas of India, and faraway lands come to see him. His maroon robes flowing over his tall frame, the Karmapa walks with clear purpose to the armchair in front of the shrine. Standing before the Buddha, he receives the traditional white khatas and gives blessings to the long line of people who pass in front of him. Once everyone is seated, he gives a reading transmission for the practice of Chenrezik, the embodiment of compassion and a special deity for Tibet. The Karmapa is also considered an emanation of Chenrezik, so he has an especially close connection with this practice. Afterward, he usually gives a talk or sometimes meets with disciples to answer questions.

The Karmapa often speaks of the importance of practicing Chenrezik and of developing bodhichitta, the awakened mind. Therefore, the first teaching in this section comprises excerpts of many talks given on this subject when he was fifteen and sixteen years old. The talks that follow this section cover a wide range of topics, from the importance of maintaining a cultural inheritance to subtle philosophical points or advice on how to meditate and work with our minds. The Karmapa's sense of humor surfaces particularly when he is interacting with students.

The first section's talks are in chronological order, starting with 2000 and extending through 2001. They illustrate the Karmapa's concerns and interests when he first arrived in India and trace how his teaching changed over the year. The final talk in this section, given in Bodh Gaya, presents the sixteen-year-old Karmapa's discussion of a song of Milarepa, the realized master and poet of Tibet. It is a condensation of three talks given to older Dharma students and may be a bit difficult for those new to Buddhism.

The next section is from 2002 and progresses from introductory to more advanced teachings. The final section presents the essentials of meditation for those who are new, and for older students, the more subtle points on deep insight. The style of all these talks reflects the traditional mode of teaching with its rhetorical questions, repetition, and humility. The audiences were always widely varied, from people who knew nothing about Buddhism to longtime meditators. The talks have a quality of distilled simplicity and a directness that will make them valuable to everyone.

Although they are not always included here, every talk ended with a dedication and prayer in which the Karmapa made supplications for the welfare of all living beings, for world peace, and especially for peace and happiness within the hearts of the people who came from all around the world to receive his generous blessing and hear his wise words.

Practicing Chenrezik and Developing Bodhichitta

TALKS FROM FEBRUARY 2000 TO JULY 2001

WHEN WE ARE TRAINING in the Dharma, the very essence of a true path is precious bodhichitta, the mind that seeks awakening for the sake of all beings. With our sincere intention and desire to benefit others, we develop bodhichitta; our intelligence and knowledge allow us to find these qualities within our own mind.

To help this process, it is important to rely on a yidam deity such as Chenrezik. Why is this so? Noble Chenrezik is the master of compassion; to speak in Dharma terms, he is the very embodiment of the compassion of all the buddhas of all times and in all directions. Inspired by his perfect bodhichitta, we can enter into a true path by reciting the six-syllable mantra of Chenrezik, which embodies his compassion. The benefits of the practice are twofold: we will attain full awakening, and we will be able to help others do the same. This is the path of bodhichitta, which the Buddha taught extensively in the sutras.

Bodhichitta can be understood as having two aspects, ultimate and relative. Ultimate bodhichitta is realizing that phenomena are empty even though they appear: they are emptiness and appearance inseparable. Relative bodhichitta is the actual practice of bodhichitta. In order to engage in this, we recognize what virtuous actions are and practice them. So that the fruit of these actions will mature, I usually give the transmission for the brief practice of Chenrezik. By meditating on it, we ourselves are benefited through perfecting the qualities of the mind's true nature, and others are benefited through our pure love and beneficial activity.

How do we further develop bodhichitta? We realize that we are individuals living on this earth and sharing it with numberless sentient beings, only a few of whom we can see. We practice so that all of them may enter into the path that leads to unexcelled awakening or perfect buddhahood. Our practice is dedicated so that, ultimately, once we have realized the essential nature of mind, pure from time without beginning, we may be able to bring all living beings to awakening in the expanse of primordial purity. On the level of temporary benefits, the dedication is for all living beings so that we may have a long life and good health. These are some of the many reasons for practicing Chenrezik.

To take myself as an example, I am a young man who analyzes, contemplates, and meditates on the Mahayana teachings. Through reciting the mantra of Chenrezik, I know its benefits. In the very same way, even if we have not entered the Mahayana path or have remained a lay person without taking ordination, we can supplicate and make aspiration prayers to Chenrezik. We can meditate on him with our mind, putting into practice the oral instructions we have received. The benefits of these practices are the same for everyone: they are not greater for one and lesser for another.

It is not enough just to believe in the benefits of practice. Our teacher, Shakyamuni Buddha, said that his teachings should be examined thoroughly with our analytical reasoning so that we may cut through any doubts and discover a profound certainty. Simply reciting the mantra or chanting it in a loud voice will not bring realization. It is also helpful to reflect on the benefits and inconceivable qualities of the profound and vast teachings of the Buddha along with the treatises composed by the great scholars and masters of the past.

Precious bodhichitta is not just a conventional teaching found in the Mahayana: it is the basis of both samsara and nirvana. Like the sun, it clears away the darkness of the two obscurations; like the moon, it cools the tormenting heat of samsara. Bodhichitta does not only reside in texts: it was practiced by the scholars and powerful masters of the past, who considered it vital. Bodhichitta is what makes one a Buddhist. For those of us who practice the Mahayana, bodhichitta is as essential as our eyes or as basic as the ground we walk on. The great masters have all traveled the path of bodhichitta to its very end.

Bodhichitta is the very basis of this life and of a stable well-being. It is the supreme path, the path to awakening, which will bring complete liberation from all sorrow. It is the skillful means that directs us toward full awakening, the cause that leads to the level of awakening where all faults are dispelled and all good qualities are present.

∿

In the world today, there exists considerable harm and injury. What is the reason for this? It is mainly that a sincere and positive motivation is not very strong within people's minds. If we have not developed a sincere motivation, we could go onto a mistaken path. Under the influence of jealousy or the desire to be the best, we hold on to negative thoughts that lead us to harm others. In this way, tremendous discord is created. To pacify and eliminate all of this, I make the aspiration prayer that the light of peace and well-being along with the sweet fragrance of immeasurable peace will come to pervade the whole world.

∿

While practicing the two kinds of bodhichitta, we understand that bodhichitta is not just something that we aspire to or engage in. In the Mahayana, the supreme bodhichitta is also known as our buddha nature or the omnipresent expanse of all phenomena. While we are caught in the world of samsara, our bodhichitta—this vast space, the heart of the victorious ones—is unclear and unknown to us. Blinded, we are swayed by habitual patterns arising from our own obscurations. Like the sun covered over by clouds, bodhichitta is present but veiled by the coarse and subtle aspects of the obscurations. It is wisdom and diligence that bring realization of the ultimate, the abiding nature of bodhichitta.

In practicing the bodhichitta of vast benefit, we are working with our inner mind and our outer conduct. The fruition is twofold: we ourselves will transcend samsara, and we will benefit beings in all realms, numerous as the atoms in all directions, by liberating them from samsaric suffering into enjoyment of perfect wisdom. It is good to make aspiration prayers like this, for they have great power and great blessing and, I believe, will be accomplished.

How to Find Peace

FEBRUARY 1, 2000

TODAY, many Tibetans have gathered here from Dharamsala and other places, along with numerous disciples from the East and West. For years, I have had the hope of being able to meet with you; however, while I was staying in Tibet it was very difficult to travel abroad, so I am particularly happy to meet with you, and I thank you from the depths of my heart for coming.

Previously, Tibetan fields of knowledge and spiritual traditions were very rich and not inferior to others, but for the last forty years or so Tibetans have suffered a great misfortune. Their spiritual traditions and knowledge in many areas have greatly deteriorated. We are putting all our strength into keeping these traditions and knowledge alive. We must study them—and not only study but give rise to a sincere intention, a pure heart.

We are a people who has experienced happiness and sadness for many years. It is crucial for each of us to generate a strong mind imbued with great courage. The teachings of the Dharma are Tibet's special heritage; they are so vast we call them limitless. They are established through the valid cognitions of their scriptures and reasonings.

Peace and well-being are to be found in this world, and even for Tibet, peace is not impossible. We should understand that just as we seek happiness for ourselves, so do others seek happiness for themselves. Many problems are created in our world today because people do not engage in what will actually lead them onto a path that benefits them and brings happiness. From the time we open our eyes in the morning until we sleep at night, if we can pass the whole day with a kind-hearted mind and cheerful face, on good terms with people and talking pleasantly to them, our mind will be relaxed when we go to sleep at night. On the other hand, if we spend the day making others upset, if we fight, and even if we win, when we are going off to sleep at night we will have regrets and our mind will not be at ease.

Our priceless pure heart is not something that can be purchased at a pharmacy, poured into our body, or obtained through a cure. If we went to a major city looking to buy it, we could not purchase this pure heart no matter what price we were willing to pay. How do we find it? With the sincere wish to discover it, we discipline our mind with our mind. When such a motivation is born within us, we and others are benefited and so our lives become meaningful. With a pure motivation that does not wane and with great courage that does not despair, may each one of us endeavor to make our lives meaningful.

The Importance of
Traditional Cultures

FEBRUARY 3, 2000

As EVERYONE KNOWS, in our world, various forms of knowledge and good qualities are needed in our lives. Among all of these, it is of great importance that the traditions of our country do not diminish and also that our positive motivation and sincerity are sustained. Further, it is crucial that the customs and practices of our country along with its arts and sciences do not decline. For example, in Tibet, there are mostly farmers and nomads, and both have their own special customs. Over a period of many centuries, a country's culture and customs are learned and passed down from generation to generation. It is very important to study and maintain these so that the thought and activity they foster may be kept alive. Each tradition is a unique resource, which includes the particular language and special culture of each country, even its people's sense of humor.

While preserving our different traditions, we should not forget that we are all persons living on this planet. We may come from different countries, languages, or peoples, but as human beings, we are all the same. Some people may be tall, others may be short, and they certainly have different feelings; however, the causes and conditions that make us human are the same.

A Discussion with Foreign Students Studying in Dharamsala

FEBRUARY 23, 2000

I have great respect for all the living beings who reside on this earth. Among these, I feel a special connection to young students, and so I am especially happy to see you here. It reminds me of my past tours when I went to many educational institutions. All of you have a good education with a background in various fields of knowledge, including the sciences. As for myself, I am an ordinary refugee from Tibet without any special qualities or training like you. However, if you should have any questions, please ask.

~

Question: In these times, is it possible for a realized master such as Milarepa to appear?

Answer: I have lived in central Tibet for about eight years and studied the Kagyu tradition of the Buddha's teachings. In these teachings, we find Milarepa, whose fame has spread throughout all realms like the drumming of summer thunder. Such a realized master as Milarepa is very rare; even masters who are able to attain some realization and experience for their own benefit are rare. It could be that a very small number of lamas have appeared who have experience and realization comparable to Milarepa's and who have attained realization in this life and this body. Masters are sometimes known as "the second Milarepa" or "the third Milarepa" and so forth, but I do not know if they have survived on nettles like Milarepa—these others probably ate noodle soup.

Seriously, these days, it would be difficult for an individual like Milarepa to appear; however, it is possible for practitioners to develop some of his qualities, such as knowing how to give up what should be given up and realize what is to be realized.

~

Question: Milarepa gave up everything in order to practice. Do we need to do this as well?

Answer: In general, if we speak of the genuine Dharma, there is the example of the fully ordained sangha who have left their homes and become renunciants. There are also the examples of lay practitioners, people involved in family life who have children, such as King Indrabodhi from ancient India or Marpa the Translator from the Karma Kamtsang tradition. All of them were able to travel along the path of the Secret Mantrayana, which is based in the Mahayana tradition. Engaging in austere practice like Milarepa, eating only nettles and wearing only cotton, is not the sole path to awakening. Why is this so? The Dharma king Indrabodhi and others all participated in worldly life. "King" is an impressive title, but it still belongs to the mundane world. Whatever else one may say about them, all these realized masters were involved in the life of a lay person; therefore, it seems that we can still move along the path to awakening even if we reside in the mundane world.

Milarepa attained awakening as a beggar, and Indrabodhi attained awakening as a king: this shows that we attain awakening through whatever skillful means is able to tame us. A great Indian master once attained realization by seeing the true nature of a large swelling in his neck. Everything depends on finding a suitable path.

~

Question: How does meditating alone in an isolated retreat bring benefit to all living beings?

Answer: What some people call "engaging in practice" involves merely staying in a cave or restricting themselves to a single place while reciting mantras and prayers without truly understanding their meaning. This is not real practice. Benefiting all living beings is central to the Buddhist tradition. We stay in retreat so that we can do this through developing bodhichitta. We practice with our mind. It is said in *The Guide to the Bodhisattva Path* that all the karma and actions of living beings come principally from their mind. For example, if we need to move something, and the thought "I will move it" does not arise in our mind, our hands will be helpless.

In the same way, it is the power of the thought "I want to engage in activity for the sake of all living beings" that should motivate us to stay in a cave or retreat house. We remain in retreat, distanced from the busyness of life, so that our bodhichitta will become stable. It is not so that we can feast during offerings and fall asleep during meditation sessions. Some go into retreat the same way that a person would check into a hotel or step into the bedroom to go to sleep. Their motivation is undermined by craving for comfort and wanting to be taken care of. This kind of retreat will not be successful. According to the Mantrayana, staying in retreat is related to the inner practice of the eighty-four thousand channels and winds. After a three-year retreat that has gone well, these are purified and we become inseparable from the mind of our yidam deity.

In Tibet, the philosophical school of the Middle Way emphasizes that mind is primary and that its nature is empty. Within retreat as well, the emphasis is on working with one's mind. Retreat makes it easier to be free of endless worldly distractions; it is a means to attain the path of awakening. Usually, it is said that to attain full awakening, we must accumulate merit for three immeasurable eons. This is not the case, however, in the Mantrayana, where Milarepa's attainment through years of retreat serves as the classic example. So retreat allows us to deepen our practice and thereby to benefit others more skillfully and powerfully.

∽

Question: How should we understand the relationship between teacher and student?

Answer: Since there are three different vehicles within Buddhism, there are different ways to look at the teacher-student relationship. Within the foundational vehicle, the teacher is known as a spiritual friend (*kalyanamitra*) and understood to be someone who has taken refuge and holds any of the seven different kinds of vows. This type of teacher is seen as a special kind of friend who gives students teachings to practice. Within the Mahayana, the spiritual friend is described in *The Guide to the Bodhisattva Path*:

> They are devoted to the vows of the Mahayana
> And will not give up the activity of supreme bodhichitta
> Even at the cost of their life.

These teachers have an intense interest—or we could say, take great delight—in the vows of the Mahayana and are able to give up even their lives for the sake of unexcelled, precious bodhichitta.

Within the Vajrayana tradition, oral instructions and initiations are passed down from a realized teacher to an appropriate disciple, who then becomes a teacher and passes the teachings on to the next generation, and so forth. In this way, genuine lamas have passed along oral instructions, commentaries, initiations, reading transmissions, and explanations on the secret and most secret levels.

∽

Question: Do we need to embrace just one spiritual tradition, or can we go around to all of them and take a little here and a little there?

Answer: All over the world, we find many diverse spiritual traditions. Within Tibet, there are mainly five that have classic descriptions: the glorious Sakyapa, the Nyingma of the Secret Mantrayana, the Gelukpa or those from the mountain of Ganden, the Kagyupa, protectors of living beings, and the Bonpo of the unchanging nature. Each one of these accords with the particular perspectives of its followers. In the realm of taste, if someone likes bread, then they are given bread; if they like tea, they are given tea. In the same way, when we are studying, whichever teaching draws our interest and devotion is the one we study and practice.

Perhaps you have studied *The Guide to the Bodhisattva Path*. It states that if there are many different spiritual traditions, many living beings can be guided along the path, and so the activity of leading them into the Dharma is more extensive. If there were only one spiritual tradition, some might like it and others not. With a variety of traditions, everyone can find something that fits. It is important to follow our inclination. For example, if some people do not eat chilies and one day you force them to eat chilies, it will only burn their mouth, and make them very uncomfortable. This has no benefit at all.

The Buddha taught for the benefit and happiness of every living being, not to force people to practice a particular spiritual tradition. For example, someone might prefer the yellow hat of the Gelukpa tradition to the red hat of the Kagyu. People should follow what they want to do, and later the reason for their preference, perhaps a hidden feeling, will surface. Therefore, from the perspective of what appears and appeals to individual beings, the different spiritual traditions were taught.

Ths spiritual tradition called Buddhism was taught by Shakyamuni Buddha so that all beings would benefit and attain happiness. There was absolutely no pressure to coerce anyone into practicing this tradition. As with the chilies, forceful tactics do not help at all. The Buddha did not teach to bring discomfort; he taught so that every living being could gather all the enrichments of life that bring well-being and happiness. Especially in this present world, independence, peace, and happiness are important. Spiritual traditions have their freedom, and we are also free to choose one that draws us and to hold its lineage. With many different traditions, the Buddhist teachings have a broader opportunity to grow and spread and bring benefit to this world.

The Oceans of Suffering

M OST OF THE TIME it is suffering that makes us cry; our tears are salty and not very pleasant to taste. If we consider the whole world, the oceans are salty, too, and it is mainly the solid land where people live and work that is most useful and pleasant. It is also true that the salty oceans are bigger than the landmasses, and in the same way, beings know more suffering than happiness. Perhaps this is a child's view, but I think that the four great oceans of our planet are like the four main sufferings of sentient beings: birth, old age, sickness, and death. Every living being in the world wishes happiness and wants to avoid suffering. How can they attain this happiness? Through the practice of genuine Dharma in all its various forms: meditation on the yidam deities and the nature of mind, the recitation of mantras, and the development of bodhichitta, the awakened mind. Developing faith and devotion is the preliminary for genuine Dharma practice. If these two are strong and uncontrived, we will ultimately attain the level of awakening, or buddhahood. This is my genuine wish for all of you.

Others Are Necessary for Practice

APRIL 19, 2000

I T IS OUR TASK to bring all living beings, who are present throughout space and have been our kind mothers, onto the path that leads to happiness free of suffering. To protect living beings from suffering and to bring them to happiness is the main responsibility of those noble beings known as bodhisattvas, who have cut through all emotional and mental obscurations.

In contrast to these noble beings, ordinary individuals are still veiled by emotional and cognitive darkness, so their minds are not able to enter into the world of pure appearance where all obscurations have vanished. To make this possible, Shakyamuni Buddha began teaching in Varanasi with discourses on the Four Noble Truths. He continued with the Mahayana and Vajrayana, and through these three sets of teachings, made it possible for all living beings to enter into the path of purification and liberation. His activity made possible the Dharma we hear today, which teaches an altruistic motivation and the activity of benefiting others.

From the perspective of Dharma and also of the mundane world, all living beings are important. On a mundane level, let us take the example of a leader who arises from a group of people. Suppose a leader was not supported by the people and had only inanimate objects, such as stones or houses, as followers. If the leader asked them to do something, they would not budge, because things like this have no consciousness that would allow them to hear. A leader exists on the basis of people who have consciousness. If there are no people, being a leader has no meaning—no one will hear what he or she says and the leader has nothing to be the leader of.

In terms of the Dharma for practitioners at every stage, all living beings are a support since they are the objects of compassionate activity. Shakyamuni Buddha and all the bodhisattvas attained awakening not just for themselves but for the sake of all living beings, who were also the focus of their compassion. If it were for themselves alone, the buddhas and bodhisattvas could not have attained awakening, as it implicates all beings. Therefore, living beings are very important. One could even say that the buddhas and sentient beings are equally kind to us.

All-Pervading Buddha Nature

T HE BUDDHA'S TEACHINGS can be divided into two main categories: the scriptures and realization. A verse states:

> The teachings of the Teacher have two aspects:
> Scripture and realization presented as they truly are.
> There is nothing else to do but
> Sustain them, speak of them, and practice them.

When we practice listening, reflecting, and meditating, the teachings will free
us from the heavy darkness of suffering. They are like a never-setting sun whose
luminous rays reach to the farthest corners of this world. Among the eighty-four
thousand teachings of the Buddha are those found in Tibet that maintain the
unity of the sutra and mantra traditions. These teachings are like a tree trunk with
numerous branches: a variety of lamas hold lineages within diverse traditions.
This multiplicity arose due to the varied characters of disciples and their particular types of confusion. In showing how to cut through the delusion of duality,
these teachings open up to every living being the possibility of attaining true
mastery over the immense and profound gates to the eighty-four thousand teachings. They are precious because they make nonconceptual wisdom manifest and
bring forth the *amrita* of all-pervading emptiness. Like placing a perfect fruit in
the palm of our hand, these teachings bring about two kinds of wisdom: the wisdom that sees the multitude of all phenomena distinctly and the wisdom that sees
clearly into their nature.

Relying on an appropriate path allows the fruition of practice to manifest.
This result is possible because buddha nature is found in the mindstream of all
living beings. In the Fourth Vajra Point of *The Supreme Continuum*, the protector Maitreya states three reasons this is so:

> The perfect buddha kaya pervades all;
> Suchness cannot be differentiated,
> And all living beings have the potential:
> Thus they always have the buddha nature.

The first line states that the *kaya*, or the heart, of the perfect buddha is all-pervasive; it is present in the mindstream of all living beings. The second line states that suchness is indivisible, which means that the buddha nature of the Buddha and the buddha nature of living beings are completely inseparable. Finally, living beings have the potential in their mindstreams, which means they possess buddha nature, or, one could say, they are similar to the Buddha.

Even though buddha nature is not the least affected by our delusions or incidental stains, our ignorance arises like clouds and temporarily blocks the light of the sun, our buddha nature. The light of the sun will shine when the clouds are swept away. This happens when we begin with developing a positive motivation and, not stinting in our efforts, we practice the quintessence of the oral instructions.

To free all living beings from samsara's suffering, we begin with freeing ourselves from samsaric existence. Once liberated from it, however, we do not follow a lower path and seek only our own benefit. Imbued with omniscience and good qualities, the fruition of our practice, we accomplish numberless deeds for the benefit of others. This altruistic motivation is a special trait of the Mahayana path.

In Tibet, the Land of Snows, the precious Dharma of the Buddha has spread like the light of the sun. Within these Vajrayana teachings, there are four great traditions, each with its great founders and teachers. For the Kagyu tradition, there are Marpa, Milarepa, and Gampopa. For the Gelukpa tradition, there are the kings of the three realms, Tsongkhapa and his chief disciples. For the Sakyapa, there are the three founding forefathers who arose as the magical display of the body, speech, and mind of Manjushri. For the Nyingma, there are Shantarakshita, Guru Rinpoche, and Trisong Deutsen. Ultimately, all of them have become perfectly awakened within the single taste of all phenomena, the essential nature of spontaneous presence, the dharmadhatu free of all elaboration. From the perspective of what appears to impure disciples, however, they demonstrate a nature that appears in different ways. For each individual, there are different forms, different types of speech, and different given names. Through all this, the great teachers reveal what is wondrous, magically arisen, and beyond thought or expression.

Not only in Tibet but for the sake of living beings throughout the world, all buddhas and bodhisattvas emanate forms and kayas that teach the inexhaustible, vast Dharma. Through the gentle rain of its methods and compassion, living beings are brought onto the path of peace and nonviolence.

Where Problems
Come From

IN THIS WORLD TODAY, there are so many troubles and difficulties, which are mainly due to pride, jealousy, and the desire to be the most important. Where do these come from? They arise from the absence of sincere, positive intentions, the lack of affection for one another, and the want of mutual respect. These are the source of many problems and terrible bloodshed, such as one finds in Tibet and in other regions of the world beset with numerous complex problems. We can see these difficult situations with our own eyes. There are other sufferings, however, that are invisible: in a billion universes, beings are caught in the vast ocean of samsaric suffering and meet with all its pain and agony. Since there is much that we do not see, it is very important to meditate on all beings with great compassion, free of any special focus. In this way, we practice not only for ourselves but for the benefit of others as well.

Everywhere in the world people say they stand for peace and well-being, but in fact, they produce the weapons of war and substances that will create conflict and harm. Day and night, soldiers move about holding guns in their hands. In the end, none of this brings much benefit. The basic problem is the lack of a sincere intention. And even if we do have a sincere motivation, we may not implement it skillfully and may miss taking the right path.

To speak from my perspective as a practitioner of Dharma, our Teacher, the Great Compassionate One, said that we should practice through listening, reflecting, and meditating on the nectar of Dharma and then give it to others through explanation, debate, and composition. Capabilities like these do not come easily. Nevertheless, whether they have such special abilities or not, all beings present throughout space always have the cause for benefit and happiness, the root of peace and well-being, which is the true nature of their mind.

Reflecting on this, I make the aspiration prayer that all sentient beings present throughout space will be free of the injuries, both mental and physical, brought about by vast wars and conflicts. To this end, I dedicate every virtue accumulated throughout all time and pray that, through these, living beings will be freed of all harm just as clouds are swept away from the sun.

Discussion with Students
from Samye Ling, Scotland

NOVEMBER 22, 2000

THE NATURE OF OUR EXISTENCE is to be born, age, fall sick, and die. The most significant of these four is the experience of death. Whether we attain a positive result from this life or whether we must continue to cycle in samsara depends on our practice. The teachings on the bardo speak of a clear light that arises just before we die. If we are great practitioners and recognize that light, we can become enlightened at that very moment. In most cases, however, due to our limited practice, when we see the light, our confusion takes over and we do not recognize it. In this way, some are born in the human realm, some in the animal realm, and some in other realms, depending on their practice.

Since we are practitioners of Buddhism and in particular the Vajrayana, we have received teachings on the process of dying. *The Bardo Thödröl* (*Liberation Based on Hearing*) explains the many appearances we will face in the bardo. If we can follow the Vajrayana path, we can achieve the result as it is explained in this text.

The meaning of *The Bardo Thödröl* can be summarized in a few words: everything depends on whether or not our mind is deluded. Appearances of the mundane world are delusive and the true nature of mind is not. Those whose minds are caught in this world are shadowed by ignorance. Incidental stains and the power of the delusions they create keep us from realizing their nature—ultimate reality itself—and so we wander on and on in cyclic existence.

Genuine lamas teach about the appearances that arise in the bardo. If we can remember the oral instructions of our lama at the same time that these apparitions emerge and think, "By their nature all of these are delusions," we will recognize the essential nature of these appearances. This is truly "liberation based on hearing."

~

Question: So many people have difficulties in their lives. I wanted to ask you for some simple and practical advice on how to deal with situations in the world that seem too hard. How do we deal with problems that seem overwhelming?

Answer: For ordinary people, the world of samsara has the nature of suffering, and so numerous problems and painful situations arise. Taking them at face value, we think they exist in the same way as they appear. Trapped in appearances, we are worthy objects of compassion. In our own lives, we meet with tremendous problems and do not see that they mainly come from our previous karma: they are a result that is the full maturation of our previous actions.

After we have done something, the consequences may seem irreversible; however, it would not be right to think, "Well, it's just karma," and give up. Whatever our problems may be, we need to find a way to eliminate them. If we are Dharma practitioners, we can clear away our problems by receiving the amrita of Dharma from a genuine teacher and by learning to look into the essential nature of these very problems. In particular, if we are ordinary individuals who work in the everyday world, it is possible to solve our problems by working hard and engaging in a variety of activities, all the while looking at the essential nature of whatever appears.

Many methods can free us from difficulties; however, precious bodhichitta, encompassing loving-kindness and compassion, is supreme. If we meditate on it well, there is nothing we cannot remedy. When we experience many different sufferings, they can be an actual support, a situation conducive to Dharma practice. If we were problem-free, we would have a hard time remembering to practice Dharma. If we are already practicing Dharma, it would be difficult for the practice to benefit us deeply. Taking all our problems and suffering as a support, we should bring them onto the path of practice. To the extent they are brought onto the path, to that extent will we attain the good qualities that result from practice.

~

Question: Through my own illusions and delusions I've caused a lot of suffering. I wonder if I can sort this out in this lifetime, or if I'll have to wait until future lifetimes. Through my practice can I actually undo what I've done?

Answer: Someone like Jetsun Milarepa, through listening, reflecting, and focusing his awareness in meditation, can attain in one lifetime and one body the level of unity that is Vajradhara. Other than such a special type of person, it is possible in these times for one to practice appropriately listening and reflecting on the teachings, yet in the future come back to samsara and wander in its cycles. In the Mantrayana, it is said that in seven or sixteen lives and so forth, awakening can be attained. Therefore, through the power of our present practice, results will definitely occur at some later time.

Until the ultimate unity, the level of Vajradhara, becomes manifest, our body, speech, and mind will be associated with the two obscurations and their habitual patterns. However long it takes to discard these, so long will faults, obscurations, adverse conditions, and fear arise. Nevertheless, if we practice listening to and reflecting on the genuine Dharma, our obscurations will become increasingly subtle and finally disappear; their ultimate disappearance is the level of buddhahood or omniscience. We should place ourselves on this path of wisdom. Until we are all able to attain awakening, however, it seems that we will be experiencing suffering and problems.

~

Question: Is the division between nirvana and samsara based on fear, that is, thought and ego? And are all creation, all tastes, all pleasure found in nirvana?

Answer: All that could possibly appear is created by the mind. Whether we speak of samsara or the level of omniscience, we are speaking of our own delusion. On the level of ultimate reality, there is no difference in the extent of qualities found in samsara and nirvana. All apparent reality issues forth as equal in nature. When this is not realized, we assign a low status to samsara, considering it negative, and a high status to liberation, considering it positive; samsara appears as suffering and liberation as bliss. On the level of ultimate reality, the sphere of experience of the buddhas, samsara is seen as the pure land of great bliss, and liberation is seen as the pure land of great bliss.

Some people think that what is called the pure land of bliss is nothing but bliss and that there are no other causes for suffering present there. But it does not seem to be like that. What is called the pure land of bliss is free of all suffering *and* all bliss. It is free of every cause for both suffering and bliss, because its nature is not deluded. What is usually called bliss is a delusion, and the cause of the delusion called bliss does not exist in the pure land; even the names "suffering" and "bliss" are not known. Great or supreme bliss is the nature of the mind; it is the primordial wisdom of great bliss or the expanse of nondual awareness and emptiness. For all these reasons, we should come to recognize both samsara and nirvana as the mind's delusions.

The Path to Full Awakening

JUNE 1, 2001

WHAT ARE THE TRUE METHODS that lead to full awakening? From the perspective of deep knowing, the method is mainly emptiness, and from the perspective of skillful means, it is mainly precious bodhichitta. This kind of path is found in all three vehicles. In the Foundational Vehicles, we can follow along an excellent path with many special attributes: it can clear away the misery of samsara and conquer the tendency to cling to an existent self.

If we would ask, however, whether the paths of the Foundational Vehicles have the qualities that enable us to completely tame our mindstream and mature the mindstreams of others, we would have to say no. Why is this? The type of realization attained by those on the foundational path cannot completely vanquish the obscurations. Although they teach meditation on the nature of the mind, their path does not lead to a stable happiness because it lacks the great compassion and loving-kindness of bodhichitta that focuses on all the living beings present throughout space.

Due to this difference between vehicles, some people consider the Foundational Vehicle inferior to the Great Vehicle and not a worthy path of practice. This is a mistaken view. There is definitely no distinction between the two vehicles: they abide in a great equality. Nevertheless, it is important to understand the special qualities belonging to each vehicle. Why is this? Individuals are naturally drawn to a particular vehicle, and in order to enter it, they need to know its particular qualities well. This is not to say that we should harbor a bias or become involved in quarrels over philosophical systems. Our teacher Shakyamuni taught so that we could attain stable happiness and so that we could help all living beings (including ourselves). Shakyamuni Buddha also held the lineages for all the vehicles—the foundational and the great—and it is not appropriate to have even the slightest discord among the teachings of the same teacher. It is important to see for ourselves the qualities specific to the Foundational and Great Vehicles, and then with respect, we should practice them. If we look at Dharma from all sides, we will see that it is important to be free of any prejudice and maintain pure vision. This applies not only to these two vehicles within Buddhism, but to all religious traditions throughout the world.

Whether we are speaking of Dharma activity, the Dharma itself, or a mundane path, the most important thing is bodhichitta. The sincere wish to benefit others is found in many religious traditions. In the future, we should do whatever we can to have an utterly pure mind and to benefit other beings through pure actions of body and speech.

When Obstacles Arise

FOR THOSE who are practicing Dharma, various negative conditions come about and different kinds of fear arise. These can cause doubts to surface: "Why should this be happening?" Such thoughts could even propel someone into abandoning the Dharma. We should remember, however, that these negative situations arise for everyone who practices the Dharma, whether they are part of the monastic sangha or lay people who have taken refuge in the Three Jewels.

The Dharma is of great value: it is an unexcelled path that brings us and all living beings equal to the extent of space onto the path of bodhichitta that leads to complete liberation. Since we are seeking to attain such a great goal, naturally there will be problems. Further, not only in relation to our Dharma practice but whatever activity we may be engaged in, it is not possible to avoid some minor, temporary problems. While practicing the path that leads to stable, unexcelled bliss, when we meet with problems, we are also meeting with the pure nature they embody: the possibility of liberation arises at the same time as the problem. We should also remember that we are practicing not just for our own benefit but for the benefit of the infinite living beings in all realms.

Negative spirits who create difficulties for Dharma practitioners will throw obstacles in the path of those who seek liberation. The harm they seek is to erase from the meditator's mind the desire to practice and attain liberation. Understanding this situation, practitioners should increase their diligence as much as possible and make as great an effort as they can to practice Dharma. This has two advantages. First, the obstacles can be stopped before they arise; and second, not losing all the work we put into practicing the path of liberation, we can continue along our journey.

These days, some practitioners think that they must meditate intensely and attain all the qualities and special attributes of the Dharma, but they do not know well the nature of the view, meditation, or conduct taught in their own tradition. Even so, they insist that sometime very soon they will be enlightened and endowed with all the major and minor marks of the Buddha. When this does not happen, they say, "The Dharma is useless. It doesn't work. I practiced hard, but it was all for nothing."

It is true that within the genuine Dharma, there is the path of the Secret Mantrayana, or the Vajrayana, which is very swift. There we find the oral instruction that states, "If you meditate right now, you'll become awakened right now."

The Buddha and all his followers continuously taught this. However, if our minds lack the mental strength or capacity to accomplish such a swift path, there is little chance of swift liberation. The *possibility* of attaining liberation depends on whether the Buddha taught this path; however, *achieving* liberation depends on us. Therefore, if we do not put forth our full strength, the Dharma will enter inside but will not become manifest. If we do not have the capacity or the necessary attributes to attain the fruition of the practice in our tradition, we might then go to another tradition and, not attaining the result once again, disparage that tradition, saying that it is not good. This pattern is the result of not being able to distinguish between a religious tradition and the individual, between the teachings and our limited self.

In Buddhism, what we call "a religious tradition" means practicing a view or philosophy of the mind. All the paths found in these traditions are related to the mind. The Buddha and the incomparable masters who followed him taught that taming our minds is extremely important. Many of us have studied the major texts of Buddhism. (How much other types of study, like the sciences, benefit the mind ultimately is not clear.) If we receive a commentary on how to meditate on the preliminary practices[207] or if we take an empowerment, these activities can benefit our minds. They are the heart of Dharma and have the purpose of establishing in our mind the habitual pattern for true happiness. If these do not help us, then receiving an empowerment does not impart its essential benefit: it is just placing a vase on our heads, and a great deal of work for the lamas.

There are other benefits from receiving an empowerment, but the main point is for us to see the very nature of our mind. It is beneficial if positive habitual patterns can be established within our mind, for example, an experience of the true nature that can blend with and benefit our mind. If this does not arise, then no matter how many texts we have studied or how many empowerments we have received, they will not be very useful. It is crucial to connect with the essential nature of our own mind.

The Source of Obstacles

IT IS SAID that the main source of obstacles in practicing Dharma is the four *maras*. Looking at them from a mundane point of view, maras are ferocious beings who create harm and prevent us from accomplishing our good intentions. Previously, when I was in Tibet, I experienced something like an apparition of what were called maras, fearsome creatures whose upper lip touched the sky and lower lip touched the earth. In Tibet, they are usually explained this way—horrific entities who devour flesh and drink blood. In the Dharma, however, the maras are not painted as such gruesome beings; it is explained that the label "mara" is given to what blocks a practitioner from attaining awakening or perfect liberation.

The four maras are the afflictions (*kleshas*), the five aggregates (*skandhas*), the children of the gods (*devaputra*), and the Lord of Death (Yama). The mara of the afflictions is usually explained as the three poisons of ignorance, attachment, and aversion. The mara of the aggregates is explained as the five components of our physical and mental makeup: form, feeling, discernment, formation, and consciousness. In general, the aggregates are known as what attracts or draws suffering upon us. The mara of the children of the gods is usually explained as the sense pleasures that draw us away from our greater purpose in life. The eighth Karmapa, Mikyö Dorje, treats this third mara as a subcategory of the first one, the afflictions. He explains that this third mara creates obstacles in the following way: first, we have a positive thought and then due to the arising of some unrelated condition, that thought does not lead to anything useful and the afflictions increase. The mara of the Lord of Death is the fearsome being who takes us to the far side of this world; he is the one we meet after death, and so this mara is also described as our fear of death. These four maras are mainly what we have to abandon while moving along the path of practice. All four are included within the phenomena of samsara and nirvana; they all arise from our conceptualizing mind and only exist for that mind.

These days, the languages, traditions, and customs of various countries, including those of Tibet, are undergoing change. What is the basis for these changes? Language, tradition, and custom all rely upon the concepts we create in our minds. When our concepts change, what is dependent on them shifts as well. For this reason, according to all the sutra and tantra traditions, the main thing to be given up is concepts in general or, specifically, those related to the four maras. Beginners will not be able to eliminate these immediately at their very root. However, having received oral instructions from a genuine lama and harmonized them with our practice, we will gradually be able to subdue them.

There are many methods to vanquish the afflictions, the first of the four maras. Among them, the best is bodhichitta. Why? Whether we consider the previous scholars and meditation masters of the snowy land of Tibet or the noble land of India, they all took bodhichitta as their personal practice. They understood it to be emptiness blended with compassion, and, in this way, they were able to benefit living beings. I, too, follow in their path. The lamas of the past, however, did not become supreme masters through practice alone: they recognized that something was true or false by analyzing and examining their own direct valid cognition to see if it was correct. The Secret Mantrayana, the king of the vehicles and the swift path of method, offers a wide variety of teachings, and all of them are related to bodhichitta. For this reason, all of us should always practice bodhichitta.

Faith and Practice

MANY OF US who practice Dharma have a great wish to see our special *yidam* deity directly and to receive his or her blessing. To bring this about, we make sincere efforts in our practice, repeating mantras and meditating on the generation and completion stages. We have great hopes of success. Yet, most ordinary practitioners have neither seen the deity directly nor attained any extraordinary signs. While we are engaging in deity practice, it is important to repeat mantras and meditate on the generation and completion stages. In addition, the meditation masters of ancient India practiced the sadhana of their particular deity with intense diligence, ignoring all problems, just as the scholar Asanga meditated on Maitreya during twelve years of retreat.

It is mainly a deeply trusting faith that allows us to see our yidam deity directly. Having faith that is free of fabrication or error is more important than practicing diligently for hundreds of years. In addition to uncontrived faith, we must realize that all states of mind are empty. If we wish only for a vision of our yidam deity and a blessing, this hope is not sufficient to attain our goal.

In general, we each have diverse habitual patterns, different karma, and a history of having made a variety of aspiration prayers. Other factors that affect us are the numerous causes and conditions that gather to shape a situation. Mainly, however, we need an utterly pure faith and, further, a mind free of grasping and concepts. Only in this way will we attain the direct meeting with the deity and the accomplishments that we seek.

Why is it that meeting our yidam deity directly and receiving the deity's blessing are so important? If we are studying texts and wish to become great scholars, there are an inconceivable number of the Buddha's teachings along with the treatises that comment on them. All these have to be studied diligently so that we can come to a basic understanding of their meaning; beyond this, it is extremely difficult to enter into the more subtle levels. In all of this practice and study, it is our own mind that is central. Without a great blessing or without awakening the generative power of previous habitual patterns, it will be extremely difficult to realize primordial wisdom.

Lord Maitreya stated that bodhisattvas abiding on the various levels are not able to attain omniscience immediately, and he also affirmed that we do not need to become expert in all five traditional Buddhist sciences. Among these are all classifications of the inner science that deals with the mind. In the practice of the

Secret Mantrayana, it is said that as long as objects continue to arise in our minds, so long will the classifications of the Secret Mantrayana last. As long as we have not realized the simultaneity of concepts and liberation, as long as we have not been blessed with the knowledge that knowing the nature of one phenomenon liberates us into knowing the nature of all, we need to train from lifetime to lifetime in the many aspects of the teachings. If we try to become expert in all five sciences or try to know all the objects of knowledge, our training will be endless. For these reasons, it is extremely important to seek accomplishments and blessings from the yidam deity, for through the blessing of the deity, our positive habitual patterns from the past will be awakened and the doubts that cloud our minds will be cleared away.

Milarepa's Song

DECEMBER 25–27, 2001

URING THIS KAGYU MÖNLAM, many of you from all parts of the world
have gathered here in Bodh Gaya, where all the buddhas of the three times
become fully awakened. Through its power and truth, augmented by the presence of all who have come, the sincere prayers made here can be fulfilled.

Today I would like to talk about a song of Milarepa's called "The Eight Ornaments of the Profound Meaning" and focus on its key points.[208] Relying on study
and reflection as the focus of their practice, people can discuss the nature of the
mind and debate important topics, but this alone will not suffice. Of course, listening and reflecting are not a fault, but if we restrict ourselves to these alone, we
will not realize the nature of the mind; for that, we need meditation practice,
which blends our mind with the Dharma. Milarepa's song describes in eight stanzas the whole Buddhist path of study and practice.

This first stanza of Milarepa's song speaks of the view:

> Cutting through assumptions from within—
> Is this not the view free of all extremes?
> Join it with scripture and reasoning
> To make it beautifully adorned.

What is view? View cuts through all that we superimpose onto reality. In
Tibetan, the word means "to look at" or "to see" and refers to seeing with the eye
of wisdom. Viewing in this way cuts through our assumptions that veil the unity
of the two truths: the relative truth of our daily life and the ultimate truth of
mind's nature.

Another way of expressing this is to say that the view pacifies all confused
thinking that would take phenomena to be truly existent. It liberates us from
extremes; for example, eternalism, thinking that something always exists, and
nihilism, thinking that nothing exists. For these reasons, it is called the Middle
Way, and the cutting through it does is from within, transcending our limiting
thoughts such as "That's a material object," "That's immaterial," "This is its
name," or "That's a new name." The phenomena of our world may appear to
us as naturally there and real, but they are merely imputed by the mind. The
mind creates labels, mere names that are imposed upon phenomena, but these

verbal marks do not exist for the phenomena themselves. Coming to see phenomena this way—through to their very nature—is the actual view of Buddhism.

Extreme views are often summarized into those of eternalism and nihilism. One side believes that things always exist and the other that they do not exist at all. For example, some think that the Buddha is permanent, which would mean that he was not born and did not die, or that the Buddhist scriptures were not begun by a particular person and are therefore permanent without beginning or end. Such assumptions take something that does not exist (a permanent phenomenon) to exist; the classic metaphor for this mistake is a lotus flowering in the sky. At the opposite extreme is the belief that nothing at all exists. This position denies the functioning of cause and effect that makes up karma and also denies the existence of wholesome and unwholesome actions. In contrast to the first mistake, the fault here lies in denying the existence of something that does exist on a relative level. For example, we might be caught up in the idea that phenomena are not truly existent. We think they are just imputed and therefore nothing at all. This view that annihilates everything would indicate an attachment to the extreme of nihilism. In the end, we should come to see that it is a mistake to be attached to what is wholesome and also a mistake to be attached to what is unwholesome. Attachment to, and eventually even the apprehension of, any extreme must be transcended.

When we think of permanence in relation to the Buddha, what we actually have in mind are the deeds and the activity of the Buddha, and not some truly existent or eternal entity. Until samsara has been emptied of all suffering beings, the Buddha's activity will be uninterrupted, and it is this quality of being consecutive that has been labeled "permanent." This does not, however, imply that there is something truly existent. In the same way, some people think that nirvana is a permanent phenomenon; however, it is not truly existent. So permanence is a quality that we have imputed onto phenomena: from the side of phenomena, there is no permanence to be posited. What can be said is that the Buddha, nirvana, and so forth, is present but not truly existent.

Further, phenomena do not take on existence by virtue of having an essence, because upon analysis, you cannot find any essential core. "Existence" is imputed by the conceptualizing mind, but it is not ultimately real. From this perspective it is possible to say that karma with its cause and effect does not exist. However, if we have not realized the ultimate nature of mind, if we have not yet arrived at that deep realization, then we are still operating from within relative truth and its delusions of dualistic perception. Until these are emptied out, the appearances of object and subject will continue to arise; until this duality of object and subject ceases to appear, there is karma with its patterns of cause and effect. Since we have not realized emptiness, we are subject to karma. If we state, therefore, that karma does not exist, we fall into the extreme of nihilism, claiming that something that does exist, does not.

Once we realize emptiness, all phenomena are included within this reality, which is not separate from the cause and effect of karma and which is free of mental constructs. On this ultimate level of realization, it is possible to state that there is no wholesome or unwholesome action. When we have realized the nature of all phenomena, negative actions naturally subside and positive ones are spontaneously accomplished. Until this time, however, we would be slipping into nihilism if we said that the phenomena of relative truth, such as positive and negative actions or karma, do not exist.

Just knowing this authentic view, however, is not enough. For others to be able to experience it, we must also know the scriptures and reasonings so that we can teach. Without the support of this knowledge, it will be difficult for others to trust what we say, and so Milarepa speaks of scripture and reasoning as an adornment to realization.

> Dissolving thoughts into the dharmakaya—
> Is this not meditation naturally arising?
> Join it with experience
> To make it beautifully adorned.

One way to understand meditation is to see it as a practice of working with the many thoughts that arise in our mind. With realization, they arise as mere appearances of the dharmakaya, the natural arising of mind's essential nature. Being clear about this true nature of thought is called "attaining the level of natural arising." At this point, there is no difference in any thought that may arise, because we see the nature of each thought to be emptiness, arising as the dharmakaya. Meditation could be defined as realizing the dharmakaya of the Buddha.

When a variety of thoughts comes to mind, we think what appears is real and has some kind of material existence. It is as if we cannot see clearly because we are looking at a mirror's surface that needs cleaning. The view wipes it clear. For meditation to go well, it is important to have the right view and also one that has been not created by someone else. The Buddha taught many different views and ways to meditate, but, in the final count, the actual view is the essential nature as it arises from our own mind. This is what is to be realized, and nothing else. This direct realization of view does not come from fabricated ideas; these can only produce what is called "the view coming from scriptures." The nature of mind—the dharmakaya or the sugatagarbha ("The One Gone into Bliss")—abides naturally; further, the view woven of assumptions also abides, and the two arise together. Therefore, this co-arising can lead to confusion and it can also lead to liberation.

We may have attained some realization from practicing meditation, but meditation itself occurs within our mind and cannot be explained to others. What can we communicate? We can say, "I practiced this meditation and then this experience arose," so we can talk about the experience, which then becomes the ornament to our meditation.

> Purifying the six sense consciousnesses—
> Is this not the conduct of equal taste?
> Join it with timing that is right
> To make it beautifully adorned.

Dualistic perception involves an object of the five senses (or six, counting mind) and a subject, one of the consciousnesses, which are explained differently in different tenet systems. However they may be explained, as long as we are experiencing in terms of a perceived object and a perceiving subject, we are caught in duality. We need to bring all these experiences into one of equal taste. For example, there are sweet tastes and sour ones. Desiring the sweet one, we become attached; turning away from the sour one, we develop aversion, and so our ignorance thickens. In Tibet, many people eat meat since there was little other food available; avoiding it would lead to hunger, and so on a relative level, eating meat was accepted. From another point of view, in the Secret Mantrayana, it is taught that whatever has been blessed and consecrated can be consumed. Whether we eat meat or not, the main point is having an equal taste in relation to food. We should not value eating one food over another but see them all as equal.

Similar to seeing the equal nature of different foods, if we realize the nature of the dharmadhatu, we know that happiness and suffering are not inherently existent. If we experience happiness, on the basis of its presence, it is possible to realize the nature of our mind, which is radiant clarity and emptiness inseparable. If suffering comes, then on that basis we practice Dharma, using the suffering to cut through assumptions. In fact, if we use the suffering to train our mind, the suffering will disappear. This is how we can come to the experience of equal taste, the equal flavor of all phenomena.

Khenpo Tsultrim once related a story about the great master Gendun Chöphel, who was on retreat. When his practice was going well and the experience of emptiness was appearing, he happened to reach out and touch his hand to the wall. It left an imprint and Gendun Chöphel thought, "I'd like to leave an even better handprint than that," so he pressed his hand hard against the surface, yet this did nothing but make his hand sore. It is like this for all of us. When an experience of emptiness is intense, or when we have arrived at the first bodhisattva level of seeing, we should be free of grasping and attachment to it. When the siddhis of the yidam deities come, or even when we are engaged in our usual practice and have not yet experienced a direct vision of the yidam, we should keep in mind that all of these experiences are without true existence. They are like an illusion or a dream.

When we are practicing any kind of Dharma, beginning or advanced, we should first generate bodhicitta, because we are practicing for the benefit of all living beings. We give rise to love and compassion and seek to benefit both ourselves and others. When we are going for refuge as well, we should be free of any fixation. While visualizing a deity in the main part of the practice, we should keep in mind that this image is not truly existent. If we can stay free of fixation, the results of the practice will come. If we grasp and cling, then no matter how much we supplicate deities for their blessing and siddhis, they will not appear. At all times, therefore, we need to maintain a view that is free of attachment.

> Experiencing bliss and emptiness—
> Is this not the instructions of the hearing lineage?
> Join these with the four empowerments
> To make them beautifully adorned.

In general, a lama's oral instruction allows us to see phenomena exactly as they are and gives rise to the experience of bliss and emptiness. Once we have seen the nature of mind, these key instructions allow us to remain within this empty nature free of fabrication. A teaching that can bring the realization of mind's nature is called "the oral instruction of the courage to persevere." This courage to persevere appears within the mind of the student while a lama is giving the key instruction. When the student is practicing the instructions of the lama, meditative experience based on these will arise in the student's mindstream. This is the kind of oral instruction we should receive.

These oral instructions in themselves are excellent, and to make them even better, the ornament of the four empowerments is added. For example, someone might already be elegant and attractive and to highlight these qualities, something extra is added; here, in this context, it is the four empowerments that are the adornment, deepening the instruction and making us confident. The four empowerments are the vase, secret, wisdom-knowledge, and precious word empowerments.

> Emptiness clearly appearing—
> Is this not the stages of the levels and paths?
> Join them with the signs of the path
> To make them beautifully adorned.

What do we mean by the bodhisattva levels and paths? In the beginning of practicing Buddhism, we study and analyze, coming to understand the view of emptiness. In looking at phenomena, we ask ourselves, "What is their nature?" and through this process of questioning, we determine that their nature is emptiness. Within this understanding or view, we rest evenly in meditation, and thereby experiences of bliss and emptiness arise. Or it could happen that from resting in meditation on an experience of radiant clarity, delight arises and from this deities and signs appear. Through our meditating on the paths and levels, flaws and concepts diminish and the play of wisdom will newly appear. In this way we move through the levels and paths, and as we do, wisdom becomes increasingly apparent. This development is based on the experience of emptiness which allows us to traverse the successive stages of the levels and paths.

The practice of the levels and paths has an adornment, for just attaining these levels is not enough: we need the ability to demonstrate the signs of realization to others so that they can know and experience them. At the first bodhisattva level, for example, we can manifest numerous buddhas in one instant and demonstrate miracles. In sum, through the practice of meditation, we have developed qualities, and when we demonstrate them outside, that becomes the ornament to the levels and paths.

> Exhausting our conceptual mind—
> Is this not enlightenment in one life?
> Join it with the four kayas
> To make it beautifully adorned.

Enlightenment in one life was attained by Milarepa. How did he accomplish this? He brought his conceptualizing mind to exhaustion: he saw its natural emptiness. Wearing through conceptual layers, he came to see that all phenomena are not truly established or real—they have no inherent existence. It is also taught that emptiness does not exist separate from our own mind. Emptiness is present in everything; and therefore, there is no appearance that can be seen as solid and real. Nevertheless, when an object appears, we see it as separate, as something other, and become attached to it; due to this clinging, we are not able to attain the ultimate result of our practice. The view from the other side of the river (seeing emptiness) is very different from the view on this side (seeing duality).

What do we need in order to realize full awakening in one life? Whatever phenomena appear within our minds, we should recognize them as empty. To attain buddhahood in this lifetime, our mind must discover the realization that all phenomena are empty and then be able to relax within that. This is called enlightenment in one lifetime.

Nevertheless, it is not enough to realize all phenomena to be empty and attain perfect buddhahood if we do not have something to demonstrate to others. What is needed is the ornament of the four kayas: the nirmanakaya (the kaya of manifestation), sambhogakaya (the kaya of enjoyment), dharmakaya (the kaya of truth), and svabhavikakaya (the inseparable union of the first three). Or, one could say, we should attain the level of realizing these four dimensions. Since people can see only our outer aspect and not our inner minds, they might doubt that we have attained realization. So we must demonstrate some visible change, and in this context, that would be manifesting the expression of the four kayas.

> Endowed with scriptures, reasoning, and key instructions—
> Is this not a lama who holds the lineage?
> Join this together with compassion
> To make them beautifully adorned.

A lama is not just someone who has obtained this title. To know if lamas are authentic or not, we must look at their mind. They should be well versed in the true teachings of the Buddha through listening to and reflecting upon them; they should also be able to teach these texts to others and apply the reasonings. Further, they should know the meaning of the ultimate nature of mind and have realized it. These are the qualities that make authentic lamas. In sum, they should have a vast understanding of the scriptures and the ability to teach them; they should have studied the reasonings of the Hinayana and Mahayana traditions, and finally, they must have inwardly trained their own mind.

In addition to these qualities, lamas must have compassion in order to benefit others. Lacking compassion, they will not foster and train disciples. For example, some lamas who have attained realization will look at the three realms of samsara and become very disheartened, thinking that they cannot free living beings from all this suffering. Authentic lamas are not like this, and through their compassion, they are able to benefit others and care for them. As described above, authentic lamas have many qualities within their minds, and compassion allows them to benefit the minds of others and cherish them.

When we take someone as our lama, that person has to be superior to us. If the lama is worse off than we are, then he or she will only drag us down and not bring us forward along the path. If the lama is the same as we are—if we know what the lama knows and the lama knows what we do—we will not be able to benefit each other. Therefore, we need a person whose qualities are superior to ours, one who knows the deeper meanings so that in our ignorance, we can turn to her or him.

> Possessing great faith and compassion—
> Are these not suitable disciples?
> Join them with sincere devotion
> To make them beautifully adorned.

Authentic lamas will not be of benefit unless there are suitable students who, after carefully examining the lama's qualities, come to rely on them. The students then should have the three kinds of faith in the lama. *Trusting faith*, or confidence, means that in following a lama, we trust that we will not be deceived by him or her, and, further, we have the feeling that in relying on this lama, there is nothing we could not do. *Inspired faith* means that when we meet the lama, we are naturally happy and through that joy, faith arises in us. *Longing faith* refers to the wish, for ourselves and others, to be free of samsara and to attain nirvana. We are drawn to take refuge through an appreciation of how profound the objects of refuge are, and subsequently, this longing faith continues to arise and inspire us as we move along the path. In addition to the three kinds of faith, qualified students also need to have compassion, which is the desire that all living beings be free of suffering and its cause. Seeing that they are caught in the depth of suffering, the practitioner's compassion yearns to set them free. All of these qualities of faith plus compassion make a worthy student.

Another way of describing a good student is through the metaphor of a suitable container. The nectar of the gods, for example, may be wonderful in itself, but to remain what it is, the nectar must be poured into a proper vessel that is free of the three faults. The container might be turned upside down so that nothing can enter; it might have leaks so that the contents flow out; and it might not be clean so that it pollutes what is poured into it. What is needed is a container that is right side up and has no leaks or contaminants. A student who has the three kinds of faith and compassion and who is free of these three faults is considered a suitable vessel. Here in the case of the student, the adornment is genuine devotion, which means that the disciple thinks of the lama as a buddha. Thus, the ideal teacher-student relationship is between an authentic lama who has all the necessary qualities and a worthy student who has faith, compassion, and the ability to retain and practice the teachings.

The last verse gives a summary of the song:

> In brief, view ascertains the mind.
> Meditation brings it into experience.
> Conduct leads to fulfillment.
> The four kayas become manifest.
> The fruition is stated to be mind itself.
> All are realized to be the same.

While we are here in this special and sacred place, it is important to dedicate all our virtue as we make aspiration prayers, not only for those we know, but also for all the living beings on this planet, among whom we count ourselves. We supplicate that everything will go well for them and that they will be happy.

Benefiting Others

AN ATTITUDE of wishing to benefit others is important whether we are working in the world or practicing Dharma. Both the environment and the people who live within it need peace and well-being. This can happen only if our minds change and we become free of seeking to harm others and develop the wish to benefit them. There are many religious traditions in the world that provide for people with different characters and aspirations, showing them a path that brings happiness and benefit to themselves and others. The tradition I am most familiar with is the Buddhist one, in which the desire to benefit others is especially important. The *shravaka* and *pratyekabuddha* vehicles emphasize the need to discard harming others and its cause. Building upon this, the Mahayana tradition emphasizes the need to benefit others and, further, to establish the causes of that benefit.

Benefiting living beings is my main practice, and I would like to give a brief introduction to the three qualities that are its basis: pure love, compassion, and bodhichitta, the awakened mind. Pure love is the desire that all living beings have happiness and its causes. Compassion is the desire that living beings be free of suffering and its causes, such as unwholesome actions. Bodhichitta is the desire that all living beings be free of suffering and that we will be able to place them on the unsurpassed level of awakening, or buddhahood.

Sometimes I see that people practicing compassion become a little sad when thinking about suffering. Continually meditating on the suffering of living beings, they become increasingly depressed and can even become sick. The very definition of compassion, however, is the wish that beings be free of suffering and its cause, so if this practice creates suffering, it is not the correct practice of compassion.

When developing pure love and compassion, we do not consider just ourselves or a few others; we expand our aspiration to include all living beings, who have been good mothers to us in the past. To repay their kindness and show our gratitude, we extend our pure love and compassion to them. We can also think that it is important to develop these qualities for all living beings simply because they are suffering. We can remember our own physical and mental suffering to understand that all living beings experience the same difficulty. Bringing to mind their suffering, we make a strong wish that it will be replaced by happiness.

In general, Buddhist teachings divide all the different kinds of coarse and subtle suffering into three categories: all-pervasive suffering, the suffering of change, and the suffering of suffering. One of the basic Buddhist teachings states that all defiled phenomena are characterized by suffering. A phenomenon is impermanent if it is corrupted (for example, by ego-clinging) or conditioned (by its situation). Whatever is impermanent arises in dependence on causes and conditions. A phenomenon appears when the right causes and conditions are present. It does not come about by its own force. If the causes and conditions are not present, a phenomenon does not appear. Reasoning along these lines, the Buddha said that all phenomena come about through the gathering of causes and conditions, and therefore they have the nature of suffering. For example, our body is impermanent, and so suffering inevitably will come to us through this physical form. We all have experienced different kinds of illness. And even when we are not sick, the five aggregates that form our physical and psychological makeup are conditioned and thus have the characteristic of suffering. Ordinary human beings, however, do not see this; only the bodhisattvas know it. The suffering of change refers to the fact that though we might be happy now, in the not-too-distant future this will change, since all phenomena are impermanent. The suffering of suffering refers to the actual experience of suffering in addition to the suffering that characterizes all phenomena. Every sentient being knows these three kinds of suffering. Keeping in mind what it is like for us when we have problems and our mind is not at peace, we should recall that others are suffering in the same way. Just as we make efforts to rid ourselves of discomfort and pain and to know joy and happiness, so should we make efforts to help others. All the while, we sustain a very clear mind that is focused on pure love and compassion.

By meditating on happiness for others, our own mind knows happiness, and eventually we will be able to benefit others as well. There is a direct correlation between helping others and the extent of our practice. As far as our practice to assist others goes, so far will its benefits and results reach.

A Spiritual Friend

THE MAIN REASON Buddhist teachings are given is to train our mind. There are a vast number of gates for entering the Buddhist Dharma, and they can be condensed into the two aspects of skillful means and wisdom, plus a third aspect of the two united. There are also the stages of the vehicles with their different dimensions. The basic vehicles of the shravaka and pratyekabuddha focus mainly on conquering everything that would harm the mind. To overcome afflictions, they teach the wisdom that realizes the lack of a permanent self in an individual. In addition, these two traditions contain instructions for giving rise to renunciation, for meditating on impermanence, and for contemplating the twelve links of dependent arising. In the higher vehicles of the Mahayana, we find mainly teachings on the six perfections,[209] the four ways of gathering disciples,[210] and many others.

The main aim of the Mahayana is to free us from the many afflictions that now becloud and disturb our minds. From time beyond time, the essential nature of our mind is peaceful and free of confusion. Nevertheless, incidental stains do arise from our ignorance, afflictions, and unwholesome actions. Although we always have our deeper knowing and mental peace, they are veiled by all these obscurations. Unwholesome actions that come from our minds circle back around to us as our own mental suffering. Therefore, the instructions found in the different vehicles are all methods to tame the mind and clear away its impurities and faults.

There are many methods to tame the mind, but in truth, we are the ones who must put them to use. Whether our minds become tamed depends on the qualities of our minds as well. For example, if it is attentive and stable, one's mind will not generate many afflictions, which spur all the unnecessary concepts that fill and distract our minds. Whether one's mind is tamed and its nature realized depends on two things: the skillful means to tame it and the person who is doing the taming. She or he must apply diligence and a deeper knowing and, further, receive the core instructions on the awakened mind and meditate on emptiness. Whether any of this is possible depends on our engaging in actual practice. If we are diligent, it is not so difficult to tame our minds.

If we do not know how to practice, however, it will be hard to attain results. When we are practicing the Dharma, in particular the core instructions, it is crucial to rely on a genuine lama. Without a lama, even if we meditate, moving along the path of Dharma will be a struggle. Sometimes obstacles loom before us, and sometimes negative situations halt our way. If we do not realize their nature as it is taught in the Dharma, we can fall into the extremes of permanence, thinking they will never go away, or extinction, denying them completely. Therefore, a spiritual friend is very important. Without one, it is not possible to enter the city of liberation. If we wish to travel to a place we have never seen before and attempt to get there with just our ignorance, we will get lost and not reach our destination. The spiritual friend is a guide for our journey, ensuring that we will not have so many problems or obstacles on our way.

A spiritual friend in name only, one who knows but a pittance of Dharma, is not helpful. One definition of a true spiritual friend is an individual who knows all the scriptures, including the sutras and the tantras. Other definitions state that the best spiritual friend has gathered all the qualities, and the least has pure love and compassion.

Not only does a spiritual friend need to have good qualities, he or she should also hold an authentic lineage. While Shakyamuni Buddha was giving the teachings, the blessing and realization that come from practicing Dharma were transferred into the mindstream of his disciples. It then passed successively from one disciple to another down to this present day. For the teachings to stay alive and the teachers to remain authentic, it is absolutely necessary that one disciple carry the lineage and that it be further transmitted to another.

If a student relies on a lama who does not hold a lineage and yet gives teachings, even though the student may practice diligently, since the lama does not have a lineage, the student will have a hard time practicing correctly and completely. Consider this analogy. The lama resembles an electrical transformer. If there is no electricity coming through the transformer, lightbulbs and electrical appliances will not work. They all depend on the transformer to provide electricity so they can function. Likewise, if a spiritual friend does not have a proper lineage, whence comes the real blessing and authentic Dharma, even though the power and the blessing of the Dharma may pierce and fill our heart, they will not increase. Therefore, we definitely need a lama who possesses not only the qualities of a spiritual friend but also a genuine lineage.

Many people who are new to Dharma practice understand that a lama is pivotal, and having an interest in receiving teachings from a lama, they search for one. I often hear it said that it is very difficult to find a good lama, and this has stayed in my mind. A Buddhist text states that if we have within the depths of our heart a great aspiration and fervent wish to meet an authentic lama, we will naturally meet one. If we have many doubts, wondering, "How is that lama? What about this one here?" we will remain in the midst of our indecision, caught in the trap of our divided mind, unable to say, "This is a genuine lama. This is a true spiritual friend." Certainty will elude us. But if we are motivated in the depths of our heart by the powerful thought "I must look for a lama," we will meet one.

Our intense desire to meet a teacher is important; however, we must also use our intelligence to analyze. In both the sutras and the tantras, it is said that before taking someone to be our lama, we should first examine that person. How to examine a lama? Not by looking at his or her wealth or the number of followers. Rather, we should look to see if a lama gives teachings based on the texts of the sutras and tantras. We ourselves should do the examining and not simply go along with a fad or another's opinion. Where do we look then? We should pay attention to the realization of the inner mind and its qualities. Does the lama really have the characteristics of having realized the mind's nature?

A lama's outer appearance and external behavior are not so important. For example, if we look at the behavior of some realized yogis in the past, we might consider it offensive and unseemly; however, their inner mind had come to a high level of realization and experience. We should therefore focus mainly on a teacher's mind and its qualities.

If we do not examine first, we might blindly follow others' opinions when they say, "That's a good lama. If you study with that one, things will go very well for you." If we follow their advice and take him or her to be our teacher, we may have problems later when the lama does not accord with our hopes and wishes. We may perceive what we consider faults and broadcast them to others: "This lama is not good. Don't go to those teachings." It could be that our own practice is not going well and we blame the lama: "That lama has no power and no understanding." When we do not rely on an authentic lama, however, the faults circle back around to us; we come to have the defect of criticizing the lama, which leads to many problems. So three faults ensue from not analyzing well: first, we rely on someone who is not to be relied upon; second, we speak of faults that are better kept to ourselves; and third, we are not focused where it counts—on our own mind. To see the fruition of our practice, we should analyze as thoroughly as we can at the very beginning. This has the twofold benefit of not making a mistake in choosing our teacher and developing our certainty as well.

In sum, the lama should have good qualities and the disciples should have faith along with devotion and respect. We should see our lama as the Buddha and offer respect through our body, speech, and mind. This is taught by the Buddha and those who have followed after him—all the scholars and masters of the noble land of India and the snowy land of Tibet. Through their kindness they have bequeathed to us texts filled with blessing and wisdom, and it would do us good to keep this in mind.

Ego-Fixation

THE PRACTICE OF DHARMA is to pacify the afflictions and concepts that fill our minds. When we blend the teachings with our minds, the power of the Dharma can act upon and pacify afflictions and concepts. If on the outside we look like Dharma practitioners while on the inside our Dharma practice has not diminished our afflictions or concepts, we merely call ourselves practitioners without actually being one. This is not to say that outer behavior, our reflection in the world, is not important, but what is crucial is to train in taming our minds.

What we tame are the three main afflictions: ignorance, attachment, and aversion. Ignorance, the root of the two others, is defined as the continual fixation on our self that we assume to be permanent and independent. This ego-clinging is the main cause for our cycling in samsara. We wish to be in paradise for our own advantage; we wish to erase all suffering for our own advantage. We cling to this "I" of ours, thinking that it is so special that we should not be bothered with problems but enjoy wealth, power, and charisma. If we honestly look into our minds, it is quite easy to see this kind of coarse and obvious grasping to a self.

There are also subtle forms of fixating on the self ("I") and what belongs to it ("mine"), like the quick thought of ourselves before another one comes. When practicing Dharma, we are taming this coarse and subtle clinging to an ego. If this does not happen, we will merely be able to suppress the afflictions temporarily, distancing ourselves for the time being. To cut through them completely, we must steadily apply ourselves to practice.

There are many means for loosening and finally uprooting ego-fixation. These practices are central, since ego-fixation functions as the cause for afflictions and the actions they motivate, creating suffering and rebirth in cyclic existence. This all happens because we do not understand a key point: samsara is like an illusion. We do not see that a deluded mind thinks "I am," clings to a self, and cherishes it. We do not realize that this "self" is not truly existent; it is like an illusion or a dream. Not knowing that we are dreaming, we cling to the self as real—and not just once but again and again. Cycling around and around in samsara, we reinforce habitual patterns that turn thick and give rise to dense afflictions and the actions they provoke. We must come to see samsara as the result of our confusion. This is crucial. If we can do this, we will have released a huge knot.

If we do not realize that samsara is delusory, then even if we engage in meditations to cut through ego-clinging, our Dharma practice will not be strong and we will not discover the Dharma's true power. While practicing, we must also be careful not to substitute attachment to the Dharma for attachment to the self. If we cling to the Dharma, it will only serve as a cause for producing ego-attachment and not function as a cause to cut through it.

Rejoicing in Virtue

IN THESE TIMES, if we can accomplish truly positive activities, they will have a special power to benefit ourselves and others. For this reason, we need to have faith in the efficacy of virtuous actions. In general, we should be trying to make everything that we do a virtuous action. Especially when things are going well, we should remember to make an extra effort to benefit others. This is important because all things have the nature of arising in interdependence. There is no phenomenon that does not come about in this way. Seeing how everything is interrelated, we should be aware of how we can help others. It is good to reflect on this.

According to Buddhist thought, happiness comes about due to a cause, and that cause is virtuous activity. The cause is dependent on many different conditions, and in order to gather all of them together, it is important to know the stages of wholesome activity, its causes and results, and how they are accomplished.

What is the key for attaining the result of any positive action? Rejoicing. Rejoicing means that in witnessing or hearing about wholesome activity, our minds are naturally happy and delighted. Just at the sight of a positive action, we are joyous.

There are two ways of looking at rejoicing: rejoicing in the virtue functioning as a cause and rejoicing in virtue as a result. If you wish to attain the level of omniscience, what is the cause? Giving up the ten unvirtuous activities and accomplishing the ten virtuous activities.[211] If we practice these positive actions ourselves, we feel good about it, and if we see someone else practicing them, we think, "That's great," and take real delight in what they have done. This is rejoicing in virtue as a cause. Rejoicing in virtue as a result means that causal virtue has come to fruition, which might be bliss or omniscience, and we rejoice in this fruition of wholesome activity.

Our rejoicing can be expressed through body, speech, and mind. In many different ways, our body can reflect the joy that is in our mind: sometimes tears come, sometimes we may even tremble. With our speech we can praise: "What you're doing is wonderful. That was great." Mentally, joy arises in our minds naturally in response to any wholesome activity, ours or another's. In this context, rejoicing is a wonderful antidote for jealousy as well.

What are the benefits of expressing this sympathetic joy? In terms of others' virtuous actions and their results—which could even be liberation—if we sincerely rejoice in their achievement, we will receive a result that is even greater than what is attained by the person who actually performed the activity. If we rejoice in the fruition of our own activity, the result will become immeasurable.

This explanation of rejoicing is based on the vast Mahayana point of view. Usually, when we perform a virtuous act, we receive the appropriate result, and it stays as just that. However, if we rejoice in the activities of others, then we attain not just the result of our activity, but also the virtue that is a result of their activity. Therefore, rejoicing has a special expansive power, and it is therefore one of the seven fundamental aspects of practice that make up the seven-branch prayer,[212] some form of which appears in almost every practice.

This has been a brief explanation of the essential nature, the categories, the practice, and the benefits of rejoicing. It is my hope that you will accomplish many virtuous acts and I hope that you will swiftly attain its result of joy—and not only this, but that through this joy, you will be able to benefit many living beings.

Feelings

THE BUDDHA turned the wheel of the vast and profound Dharma three times with the purpose of teaching human beings how to tame their conceptual minds. The practice of Buddhism should be the practice of taming our minds. First, we need to make a connection between the Dharma and our minds. This happens through a joyful diligence, a sharp intelligence, and a deep affection for all beings. With the blessing of the lama added, these all help to gather the accumulation of merit.

The special attribute of the Dharma is its ability to conquer all the unwholesome thoughts in our minds that arise due to the darkness of ignorance. When our practice is one-pointed, our minds can connect with the Dharma and its strength can enter within. The benefits of this are unsurpassed. These days, people are experiencing many strong feelings, which are intense and often difficult, and so I thought it would be helpful to speak about them and how the Dharma can help.

Since we live in this world, we have feelings. They usually arise in dependence on outer objects, which bring about experiences and ideas in our mind. Traditionally, it is said that all feelings can be included within the three categories of happiness, suffering, and neutrality, which is neither of the first two. All human beings have these feelings, and a good argument can be made that other living beings have them as well.

The reason that I chose to speak about feelings is that they tend to be excessive. When happiness comes, it is huge and uncontained. When some situations create suffering, it is immense and deeply painful. In this life, we need happiness but in the right measure. It is our minds that create the balance we need. If we let our feelings go to the extreme, many faults and problems will arise. I have heard (whether it's true or not I do not know) of some people who have actually died of unbearable happiness. I am not a person who has had this type of experience, so I do not have much to say about it. However, I do know a little bit about suffering.

The feeling of suffering will naturally arise in our minds, and we can learn to adjust it by keeping a certain balance. If our mind is filled with sadness and misery, it is a fault, since our minds can shrink and become very limited. For some people suffering becomes so extreme that they take their own lives. Therefore, I think that if a feeling becomes extremely strong, it is a mistake. Wishing to have such strong feelings would also be a mistake.

Since the very nature of samsara is suffering, there is no reason for us to be preoccupied with this suffering. Rather, we should focus on and develop what brings about happiness. In our contemporary world, we often make decisions based on our feelings, which are impermanent and can change easily. Feelings arise from the mind, and its thoughts are changing all the time. For example, some of us might meet a lama and be very impressed, thinking, "I had a really good feeling," and so we decide to take the person as our teacher. On the other hand, we could meet another lama and, not having a good feeling at all, think that this person is probably not a good teacher. We make decisions by looking at and evaluating our experience of various feelings. Rather than analyzing a situation, we trust our feelings when it comes to making decisions, yet feelings can change in a breath. When the path of our lives takes many different turns, our experience may not be stable, excellent, or easy. Feelings are important; however, if we make them central, we will have a difficult time. It is much better to seek a pure and profound path that will benefit us in this life, and enter into it.

Not attached to happiness nor depressed about suffering, we should seek a stable and constant path. If we are always looking to feel good, and if on top of that our minds are lost in distraction thinking about feeling good, then what will become of our life? We will be diverted from our true purpose and open ourselves to harm.

Feelings ranging from all shades of happiness to the echoes of sadness will come into our mind. It is not possible to eliminate them completely. If suffering appears and we meet it with patience and perseverance, we will be able to continue along the path we have chosen. If a feeling of happiness arises and, deluding ourselves, we cling to it, where will it lead us? It is important to think for the long term.

All of us have our own life's path, and while moving along it, we will meet with various kinds of problems and suffering. No matter how many difficulties may arise, we should look back at what we have accomplished and keep in mind the path we wish to travel along. This will help us to remain stable. However much we may have to endure, we should develop tolerance so that we can progress along our way. Until we have come to the end of our path and accomplished all our goals, we should heed neither suffering nor joy; otherwise, the goal we seek will never come within our reach.

This is my own way of thinking, and I am not insisting that everyone follow it. Our own wishes and aspirations are central. If we can travel along the path of happiness and delight, this is infinitely better than all the riches in the world. Our wishes are important; nevertheless, we have to examine them well: "What will be the result of this in the future? Where will it lead me?" We also should consider well the situations that presently surround us, asking ourselves, "How can I work with this skillfully?" Not following our wishes or impulses blindly, we can reflect on them as we move along our life's path. Individuals are important, and our own particular life is unique. No one else can be us or replace us. Whether future lives exist or not, they cannot create our present life. Our present life is precious and we should use it well and wisely.

Taking Responsibility for Ourselves

WE SHOULD BECOME our own discipline master. We are the ones to main-tain our own discipline, taking up what is to be taken up and giving up what is to be given up. Success and failure depend on us.

Our peace and happiness come through our own minds: they are not an illu-sion we create or something fabricated by scientists or even by the Buddha. Our own peace and happiness have been present from time beyond time. It's not that some person could come along and eliminate them, as they mainly depend on us. We ourselves destroy our happiness and keep ourselves from attaining it. For this reason, we also can experience the joy that is within our mind. It is not another person who experiences it. Whether we find this inner joy also depends on the strength of our aspiration.

On the other hand, we also must keep in mind that we all live in dependence on harmonious conditions. They are necessary and must include freedom, peace, and genuine happiness. If a generally positive situation lacks these three, then life becomes meaningless. When we have freedom, especially, we will see greater pos-itive results and benefits in our lives.

Emptiness

USUALLY, WE LOOK at samsara in a rough or superficial way. Take the concept of time. We tend to think of one year as a solid unit; however, if we analyze it with reasoning, nothing concrete will appear. The same is true for other units of time—one month, one day, or one moment—which we assume exist. If we take many of these single moments and combine them, they can add up to a year. However, if you consider the nature of one moment, you will not find an inherently established unit of time; there is no concrete object that can be brought before our eyes. The true nature of a phenomenon does not appear because someone has realized it, nor does it arise because it was newly discovered. Emptiness is present from time beyond time.

The many volumes of the Buddhist canon found in the Kangyur and Tengyur are based on the teachings of the Buddha and the writings of his followers, who were scholars and meditation masters. They present a philosophy that elucidates the nature of emptiness or pure reality. In general when we are practicing meditation on emptiness, we first use our deeper knowing to analyze in order to discover emptiness, taking either an outer object, such as the possessions we take to be ours, or an inner one, such as the "I" we consider ourselves to be. Through various kinds of reasonings, we analyze all these objects using our deeper knowing to ascertain their emptiness.

This, however, is different from directly realizing emptiness through meditation upon it. We use our deeper knowing first to determine what emptiness is, and from this process come the thoughts: "This is emptiness. All phenomena are empty. All phenomena are free of coming and going. No phenomenon arises from itself, nor from another, and so forth." Many different kinds of statements and reasonings are used to explain emptiness. These are all something new that our intelligence has created, bringing forth emptiness as ideas born within our mind. This is not, however, actual emptiness, since it is our intelligence that has produced it.

When we are *analyzing* through listening and reflecting, emptiness is the object. When we are actually *meditating* on emptiness, there is no examination or analysis, for the mind needs to abide peacefully. When analyzing, we need a sharp and accurate intellect, but if this arises during meditation, we cannot stay settled into the practice, so at that time, we do not need to analyze emptiness. While we are meditating, the meaning of emptiness will naturally dawn in our minds. It is through the stages of practice that the nature of emptiness arises in our mind. First, if we do not know the true nature of emptiness, we should come to know it. Once we know it, we should become familiar with it. Only after this will meditation allow primordial wisdom to dawn within.

The mind must be able to realize emptiness directly. The empty nature of all phenomena will never be ascertained if we stay with reasoning alone, because it will prevent us from letting phenomena abide in their empty nature. No matter how many reasonings we might use, the nature of phenomena remains as it is. For example, we might look at a table and reflect on emptiness using powerful logic. Although the table is not inherently existent, our reasonings will never make it disappear. Reason alone cannot counter our tendency to take all phenomena to be concrete and existent. What can we do then? We need to purify our attachment to conceptual thinking. Only afterward can we come to know the empty nature of phenomena. What is most important is to turn inward and meditate on our mind.

When we do this, we will see that the nature of all phenomena is not just emptiness; they also have the aspect of radiant clarity. If we just say "emptiness," that could mean mere non-existence: from time beyond time, phenomena are not truly existent even though they appear so to most people. Analyzing with the aim of discovering the empty nature of phenomena defeats this ancient habit. However, we should not mistake emptiness and think that it is a vacuum or blank nothingness. The nature of the mind also has the aspect of radiant clarity, which refers to the mind's ability to know and manifest. When we are seeing the empty nature of phenomena, it appears clearly. We can say, therefore, that clarity and emptiness arise as a unity. If they did not, I do not think we could realize emptiness.

The Two Truths

WHETHER WE ARE PRACTICING listening, reflecting, or meditating on the teachings, it is indispensable to understand the two truths, the relative and the ultimate. They are an essential part of the teachings. How do we distinguish the two? If we carefully examine and analyze an object, we can come to see that it does not truly exist. This points to the ultimate truth. If we have not examined and analyzed, however, we think it does exist, and this is relative truth. How are the two truths defined? The relative truth is a mistaken seeing; it is the object discovered by our mind when it is embedded in this world. The ultimate truth is a correct seeing; it is the object discovered by the awareness of those who have realized the nature of their mind.

There is almost no difference in the way the definitions of the two truths are posited by the various schools of philosophy; however, concerning the basis for the definitions—what they actually indicate—there is a great variety of views found in the philosophical systems of the Vaibhashika, Sautrantika, Chittamatrin, and Madhyamaka schools. These days, the most widespread practice, whether related to listening, reflecting, or meditating, belongs to the Consequentialist school (Prasangika) of the Middle Way (Madhyamaka).

According to this view, the basis for the definition of relative truth is the following: from the hell realms up to the level of full awakening, whatever is an object that can be expressed in words or thought is considered relative truth. What appears to us—mountains, walls, stones, houses, and so on, all phenomena—are objects that can be expressed in words and thought, and therefore they are considered relative truth. This relative truth of all phenomena is seen by both worldly people who have not realized emptiness and, in the post-meditation phase, bodhisattvas who have realized emptiness and abide on the first up to the tenth levels.

Ultimate truth is defined as the emptiness seen by the primordial wisdom of the bodhisattvas who rest in meditation on the first level through all ten levels up to the emptiness seen by the primordial wisdom of the Buddha. Ultimate truth transcends expression in words and thought.

In the Prasangika school, the two truths have different bases for their definitions. Are they the same or different? In terms of relative truth, the two truths are understood to have the same essential nature, but to reflect different aspects, so on the one hand, they are alike, and on the other, they are different. From the perspective of ultimate truth, the two truths are neither the same nor different.

Knowing the two truths in detail is very useful. In Buddhist teachings, all the objects we can know are summarized into the categories of the two truths. If you know the complete description of the two truths, you will know perfectly the meaning of the Buddhist texts. In particular, if you know the meaning of relative truth, you will understand clearly the presentation of what is wholesome and what is not; consequently, you will avoid unnecessary problems and discover the joy of the higher realms. If you know correctly the complete description of ultimate truth, you will cross the ocean of samsara and reach omniscience. For these reasons, there is a great purpose and benefit in studying and meditating on the two truths.

This brief explanation of the two truths is a mere drop from the ocean of the Buddha's scriptures and their commentaries, in which the two truths are discussed extensively. Knowing about the two truths is indispensable for understanding the teachings, and if you would like to know more, it would be very good to consult the many texts that are available.

Taking Refuge

WHATEVER RELIGIOUS TRADITION we follow, we must first understand the basis of that tradition. For Buddhism, taking refuge is the foundation, the ground for the arising of all Buddhist practice. This is true for the shravakas and pratyekabuddhas belonging to the Foundational Vehicle, for the Mind Only school and the Middle Way schools, and for the Secret Mantrayana with its four divisions of tantra. For all paths of sutra and tantra, the gate that opens the way is the refuge vow. All Buddhists have taken this vow, the basis for truly receiving Buddhist teachings.

If we look further, it can be said that discipline is the actual basis of Buddhist practice and that every vow embracing discipline takes the refuge vow as its support. Actually, without the refuge vow, we cannot receive any other vows, such as the Pratimoksha vows of the Foundational Vehicle, the bodhisattva vows of the Mahayana, or the many vows of the Secret Mantrayana. The refuge vow is indispensable.

It is also the source of all good qualities. The practice of the ten wholesome actions, such as not killing, stealing, or lying, is found as well among other religious traditions and also among those who live a moral life in the secular world. But ultimately, good behavior alone is not enough, because it cannot cut through what keeps us rooted in samsara. What is primary among all the causes that release us from samsara's suffering? The refuge vows. If we have taken these, whatever positive actions we do will become causes for liberation.

The Secret Mantrayana contains the profound teachings of the channels, winds, and spheres. A strong basis is needed to be able to practice these subtle instructions. Without it, even if we do engage in the practice, we will not come to the ultimate result of full awakening. Some people disdain the refuge vow, thinking that it is a small thing and not very deep. They feel that they must have the higher Secret Mantrayana practices, mahamudra, or *mahasandhi*. But if we do not value the refuge vows and toss them aside, we will not be able to take these other paths. This is a very important point.

The essence of the refuge vows is to free us from the fear of being trapped in samsara. Taking refuge is divided into three main categories: taking the vows according to the mundane world, according to the Foundational Vehicle, and according to the Mahayana. The first category refers to taking refuge in mundane deities, which are believed to inhabit rocks, trees, and so forth. If everything goes well, these can bring only temporary happiness or relief from suffering. They cannot bring ultimate happiness or ultimate release from suffering, because they too are caught in suffering. The difference between worldly deities and those who transcend the world is determined by whether they have realized the absence of a permanent and autonomous self. In terms of Buddhism, those who have transcended the world are the Three Jewels—the Buddha, Dharma, and Sangha—and so they can function as a true refuge.

Though the refuge vow is the foundation of all the Buddhist schools, there are some differences in the depth of the motivation, in the understanding of the Three Jewels, and in the duration of the vows. The greatest difference comes in the kind of motivation found in the Foundational Vehicle and in the Mahayana. In the former, we take refuge in order to free ourselves from the suffering of samsara. In the latter, we take refuge so that we may bring all sentient beings who extend throughout space to full awakening.

How should we understand the Three Jewels? The Buddha is the one who taught the Dharma. He is the source of all the teachings, so we keep him in mind as the teacher. The Dharma is the path we travel to reach the ultimate goal, so we keep it in mind as the path. The Sangha is our companion on the path, those who have experienced it fully or who are now practicing it. If no one has experienced the path, including us, how could we understand its nature?

Taking refuge vows from a genuine teacher, however, is not enough; we need to practice the advice that is given along with the vows. The principal advice is related to the Three Jewels. Once we have gone for refuge to the Buddha, we do not take refuge in mundane deities. The Buddha is fully capable of giving temporary and ultimate refuge, and so we do not need to look anywhere else. Once we have gone for refuge to the genuine Dharma, we do not harm living beings in any way. Once we have gone for refuge to the Sangha, we do not associate with destructive friends, because our thought and behavior could become like theirs and we would risk contravening our refuge vows, such as not harming others. If we must spend time with them, we should be careful that our thinking and behavior do not turn into theirs.

This is brief advice for those who have taken refuge vows, the source of all good qualities. We have taken the vows knowing how fearsome samsara is. Or perhaps we have tried many ways to be free of suffering, but to no avail, so we finally turn to the refuge vow. If we can sustain it and practice the Buddhist path well, then in the future we will not have to fear the suffering of this world. Not needing to seek another refuge, we will be able give ourselves refuge from fear. This outcome mainly relies on our own efforts and diligence.

Giving Rise to Bodhichitta

THOSE ON THE BUDDHIST PATH seek to bring all living beings into happiness and, ultimately, into full awakening. When this has been attained, all that should be removed has been eliminated—the obscurations of the afflictions, the cognitive obscurations, and the obscurations of habitual patterns—and all that should be realized has been accomplished—the wisdom that realizes the nature of phenomena and the wisdom that sees them in their vast multiplicity. In brief, full awakening is a level where all faults have been discarded and all qualities have been attained. This is an important point, since the Buddha is not simply a great scholar; he is also endowed with unexcelled qualities that arise from meditation. To come to this level of awakening, we need a perfect cause, which is the awakened mind, or bodhichitta. Once we have given rise to bodhichitta, we practice it in order to attain the ultimate fruition. In the core instructions on how to generate bodhichitta, many methods are taught, and an outstanding one was explained by the great master Atisha.

Of seven stages, Atisha first presents bodhichitta (1) as the perfect cause for attaining full awakening and as divided into two types, the bodhichitta of aspiration and the bodhichitta of engagement. The first is defined as the mind that aspires to carry all living beings across the ocean of samsara's suffering and bring them to enlightenment. Once this motivation has permeated our being, we engage with a one-pointed mind in beneficial activities related to our body, speech, and mind. This is the bodhichitta of engagement. These two kinds of bodhichitta come about due to a cause, which is altruism (2). Everyone wishes to gather happiness and avoid the torment of suffering. With an altruistic mind, we must take up the burden of providing this for them. What is altruism? Not only do we wish to place beings in happiness and free them from suffering, we actually engage in doing so.

Compassion (3) is what allows for altruism. Once compassion has been born within, an altruistic mind can arise. How to understand compassion? With all suffering living beings as our object of reference, we think, "I am going to free them from all suffering." This includes actual suffering and its cause as well.

Compassion arises based on pure love (4). Holding within our mind all living beings who are unhappy, we think, "I want everyone to be happy." And this is not just for a short while but continuously, and that implies that we also wish for them to have the cause of happiness. How is pure love born? It is born on the basis of what engages or moves our mind (5), which has two aspects: what engages our mind and what engages another's. If we look at this closely, we can see that all sentient beings, including ourselves, are quite the same in wanting to be happy and free of suffering. Our concerns are similar, and this allows us to extend ourselves and empathize with others. We can also contemplate that from time beyond beginning, living beings have been our close relatives, and so we wish them happiness and freedom from suffering. Just as we would wish this for our friends and relatives, so should we extend that wish to encompass all living beings, who have been our close relatives from time without beginning. As we follow this path, pure love and happiness arise from what engages our mind.

As the other stages have arisen from a cause, so does the stage of what engages us: it comes from recognizing what others have done and being grateful for it (6). If someone else has helped us, we remember it. Not letting their kindness slip from our mind, we remain grateful. And this gratitude is not for just one or a few people, but for all living beings, who have been kind and good mothers to us (7). They gave birth to us, looked after our needs, and taught us what to accept and what to reject. In return for this kindness, we can express our gratitude by thinking, "I will lead all living beings out of samsara and bring them into awakening." This is being grateful for another's kindness through recognizing a close and ancient connection with all living beings.

These condensed stages of meditation are related through a sequence in which one is the cause of the next, which then serves as a cause for the subsequent stage, and so forth. If we cannot consider all beings as our mothers (1), then being grateful for others' kindness (2) will not come about. If this is not present, then what engages our mind (3) will not arise, and if that does not exist, then pure love (4) is absent. Without that, compassion (5) is not generated, and if we lack compassion, altruism (6) will not appear, and without this, bodhichitta (7) is difficult to find. If we can follow this sequence of cause and effect, bodhichitta, the awakened mind, will arise within our being and the fruition of the practice will swiftly arise for us.

This core instruction on bodhichitta from the incomparable Atisha teaches how to generate the awakened mind and is very helpful for people new to practice. If we wish for true happiness and follow this practice, I have no doubt that it will benefit us. I make the aspiration prayer that you will be able to discover the ultimate fruition of this practice.

Counting the Breath

THE BUDDHA TAUGHT the Dharma to a multitude of different living beings in accordance with their individual characters, aspirations, and capacities. Because of this, there are numerous ways of practicing the Dharma and many aspects to the path, which include the stages of the various vehicles. The genuine Dharma is the root of all of these. All the paths and the core instructions to practice them can be summarized into the two categories of study and practice, or scripture and realization. "Scripture" refers to all the teachings of the Buddha and "realization" can be defined as "what the manifestation of our own deeper knowing brings forth," such as the samadhis, or meditative stabilizations.

If we rely on the Buddhist path and wish to attain liberation, we should study the teachings, which were perfectly given by the Buddha, and follow the sequence of studying, reflecting, and meditating on them. These three form the core of the stages for entering the Buddhist path. In addition to engaging in these practices, we need a fine character, which makes us an appropriate vehicle for the Dharma and allows us to attain the ultimate result.

Meditation belongs to the field of working with our mind. For it to go well, we need a very pure mind and one that is relatively free of concepts and the distractions of mundane entertainments; otherwise, afflictions and concepts will arise—the opposite of the qualities we want to cultivate through meditation. The methods to do this are found in the Foundational and Greater Vehicles as well as the Secret Mantrayana, where numerous core instructions teach how to traverse the stages of the vehicles and paths.

From among these teachings, focusing on the inhalation and exhalation of the breath is a practice that helps beginners to still their concepts. Everyone experiences the breath moving out and coming back in again. What is the benefit of focusing on this? The concepts in our minds mainly arise based on the nature of the winds that circulate in the channels of the subtle body. If we can balance the winds, the concepts in our minds will diminish and eventually come to stillness.

To practice stable contemplation using the breath, we first take a certain posture: our legs are in the lotus position or a related posture and our back is lengthened. Why is it necessary to sit in a special way? The mind moves relying on the winds, and the winds move along the paths of the channels. If we do not have a good posture, the channels will be crooked, not straight like a good road, and the winds will not be able to flow easily within them. When this happens, it is difficult for the mind to remain in stable contemplation. Therefore, it is important for the body to remain in a posture of meditation in which the channels can be straight.

After taking a correct posture, we begin meditation on the breath. This meditation is not as profound as meditation on emptiness and not as vast as meditation on the awakened mind. In this practice, we count both the exhalation and the inhalation. For example, on the exhalation, we think "one" and on the inhalation, "one." Without slipping, we maintain this counting, "one, two, three" as the breath goes out and in. Focusing one-pointedly on the counting keeps many distractions from our minds, since it holds the mind's attention and prevents other things from coming up to block our path of practice. So we count the breath as it exits and enters, not saying the numbers aloud but counting silently in our mind.

Three kinds of faults can happen with this practice and should be avoided. (1) We can mistake one number for another, saying "two" when we should say "one"—for example, counting the exhalation as "one" and the inhalation as "two." Generally, exhalation and inhalation are distinct and appear as two different aspects, yet sometimes when we are confused, (2) we take one of them to be two, increasing the count, or (3) we take the two of them to be one, decreasing it. For example, we think that an inhalation is an exhalation and so we count one part of the cycle of the breath as two. Or we think that an exhalation is an inhalation and miss a count. In this way our numbers become too large or too little.

When we are meditating on exhalation and inhalation, we should leave our breathing the way it usually is and not try to alter it. Not trying to speed it up or slow it down, we simply let the breath follow its natural course. If we try to speed up our breathing, we could do harm to our minds; blocking the breath and trying to slow it down will also impede our meditation. Count the flow of breath naturally just as it is. Do not count above ten. Extending the count for too long could allow confusion and many distractions to appear, negating the benefit of the practice. Less than ten is also not good, since we will not be able to develop the stable contemplation of following the breath. Therefore, ten, not more or less, is just the right amount.

How to do the daily practice? At first, we do not need to do many sets of ten in one sitting. On the first day, practice a little bit, and then the next day, do a little bit more, building up to ten sets of ten. Then we can successively develop the practice by meditating in the morning the first day, in the morning and evening on the next day, and in the morning, afternoon, and evening on the following day. If we follow this progressive path, then concepts and distractions will diminish. This is one of the benefits that come from the practice.

Working with the breathing this way is not so difficult or demanding. If we can hold the mind to the movement of the breath, it will benefit our body and can help to heal some kinds of illness. *Meditation* means "to become accustomed to." If we practice daily, we will become accustomed to or familiar with the practice; finally, the wisdom that arises from meditation will appear in our mind.

Sometimes when people are in a rush, they force themselves to meditate. Of course, we can meditate in this way; however, it will be difficult for the mind to rest one-pointedly or be tamed and stilled. When we are in a hurry, rather than push ourselves to meditate, it is better to wait for a more convenient time. If we can come to practice without missing a day and bring one path to perfection, our practice will go well.

Calm Abiding

DIFFERENT THINGS in this world can bring happiness and enjoyment. The most important of them all is what brings peace and happiness to our minds. How can we develop these? Usually, our minds are filled with the movement of concepts that disturb it. When the mind is set in motion this way, it cannot remain one-pointed and goes astray, unable to rest within. For this reason, mental happiness eludes us. When these concepts are dissolved into the nature of mind, we will experience the feeling of mental happiness.

There are many methods for creating a mind that is one-pointed and joyful, the most important of which is meditation. The Buddhist tradition offers a multitude of diverse meditations, such as those found in the Mahayana tradition or in the Secret Mantrayana with its many graduated practices, including those of the channels, winds, and spheres. It is said that the Buddha taught eighty-four thousand gates of samadhi. If they were all condensed, what would be central? Calm abiding (*shamatha*) and deeper insight (*vipashyana*). Of the two, we first meditate on calm abiding, as it is indispensable and the easiest for those who are beginning to practice.

In order to practice calm abiding, we need to know its characteristics, its essential nature, and its various categories. Unless we know these things, we will not know how to meditate. First, we take a posture that is different from our normal one, more specific than the one described in counting our breath. Among the many postures that are taught for practitioners engaging in samadhi, the seven-point posture of Vairochana is one of the best.[213] As mentioned earlier, if we sit in a straight posture and maintain a good meditation, all the winds will flow smoothly in the channels. The posture helps to keep a stable center while we are focusing on the mind and for this reason, it is important. If our posture is good, calm abiding will go well.

Generally, calm abiding is defined in this way: "Relying on a correct referent, the mind rests one-pointedly." It can be divided into three ways of meditating: placing the mind using a support, placing the mind without using a support, and placing the mind on the essential nature itself.

When using an external support or object, we place an article in front of our eyes, for example, a flower. By focusing one-pointedly on it, we keep numerous concepts from forming and revolving in our mind. This practice of focusing one-pointedly on an ordinary object in front of us—often a pebble or little stick—is called "calm abiding with an impure external support." When we focus in the same way on an object that is related to the Dharma—a statue or image of the Buddha, a hand-held symbol of a deity, a Dharma text, and so forth—that is known as "calm abiding with a pure external support."

When we have become familiar with these first practices and our mind can rest without moving from its object, then we can start the second type of calm abiding, which is without a support. Here, we turn our focus inward and bring to mind an image of the Buddha. If we begin this second practice before we can do the basic one, it will be difficult, since here there is no external object to serve as a referent. With our mind unable to remain focused, concepts will crowd in. So practice the first meditation until it goes very well, and then move on to the second. If we follow these steps, practice will go well.

The third kind of calm abiding is placing the mind on the essential nature itself. Here, there is neither an external nor an internal support. With our mind staying very focused, we meditate free of concepts, which is the highest level of calm abiding meditation. Mastery of the two earlier practices allows this one to be stable. When our mind is undisturbed by any concept that might arise, the natural joy and clarity of the mind will dawn. When we have this experience of calm abiding, we will appreciate its great value.

Many ways of placing the mind have been taught by the great lamas in their core instructions. They have taught, for example, that we should not run after the past, not call the future to us, and not be moved by the thought present in our minds now: we should remain completely focused on our reference point, abiding within the essential nature, not affected by thoughts of the past, present, or future. When we become accustomed to this through study and practice, various meditative experiences will arise. The sutras and the tantras give many explanations of these, which can be condensed into five.

The first is known as the experience of *movement*. When we first begin practicing calm abiding, it seems that our afflictions multiply and our concepts increase. Is this a fault? No, this happens because we had not practiced calm abiding before and did not notice whether we had many concepts. Now that we are practicing calm abiding, we begin to see all the afflictions and concepts in our mind. It is not that the practice has created more of them; by simply looking into our mind, we are noticing what was already there. For this first stage, the feeling we have when experiencing the onrush of powerful concepts and afflictions is compared to a turbulent river plunging through a gorge.

The second stage of calm abiding is known as *attainment*. Through our meditating on the first stage, concepts have decreased a little and the afflictions are somewhat reduced. Our experience, however, is not stable: sometimes we have an onrush of concepts, and afflictions and sometimes we are freer of them. They are not constant as in the first stage; their appearances come more slowly. At this point, the river has exited the gorge and flows more slowly in a wider bed.

The third stage of calm abiding refers to the experience of *familiarization.* Here afflictions and concepts do arise but not with the force they had before. The feeling of an onrush or a narrow space has subsided, and the river moves leisurely along its course. This does not mean that all concepts and afflictions have vanished, but they are naturally pacified and the afflictions are softer, more gentle, like a broad river flowing peacefully.

Having practiced the first three stages, we come to the fourth, the experience of *stability,* where our practice of calm abiding has become constant. The example is a vast and peaceful ocean unmoved by waves. Concepts naturally do not arise. A sense of vastness contrasts with the narrow feeling of the first stage. Within this wide expanse, the waves of concepts and afflictions have been stilled.

The fifth stage is known as the experience of *complete stability.* When we have become completely familiar with the practice of calm abiding, not only do we attain true stability, we also begin to have a slight experience of the clear, radiant aspect of the mind. This knowing aspect of primordial wisdom appears due to our practice of calm abiding. The example here is a large ocean that is not only free of waves but also clear and transparent. Some oceans are polluted; this one is pellucid by nature. So at this fifth stage, in addition to a very steady mind, the clear and cognizant aspect of its ultimate nature starts to manifest. This is the fruition of the practice of calm abiding: temporary experiences of the clear, radiant nature of primordial wisdom or the *dharmata.*

This has been a brief explanation of how to place our mind in calm abiding and how meditative experiences arise. The Buddhist teachings move along a graduated path: first the stages of calm abiding and then the stages of deep insight. Through such gradual practices, lamas of the past gave birth to realization in their mental continuum and discovered primordial wisdom. All the qualities that the great masters found, we can attain as well. It all depends on our own efforts, our diligence, our deeper knowing, and our correct motivation.

When we first enter the Dharma, we need to give rise to faith or confidence, and we also need to know why this is necessary. If we just rely on an unthinking devotion, we will be caught in blind faith. Therefore, through examining and analyzing, we should give rise to genuine faith. Afterward, it is important to maintain good discipline, such as keeping the refuge vows. We should then practice studying, reflecting, and meditating on the teachings. First we hear core instructions from a genuine lama and analyze them with our reasoning. But we do not stop there. The special mark of Buddhism is that it goes beyond study and reflection to emphasize meditation. In the ordinary world, we will also find study and analysis but not meditation. In Buddhism, we study and reflect on the

Dharma; and then, fully blending what we have understood with our mind, we practice resting evenly in meditation.

We cannot immediately grasp the more advanced practices, such as the Great Seal (mahamudra) or the Great Completion (mahasandhi), both of which lead to the result of primordial wisdom. For all of these higher-level practices, we need a steady basis, which is none other than the correct practice of calm abiding. If the untamed mind is filled with concepts and afflictions, these higher practices are not possible. In the beginning, a tree needs strong roots. Similarly, what is most important for meditation is calm abiding. For this reason I have explained it for those of us who are practicing meditation to help us find mental happiness and well-being. This is my great hope.

An Introduction to Deep Insight

I F WE CAN PRACTICE calm abiding well, we will be able to suppress the afflictions or set them at some distance. We can also diminish our suffering, sometimes even get rid of it for a while, but the practice of calm abiding will not totally remove it. Deep insight is the remedy that allows us to completely eliminate the afflictions and suffering. To practice deep insight, we first need to know its essential nature. Deep insight includes examining with our deeper knowing to discover the nature or makeup of each phenomenon. As with calm abiding, when we first practice deep insight, we need to take a meditation posture so that our mind can hold its focus.[214]

With our mind steady, we use our deeper knowing to analyze in order to discover the ultimate nature. The objects of the analysis are actually all phenomena, but since they cannot fit into our mind, they are summarized into two categories: those with form and those without. To the first one belong such things as a pillar or a vase—basically, what we can see with our eyes. Our physical form also belongs here. How to analyze it? We look at each part, which is composed of many other parts put together, and then we analyze these other parts into increasingly smaller divisions.

Our body, for example, has two arms, two legs, and a head. While analyzing the arm, for example, we can see that it does not really exist as one indivisible unit, but is made up of parts: the hand, the forearm, and the upper arm. If we analyze the hand, we can see that it too is made up of parts: the five fingers and the palm. By continuing to analyze in this way, we finally come down to coarse and then even subtle particles. These, however, are not without parts, nor are they unchanging. If we look at one particle, we can see that it has an eastern part, a southern part, a western part, a northern part, and a top and a bottom part, too. It is made of different sections put together, and this allows us to say that a particle, whether coarse or subtle, does not exist as an independent entity. From the perspective of the way they appear, all phenomena with form, all composite things, seem to exist on this coarse level. However, if we analyze carefully, not only do coarse particles not exist, but even subtle particles are not inherently existent. This is the way to analyze phenomena with form using our deeper knowing: taking an object down to its smallest part and seeing that even that does not exist.

The second category, phenomena without form, refers to the central mind and its mental factors. All these mental phenomena are considered formless. And the mind itself cannot be proven to exist through possessing characteristics that define it on a relative level. The mind has multiple aspects, which can be summarized into the three categories of past, future, and present. If we analyze these three, we can see that the mind of the past has gone by and does not exist now. The mind of the future is still to be born and does not exist now. This present mind is just one moment, which will soon cease. We may think that a separate moment is there, but if we analyze it, we can see a past aspect, a future aspect and a present one, so it is not one moment, one entity, but made up of many parts. Analyzing in this way, we cannot find what is called "a present moment." Therefore, it does not actually have the characteristics that would define and establish it as being this present moment, nor does it have an inherent nature. Mind is not established as a color or shape belonging to a form. No matter where we look, a separate mind cannot be found: it is like space. Analyzing the mind relative to the three times, we can see that it is not inherently present in any one of them. A mind that exists cannot be established by any valid logic.

In Buddhist philosophy, all phenomena with or without form are presented in this way. When our deeper knowing analyzes any object, it is found to lack ultimate reality. And not only is the object of analysis not inherently existent, the subject itself, our deeper knowing that analyzes the object, does not inherently exist either. How is this so? If we rub two pieces of wood together, a fire will ignite and burn the wood. Once all the wood is consumed, the fire will naturally die out. Correspondingly, a permanent, inherently existent object does not exist and, further, the deeper knowing that is the investigating subject does not inherently exist either. The wood and the fire both cease to exist.

When we see that ultimately neither the object nor the subject exists, concepts cease. There is no basis for objects, whether they be physical or mental. There are no characteristics to be apprehended and therefore there is nothing truly existent to be discovered. There are no thoughts that remember the past and none that fabricate the future. Resting evenly in this free expanse that is the mind's nature is practicing deep insight. When we continue in this state, looking at whatever arises to see its nature, we become accustomed to it and trust that it is true.

How do we continue our practice once we have finished a session? We hold the thought that whatever arises in our mind resembles an illusion or a movie: although these phenomena are nonexistent, they appear; although they appear, they are nonexistent. If we see someone in a movie, that person is not really there, yet a person appears. Someone is appearing to our eyes, but, we question, is that a real appearance? No, it's like an image from last night's dream. In this same way, all phenomena resemble an illusion. This is true because their nature is emptiness. In sum, during this postmeditation phase, we train in recognizing the empty nature of these phenomena, seeing them as an illusion or an image from a film.

If we study and practice deep insight again and again—how to rest evenly in meditation and then how to practice afterward—we will gradually become accustomed to the practice. Finally, with the realization of mind's empty nature, or the direct realization of the dharmata, it is not necessary to suppose that phenomena are illusionlike; we will directly see the truth that all phenomena do resemble an illusion. This direct realization of the dharmata's truth and the final freedom from all of our suffering depend mainly on our skillful practice of deep insight and our diligence in following step by step the Buddha's teaching of calm abiding and deep insight. There are many texts by the scholars and meditation masters of India and Tibet that elucidate his thought and the various stages of these practices. If we become familiar with these and engage in the practices again and again, the future will bring us a positive result. That is my hope for you.

The Many Ways to Practice Deep Insight

IT IS IMPORTANT for us to have a stable and peaceful mind, for it is mostly through our mind that we experience suffering and problems. With diligence, we can establish our minds in peace by abandoning the afflictions that create obstacles. Meditation makes this possible because it establishes a steady mind. Among the many types of meditation, calm abiding (shamatha) and deep insight (vipashyana) are central to this process. In calm abiding, our mind is focused inwardly, which allows us to suppress the afflictions so that they do not actually manifest. There is a sense of distance between us and the afflictions. It is not possible, however, to eradicate them with calm abiding alone; deep insight is necessary to remove them at the root.

While training on the path of deep insight, there are three main stages: the cause for the arising of deep insight, the various aspects or ways of practice, and postmeditation. The cause involves relying on a genuine teacher, listening to the authentic Dharma, and maintaining it in the correct way. If all three aspects are not complete, a phenomenon is not considered a cause since it cannot bring about the appearance of deep insight through a more profound knowing.

Genuine teachers have perfectly blended their own mind with the Buddha's thought as it is found in the scriptures. Relying on such a teacher is important; however, we do not just rely on a teacher but also listen correctly to presentations of the Dharma on both the provisional and the definitive levels.[215] And we do not stop here but continue to use our deeper knowing to cut through doubts and establish the correct view within our mindstream. If this does not happen, the wisdom of deep insight will not be born. If we follow a worldly or non-Buddhist view, the wisdom of deep insight will not arise, since these views are not free of error.

By listening to and reflecting on the scriptures and their commentaries, we cut through doubts and ascertain the view through various reasonings. We gain certainty in the view and in the nature of mind that the view presents, and then we blend this together with our own mind. If we can do this, the perfect cause for deep insight will be established.

Lamas of the past first trained by reflecting on the nature of mind as presented in the view and thereby came to the unmistaken view that the nature of the mind is emptiness. This refined understanding served as a basis for their subsequent practice of meditation. This is called training in the path. Otherwise, if we practice without having the right view in mind, it is like trying to climb a steep cliff without hands. It will be very difficult to reach our goal of giving rise to realization in our mindstream. If we have the correct view first and then practice meditation, traveling along the path will be completely free of obstructions, just like the flight of the *garuda* as it soars through space.[216] Our meditation will go well and realization will arise in our mind. For all these reasons, it is important that we have an utterly pure view in our mental continuum.

The second point concerns the ways to hold or practice deep insight, which are numerous. There are the practices common to a worldly path and non-Buddhists, the practice according to the shravakas and pratyekabuddhas, the practice according to the Mahayana, and, within this, the tradition of the Secret Mantrayana.

The mundane practice of deep insight has much in common with non-Buddhist traditions, where we rest in meditation and move from coarser to more subtle levels. For example, when we come to the first level of stable contemplation,[217] we look back at the previous, lower realm of desire and see that it is not a suitable object of meditation, since it has faults, such as violence and hatred. We also see that the first level of stable contemplation is free of such faults. In this way, seeing the preceding, lower level as having faults that the superior one does not, we move progressively through the four levels of stable contemplation, each one having pacified the faults of the previous one and become more subtle.

While we are practicing deep insight based on this mundane path, we can suppress the afflictions and temporarily prevent them from manifesting, but we cannot eliminate them completely, and therefore it is possible to fall back into samsara and cycle again through various states of existence. However, if someone is free of the attachment and wantingness found in the desire realm and practices this worldly path of profound insight, she or he can attain the great and wonderful qualities that belong to our deeper knowing.

Deep insight is also practiced in the shravaka tradition, where the focus is on the Four Noble Truths and their sixteen different aspects. The Buddha turned the wheel of Dharma three times, and during the first turning, he taught about the Four Noble Truths: the truth of suffering, the truth of its origin, the truth of its cessation, and the truth of the path that leads to cessation. These can be explained in different ways, for example, through the twelve repetitions, which refer to the three categories of essential nature, function, and result, applied to each of the four truths, making twelve in all.[218] Alternatively, it is taught that each one of the four truths has four aspects, such as being impermanent, empty, having no self, and so forth, adding up to sixteen. The shravaka practice of deep insight is to rest in meditation on these sixteen aspects or sixteen ways of holding the mind. The pratyekabuddha tradition focuses on the twelve links of dependent arising, beginning with ignorance.[219] When they practice deep insight, they meditate on these twelve aspects or ways of holding the mind.

In the Buddhist scriptural tradition, dependent arising is key, and there are many ways to understand it from the lower to the higher philosophical systems. However, when it comes to how the twelve links arise, the explanations are basically the same. For example, the Madhyamaka states that all phenomena appear through arising in dependence on causes and conditions. Phenomena are impermanent and do not exist inherently. The true nature of all phenomena is emptiness, free of mental elaborations. However, on the mere ordinary or relative level, what we experience are appearances and what we think about them: these all come about through dependent arising, through causes and conditions relying one upon the other. For the Buddhist teachings in general, dependent arising is important, and this is especially true for the Madhyamaka school.

Of all the different ways to practice deep insight, the most important is that of the Mahayana path, which is based on the six perfections. Within this tradition of meditation are found three main schools: the Svatantrika or Autonomy school; the Prasangika, or Consequentialist School, also known as the Rangtong or "empty of self" school; and finally, the Shentong, or "empty of what is other to it" school. Followers of the Svatantrika school meditate on deep insight by dividing the process of meditation into two aspects: the one who meditates and the object of meditation. The first refers to the mind of the one who is meditating on the dharmadhatu, and the second refers to the object of meditation—the dharmadhatu itself upon which the mind is meditating. How does the meditation proceed? We bring to rest all mental constructs, such as those positing existence and nonexistence, in relation to the consciousness of the subject who is meditating and in relation to the object of meditation, the expanse of all phenomena. We then rest in the wake of that negation, which resembles an empty sky. This is the way that the Svatantrika school presents the practice of deep insight.

The Prasangika or Rangtong school has a slightly different approach. The object of meditation is the dharmadhatu, and the subject is the mind that is cognizant. One then asks, "Are these two the same or different?" Through examining, we discover that they are neither the same nor different; they are actually inseparable just like water poured into water. Once two glasses of water have been blended together, it is impossible to tell which one was poured into the other. We rest evenly in this state where there is no differentiation between the consciousness of the subject and the expanse of all phenomena that is the object. This is deep insight meditation according to the Prasangika school.

The Shentong school describes primordial wisdom as empty of the subject/object duality; it is aware of its own nature and naturally clear. A synonym for this wisdom is reflexive awareness free of duality and present from time beyond time. From this ultimate point of view, there is nothing to be subtracted and nothing to be added. There are no obscurations of the afflictions to be eliminated and no qualities of the Buddha to be attained. Without contrivance, we rest within the nature of mind just as it is. In other words, we rest evenly in the radiant clarity that is mind's nature. This is the practice of deep insight according to the Madhyamaka Shentong school.

In all of these schools belonging to the Mahayana tradition, we rest evenly in meditation on the expanse of all phenomena free of complexity; we are free of mental constructs posited on the basis of existence and nonexistence.

In the unsurpassed Secret Mantrayana, the way of practicing deep insight is slightly different from the Mahayana. Emptiness free of duality is explained as the nature of mind, but it is emphasized that this emptiness is not just nonexistence, not a vacuum or a mere void. The essential nature is emptiness, but it has the aspect or capacity of appearing as anything, so it is said to have the aspect of radiant clarity. Not only does emptiness have the aspect of radiant clarity, but within the essential nature of this clear aspect there is also the appearance of great bliss. Resting evenly within emptiness just as it is, endowed with great bliss, is the Mantrayana's view of deep insight.

These ways of practicing deep insight—of the Shravaka and the Pratyekabuddha, the Svatantrika, Prasangika, Shentong, and Secret Mantrayana—allow us to cut through the very root of the afflictions. The worldly path of deep insight does lead to higher levels of meditative absorption and to the development of deeper knowing, but it is only able to suppress the afflictions, not to uproot them. It is only the Buddhist path of deep insight that is able to cut through the roots of samsara and lead to true freedom.

The third and last category of training in deep insight belongs to the postmeditation stage, or how we work with our mind once the session of meditation is over. Usually, the first thing we notice is our body. Our ignorance would tell us that it actually exists, but with the help of meditation, we can see that it has no inherent nature, which means that it is like an illusion, appearing though it does not exist. What we see is a fiction, something a magician would conjure. So in relation to our body, we hold the thought that it is like an illusion. In addition to physical sensations, we will also experience a range of feelings from happiness to suffering. These, too, are not truly existent, though we do experience them; they resemble the feelings in a dream. We might dream that we cut our arm and while dreaming would experience pain just as if we were awake. Yet cutting our arm and the cut itself are present only in the dream. When we wake up, our arm shows nothing. Our ordinary feelings are like this: though nonexistent, they appear seeming to be real.

The essential nature of the mind is like space. There is no such thing as a mind that truly exists or a mind that is inherently established even though we might find reasonings, scriptures, or experience to the contrary. Mind is empty. Our ordinary mind, however, becomes confused in thinking that things really exist. The nature of our mind is emptiness, but not a blankness, not the result of mere negation: emptiness is also radiant clarity, the basis for the appearances of both samsara and nirvana. The mind is like space and it also has a clear and knowing aspect, which allows us to say, "This is space." Resting in mind's empty, clear nature, we will be at ease as we move along the path of practice.

Body, feelings, and mind are all phenomena that merely appear like clouds in the sky. Where do clouds come from? When they disappear, where do they go? We can't say. Like body, speech, and mind, other phenomena also are free of arising and ceasing, of coming and going. Their essential nature is emptiness.

Most living beings seek mental happiness and want to eliminate suffering, but just wishing will not bring this about. We may even create the opposite. So we must search for the cause of suffering and the cause of happiness. The afflictions are the cause of samsara, of all mental discomfort and suffering. The remedy is meditation. Among all types of practice, deep insight is the best. Without practicing, hoping and making prayers for liberation will not bring it about. To attain liberation, we must eliminate the afflictions by relying on a remedy that can cut through their root, and deep insight is this profound antidote. For this reason I have given this longer explanation and hope that it will benefit your practice and that you will be able to tame your mind and swiftly attain liberation.

The Importance of Dedication

WE HAVE ALL ENGAGED in wholesome activity. Whether this will bring about a vast result or not mainly depends upon dedicating the merit, and so an excellent dedication is very important. All the various factors belonging to dedication must come together for it to be complete.

First we need to know the virtues that we are dedicating. They are traditionally divided into two categories: those we ourselves have gathered and those gathered by others. The first category contains the roots of virtue that come from our studying and reflecting on the teachings and also the virtuous actions that others have encouraged us to do. The second category covers the virtues others have gathered in which we have rejoiced, and the virtues others have done to which we have no obvious connection.

Second, there are various objectives to which we can dedicate our virtuous or wholesome actions. We can dedicate our wholesome activity so that we become a powerful and benevolent leader or so that we are reborn in a higher realm and attain its happiness. This kind of dedication is all right; however, once we attain the result of this kind of dedication, the virtue will be exhausted. Further, the virtue can be destroyed if we become angry before attaining the results of our dedication. Therefore, we should look for a better purpose for our dedication. The most supreme goal is the attainment of full awakening. If we make this kind of dedication, then until attaining complete realization, our virtue will not diminish but increase. Further, if we become angry or engulfed by some other negative emotion before attaining our result, this event will not destroy our virtue since it has become powerful and extensive due to the dedication. These are the attributes belonging to the highest objective for our dedication.

Third, we make the dedication for the benefit of others, so that measureless numbers of living beings may be freed of suffering and attain genuine happiness and the ultimate place of happiness, the level of precious awakening. It is also acceptable to make the dedication for our own benefit; however, that virtue will not become vast. For example, if I have one mirror, I can see only one face in it, but if I have thousands of mirrors, even though there is only one face, I can see thousands. In this way, it is all right to make the dedication for the benefit of ourselves, but it will not extend very far. Therefore, it is good to make the expansive dedication for the benefit of others.

We can also dedicate our virtue along with the virtue of others. How is this possible? Using myself as an example, I know of four kinds of virtue: the virtue I have accumulated and the virtue that others have encouraged, plus the virtue of others that I rejoice in and their own virtue that stands separate. The first two I can dedicate, but what about the virtue of others, including the Buddha or Manjushri? I can combine their virtue together with my own and then dedicate all of it for the attainment of awakening by myself and all living beings.

What are the benefits of a dedication made for the pure purpose of attaining full awakening and for the benefit of others? Our mind will become peaceful, and that in itself is the source of vast benefits. Temporarily, we will be free of harm and illness. In the future, we will attain a more pleasant or higher rebirth. Further, from now until complete realization, the power and virtue of this dedication will remain with us. Therefore, it is said that this kind of dedication is vast and lasting.

There is one more important point. While making a dedication, the three aspects of an action (also known as the three spheres or wheels) should be utterly pure or empty: the subject who is dedicating, the act of dedicating, and the object of the dedication. All three have the essential nature of emptiness and, aware of this, we dedicate. If our dedication has these three aspects, then it is completely pure and effective.

For beginners, however, it will be a bit difficult to dedicate merit through knowing that the three aspects of an action are empty. This kind of focus is not so easy. If we cannot make this kind of dedication, we can make an aspiration: "Just as the great bodhisattvas, such as Chenrezik and Manjushri, made their dedications seeing the three aspects in their empty nature, I also aspire to make such dedications."

A ritual for dedicating can also be added; for example, we can recite verses of dedication composed by the Buddha or by the great lamas who have followed him. We can then recite whatever aspiration prayers we like. If, with a pure mind, we can make our dedication and aspirations in front of representations of the Three Jewels, they will be free of obstacles and very powerful.

If we understand the way to dedicate, the objective, the benefits, and the different virtues of making the right kind of dedication, we can dedicate the wholesome actions we have worked so hard to accomplish toward the ultimate result—full awakening, vast and inexhaustible. It is also important that we rejoice in all the merit occurring in the world. Through our lives and virtuous actions, we are all accumulating merit; however, a good result is not easy to find, and that is why the dedication is so important. I am glad to have been able to explain this to you and to dedicate all the merit we have accumulated, along with that of all the buddhas, for the benefit of all living beings that they may attain full awakening, and also to make the aspiration that you will be able to practice in this excellent way.

Part III

The Poetry of the
Seventeenth Karmapa

Introduction to the Poetry
of the Seventeenth Karmapa

POETRY PERMEATES Tibetan literature. Almost all the meditative practices and many of the philosophical texts are in verse. Poetic form inspires insight and also serves as a mnemonic device, the metric counts settling the words into mind. The main poetic strategies used are metaphor, simile, euphony, wordplay, and meter in odd-numbered beats, usually seven, nine, or eleven to a line. The poems by the seventeenth Karmapa presented here reflect the many modes of Tibetan poetry. Some are short four-line verses that point out the nature of mind and are meant to be aids for meditation. Others are visionary poems, which come from a pure, deeper seeing and envision other realms and times, or other states of being, often presented as evocations of pure lands or a golden age. There are praises of a particular place, and prayers for peace and happiness, for positive outcomes, and for auspicious times. The long-life prayers for great lamas are entreaties for their longevity and also contain profound teachings. Some poems evoke a certain state of mind. The songs are lighter in feeling, with their melodious sounds of "a la la" and repeating lines creating a refrain. The language of these texts varies as well. In some poems, it is simple and unadorned, and in others it is complex, dense with intertwining metaphors and rich in the textures of classical Sanskrit imagery that resonate with high Tibetan culture. These verses are meant to be read again and again; often poems about the Dharma are memorized to blend them more intimately with our mind.

Some of the poems have double titles, one descriptive and the other poetic. At the end of many of the poems, as in most texts in Tibetan, is found a colophon describing the occasion of the work's composition: who requested it, where and when it was written, who wrote it, and, when appropriate, the translator, editor, and sometimes the publisher. Authors are often difficult to identify, as they can have many names, which are used on different occasions. Also traditional is the humble mode of referring to oneself—"a jester in king's clothes," and so forth— aimed at removing any suspicion of arrogance at having created this work. Following the colophon are my brief comments on the poem itself, including explanations of Buddhist terms. Unusual words or phrases that appear in more than one poem are usually explained at their first occurrence only.

The seventeenth Karmapa has a great interest in poetry and has studied traditional Tibetan poetics extensively. About these studies he said, "In this world of ours, there are many types of knowledge, including the various religious traditions and a range of cultures that are very diverse. Among these, one that I have studied intensively is the philosophy of India's Vedas as it is reflected in the classic text on poetics, *The Mirror of Poetry*. Found here are praises to deities, such as Maheshvara and Brahma, references to the ten avatars of Vishnu, the golden dorje of Indra, and so forth. When creating poetic metaphors, this text gives the correspondences between the meanings to be expressed and the words that express them, and this resonance results in an effective composition. In the Nyingma tradition of the Secret Mantrayana, all these Indian deities became guides for the Buddha's teachings and individuals worthy of respect; they gather in all good things, all benefits and well-being."[220] On the subject of deities, many of which are common to Hinduism and Buddhism, the Karmapa remarked, "The goddess of poetry is Yangchenma (Sarasvati),[221] so as a writer of poetry, I do feel a special connection with her."[222]

On a more personal level, he stated, "I began to write poetry about three or four years after I came to Tsurphu. My first teacher of poetry was Lama Nyima, who explained *The Mirror of Poetry*. After this I began to compose a little and have continued up to now. Usually, I write when I don't have too many feelings. The feeling of happiness is not strong, nor is the feeling of suffering. Sometimes, when I have a joyful feeling, I write as well. When I'm sad, I write only a little bit, not much.

"When I write a poem, I need to reflect on it, yet as I'm thinking, I do not remember how to compose the words. Then, suddenly, the poem comes right through and it reads well. Mostly my writing happens like this. That is my way of composing."[223]

In response to a question about when he began painting, the Karmapa replied, "I really began here at Gyütö, but while in Tibet, I worked with colors some, filling in outline drawings. Once here in India I actually began to draw. There is a close connection between poetry and painting. In painting, you use beautifully drawn forms, such as mountains, lakes, and trees, to create something pleasing to the eyes. In poetry, related to speech, you use words to make something interesting and beautiful. Music and song are pleasing to the ears and closely connected to poetry. When I came to like poetry, I came to like all these other arts as well."[224]

The Karmapa also likes to write music and spoke of the connection between music and meditation: "Hearing a beautiful melody can invoke your wisdom body and thereby have a peaceful and harmonious effect on your mind, in the same way that the meditation of calm abiding brings inner peace. If you can sustain this calmness, you will develop inwardly, moving through deeper insight all the way up to the ultimate level of realization."[225]

In speaking of his own work, the Karmapa is typically humble, yet the Dalai Lama has praised him highly for his poetry, especially the verse the Karmapa presented to him called, "A Joyful Aspiration":

I was so very surprised and happy when I read the profound poem by the 17th Karmapa as he wrote about his escape from Tibet in a poetic form. Even my poems do not have this quality or profundity. From that point onwards, I realized that the Karmapa is in fact a being who possesses the clarity of inner wisdom, who is very keen to learn Buddhist logic and philosophy. I told many others about the poem and how wonderful it was from the point of view of his knowledge of Dharma and the wisdom within.[226]

This poem is the first in the selection that follows.

A Joyful Aspiration

SWEET MELODY FOR THE FORTUNATE ONES

Om Swasti. The right-turning conch of pure compassion in body,
    speech, and mind
Pours forth a stream of good intentions that never change.
Thereby, may a sweet, resonant melody beyond compare, such music
    for the ears,
Open the lotus petals of virtue, excellence, and goodness.

It has the supreme name of the Wish-Fulfilling Tree, the ambrosial one.
Musical tones of this flawless tree, granting every wish, are dulcet and
    pleasing.
Throughout its branches gems of lasting happiness nestle among their
    leaves.
Sovereign in our realm, may the world be resplendent with the beauty
    of this tree.

ASPIRATION FOR TIBET
A string of fragrant flowers, these snow mountains are tranquil and
    fresh.
In a healing land where white incense rises sweet,
May the gracious beauty of luminous moonbeams, light of the spiritual
    and temporal worlds,
Conquer all strife, this darkness of the shadow side.

ASPIRATION FOR THE DALAI LAMA
Inspiring festivals of merit in the Land of Snow,
You are the Supreme One holding a pure white lotus.
With the beauty of all good qualities, a treasure for eyes to behold,
May your life be long, steadfast as a diamond vajra.

ASPIRATION FOR CULTURE AND KNOWLEDGE
The most excellent virtue is the brilliant, calm flow of culture:
Those with fine minds play in a clear lotus lake;
Through this excellent path, a songline sweet like the pollen's honey,
May they sip the fragrant dew of splendid knowledge.

ASPIRATION FOR THE WORLD
Over the expanse of the treasured earth in this vast world,
May benefit for beings appear like infinite moons' reflections;
Their refreshing presence brings lasting welfare and happiness
To open a lovely array of night-blooming lilies, signs of peace and joy.

CONCLUSION
Descending from a canopy of white clouds, the gathering of two
    accumulations,
May these true words, like pearled drops of light or pouring rain
Falling in a lovely park where fortunate disciples are free of bias,
Open the flowers of friendship and let well-being and joy blossom forth.

These words of aspiration, sprung from a sincere intention, were written
down by Ogyen Trinley, the one who bears the noble name of the
Karmapa, while he was escaping from Tibet. One night in the illusory
appearance of a dream, there arose a lake bathed in clear moonlight and
rippled with blooming lotus flowers that served as a seat for three
Brahmins, wearing pure white silk and playing a drum, guitar, flute, and
other instruments. Created in pleasing and lyric tones, their melodious
song came to my ears, and so I composed this aspiration prayer with a
one-pointed mind, filled with an intense and sincere intention to benefit
all the people of Tibet. Within a beautiful, auspicious chain of snow
mountains, this land of Tibet, may the sun rays of this supreme aspiration
for awakening swiftly appear. (Khenchen Thrangu Rinpoche added the
headings.)

Notes

As stated in the colophon, this poem is based on a vision that appeared to the
Karmapa while escaping from Tibet. It was immediately taken up by the Tibetans
in exile, put to music, and recorded by the Tibetan Institute of Performing Arts.
In English, it found its way to many sites on the Internet. The poem begins with
an aspiration that the teachings of the Buddha, like a resonant song, reach everywhere and benefit all beings. As one of the eight auspicious symbols,[227] the right-
turning conch shell symbolizes the resonant speech of the Buddha and, by
extension, his teachings. It is one of the musical instruments played during rituals and ceremonies. Its turning to the right marks the conch as rare and also
reflects the clockwise turn of the planets in the heavens and the right-turning spi-
ral of the Buddha's hair. The wish-fulfilling tree, along with the wish-fulfilling
jewel, is a classic image for a numinous object that will bring all that is needed

and wished for; here, the great tree stands as a wish for abundance and happiness. In Hindu mythology, it is the central tree in the main garden of the god Indra's paradise. "These celestial trees change their appearance in each season, are laden with beautiful blossoms and fruit, radiate divine perfumes, and are as brilliant as precious jewels."[228]

The two opening verses are followed by four aspirations: for Tibet to know peace, for the Dalai Lama to live long, for the precious knowledge of Tibetan culture to be preserved and enjoyed, and for peace and happiness to spread throughout the world. In his aspiration for Tibet, the Karmapa envisions his homeland as a land of healing where the spiritual and temporal worlds complement each other and can reverse the darkness that has settled over his country. The *Land of Snow* refers to Tibet, and the *vajra* is the symbol for what is indestructible, brilliant, and unchanging, associated with the Vajrayana Buddhism of Tibet and the full awakening of the Buddha.

In the wish for the Dalai Lama's long life, *the Supreme One holding a pure white lotus* refers to Chenrezik, the embodiment of compassion, of whom the Dalai Lama is an emanation. Culture is envisioned as a sweet path where knowledge is enjoyed as ambrosia. In the next verse, the white of infinite moons throughout space is reflected on earth in the white of lilies whose blossoms are opened by moonlight. It is an image of peace and harmony pervading the entire universe. In the last verse, the *two accumulations* refer to (1) gathering merit by engaging in wholesome activity to benefit others, and (2) gaining wisdom through study, reflection, and meditation, and coming to see the emptiness of all phenomena. In conclusion, the Karmapa makes the wish that his words will help to create the better world envisioned in the poem.

Entering the Middle Way

The sun of vajra mind, simplicity itself,
     pervades the entire expanse of phenomena's space;
The primordial nature of mind cannot be destroyed:
    it is radiant clarity, great bliss, and the vast extent of emptiness.

Your profound wisdom, a knowing free of veils,
     dawns for every living being.
Guide of the fortunate kalpa, through your name, "Gautama,"
    may a rain of auspicious flowers descend.

Notes

This poem was written on the occasion of the publication of *The Ocean of Reasoning* by the seventh Karmapa, Chödrak Gyatso.[229] The text belongs to the Madhyamaka or *Middle Way* school, which follows a path that avoids extremes, such as nihilism or eternalism. As its title indicates, this text is a vast and detailed study of the elements of reasoning and how they interrelate. It presents subtle discussions of perception, of what we can know, and of how we know what we think we know. As our understanding becomes increasingly refined, it can deepen into realization.

What constitutes this realization is the topic of the first verse. (The lines are in a longer, fifteen-beat meter, here split into two lines.) The first line speaks of the two aspects of mind's nature: its radiant, clear, and knowing aspect, imaged by the sun, and its empty aspect, imaged by the expanse of space; these two aspects are inseparable, just as the sky is pervaded by sunlight. *Simplicity* is another way to translate "free of mental constructs" or "free of mental elaboration," a time when the mind remains undisturbed by discriminating thought; it is simple and free of conceptual clutter. *The expanse of phenomena's space* (the dharmadhatu) refers to the empty and spacious nature of everything that arises. The second line describes the mind's nature: indestructible, luminous, blissful, spacious, and empty. *Fortunate kalpa* is a synonym for a golden age. *Gautama* is another name for the Buddha, who was given the name Siddhartha Gautama at birth. The next two lines speak of the potential for every living being to come into this wisdom, free of the two *veils*, or obscurations—the obscuration of afflictions and of cognitive obscurations. The poem concludes with an aspiration for an auspicious era.

The Three Kayas

The dharmakaya is naturally arisen, the ultimate;
The sambhogakaya is all-pervading, bliss-emptiness unceasing;
Through the nirmanakaya pouring forth a rain of joy,
May auspiciousness in all its glory be present.

Notes

Naturally arisen can also be translated as "self-arisen," in the sense that it does not depend on anything else: it arises from within and as its own nature. (The "self" of self-arisen does not mean that a permanent, autonomous self is posited.) The *dharmakaya* is variously translated as the ultimate kaya, the body of truth, the dimension of truth, the body of reality, and so forth. Ultimately beyond expression in words or speech, dharmakaya is another synonym for ultimate reality and is the basis for the two other kayas (bodies or dimensions) which arise from it. The *sambhogakaya*, the enjoyment body or the luminous body, encompasses the richly arrayed mandalas of the myriad deities. It can be perceived only by individuals who have realized the nature of their mind. The *nirmanakaya* is the manifestation body (the tulku), the buddhas whom ordinary individuals can meet. Shakyamuni Buddha was a nirmanakaya manifestation. In general, this stanza resembles a teaching poem. Often a lama will summarize a philosophical position or a set of concepts by putting them into verse. This concise version clarifies the meaning and makes it easier to keep in memory.

The Peaceful and Calming Victory Flag

MELODIOUS SONG OF THE BATTLE VICTORIOUS OVER MARAS

This wisdom, profound and clear, a garland of dawn's glowing
    moonlight, sheds luminous joy.
This cluster of lively moons, the positive signs of radiant clarity, turns in
    the gracious dance of emptiness and luminosity, free of fabrication,
    cool and fresh;
A broad and calming shade that benefits and brings joy permeates the
    whole universe.
The sweet melody of auspicious virtue and excellence for all beings
    resonates as the glorious ornament of the three realms.

Two rising curves of pure gold are great joy's loving, radiant smile;
Vibrant blue reflects the ultimate, the dharmakaya lit by a vigorous and
    youthful sun; sphere of light, this hand draws
And plays, gathering into the glide of an image the unity of the
    profound and vast, the peaceful and soothing.
Throughout existence, may the victory banner of the Buddha's teachings
    resound its famous and melodious song.

In order to liberate beings from the four maras, this aspiration prayer was
made by the seventeenth one to hold the Karmapa's lineage. (Translated
with advice from Khenchen Thrangu Rinpoche. See the color plates for an
image of the flag.)

Notes

The image this poem describes is generally known in the West as the Dream Flag
since the sixteenth Karmapa saw it in a dream one night at his monastery in
Rumtek in the mid-1970s. Describing his vision, he asked that a flag be made.
Its purpose was to enable the spread of the Buddhist teachings and the flourishing of happiness and well-being for everyone. These flags now fly in many places
throughout the world and are also a design element in many Dharma articles.

    The name of the flag is "the peaceful and calming victory flag." The subtitle
of the poem speaks of being *victorious over maras* or the obstacles to Dharma
practice.[230] What follows in the first four lines of the poem is a richly layered,

luminous evocation of clarity and emptiness in play, imaged as dancing moons. For Indian poetics, the moon's more subtle light is known for its welcome coolness, associated with the night; in a very hot country, shade can have a positive connotation.

Free of fabrication means free of mental constructs, free of cogitation. Among *the three realms,* the realm of desire is divided into the six realms of gods, demigods, humans, animals, hungry ghosts, and hells. This is what Buddhists usually think of when "cycling in samsara" is mentioned: beings move around the wheel of existence taking successive births in these six places, which can also be understood as mental states. The other two realms, the form and formless, are inhabited by different types of gods, or, from another perspective, they represent different states of mental concentration.

This first stanza sets the stage for the second which describes the flag's design of two golden waves rising up into a deep blue sky. The golden waves represent joy and the blue sky is the dharmakaya, the ultimate nature of mind, which is not just empty but radiant, too. In the sixteenth Karmapa's original conception of the flag, the pure gold of joy and the deep blue of the dharmakaya were overlapping; this lack of a sharp edge between the two was meant to signify that bliss and emptiness are inseparable.[231] The poem speaks of another kind of inseparability in the *unity of the profound and the vast* and ends with an aspiration that the teachings resound throughout the world.

A Festival of the Field for Gathering Merit

Om tare tuttare ture soha.
Ah ho.
The essential nature of simplicity is the ground's ever pure expanse.
When set to the enchanting music of a clear and radiant knowing,
     naturally present,
And matured by the jeweled rain of joy descending as the union of the
     three kayas,
The sovereign one, the ultimate lama, arises remembered in the center
     of my heart.

The enlightened activity of your three gates illuminates like a garland of
     the sun's rays.
The hundred thousand lights of your virtuous actions spontaneously
Create a cooling shade to ease the pain of fortunate disciples;
A lotus of the three joys unfolds in the center of their hearts.

The lotus of this life with its leisure and resources holds in its center
A stamen that befriends a mellifluous bee with its honey of
     renunciation.
Grant your blessing that the true lama's lotus feet are bathed by the sun
And the abundant petals of benefit for others open forth.

Gazing at the very face of primordial wisdom, luminous and self-arisen
     from the natural state,
And resting at ease on the path, with nothing to add or take away,
Grant your blessing that I take the royal seat, present from time without
     beginning
In the expanse of emptiness—dharmakaya's true nature, ultimate reality.

In the sky, an umbrella of white clouds forms a rainbow canopy above.
Between sky and earth, flowers of virtue and excellence fall in a gentle
     rain.
On the earth, filled with happiness, people sing in great delight;
May this joy enrapture the whole world.

A sincere intention free of fault is a jeweled lamp, a luminous treasury
That liberates every being from a dense darkness where virtue cannot go.
May the dulcet melody of incomparable fame, this celestial music
For the festival of a golden age without end, resound throughout the
    three realms.

This prayer was written by Ogyen Trinley Dorje on September 4, 2001 as
the sun came over the dome of the eastern mountain. May it be a cause
for virtue.

Notes

The title refers to the *ganachakra* celebrations, Vajrayana feasts, which are extensive deity practices gathering merit for the participants. The Karmapa sees them
as festivals and this song is often sung during these gatherings. *Om tare tuttare
ture soha* is the mantra of the female buddha Tara, who along with Chenrezik is
the most beloved deity in Tibet. She is known for her ability to protect from
danger and is especially invoked before a journey. Since these verses were written "on the verge of escaping to India," it would be natural for the Karmapa to
be thinking of her. (The original title was "Calling the Lama from Afar.") *Ah ho*
is an expression of wonderment, and *ho* is usually associated with joy, so it could
be translated as "wondrous joy." As in other poems, this one begins with an evocation of the basic ground, emptiness or simplicity, which is a pure expanse, an
openness never constricted or blocked.

Ground refers to the foundation, the mind's nature that functions as the
unseen support for all that we do. The term often appears in the sequence of
ground, path, and fruition, where the ground is the place whence we start, the
path is what we practice to remove the veils of ignorance covering mind's nature,
and the fruition is the clear manifestation of mind's ultimate nature, which was
always there at the ground but not perceived due to our ignorance. This fruition
can also be described as *the union of the three kayas.*[232] Present during the ground,
path, and fruition, emptiness, which is inseparable from a *radiant knowing*,
allows *joy to descend* and the *ultimate lama to arise* in the center of his heart.

In the second verse, the Karmapa envisions joy unfolding in the center of disciples' hearts through the influence of Tara's *enlightened activity*. The *three gates*
signify the body, speech, and mind, the avenues of interaction with other worlds.
The *three joys* are what appear when body, speech, and mind are clear. *Leisure*
refers to being free of eight unfavorable states of rebirth in which it is difficult to
practice, and *resources* refers to being endowed with ten positive conditions for
practice, such as taking birth in a land where Buddhist teachings are available.

In the third verse, the image of the lotus is transferred from the disciples' hearts to their lives and to the lama, with prayers for his welfare (*bathed by the sun*) and flourishing activity. The fourth verse is an aspiration that our practice go well, so that we are able to look directly into wisdom in a nondual manner and abide there on the *royal seat* of ultimate reality, with no need to add or subtract anything. The fifth and six verses envision a perfect time on earth through rich overlays of visual and aural images.

Pointing Out Mahamudra

Like the illusory face of this appearing world,
The movement of mind is not touched by artifice;
It is not altered by action, freedom, or realization.
To remain in the depths of mind free of reference
Is known as mahamudra.

Notes

The Karmapa gave this verse to Lama Tenam to use in his meditation practice. Within the Kagyu lineage, the practice of *mahamudra* is the deepest form of meditation. It is deceptively simple to describe and quite difficult to practice. Mahamudra practice could be described as remaining settled into the nature of mind, immersed in its nature that is awareness and emptiness inseparable, *not touched by artifice*, which means that there is no effort to do anything, and *free of reference*, which means that the mind is not grasping at anything at all. If you were working with this verse, you would first memorize it and reflect on its meaning until it became very clear. Then resting in meditation, you would float the verse in your mindstream, keeping a gentle focus, much as a koan is held. Then, after a while, you would let it go and rest in the space it has opened out, free of referent or mental activity. When thoughts arose again, you would fold them into the verse, which would become your referent again, and so you would continue, naturally shifting between resting in meditation and reflecting on the verse.

A New Arising of My Homeland, the Snowy Land of Tibet

Amid a healing grove of refreshing sala trees,
We discuss this time of the year two thousand.
From the lakeshore, the melting white moon of merit is seen;
Its rays illuminating like the body of the Buddha with all its signs.

Bodhichitta is a band of lamplight in the dusky horizon
Bringing joy to the weary mind.
Freedom from harm, like the fragrance of perfect joy,
Permeates the wide reach of this world.

White flowers of snow lightly fall like honeyed rain,
The glory of the mind comes softly to the ear.
The young, flawless sun is a good friend of the opening lotus;
The joyful amrita of benefiting others brings delight.

With a resonant song of long life, the drums of summer thunder
    fill the world,
Arousing the play of myriad songs and dances of great bliss.
Flowers from a golden age fill the celestial path of the sky. . .
    Fill the celestial path of the sky.

Notes

With the ambience of a conversation among friends, this poem envisions a renaissance for Tibet. *Sala trees* are hardwood trees found in India and associated with the Buddha's birth in Lumbini, where his mother reached up to hold one of its branches, and also with his parinirvana in Kushinagara, where he passed away in a grove of sala trees. *The melting white moon of merit* is a blending of the white usually associated with merit (and all that is positive) and the pale light of the moon. The radiance of the moon is compared to the body of *the Buddha with all its signs*. These refer to the thirty-two major and the eighty minor marks of the Buddha's body that became manifest when he was enlightened. They include many different features: his eyes are clear and wide, his body looks as if it were polished, and the sign of the wheel marks both the palms of his hands and soles of his feet. *Bodhichitta*, the desire to attain full awakening for the sake of others, is here likened to a band of light on the horizon, an image for the dawning of bodhichitta within the expanse of one's own mind. Its appearance brings joy.

This blending of inner and outer images continues in the next stanza with *white flowers of snow* that elicit the glory of the mind. One practice of mahamudra is to look into the nature of each concept to find its pure nature. From this perspective, it is almost as if he is seeing the nature of each concept rising in the space of mind, like the clear and radiant crystal of a snowflake, falling for a while and then disappearing, the way a sound comes into the ear and fades away. This transposition between the senses, here the visual becoming aural, is not unusual; it is said that for the Buddha, sense experience is completely synesthetic: he sees sounds, hears images, and tastes touch. *The drums of summer* is a classic image for thunder and the rousing energy of a season when all is growing and pushing upward. The poem ends on an upbeat with a sense of trumpeting and celebration.

Equal Nature

From the space of the utterly pure extent of phenomena,
      deep and clear wisdom expands.
Mind's primordial nature is forever free of elaboration.
Not deluded by habitual mind or samsara and nirvana as they naturally
    arise,
To this expanse, the equal nature of all things, I bow.

Notes

This brief homage to the equal nature of all phenomena could also be used for meditation. The *pure extent of phenomena* is another way to signal emptiness. From this vast space, the wisdom intrinsic to it unfolds. *Habitual mind* is the collection of tendencies lodged in the all-basis consciousness; when the right conditions appear, the habits are activated into concepts that bring experience. This again leaves its traces in the all-basis consciousness, and so continues the cycle of samsara, understood here as the uninterrupted linking of one concept to another. Mind's primordial nature, however, is *free of* such *elaboration* or concepts. As you rest in this nature, *samsara and nirvana naturally arise.* Appearance and emptiness are inseparable; seeing this, you know that all phenomena have the same or *equal nature.* To *bow* to this nature is to recognize and appreciate it and, through humility, perhaps to move the ego aside long enough to make a true connection with it. This verse is another that the Karmapa gave to Lama Tenam to use in his practice of meditation and which he has generously shared.

An Aspiration Prayer in Verse

THE MELODIOUS SONG OF THE RIGHT-TURNING CONCH
THE MESSENGER WHO CALLS FORTH THE YOUTH
OF A GOLDEN AGE

Om Swasti.
Blazing with the full brilliance of the signs and marks, the supreme body
Liberates when seen and brings a festive joy never known before.
Through the virtue of creating such an offering to benefit beings
Just as a wish-fulfilling tree, an excellent action is accomplished.

This tree gives a fragrant aroma of Dharma as a companion for the
  golden age.
Total sincerity and pure virtue are its refreshing shade.
May it always be present as a calm repose to ease the mind.

The flawless sutra and mantra traditions are like refined gold.
Study and practice are perfect like the lustrous image of a thousand-
  spoked wheel.
Through the Buddha's teachings circling in the sky over the four
  continents,
May the sovereignty of the fearless Dharma remain supreme forever.

Here in this land of medicinal herbs and sala trees,
Ringed by snow mountains, these lotus flowers in white,
The Buddha's teachings have the radiant qualities of a nascent sun;
May the Dharma always be present in this sky of living beings' merit.

May all those connected to me throughout the three times—
Fathers and mothers, their eyes filled with pure love, rulers, their
  partners,
Ministers, and attendants, every level of society, winged creatures,
  wild beasts,
Every single one—be completely filled with the ambrosia of awakening.

Chenrezik, unique protector of the Land of Snow,
And masters holding the lineage of teachings free of bias:
Residing on your fearless lion thrones,
May you remain firm and invincible in the vajra realm.

These elegant sayings, like a garland of fresh lotus blooms,
Are embellished with the gems of sparkling verse.
May dakinis adorned with jeweled earrings
Accomplish their myriad activities in brilliant glory.

At the request of Lama Jigme, who has incomparable faith and samaya, this was written down by the one called He Who Holds the Bodhisattva's Crown, The Wise One Delighting the Noble Lady Who Grants Long Life [White Tara] and He Who Has Attained the Youth Bestowing Nectar of Immortality. A jester in king's clothes, he composed it having just turned fifteen. May all be auspicious. May it be a cause of virtue.

Notes

Tibetan verse often begins with a Sanskrit invocation, such as *Om swasti,* which means "may all be auspicious." The occasion of this verse was the offering of a beautiful statue. This is the *excellent action* spoken of in the first verse. In the beginning of the poem, the overarching image is that of a splendid and bountiful tree, a symbol of the Dharma, which continues to be the central subject of the next two verses. The *supreme body* in the second line of the poem refers to a nirmanakaya buddha or, more broadly, a tulku, one who has manifested in physical form and whom we can meet. The *sutra* tradition refers to the teachings presented the second time the Buddha turned the wheel of Dharma. They focus on compassion and emptiness, and on the wisdom that realizes emptiness and engages compassionately and skillfully in the world to help living beings. The *mantra* tradition is a synonym for the Vajrayana, the path of skillful means (often using mantra repetition) that swiftly leads to liberation.

A thousand-spoked wheel of special gold was offered to the Buddha before he gave his first teaching at the Deer Park in Sarnath, and so the wheel has become the symbol of the Buddhist teachings. It is found atop all Vajrayana monasteries flanked by two deer. Here the wheel is imaged as majestically spinning in the sky of this world. In the cosmology used for visualization practices, this universe is pictured as a disk with Mount Meru in the center and *four continents*, an island on each side, grouped around Mount Meru in the four directions. *Ringed by snow mountains* refers to Tibet, which is encircled by high mountains: the

Himalayas to the south and east, the Karakoram to the northeast, the Kunlun arching across the north, and many smaller ranges to the west, including the famous Amnye Machen.

The fifth verse makes the aspiration that all beings attain the *ambrosia of awakening*, the fruition of Dharma practice. *The three times* are the past, present, and future. Since Buddhists believe in past and future lives, the Karmapa prays for all those connected to him from the distant past into the far future. The *teachings free of bias* means that, in general, they are free of a prejudice that would value one religious tradition over another; specifically, they refer to the renaissance of Dharma that was the nonsectarian movement of nineteenth-century Tibet. The sixth prays that the Buddhist teachings remain. The *fearless lion thrones* refers to the four pairs of lions, emblems of courage, who hold up the thrones of enlightened beings. The *vajra realm* could be interpreted as emptiness or as the dharmakaya. The final verse aspires that the beauty of these verses will cause the beneficial activity of the teachings to flourish. *Dakinis* (a Sanskrit term whose meaning in Tibetan is "women who move through space") can be understood in many ways; here, they are presented as those who accomplish enlightened activities related to the Dharma. It is almost as if they have playfully picked up these gems of words and worn them as their ornaments.

The Moon of Bliss

Treasury of the mind, this young white moon is brilliant with
  the signs and marks.
An aural ambrosia thrums a sweet melody of the teachings that mature
  and free.
May a gladdening rain of nectar from this moon of great bliss
Bring auspicious splendor above, below, and upon this earth.

Notes

This richly textured prayer belongs to the tradition of Tashi prayers, or prayers
for auspiciousness, that come at the end of a practice as part of the dedication.
The effect is to make the universe glorious, spreading all the merit and goodness
everywhere. The *signs and marks* are those of the Buddha, and *the teachings that
mature and free* refers to the Vajrayana.

The Homage

Om Swasti.
In the expanse of great bliss—this clear sky—the moon face of a radiant
    clarity, limpid like the eye of a deer,
Shines forth its brilliance, enveloping the world in a gossamer of white.
In the splendid shrine of vast space that is ultimate reality,
A reverberating air delights with its dulcet tones.

A moonbeam lamp, the melodious fame of Lozang Drakpa spreads its
    light.
The luminous chariot of the sun comes through the glow of dusk
And leads to the throne of the Buddha's teachings, this lotus, fresh and
    open;
On its anthers, the liquid moonlight of his body, speech, and mind
    sways gently to and fro.

Like a waxing moon, the virtuous activity of a sincere intention
Melts happiness into the mind, its lambent rays making mind's nature
    known.
With a beautiful throat like a right-turning conch,
Saraswati, Melodious One of Powerful Speech, plays her lute here.

Written by the 17th in the lineage of the Karmapas, Ogyen Trinley Wangi
Dorje. May the stainless teachings of the Buddha expand like [the spokes
of] a wheel in all directions. January 21, 2001.

Notes

Praise of a locale is a typical theme of Tibetan poetry. Milarepa would often begin
his songs with a tribute to the area where he was practicing. This verse is a section of a longer tribute to Gyutö in prose. Bathed in liquid light, these stanzas
give luminous praise to Gyutö Ramoche University, where the Karmapa has been
in temporary residence since 2000. Belonging to the Dalai Lama's Gelukpa tra-

dition, Gyutö is located near Dharamsala. When the Karmapa first arrived, the main temple with its *shrine* hall was the only completed structure. *Lozang Drakpa* is a name of Je Tsongkhapa, the greatest scholar of the Gelukpa tradition. The first two lines of the last verse depict, with a clarity that only metaphor can bring, how altruistic motivation can transmute into the realization of mind's nature, taking us from words into experience. *Saraswati*, usually depicted playing a *lute*, represents culture and the arts. She is a deity to whom the Karmapa feels a special connection.

A Song of Blossoming Goodness to Celebrate the Youth's Golden Age

In Tibet, land of medicine, where snow falls and moonlight refreshes,
A golden age never fades, like the fullness of summer when a guest
  arrives.
Melodious good news brings joy to the three realms.
Always awake, the deer's eyes are wide open.

The two traditions of religion and politics are a necklace perfectly
  aligned;
The brilliance of its gold radiates happiness to everyone.
Since these two are respected by all beings and gods as well,
The sweet melody of virtue and excellence resounds throughout the
  earth.
The drumbeat of fine writing, deep and secret like a calm, refreshing
  melody,
Is a splendid friend of the Buddha's teachings that increase like the
  waxing moon.
All this you'll know the moment the baton of priceless study and
  reflection strikes.

Radiating their brilliant sunlight to all beings,
Lineage holders are free of all bias
And not covered by the dusky veils of wrongdoing.
Present above our crown and seated on a swaying lotus,
They play the victorious drum of true Dharma that never fades.
May the memory of these warriors without compare,
Who, for the sake of honesty and truth, risk even their treasured body
  or life,
Always burn within the heart and mind of our Tibetan people
Right here, where their fame has found a home.

Ah la la, in this most pleasant and refreshing land
May all that's auspicious and good be present
At this feast of the golden age, abundant in harvests.
Ah la la calls forth a sweet and auspicious song.
In the cool country, may there be great goodness and excellence;

Ah la la, may both of these and freedom, too, increase.
May all that is auspicious and good be present at this feast.
Ah la la calls forth a sweet, auspicious song.

As the pure white flower of good fortune opens smiling,
May this festival of goodness not fade but always appear.
Youth of the golden age are invited to come here.
May joy, delight, happiness, and good fortune flourish.
May the radiant smile of an awakened heart and the clear signs of
     realization
Always shine forth from the Potala's pure land.
May the music of good news to gladden Tibetans
Resound in that land like summertime thunder.
Let us create this festival of good fortune there.
May it not fade but always appear and abide.

At the request of Drongpa Tsultrim Luwang, who has the three kinds of
faith and who offered a white scarf along with representations of the
Buddha's body, speech, and mind, this was composed by Ogyen Trinley
during his flight from Tibet. May what is here prayed for be accomplished.

Notes

Envisioning a golden age, these are further verses that the Karmapa composed
while escaping from Tibet. They are more songlike than the others, with the
repeating "ah la la" and drums playing. The structure, words, and phrasing are
simpler than usual, making it easier to sing. The poem has something of a
medieval feel, almost as if King Arthur and his knights were transposed in time
and place, becoming dharmic warriors who have brought freedom and excellence to their land and now celebrate with a great feast where they are memorialized in song. This scene would also be an inspiring image to sustain the
Karmapa's party while they were escaping from Tibet.

The fullness of summer when a guest arrives points to the easier travel in Tibetan
summer months, when many guests arrive as do the summer rains and their thunder. *Lineage holders* refers to those within a particular tradition who have mastered
its meditative practices, conduct, and philosophy. On this basis, they have been
authorized by their lama to teach and transmit the lineage to their students. One's
teacher or a special deity is often visualized *above the crown* of one's head. The
Potala can refer to the pure land of Chenrezik, the embodiment of compassion,
or to the Dalai Lama's residence in Lhasa. In the colophon, the *three kinds of faith*

are trusting faith (in the teachings of karma with its linkage of cause and effect and in the truths of suffering and its origin), longing faith (for full awakening), and inspired faith (in the Buddha, Dharma, and Sangha).

The Song of Natural Awareness

Om Swasti Jayentu.
Primordially pure, the expanse of all phenomena is great bliss.
All signs of elaboration stilled, it is spontaneously present.
In that glad realm, where the joyous ambrosia of the three vehicles
  is found,
May the sun of naturally arising awareness be victorious.

Notes

This verse begins with a description of the nature of mind and ends with an aspiration to realize it. *Om Swasti Jayentu* is an invocation meaning "may all be auspicious, and may the good be victorious." *Primordially pure* means that from time beyond time, the nature of the mind has never been tainted or corrupted by anything at all. *The expanse of all phenomena* refers to the dharmadhatu. *Great bliss* is a transcendent joy; what makes it great, or beyond this world, is its union with emptiness. Here, bliss and emptiness are realized as inseparable. *Signs of elaboration* are concepts or the actions based on them. With this mental interference stilled, the nature of mind is *spontaneously present*; there is no need to do anything or make up anything: it simply, naturally arises as what it is. The *three vehicles* (*yanas* in Sanskrit) refer to the three major traditions of Buddhism: the Hinayana, or the foundational vehicle, which is the earliest one and found mostly in Sri Lanka, Thailand, and Burma; the Mahayana, or great vehicle, which came next in time and is found mostly in China and Japan; and the Vajrayana, the diamond or vajra vehicle, which was the last to develop and is found mostly in Tibet. The Buddhism of Tibet combines all three vehicles in the following way: the Hinayana is followed in terms of ordination and vows; the Mahayana is followed for its teachings on emptiness and compassion and for its Middle Way philosophy; and the Vajrayana is followed for its myriad and swift methods of practice. *Awareness* is another way of expressing the clear and knowing aspect of mind, here imaged as the sun.

A Long-life Prayer for the Embodiment of Chenrezik, Perfect Guide for Samsara and Nirvana [His Holiness the Dalai Lama]

SWEET DEW FROM THE WISH-FULFILLING TREE OF IMMORTALITY

The nature of coemergent awareness is utterly pure from time
    beyond time;
The expanse of wisdom, never departing or returning, is present at
    the ground.
A vast dimension imbued with profound and clear wisdom,
You who made manifest this dharmakaya, may you live long.

Within awareness-emptiness, perfectly pure and free of elaboration,
You are the graceful play of great bliss and emptiness in unity.
Sambhogakaya continually pervaded by the five certainties,
Vajradhara, powerful and glorious one, may you live long.

Not moving from the space of the dharmadhatu, profound and
    peaceful,
This perfectly pure nirmanakaya, from beautiful clouds of emanations
Sends down a joyous rain of Dharma in three sequential stages.
Supreme guide for those above, below, and on the earth, may you
    live long.

The wisdom of the natural state, primordially pure and deeply clear,
Spontaneously arises as the true forms of the vajra rainbow body.
In the expanse of the youthful vase body, the phenomena of samsara and
    nirvana come to an end.
Samantabhadra, vajra of the mind, may you live long.

In the avadhuti's expanse, great emptiness as the total purity of
    the nadis,
Is the splendor of accomplishment—the chakras of life-force prana,
The letters, and the superb bindu of great bliss.
Endowed with all of these supreme aspects, may you live long.

Possessing the root of victory over the five bases
And with the fine petals of the nature of the three imputed bases,
You play with the fruition that sees all phenomena as truly mind.
Wish-fulfilling tree of the timeless Madhyamaka, may you live long.

From the expanse of radiant clarity, this pure prana mind in the
    avadhuti
Arises inseparable from the three kayas, the form bodies with the major
    and minor marks.
Abiding in the essential nature, which is permanent, stable, and
    unconditioned,
On the immutable lion throne, may you live long.

In that year on a throne like an opened flower, for the three types of
    beings,
The smiling rays of moonlight nectar that is your bodhichitta
Are victorious in battle with the shadows of the dark side.
Resting in your three secrets on the Dharma throne, may you live long.

Through the unexcelled truth bestowed by the Three Jewels
And the vast interdependence arising from the dharmata,
May the excellent aspirations I have put into words be swiftly
    accomplished
And may the three worlds be beautiful in auspicious glory.

Soon after he escaped to the noble land of Dharma, while the sun
wandered over a meadow of the eastern mountain, on January 14, 2000,
this supplication was made one-pointedly by an ordinary Tibetan called
Tendzin Kunkhyab Wangi Dorje, one fortunate to take respite in the
cooling shadow of His Holiness's unexcelled bodhichitta. Mangalam.

Notes

This long-life prayer for the Dalai Lama, a realized master, great scholar, and
monk, is replete with references to advanced meditation practice and philosophy
and to the special conduct of the ordained sangha, and therefore, it may be difficult for those new to Buddhism to understand. The first three verses focus in
sequence on the Dalai Lama as the embodiment of the three kayas. In the first
one, the Dalai Lama is praised as one who has made manifest, or fully realized,
the dharmakaya. This is described by a series of phrases that are basically

synonyms but with slightly different perspectives. *The nature of coemergent awareness* has the meaning that each phenomenon arises from emptiness, and yet, while appearing it has no reified or inherent nature. Awareness arises simultaneously with its empty nature; the two are never separate. This nature has always, *from time beyond time*, been pure and *present*. The Sanskrit *kaya*, usually translated as "body," here takes on the meaning of *dimension*, clearly indicating that it is the *vast*, ultimate reality of mind that is intended.

The second verse addresses the Dalai Lama as *Vajradhara* (Holder of the Vajra), the ultimate deity manifesting on the sambhogakaya level. Often translated as the "enjoyment body," the sambhogakaya is here described as the *graceful play of great bliss and emptiness*. It is *pervaded by the five certainties* of time, place, teacher, teachings, and retinue, which indicate the particular qualities of a teaching given on this exalted level, not available to ordinary beings. The third verse speaks of the Dalai Lama as the nirmanakaya, or an emanated body, which remains anchored in *the space of the dharmadhatu*, while appearing as a supreme guide for all beings. The *three sequential stages* refer to the three successive times the Buddha turned the wheel of Dharma.

The fourth verse addresses the Dalai Lama as *Samantabhadra* (*Kun tu bzang po*, the All-Good), the emblem of ultimate reality, the primordially pure body in the Nyingma tradition. The terminology and concepts of this verse reflect the dzogchen, or Great Completion, teachings of this tradition, pointing to the close relationship of the Dalai Lama to great Nyingma teachers, among them Dudjom Rinpoche and Dilgo Khyentse Rinpoche. *Primordially pure* refers to the advanced stage of dzogchen practice called "cutting through," and *deeply clear* refers to the stage called "leap over." The *rainbow body* is the manifestation of the highest attainment of dzogchen practitioners. When their physical bodies are dissolved into purity, after death they gradually dissolve until only nails and hair are left behind. With the rainbow body of great transformation, the physical body is transformed into a body of subtle light, which remains for as long as living beings need their help.[233] *The youthful vase body* is a synonym for Samantabhadra and focuses on the pristine awareness that is radiant within this ultimate body as light within a crystal. *The phenomena of samsara and nirvana come to an end* refers to the highest realization, the fourth appearance or vision where all phenomena have dissolved back into their ultimate nature.

The fifth verse addresses the Dalai Lama as a great yogic practitioner. It speaks of the vajra or subtle body, made of *nadis* (channels), *prana* (winds), and *bindu* (spheres). The *avadhuti* is the central one of three main channels, and the *letters* are seed syllables, giving rise to various manifestations. The first two lines of the sixth verse address the Dalai Lama as the perfect monk, who has kept his vows in relation to the *five bases*, which are five types of action to be avoided. The *three imputed bases* refer to three commitments kept by the ordained sangha to engage in certain rituals and keep the summer retreat.[234] The next two lines refer to the two Mahayana schools of philosophy, the Mind Only School that *sees all phenomena as truly mind*, and the ultimate view of the *Madhyamaka* or Middle Way school.

The seventh verse reflects the Shentong Madhyamaka view, whose name—literally, "empty of other"— indicates that the pure nature of the mind is empty of what is other to it—the temporary flaws or blockages produced by a confused mind. This philosophy emphasizes the radiant and clear aspect of mind and complements the emphasis on the empty aspect of mind in the Rangtong Madhyamaka view, whose name—literally, empty of self—indicates that the nature of mind is empty in and of itself. The Shentong view also speaks extensively of buddha nature, the true nature of mind (or basic goodness), that is found in every living being.

Within the Shentong school there are different views, and one of them is reflected in the first line of the verse: *prana mind in the avadhuti* reflects the writings of the great scholar and practitioner Dölpopa Sherab Gyaltsen, who, following his understanding of the Kalachakra teachings, stated that realization comes about only when the prana enters the central channel. The second line reflects the Shentong view that the three kayas are spontaneously present at the time of realization, refuting a Rangtong position stating the form kayas are created during the path of practice. Tibet's most famous poet and yogi, Milarepa, sings, "The three kayas inseparable, how wondrous!"[235] This reflects the Shentong view where all three kayas are seen to be spontaneously present and not created. The third line refers to the mind's nature as *permanent, stable, and unconditioned*, reflecting the view of Maitreya's *Supreme Continuum*, a main source for Shentong, wherein the dharmakaya is described as "permanent, stable, peaceful, and immutable."[236] It is important to note that here "permanent" does not have its usual meaning, but refers to a permanent that is beyond the permanent posited in a dualistic framework of permanent and impermanent. It transcends this dualistic thinking and points beyond to the essential qualities of mind, which are inseparable from their empty nature.

The eighth verse begins *In that year*, referring to a prediction the Karmapa has made that around 2003 something significant will happen in relation to Tibet. The *three types of beings* are those of three levels, of greater, average, and lesser ability, whom the Dalai Lama will benefit. The *three secrets* are the enlightened body, speech, and mind. The last verse is an aspiration for the realization of all that has been prayed for. The name Tendzin Kunkhyab Wangi Dorje in the colophon was given to the Karmapa by the Dalai Lama along with his prayer for the Karmapa's long life. *Mangalam* is a Sanskrit word meaning "may all be auspicious."

A Radiant Smile of Spontaneous Confidence

A PRAYER FOR THE LONG LIFE OF PEMA DÖNYÖ DRUPA, THE PROTECTOR MAITREYA IN HUMAN FORM

Om Swasti. Buddha nature is the expanse of bliss, infinite and
   unchanging.
The major and minor marks are perfect like the pristine rim of
   Brahma's wheel.
You who know rituals to bring eternal happiness, noble and immortal
   lady,
Mother of the Victorious Ones, grant that all be auspicious.

The high and mighty of this world along with the gods
Bow down their heads to your lotus feet.
You are a treasury, a mandala adorned with the three secrets and
   the three kayas.
Protector Maitreya, Pema Dönyö, please live long.

Through a clear and luminous image of what is invariably good,
You give a vision of the path to all beings blinded by prejudice.
Accomplishing millions of beneficial actions,
You who bring the sunlight to beings, please live long.

Through generating bodhichitta and being immersed in it for
   countless eons,
You have fully gathered the two accumulations, infinite and precious
   by nature.
Embraced by the beauty of youth and wearing robes of saffron hue,
Powerful Vajradhara, you who keep the three vows, please live long.

Like a dark cave facing north, people have the faults of the five
   degenerations,
Yet they enter into the clear light of the sun's rays, shining from the orb
Of your perfect compassion, opening lotuses petal by petal.
You who radiate enlightened activity in a hundred directions, please
   live long.

The field of disciples' minds, sown with hope, is saturated
With a rain of blessing that fills their wishes and clears away pain.
Embodying myriad, inconceivable qualities,
Master and genuine guide, please live long.

Through the power of the blessing of ultimate truth, the eternal
    dharmadhatu,
And the power of relative truth, unceasing dependent arising,
May you live stable and unchanging for hundreds of eons.
May your activity of purifying and liberating never subside and always
    flourish.

With a sincere and one-pointed mind, this was written by Ogyen Trinley
Dorje, an inferior disciple of the Protector [Situ Rinpoche]. As prayed for
here, may all these hopes be gathered together and fulfilled as I have
wished. (Translated with the kind assistance of Khenpo Tashi Gyaltsen,
2001.)

Notes

This is a prayer for the long life of Tai Situ Rinpoche, who, together with Gyaltsap Rinpoche, is the main teacher of the Karmapa. Situ Rinpoche is considered
an emanation of *Maitreya*, the fifth and next Buddha, who waits to take rebirth
in the realm of Tushita as Shakyamuni did before him. It was to Situ Rinpoche
that the previous Karmapa gave his Last Testament, or letter of prediction. In Situ
Rinpoche's name, *Pema Dönyö Drupa*, Pema (Lotus) connects him with Guru
Rinpoche (Padmasambhava, the Lotus Born) and Dönyö relates him to the buddha Dönyö Drupa (Amoghasiddhi), who, like the Karmapa, is especially connected with enlightened activity.

Once again, the first verse invokes the ultimate, and here it is in the form of
the buddha nature, which the Shentong tradition teaches to be present within
each individual. The deity invoked is White Tara, who is considered a female
buddha and especially known for granting long life (*immortal lady*). *The pristine
rim of Brahma's wheel* makes a double allusion: (1) to Brahma, the god of creation
in Hindu theology, who gave a thousand-spoked wheel to the Buddha after his
full awakening, and by extension, this points to Tara as an enlightened buddha;
and (2) in the actual longevity practice of White Tara, a pristine wheel is imagined within one's heart. White Tara is also addressed as Prajnaparamita or transcendent wisdom, which is given female form as the *Mother of the Victorious
Ones*. It is from the depths of this wisdom that buddhas come forth.

The second verse envisions Situ Rinpoche as a rich mandala of the *three secrets* and *the three kayas*. The third verse speaks of him as an inspiring and compassionate teacher. In the fourth, he is called *Vajradhara*, the ultimate deity. It is traditionally taught that the best way to relate to one's lama is to see him or her as Vajradhara. Situ Rinpoche is also wearing the *robes of saffron hue* of a monk, who keeps *the three vows* of the Foundational Vehicle (the vows of individual liberation), the Mahayana (the vows of a bodhisattva), and the Vajrayana (the samaya vows with one's teacher). The fifth verse speaks of the beneficial effect of his compassion on people, who have *the faults of the five degenerations*, (of life span, the times, view, physical form, and afflictions). The sixth speaks of his qualities, and the seventh begins with a succinct statement of the two truths, the *ultimate* as the expanse of all phenomena, and the *relative* as the gathering of causes and conditions that bring about the dependent arising of all phenomena. It ends with a final prayer for his long life and the success of his *activity of purifying* obscurations *and liberating* beings into the realization of their own buddha nature.

The fourteen-year-old Karmapa on top of the monastery at Tsurphu in mid-1999, several months before his escape.

Photographer unknown

On the exploratory trip to Mustang in late 1999, Lama Tsultrim with his horse in front of Khuyug Monastery, Tibet.

Photo: courtesy of Lama Tsultrim

From this same trip, Lama Pema and Lama Tsultrim on the road from Khuyug Monastery to the first army camp, where the escaping party will pass.

Photo: courtesy of Lama Tsultrim

The road between the two army camps near the southern border of Tibet.

Photo: courtesy of Lama Tsultrim

Near Zangzang, Tibet, during the escape. In front of the jeep from left to right: Dargye, Drubngak, the Karmapa, Lama Tsewang, and Tsewang Tashi. Without changing into ordinary clothes, the Karmapa would not have been able to escape.

Photo: Lama Tsultrim

Riding horseback on the trail from Lo Monthang to Chele during the escape.
From left to right: horse assistant, the Karmapa, Tsering Tashi, Lama Tsultrim, and
another horse assistant.

Photo: Dargye

The Karmapa's sister, Ngödrup Pelzom, who had left Tibet before his escape, at a
gathering in Gyutö Ramoche University.

Photo: Michele Martin

At the end of his escape, the Karmapa's first meeting with the Dalai Lama on the morning of January 5, 2000. Only the Karmapa could change into robes. Left to right: Lama Tsultrim, Nenang Lama, the Karmapa, the Dalai Lama, Tsimpön Drubngak, and Ngödrup Pelzom.

Photo: courtesy of Lama Tsultrim

At Gyutö Ramoche University, all those who escaped with the Karmapa. Left to right: Tsewang Tashi, Nenang Lama, Tsimpön Drubngak, the Karmapa, Lama Tsultrim, Dargye.

Photo: Angus McDonald

The Dalai Lama and the Karmapa

Photographer unknown

The Karmapa in the shrine hall of Gyutö Ramoche University.

Photo: courtesy of Tashi Gawa

Situ Rinpoche, one of the Karmapa's root lamas. Situ Rinpoche lives in northern India at his monastery, Sherab Ling.

Photo: courtesy of Lama Tenam

Gyaltsap Rinpoche, also a root lama of the Karmapa. Gyaltsap Rinpoche lives in his monastery, Ralang, in Sikkim, India.

Photographer unknown

Thrangu Rinpoche, tutor to the Karmapa, on retreat in the Himalayas.

Photo: Michele Martin

Khenpo Tsultrim Gyamtso, also a teacher of the Karmapa, meditating in the Rocky Mountains.

Photo: Blair Hansen

The Karmapa in the shrine hall at Gyutö Ramoche University, where he gives talks and celebrates major events.

Photo: Angus McDonald

Gyütö Ramoche University near Dharamsala, temporary residence of the Karmapa.

Photo: Michele Martin

Situ Rinpoche offers an empowerment to the Karmapa.

Photo: Michele Martin

At his birthday celebration in 2002, the Karmapa receives a statue during a ceremony for his long life.

Photo: Angus McDonald

The Karmapa's main seat in Rumtek, Sikkim, India.

Photo: Scott Unterberg

The Karmapa performing a purification ritutal before an Amitayus Empowerment at the Stupa in Bodghaya,India, December 29, 2001

Photo: Tom Schmidt

The Karmapa visiting Thrangu Rinpoche's Vajra Vidya Institute, March, 2001.

Photo: Scott Unterberg

The Karmapa in his quarters on the top floor of Gyutö Ramoche University.

Photo: Angus McDonald

The Karmapa leaving Gyutö Ramoche University for Dharamsala in June 2002.
Photo: Michele Martin

Calligraphy by the Karmapa of the Tibetan for Karmapa khyenno, "Karmapa, think of me."

The Peaceful and Calming Victory Flag, a vision of the sixteenth Karmapa.

In this drawing by the Karmapa, the Tibetan letters nga mong *mean "camel."*

In this drawing by the Karmapa, the Tibetan words sel nang *mean "clear appearance."*

The Karmapa and the Dalai Lama.

Photographer unknown

The Karmapa in Ladakh, fall 2001.

Photographer unknown

A Long-life Prayer for the Glorious Lama, Scholar, and Siddha Thrangu Tulku, Karma Lodrö Lungrik Mawe Senge

THE YOUTHFUL VITALITY OF IMMORTAL NECTAR

Om Swasti Dziwentu.
The dharmakaya, free of elaborations, is always stable and never
   destroyed.
Your speech is the melody of the nada, the invincible vajra.
With the enlightened mind that sees all possible phenomena,
Amitayus, perfect guide, you accomplish all goodness.

From the golden age arose a new mansion of clouds poised in the depth
   of space,
Where your signs and marks arose as a clear and radiant mountain,
Creating festive occasions for beings to increase their merit.
May you remain for the longest time.

Your flawless knowledge, like a blooming, full lotus,
Suffuses your writings with great love and compassion.
Through your limitless abilities, you satisfy a multitude of beings
   seeking liberation.
Guide of beings, may your life be long.

Through explaining the Dharma, you release beings
   from the tangled net of ignorance and confusion.
In debate, you defeat the opponent's bold stance.
By their very nature, your writings carry away our minds with joy.
You of genuine and powerful speech, may your life be long.

Rising from the jeweled ocean of your immeasurable merit,
The white moon, clear mandala of your wisdom,
Pours forth a nectar that is the light of your activity.
Lion of speech, teaching scripture and reasoning, may your life be long.

From churning an ocean of milk with these good intentions,
A white lotus garland, these words of aspiration, comes to the surface.
Protector, through the merit of offering this to all the buddhas and
bodhisattvas,
May the benefit of your life last for hundreds of eons.

Glorious Lama, through the power of the truth of the Victorious One,
Amitayus,
And the power of a good connection with this sincere, pure intention,
May your life remain stable until the end of the world.
May the vitality of perfect Dharma, wealth, enjoyment, and liberation
flourish.

This [prayer] was requested by the one responsible for Nenang Monastery, Lama Tsewang Tashi, who offered representations of the Buddha's body, speech, and mind, and was written by the seventeenth Karmapa Ogyen Trinley Dorje during a fine waxing moon of Saga Dawa. Shubam.May it be a cause for virtue.

Notes

This is a long-life prayer composed by the Karmapa for his tutor, Thrangu Rinpoche, who is also an incarnate lama. *Om Swasti Dziwentu* is an aspiration that what is excellent and good continue and be sustained.The *melody of the nada* is a metaphor to describe very refined and subtle speech. As the tip of the bindu (sphere) in visualization practice, the nada is the last reference point before everything becomes emptiness. It is the most subtle thing we can imagine. *Amitayus* is another of the deities associated with long life, forming a triad with two other deities of long life, White Tara and Ushnisha-Vijaya. He is invoked here to grant long life to Thrangu Rinpoche.

The first two lines of the second verse refer to Thrangu Rinpoche's manifestation as a tulku, arising as a buddha impressive as a *mountain* and sheltered in a cloud mansion *poised in the depth of space.* The next two verses praise him as a scholar and reference the three activities of the learned ones, *writing, explaining,* and *debate.* The fifth verse continues this theme, addressing Thrangu Rinpoche as a *lion of speech* and alluding to Manjushri, the deity of wisdom.

The sixth verse begins with a reference to the Karmapa's composition of this prayer. *Churning an ocean of milk* comes from the Hindu creation legends, which were often adopted into Buddhism. In brief, the legend relates that the gods and demigods churned the ocean to find its treasures, mainly seeking amrita, the nectar of immortality. As they churned the ocean, it turned into milk and then clarified butter. Last to emerge from the ocean was the physician of the gods, who carried a vase of amrita. This image is entirely appropriate in a long-life prayer, and the Karmapa has given it his own turn, imagining that the words of this aspiration, too, have emerged from the swirling primal ocean like whorls of lotus petals, white as milk and strung as the lines of his poem. The last verse invokes *Amitayus* to bless Thrangu Rinpoche with long life, which would bring to others the benefits of the *Dharma, wealth, enjoyment,* and, ultimately, *liberation.*

In Commemoration

THE CLEAR VOICE OF THE CONCH

Doctor, dear friend within my heart,
You are a healer of great diligence and refinement,
A doctor of great fame,
A physician who left a great legacy.

Doctor, dear friend within my heart,
As the warmth and essence of your mother
Placed you newly in this world with its winding ways,
Did you not see and hear the array of wonders on this planet?
How vast. How deep and profound. How myriad!

Doctor, dear friend within my heart,
During this life, a vessel of mist,
Did you not experience the many sounds of joy and pain
And tread with measured step a path among the people?

Doctor, dear friend within my heart,
Counting each bead of the years,
You did not waste this life's thread.
Medical wisdom—vast, profound, long-lasting, and beneficial—
Is an ocean of amrita.
Your hand, steady and constant, took up the ladle of discipline.
Are you not the great hero who eagerly drank, never satisfied?

Doctor, dear friend within my heart,
On the wings of discernment, you flew
Higher and higher into the expanse of knowledge,
Your fame increasing like the secret drum of summer thunder;
At last, wasn't the blue sky, heart of the gods' daughter, almost
    broken apart?

Doctor, dear friend within my heart,
Skilled in vast knowledge of medical care,
You were the field producing a new growth of learning

To nurture generations of doctors to come.
From you flowed a deep river of healing lore.

Doctor, dear friend within my heart,
You were flawless, free of defilement.
Your footprints of moonlight, pure and white,
Came in a great wave, leaving their trail on the hard, solid stone.
Who could ever conceal the trace of your steps?

Composed by the seventeenth in the succession of Karmapas, Ogyen
Drodul Trinley Wangi Dorje, at Gyutö Ramoche University and offered
to His Holiness the Dalai Lama's physician, Tendzin Chödrak, April 25,
2002.

Notes

In a simple and touching way, this poem is an outpouring of love to commemorate the great healer, Tendzin Chödrak, who passed away in early 2002. It traces his life from birth into the wonders of this world through to the joys and pains he saw as he walked along life's path. Mala beads, used to count mantra practice, are imaged as the years passing along the thread of his life, while he constantly worked to benefit others and constantly increased his knowledge, which grew so vast the sky could hardly contain it. And as all great men, he passed his knowledge on to the new generation so that it might continue to help others. He will be remembered—his *footprints of moonlight* have left their mark.

The Excellent Tree, Free of Death and Sorrow

A PRAYER FOR THE LONGEVITY OF THE VICTORIOUS FATHER
AND SONS OF THE GLORIOUS KARMA KAGYU

Om swasti.
Powerful One, who continues the deeds that are an ocean of activity
Of the kayas and wisdom belonging to infinite buddhas,
Knower of past, present, and future, Gyalwang Karmapa,
May your life be long and your activity flourish.

As Amitabha, protector of the joyous realm,
Through the play of wondrous emanations arising from your intention,
Lord of the dance, you are skilled in upholding the banner of the
    teachings.
I bow to the peerless line of your previous incarnations.

From time beyond time, not vanquished by existence or peace,
You attained the vajra body of union, yet appear as one on the pure
    levels.
Situpa, display of the Victorious One, great Maitreya,
May your life be long and your activity flourish.

Bestowing brilliant treasuries of wisdom to defeat the darkness of
    ignorance,
The actual appearance of Manjushri, you are a vast life-tree of the
    teachings.
Jamgön Lama, protector for these degenerate times,
May your life be long and your activity flourish.

Creative play of the great sphere, indestructible and beyond time,
As the Lord of Secrets, you are the vajra dancer of bliss and emptiness.
Goshir Gyaltsap, appearing in forms able to tame everyone,
May your life be long and your activity flourish.

Subduing with brilliance all that appears and master of the four
    elements,
You are a chakravartin of activity, endowed with the vajra body.

Glorious, great Pawo, the actual appearance of the Lotus Born,
May your life be long and your activity flourish.

You are the magical display of the wisdom of Amitayus,
Your expertise in method is deep and vast; your glorious activity,
     spontaneous and complete.
Treho Tulku, your spreading roots bring forth joy and benefit.
May your life be long and your activity flourish.

Through the power of supplicating with unchanging respect,
May the blessings of the lamas enter my mind;
May I be able to mirror all the vast qualities
Reflected in the deeds of their body, speech, and mind.

Gate to the source of every perfect joy and benefit,
May the teachings of the Buddha endure a long time.
May all the communities who hold the teachings and explain and
     practice them
Flourish through engaging in the ten Dharma activities.

May I and all those who are connected to them,
From now until the youth of great joy's heart is mature,
Be unaffected by the faults of obstacles or harm;
May all dharmic intentions of the fortunate ones be spontaneously
     fulfilled.

All samsara's joys and riches resemble last night's dream.
Once you have seen them to be trivial and futile,
With all doubts settled, take up the genuine Dharma.
Practice with diligence and without any pretense.

Resolve that your mind is the Buddha; know that mind itself
Is clarity and emptiness, spontaneous and by nature free;
Beyond hope and fear of samsara or nirvana,
May you gain certainty that you are fully awakened and free.

This is a brief supplication for the long life and flourishing activity of the
father and sons, genuine objects of offering for gods and humans.
Reminding myself of their kindness and at the urging of many who strive
to benefit others, the one to whom has come the blessing of the name

Buddha Karmapa, the seventeenth, Ogyen Trinley Palden Wangi Dorje, wrote down this supplication during the nineteenth Great Kagyu Sangha Prayer Festival in Bodh Gaya [December 23-29, 2001], supreme place where the Tathagata attained complete and perfect awakening. May it be a cause for the blessing of the lamas to enter the mindstream of every living being.

Notes

This long-life prayer is for the Karmapa and the six great masters who are traditionally considered the main incarnate lamas of the Karma Kagyu tradition. The *father* is the *Gyalwang Karmapa* of the first verse, and each of the following six verses is devoted to one of his heart sons, summarizing their particular qualities or achievements and identifying the deity of whom they are considered an emanation. Of the last five verses, three are aspirations and two are Dharma teachings.

The first verse speaks of the Karmapa, who is considered an embodiment of all the buddhas' *activity*. *Knower of the past, present, and future* refers to the first Karmapa, Dusum Khyenpa, "Knower of the Three Times." The second verse describes Shamar Rinpoche's previous incarnations as emanations of *Amitabha*, the Buddha of the *joyous realm*, or Sukhavati. The emanations of tulkus are said to come from their pure intention to benefit beings. *Lord of the dance* is a traditional epithet of the Shamar incarnations. The third verse is devoted to *Situpa*, or Tai Situ Rinpoche, who is the *display* or emanation of *Maitreya*, the future Buddha. *Not vanquished by existence or peace* means that he is not caught by the attractions of samsara nor submerged in the static peace of nirvana. Attaining the *vajra body of union* is a synonym for full awakening, in which bliss and emptiness are realized to be an inseparable unity. Even though he has reached this great attainment, Situ Rinpoche continues to manifest for the benefit of beings, appearing as a highly developed bodhisattva. The *pure levels* refer to the eighth to tenth levels of bodhisattvas, when all the afflictions have been overcome and only the cognitive obscurations remain.

The fourth verse is dedicated to *Jamgön Lama*, Jamgön Kongtrul Rinpoche, who is an emanation or *actual appearance of Manjushri*, the embodiment of wisdom. The first Jamgön Kongtrul, Lodrö Thaye, is famous for his Five *Treasuries*, which preserve the *wisdom* of all the Tibetan traditions, their important core instructions, the empowerments and main ritual practices of the Kagyu and Nyingma traditions, plus Lodrö Thaye's own writings on an impressive range of topics. *Life-tree* refers to the axis of a stupa or a statue, functioning as its main support; it was an epithet often applied to Lodrö Thaye, indicating his central role in sustaining the Dharma. He was especially important in the nonsectarian movement of nineteenth-century Tibet.

The fifth verse speaks of *Goshir Gyaltsap* Rinpoche, who is considered an emanation of the *Lord of Secrets*, an epithet of Vajrapani, who is the holder of the Secret Mantrayana or Vajrayana teachings. Gyaltsap Rinpoche is renowned as a practitioner in this tradition. Especially in the context of mahamudra and dzogchen, or mahasandhi, teachings, *the great sphere* is a synonym for the primordial and enduring nature of mind, and *creative play* is the inventive energy, the unlimited display of that nature. Gyaltsap Rinpoche is praised as the *dancer of bliss and emptiness*, the ultimate as movement, which allows him to manifest in whatever way is needed to benefit his disciples.

The sixth verse is devoted to *Pawo* Rinpoche, considered an emanation of Padmasambhava, *the Lotus Born*, another name for Guru Rinpoche. His charisma is so radiant that he conquers all and masters *the four elements* of earth, water, fire, and air. *Chakravartin* is a term adopted from Indian mythology and refers to a world ruler. Within Buddhism, the chakravartins are bodhisattvas who have accumulated tremendous merit and use their power to promote the well-being of their subjects and to make the Dharma more widely available.

The seventh verse centers on *Treho Tulku*, who is considered an emanation or *magical display* of Amitayus, one of the three deities connected with long life. *Method* refers to the path of method, the array of powerful, precise, and swift skillful means available in the Vajrayana to lead practitioners into full awakening. In particular, the term covers the generation stage of visualization practice, the practices related to the subtle body in the completion stage, and, finally, the advanced practices of the Six Yogas of Naropa. The complementary practices are the path of liberation, which basically refers to mahamudra. *Activity* that is *spontaneous* is uncontrived, arising straight from the nature of mind. This verse concludes the section of the prayer focused on the father and six sons.

The eighth, ninth, and tenth verses are traditional aspirations to receive the *blessings of the lamas,* for the teachings to *endure,* and for the Buddhist communities to flourish through practicing the *ten Dharma activities,* which include listening to the Dharma, reading Dharma texts, making offerings, memorizing texts, meditating, and so forth.[237] The tenth verse ends with a prayer that until our realization of bliss-emptiness *matures,* we will be free of *obstacles* and *harm* along the path and that our positive *intentions* will be fulfilled.

The last two verses are beautifully condensed teachings on the ephemeral quality of all that attracts us to *samsara;* it is no more real than a *dream* gone by. Seeing how senseless and *futile* it is to be caught up in the mundane, we are encouraged to resolve our doubts and practice simply and wholeheartedly. Seeing that our *mind* and the mind of *the Buddha* are not different, we come to the

Shentong understanding of mind's nature: its aspects of *clarity and emptiness* are inseparable; it is *spontaneously* present and therefore unfabricated; and it is naturally *free*. When this liberation arrives, there is no hope of attaining nirvana and no fear of falling into samsara, because their equal nature has been realized. The Karmapa's parting wish is that we *gain the certainty* of having realized all this; in other words, that we attain full awakening.

Part IV

The History of the Karmapas

Introduction to the
History of the Karmapas

IN THE BUDDHISM OF TIBET, one of the functions of history is to trace a lineage to other times (sometimes many eons into the past or future) and to other places (including pure lands and billions of other universes) in order to make connections with buddhas or bodhisattvas, to yidam deities or siddhas. This linking to another time and space helps to define the lineage, to give it legitimacy, and to record the sources of its philosophy and practice. Specific dates are not so important as who the people were, how they were, and what they did or taught. Traditional accounts take for granted life spans of several hundred years, travel to other universes, higher modes of perception such as precognition, and also flying beings, both human and not—ideas that we usually associate with myths, fairy tales, and science fiction.

A classic biography in Tibet is called *namthar*, "complete liberation," which chronicles the events of a lama's life that lead to realization and the ensuing activity to benefit others. For this reason, namthars are sometimes called "spiritual biographies." They have a hagiographic tendency, presenting the illustrious lives of masters and the teachings of a tradition. Often their main figure seems larger than life, which can be a way of bringing in the larger dimensions of mind that they inhabited.

The following narrative of the Karmapas' lives incorporates the writing of Tendzin Namgyal, a scholar and practitioner, especially well-versed in the histories of the Karmapas. This portrayal follows in the tradition of namthars, citing the prophecies about the Karmapa and the texts that have spoken of him, his activity, and lineage.[238] Focusing on the first Karmapa, it shows how the tradition of tulkus began with the second Karmapa and then explains two of the particular attributes of the Karmapa, the Black Crown and the Last Testament. The next section, written by Dzogchen Ponlop Rinpoche, consists of brief histories of each of the previous sixteen Karmapas.[239] These serve as a general reference, and also as a setting for the story of the seventeenth Karmapa, showing how the pattern of his life relates to that of his predecessors. The final section presents three songs of the sixteenth Karmapa, included here with the histories as they are prophetic of what would happen decades later—history seen from its future.

Concluding with the history and poetry of the sixteenth Karmapa, this last section brings the book full circle to its beginning and the telling of how the sixteenth Karmapa gave to Situ Rinpoche the Last Testament, predicting his next incarnation, Ogyen Trinley Dorje.

A Traditional Narrative of the Karmapas

THE KARMAPA is known as the one who performs the enlightened activities of all the buddhas of the past, present, and future. His lineage of incarnations extends back to twelfth-century Tibet and the first Karmapa, who originated the tradition of recognizing incarnate lamas. Many ancient texts speak of the Karmapas. Traditionally, within his own Karma Kagyu lineage, several prophecies about him are cited.

From *The King of Samadhi Sutra (Samadhiraja Sutra)*:

> The teachings will come to the land of the red-faced,
> The ones to be tamed by Chenrezik.
> The Bodhisattva Lion's Roar (Simhanada)
> Will appear as the Karmapa.
> He will tame beings through his mastery of samadhi,
> Bringing into bliss those who see, hear, touch, or remember him.[240]

From *The Descent into Lanka Sutra* (*Lankavatara Sutra*):

> Wearing the robes of a monk and a black crown,
> He will benefit beings without interruption
> For as long as the teachings of one thousand buddhas last.[241]

From *The Tantra of the Blazing, Wrathful Meteorite*:

> In the utterly pure mandala,
> Embodying the buddhas of the ten directions,
> The one renowned as Karmapa will arise
> To reveal the results of practice in this life.

The *Root Tantra of Manjushri* also speaks of his name:

> Having a name with *ka* at the beginning and *ma* at the end
> There will arise a noble being who will clarify the teachings.[242]

From Zhang Rinpoche's *Hidden Treasure of the Steep Rock,* there emerged a yellow scroll that told of the first Karmapa, Dusum Khyenpa (Knower of the Three Times), of his relation to the great Indian scholar Dharmakirti, and of his future birth as the sixth Buddha:

> The lama who is Dusum Khyenpa
> Has the name Dharmakirti.
> After the teachings of the Buddha Maitreya,
> At the time of the one called "Lion Buddha,"
> The teachings will spread widely.
> He is Dharmakirti himself.

The great scholar Situ Panchen also spoke of this relationship in his history of the Kagyu lineage. Tushita is the heaven where a future buddha reigns and whence he descends to earth. As the fourth buddha of our era, Shakyamuni, came from Tushita to take birth on earth, so now the Lord Maitreya waits to take rebirth as the fifth buddha. Succeeding him as the sixth Buddha will be the Karmapa, and according to Buddhist scriptures he will be called "the Lion."

The revealed scriptures of the Tertön Sangye Lingpa speak of Gyalwa Chokyang (Supreme Melody of the Victorious One), who was one of the twenty-five main disciples of Guru Rinpoche and a previous incarnation of the Karmapa:

> At the great temple of Samye, where Guru Rinpoche, King Trisong Deutsen, and the main disciples were present, the king asked Guru Rinpoche about Gyalwa Chokyang: "In the future, what will become of this present Gyalwa Chokyang? Where will his fame spread?" Guru Rinpoche replied: "Listen well, Sovereign. In the future, the present Gyalwa Chokyang will be known everywhere. He will introduce living beings to the fruition of the three kayas and bring them into great bliss. [As the sixth Buddha] he will have the name 'Lion.' As the son of the protector Maitreya, the Great Compassionate One, he will overturn the foundations of samsara." Thus the Sugata predicted.

The terma texts of the master Nyang Ral Nyima Özer[243] describe the Karmapa as an emanation of Chenrezik, who resides at Tsurphu, the main seat of the Karmapas in Tibet.

> Chenrezik, the Great Compassionate One,
> In order to tame China, Tibet, and Mongolia
> With the enlightened activity of Gyalwa Gyamtso[244]

Appears as one named Karmapa;
Residing in Tsurphu, he is Dusum Khyenpa.

The Black Crown

The story of the Black Crown extends far back in time. In describing great masters, Sangye Lingpa (1340-1396) speaks of the famous Black Crown of the Karmapas:

> A supreme being who holds the Black Crown,
> The yogi who has mastered Dharma and places the world in bliss,
> Sustaining the enlightened activity of Chenrezik,
> Dusum Khyenpa [resides] at Tsurphu.

The *Root Tantra of Manjushri* also describes the Black Crown:

> At the peak of his fine blue-black topknot
> Appears the great blue-black [hat] made of supreme strands
> And adorned with a great and luminous jewel.
> This is the ornament of the buddhas' emanation.

It is said that countless eons before this one, the third Buddha, the Sugata Dipamkara, came into this world. In numberless eons previous to that,[245] in a place to the west of Mt. Meru, King Yulkhor Kyong (Protector of Country and Subjects) had a son.[246] He was very skilled at resting evenly in meditative absorption. Later known as Drangsong Könpakye (Rishi of Rare Birth), he had remained stable in one-pointed samadhi for eight hundred thousand years. When the realization of vajralike samadhi finally arose for him, one million, three hundred thousand dakinis of the ten directions were filled with amazement. They gathered in one place and fashioned a precious hat that was made of the hair offered by each one of the dakinis and adorned at the top by a sun and moon. As the appearance of primordial wisdom itself, the crown appeared naturally over the head of Drangsong Könpakye.

In his next life, he was Lha'i Pu Drime Karpo (Stainless White Son of the Gods), and then Luyang Nyingpo (Heart of a Song's Melody), followed by Karma Denu, the Brahmin Saraha in India, and so forth. During all of these incarnations, the wisdom crown appeared above his head for all of those who had the capacity to see it. Afterward in Tibet, from the glorious first Karmapa, Dusum Khyenpa, through the remaining incarnations of the Karmapa, it was known that this crown of naturally arising primordial wisdom appeared above their heads.

There are many scriptures that praise the Karmapa as embodying the essential nature of the body, speech, mind, qualities, and activity of the tathagatas of the ten directions and three times. Several stories of the Karmapas' incarnations are presented here in brief. The first Karmapa was Dusum Khyenpa, born in 1110 C.E., the Tibetan Year of the Iron Tiger, in Teshö, located in the eastern area of Tibet known as Kham.[247] In his young years, his genuine potential to be a bodhisattva or buddha was awakened and he possessed signs of actual realization. Accompanying him as closely as his shadow were lamas, gods, and protectors.

He studied and reflected on all the infinite and nonsectarian ways of understanding and practicing Dharma, receiving visions of the deities and also prophecies. He arrived at all the successive levels of realization through the practice of giving up what is to be given up (all faults) and taking up what is to be taken up (all good qualities). Not content with just this, by merely hearing the name of the unequaled Dakpo Lhaje (Gampopa) he felt unwavering faith arise in him. Understanding that he had a karmic connection with Gampopa during many lifetimes, Dusum Khyenpa bowed at his feet and received from Gampopa detailed empowerments, reading transmissions, and oral instructions.

Through his meditation, Dusum Khyenpa became famous for having greater exertion than eight hundred great practitioners, and he arrived at the zenith of experience and realization. Placing his hand on Dusum Khyenpa's head, Gampopa prophesied the spread of his teachings to central Tibet (U and Tsang) and eastern Tibet (Kham): "My son, you have cut the ties to samsara. Son, practice at Kampo Gangra in Kham. Your benefit for living beings will spread to U, Tsang, and Kham." Dusum Khyenpa practiced at Karma Gön, Kampo Nenang, Drama Drushi, and other places, and his realization of mahamudra, the brilliant nature of mind, became manifest. So that sentient beings could accumulate merit, he established new monasteries, among them Tölung Tsurphu, which became the seat of the Karmapas. Dusum Khyenpa also founded their sanghas; capable of benefiting others, his disciples and their disciples grew in number. It is said that his Dharma lineage will be longer than the current of a great river. From the first Karmapa, the study and practice of the special teachings of the Karma Kagyu would extend throughout Tibet and to other countries.

In the advice of Dusum Khyenpa, we find the first prediction of a reincarnation in Tibet: "At a future time, in Ngothong near the Yangtse River, one will come to fulfill my intention." History confirms that this was the second Karmapa, Karma Pakshi, an event confirmed by scholars and meditation masters alike.

The first Karmapa's practice of predicting his reincarnation was continued by Karma Pakshi. To Drubthop Orgyenpa (Master of Meditation from Orgyen), who was a direct disciple and held the Karmapa's lineage of teachings the second Karmapa said:

> From the direction of the setting sun will come one who wears the Black Crown. This is the prophecy concerning Rangjung Dorje. There will come a reason for entrusting you [Orgyenpa] with the Black Crown and texts for your safekeeping. Look after them well.

Over a period of three days, Karma Pakshi gave Orgyenpa numerous oral instructions. During this time, Orgyenpa said to him with complete conviction, "Your lineage is that of the Black Crown." The vision of his higher powers of perception foresaw that the successive incarnations of the Karmapas would possess the Black Crown.

Later, when the fifth Karmapa, Dezhin Shekpa, was visiting China, Yung Lo, emperor of the Ming dynasty, saw directly above the head of the Karmapa the crown that is the continual and natural appearance of wisdom. He inquired of the Karmapa, "Would it not be beneficial if I offered a crown that ordinary living beings could perceive?" And the Karmapa replied, "It would bring benefit." Accordingly, the emperor offered "the precious Black Crown that frees upon seeing," and the custom of wearing the Black Crown has continued from that time onward.

The Last Testament

Unlike other incarnate lamas in Tibet, the Karmapas are not recognized through divinations, or through the prophecy of one possessed by a deity, or by a single name dropping out from many contained in a vessel. As their special accomplishment, almost all the successive incarnations of the Karmapa have left what is traditionally known as "the Sealed Words of the Last Testament." Through the Karmapa's wisdom that knows what will come, the Last Testament clearly gives information about the next Karmapa, which can include the name of his family, the place, the animal of the twelve-year cycle, and the various signs that will appear linked to him. These wondrous predictions belong to the tradition of how the birthplace and the family of the Karmapas are recognized.

Following this custom, just before the fifteenth Karmapa, Khakhyab Dorje, withdrew the manifestation of his form body, he left a text concerning the next Karmapa, Rangjung Rigpe Dorje, with a close disciple.[248] Called "The Last Song: A Reed's Flower to Embellish the Ear," the text was kept secret until the appropriate time. Relying on its words, the eleventh Tai Situ[249] took the responsibility of searching for the reincarnation and recognizing him. On the basis of this research, the thirteenth incarnation of His Holiness the Dalai Lama, Gyalchok Thubten Gyatso, gave his final confirmation of the Karmapa's recognition. In this way, continuing through many centuries down to the present time, the history of how the Karmapas are recognized has very deep roots.

The tertön Chokgyur Lingpa[250] (1829-1870) was a great master and visionary who discovered many Dharma treasures. He was a prominent member of the vibrant nonsectarian movement that blossomed in nineteenth-century Tibet. In his prophecies about the Karmapa, he began by invoking Gyalwa Chokyang, the Karmapa's incarnation as one of the main disciples of Guru Rinpoche:

> Lotsawa Gyalwa Chokyang, listen to me.
> In the supreme place of speech, Palace of the Half Moon,
> You will have twenty-one future rebirths.
> An emanation of Chenrezik, you know all three times.

Chokgyur Lingpa then continued to give the names of the Karmapas who would be born after his time:

> The names needed after Thekchok (Supreme Vehicle, the fourteenth
>   Karmapa) passes into nirvana
> Are the Dewe Dagnyi (Very Nature of Bliss, the fifteenth Karmapa),
>   Rigpe Dorje (Vajra of Awareness, the sixteenth Karmapa),
> Ogyen Trinley (Enlightened Activity of Guru Rinpoche, the seven-
>   teenth Karmapa), and Samten (Stable Contemplation, the future
>   eighteenth Karmapa), and so forth.

He also spoke individually of each incarnation and made the following prediction of the seventeenth Karmapa:

> Nearby, at the foot of a verdant tree that grows on rocky mountains is the seventeenth incarnation of the Karmapa together with Kenting Tai Situ. This is a symbol that through their minds being fused as one, the leaves and petals of the Buddha's teaching will unfold and the fruit, the essence of the Dakpo Kagyu, will be plentiful.[251]

The text of Guru Rinpoche, *Hidden Predictions* (*mDo byang gud sbas*), gives the vast perspective:

> The teachings of my emanation, the Karmapa,
> Will not come to an end until the teachings of the fortunate kalpa
>   have come to a close.

Brief Histories of the Sixteen Karmapas

BY DZOGCHEN PONLOP RINPOCHE

The First Karmapa Dusum Khyenpa 1110–1193

DUSUM KHYENPA means "Knower of the Three Times" (past, present and future), referring to the total lucidity he attained at enlightenment, giving him knowledge of the three modes of time and the "timeless time" of enlightened awareness.

Born to a family of devoted Buddhist practitioners in Teshö of eastern Tibet, the boy who was to become known as the first Karmapa was called Gephel as a child. He first studied with his father and became a knowledgeable and seasoned practitioner even as a young boy, continuing his education with other Buddhist teachers of the region. Already quite learned by the age of twenty, he moved to central Tibet, became a monk, and spent the next twelve years or so engaging in study and meditation practices. He studied with very well known masters of the time, such as Chapa Chökyi Senge (1109-1169), a great logician and the founder of the debate system in Tibet, and Patsab Lotsawa Nyima Drakpa (1055-?), who was a great master of the Prasangika Madhyamaka tradition and translated many Madhyamaka texts into Tibetan.

At the age of thirty, he received teachings from Gampopa, the heart son of the greatest yogi in Tibetan history, Milarepa. Dusum Khyenpa first trained in the foundation practices of the Kadampa tradition and, following that, in the general philosophy of the sutras. This training in the foundation of all Buddhist traditions established a pattern for all future Kagyu followers by demonstrating the importance of establishing a correct basis of knowledge. This is true even for engaging in the most powerful of advanced Vajrayana practices. Dusum Khyenpa also received and unified the lineage teachings given to him by Rechungpa and other students of Milarepa.

The Karmapa's accomplishment in meditation and in the practices transmitted to him by his teachers was greatly enhanced by his own natural compassion. His practice produced rapid results and great accomplishments, or *siddhis*. Such accomplishment is often perceived by followers as the ability to perform miraculous activity, and the legends of the Karmapas through the ages speak of their ability, through the manifestation of this seemingly miraculous activity, to create a great sense of wonder and faith in their students. All the Karmapas have since been known for their ability to inspire, through their simple presence, this profound sense of wonder and faith in the reality of the accomplishment that is the fruition of the Buddhist path.

In 1164, at the age of 55, Dusum Khyenpa founded a monastery at Kampo Nenang; five years later he started Pangphuk Monastery in Lithang, in east Tibet. Later, at the age of seventy-six, he established an important seat at Karma Gön, in eastern Tibet. In 1189, when he was eighty, he established his main seat at Tsurphu, in the Tölung Valley, whose river feeds into the Brahmaputra in central Tibet.

The first Karmapa made predictions about future Karmapas. In particular, he was the first Karmapa to present a prediction letter detailing his future incarnation. He gave it to his main disciple, Drogön Rechen, whom he chose to become the next lineage holder.

Dusum Khyenpa passed away at the age of eighty-four. Among his other main disciples were Tak-lungpa, founder of the Talung Kagyu; Tsangpa Gyare, founder of the Drukpa Kagyu; and Lama Kadampa Deshek, founder of the Katok Nyingma lineage.

The Second Karmapa Karma Pakshi 1204–1283

"P AKSHI" means "Great Master," a term of Mongolian origin, indicating a special honorific status or position conferred by the Mongolian emperors.

Born in Kyille Tsakto in eastern Tibet to a noble family of yogins, the young boy was named Chözin by Khache Panchen. He was a child prodigy who already had a broad understanding of Buddhist philosophy and practice before the age of ten.

On his way to central Tibet for further education, he encountered Pomdrakpa, who had received the full Kagyu transmission from Drogön Rechen, the first Karmapa's spiritual heir. Pomdrakpa realized, through certain very clear visions, that the child he met was the reincarnation of Dusum Khyenpa, as indicated in the letter given to Drogön Rechen. Pomdrakpa conferred on the young Karma Pakshi all the teachings through traditional empowerments and formally passed on the lineage in full. Ever since this time, each young Karmapa, despite his preexisting knowledge and accomplishment of the teachings, formally receives all the transmissions of the teachings from a lineage holder.

The second Karmapa spent much of the first half of his life in meditation retreat. He also visited and restored the monasteries established by the first Karmapa. He is famous for having introduced the melodious chanting of the *Om mani padme hung*, the mantra of compassion, to the Tibetan people.

At the age of forty-seven, he set out on a three-year journey to China, at the invitation of Kublai, grandson of Genghis Khan. While he was there, Chinese and Tibetan histories as well as statements of European visitors record that the Karmapa performed many spectacular miracles at the court. He also played an important role as a peacemaker. However, the Karmapa declined to stay permanently at the court, which caused Kublai Khan's displeasure.

Over the next ten years the Karmapa traveled widely in China, Mongolia, and Tibet and became a teacher of the greatest renown. He was particularly honored by Munga Khan, Kublai's brother, the Mongol ruler at that time.

After Munga's death, Kublai became the Khan and ruled a vast empire. However, harboring resentment against the Karmapa for his refusal to stay at the court of Kublai, and due to his perception that the Karmapa had paid more attention to the Munga Khan many years before, Kublai Khan ordered the arrest of the second Karmapa. However, the Karmapa thwarted each attempt to capture, and even kill, him, despite the overwhelming forces sent against him. As the Karmapa continually responded with compassion, Kublai Khan eventually had a change of heart and came to regret his actions against the Karmapa. He finally approached the Karmapa, confessing his misdeeds, and requested Karma Pakshi to teach him.

In fulfillment of a long-standing vision, the Karmapa returned to Tibet and directed the building of a Buddha statue at Tsurphu well over fifty feet in height. The finished statue was slightly tilted. In one of the best-known stories of the miracles of the Karmapas, Karma Pakshi was said to have straightened the statue by assuming its same tilted posture and then straightening himself. The statue simultaneously righted itself.

The histories record that the second Karmapa composed over one hundred volumes of texts, which once were enshrined at the monastic library at Tsurphu. Before passing into parinirvana, he told the details of the next Karmapa's birth to his main disciple, Orgyenpa.

The Third Karmapa Rangjung Dorje 1284–1339

BORN TO A FAMILY of tantric practitioners of the Nyingma lineage in Dingri Langkor, in the Tsang region of central Tibet, Rangjung Dorje sat up straight at the age of three and proclaimed that he was the Karmapa. At the age of five, he went to see Orgyenpa, who had prepared for his visit on the basis of a prescient dream. Orgyenpa recognized the child as the reincarnation of Karma Pakshi and gave him the Black Crown and all the possessions of the second Karmapa.

Rangjung Dorje grew up in Tsurphu, receiving the full transmissions of both the Kagyu and Nyingma traditions. At the age of eighteen, he received the preliminary monastic ordination. After a retreat on the slopes of Mount Everest, he took full ordination, and further broadened his studies at a great seat of the Kadampa lineage. Not content with this, Rangjung Dorje sought out and studied with the greatest scholars and experts of all the Buddhist traditions of the time. By the end of his studies, he had mastered nearly all of the Buddhist teachings brought to Tibet from India.

In particular, during a retreat in his early twenties, he had a vision at sunrise of Vimalamitra and then Padmasambhava, who dissolved into him at a point between his eyebrows. At that moment, he realized and received all the teachings and transmissions of the dzogchen tantras of the Nyingma lineage. He wrote many volumes of teachings on dzogchen and founded the Karma Nyingtik lineage. Through his mastery of the profound Nyingmapa teachings of Vimalamitra, he unified the Kagyu mahamudra and the Nyingma dzogchen.

At the age of thirty-five, through visions he received of the Kalachakra teachings, he introduced a revised system of astrology, which continues to this day. Called the Tsur-tsi, or the Tsurphu tradition of astrology, it forms the basis for the calculation of the Tibetan calendar in the Tsurphu system. He also studied and mastered medicine, which is related in part to astrological studies in the Tibetan system. Over the course of his life, Rangjung Dorje also wrote many treatises, including the universally renowned *Profound Inner Meaning* (*Zab mo nang don*), one of the most famous Tibetan treatises on Vajrayana.

The third Karmapa established many monasteries in Tibet and China. He visited China in 1332, where he enthroned his disciple, the new emperor, Toghon Temur. Rangjung Dorje later passed away in China. It is said his image appeared in the moon on the night of his passing. Among his many disciples, some of the main ones were Gyalwa Yungtönpa, who was to become the next lineage holder, Khedrup Drakpa Senge, Dölpopa, and Yakde Panchen.

The Fourth Karmapa Rolpe Dorje 1340–1383

THE FOURTH KARMAPA was born in Kongpo Province in central Tibet. It is said that during her pregnancy, his mother could hear the sound of the mantra *Om mani padme hung* coming from her womb, and that the baby said the mantra as soon as he was born. At the age of three, he announced that he was the Karmapa.

At a young age, he manifested the ability of the Karmapas to perform extraordinary activities, such as spontaneously reading books and receiving many profound teachings in his dreams. As a teenager, he received the formal transmissions of both the Kagyu and Nyingma lineages from the great Nyingma guru Yungtönpa, the third Karmapa's spiritual heir. Emperor Toghon Temur invited the nineteen-year-old Karmapa to return to China. He accepted and began an extended journey, stopping at many places along the way to give teachings. He taught for three years in China, establishing many temples and monasteries there. Temur was the last Mongol emperor of China. The subsequent emperor of the Ming dynasty later invited the Karmapa to China, but Rolpe Dorje sent a lama in his place.

During his return to Tibet from China, Rolpe Dorje gave *upasaka* (lay ordination) to a very special child from the Tsongkha region, whom he named Kunga Nyingpo. Rolpe Dorje predicted that this child would play an important role in the Buddhism of Tibet. The child was to become known as the great master Tsongkhapa, the founder of the Gelukpa school.

An accomplished poet, Rolpe Dorje was fond of Indian poetics and composed many wonderful dohas, or songs of realization, a form of composition for which the Kagyu lineage is famous. After one of his students had a vision of a Buddha image over three hundred feet tall, the fourth Karmapa orchestrated the painting of a huge thangka of the Buddha. It is said that the Karmapa traced the design of the Buddha's outline with the hoofprints of a horse he was riding. The design was measured and traced on cloth, and after laboring for over a year, five hundred workers completed the cloth painting of the Buddha and founders of the Mahayana.

Rolpe Dorje passed into parinirvana in eastern Tibet. Among his many disciples, the main one was Khachö Wangpo, second Shamar Rinpoche, who became the next lineage holder.

The Fifth Karmapa Dezhin Shekpa 1384–1415

THE FIFTH KARMAPA was born in the Nyang Dam region of southern Tibet to yogin parents. During the pregnancy, they heard the recitation of the Sanskrit alphabet and *Om ah hung* mantras. Soon after birth, the infant sat upright, wiped his face, and said, "I am the Karmapa. *Om mani padme hung hri.*"

When the child was brought to Tsawa Phu in Kongpo, Khachö Wangpo immediately recognized him as the incarnation of Rolpe Dorje and presented him with the Black Crown and other possessions of the fourth Karmapa. He went on to give the Karmapa the full cycle of Kagyu teachings, and the Karmapa soon completed his traditional training.

After Emperor Yung Lo of China had a vision of the Karmapa as Chenrezik, Dezhin Shekpa received a invitation to visit China. At the age of twenty-three, he started on a three-year journey to reach the imperial palace. Yung Lo was an extraordinarily devoted student of the Karmapa, whom he took as his guru. Chinese records speak of the Karmapa's manifestation in response to such devotion as a hundred days of miracles. The emperor recorded these events for posterity in silk paintings with a multilingual commentary. Following in the footsteps of the two previous Karmapas, Dezhin Shekpa subsequently made a pilgrimage to the famous Wu-tai Shan sacred mountains, to visit his monasteries there.

The emperor achieved some realization and had a vision in which he saw the wisdom vajra crown above the Karmapa's head. So that all beings might benefit from seeing something of this transcendent aspect of the Karmapa, the emperor commissioned the creation of a physical replica of the wisdom vajra crown, which he saw as a black hat. He presented it to his guru, requesting him to liberate those who saw it by wearing the crown on special occasions. This was the beginning of the Black Crown ceremony. The emperor also offered Karmapa the highest-ranking title.

In 1410, Dezhin Shekpa returned to Tsurphu to oversee its reconstruction; the monastery had been damaged by an earthquake. He recognized the Shamar reincarnation of Chöpal Yeshe and spent three years in contemplative retreat. The next lineage holder, however, was the Karmapa's student Ratnabhadra.

Realizing that he would die at a young age, he left indications of his future rebirth and passed away into parinirvana at the age of 31. In the ashes of his cremation fire were found relics, naturally formed images of many buddhas.

The Sixth Karmapa Thongwa Dönden 1416–1453

THE SIXTH KARMAPA was born in Ngomtö Shakyam, near Karma Gön in eastern Tibet, to a family of devoted yogins. Shortly after his birth, while his mother was carrying the young child, he suddenly became very excited when their path crossed that of Ngompa Chadral, a student of the fifth Karmapa. Ngompa Chadral asked the name of the child, who smiled and replied, "I'm the Karmapa." Ngompa Chadral cared for the infant for seven months and then took him to Karma Gön.

The young Thongwa Dönden immediately began to teach. Shamar Chöpal

Yeshe came to Karma Gön during this period to crown the Karmapa. Thongwa Dönden received teachings and transmissions of the Kagyu lineage from Shamar Chöpal Yeshe, Jamyang Drakpa, and Khenchen Nyephuwa. In particular, he received the full lineage transmission from Ratnabhadra, who was his principal teacher. At a young age, he began to compose many tantric rituals, eventually establishing a body of liturgies for the Kamtsang lineage. He also joined the lineages of the Shangpa Kagyu and the Shije (the teachings of Chö, cutting through egotism) into the main Kagyu lineage transmissions.

He dedicated his activity to composition, teaching, restoring many monasteries within Tibet, printing books, and strengthening the sangha. He began to develop the *shedra* (the monastic university) system in the Karma Kagyu lineage.

Realizing that he would die at an early age, he entered retreat and conferred a regency on the first Gyaltsap, Goshir Paljor Döndrub, indicating where he would next take birth. The sixth Karmapa's main spiritual heir was Pengar Jampal Zangpo, author of the "Mahamudra Lineage Supplication." This renowned prayer of the Kagyu lineage represents his spontaneous utterance upon realizing mahamudra. Thongwa Dönden passed into parinirvana in 1453 at the age of thirty-eight.

The Seventh Karmapa Chödrak Gyatso 1454–1506

BORN TO A FAMILY of tantric practitioners in Chida in northern Tibet, the seventh Karmapa was heard to say "Ama-la" (mother) while he was still in his mother's womb. At birth, he spoke the Sanskrit mantra *Ah hung*, which symbolizes the ultimate (emptiness-luminosity). At five months of age he said, "There is nothing in the world but emptiness."

When he was nine months of age, his parents took him to Goshir Gyaltsap Rinpoche, who recognized him as the seventh Karmapa in accordance with the instruction letter of the sixth Karmapa, Thongwa Dönden. At four, he was given a series of empowerments by Goshir Paljor Döndrup, and at eight, he was given the Kagyu teachings from Pengar Jampal Zangpo and Goshir Paljor Döndrub at Karma Gön.

Chödrak Gyatso dedicated much of his life to retreat. He was also an extremely accomplished scholar who authored many texts, such as a commentary on *Abhisamayalamkara* called *The Lamp of the Three Worlds*. His most famous, multivolume text is *The Ocean of Reasoning*, his commentary on *pramana* literature.

The Karmapa formally established monastic universities at Tsurphu and other places. He also restored the large Buddha statue commissioned by Karma Pakshi at Tsurphu. Something of an activist, he settled disputes, worked to protect animals, initiated bridge construction, and sent gold to Bodh Gaya for the gilding of the statue of the Buddha at the place of the Buddha's enlightenment. He also convinced numerous people to recite millions of *Om mani padme hung* mantras as a cure for all ills. Before passing into parinirvana at the age of fifty-three, he provided details of his next incarnation and passed on the lineage to Tai Situ Tashi Paljor.

The Eighth Karmapa Mikyö Dorje 1507–1554

ORN IN A SMALL VILLAGE called Satam, in the region of Kartiphuk of Ngom-chu in eastern Tibet, to a family of devoted yogins, the eighth Karmapa was said to have spoken the words "I am the Karmapa" at birth. Upon hearing this report, Tai Situpa confirmed the child to be the new Karmapa. He spent the next years at Karma Gön.

When he was five, a child from Amdo was put forward as the Karmapa. The Karmapa's regent, Gyaltsap Rinpoche, set out from Tsurphu to investigate the two children. However, on meeting Mikyö Dorje, he found himself spontaneously prostrating and knew that he was the real Karmapa.

Tai Situ Rinpoche, along with Goshir Gyaltsap Rinpoche and other students of the previous Karmapa, devised a test, which the child not only passed but to which he was heard to say, "*E ma ho!* Have no doubts, I am the Karmapa." Gyaltsap Rinpoche enthroned him the following year when he was six.

Mikyö Dorje studied with Sangye Nyenpa Tashi Paljor, Dulmo Tashi Öser, Dakpo Tashi Namgyal, and Karma Trinleypa. He took the essential Kagyu teachings from Sangye Nyenpa Tashi Paljor. When quite young, the Karmapa declined an invitation to China on the ground that the emperor would pass away before he could arrive, a prediction that turned out to be true.

Mikyö Dorje was one of the most renowned of the Karmapas, a great meditation master as well as a prolific and learned scholar, author of over thirty volumes of work, including important commentaries on the sutrayana treatises and pithy instructions on tantras. The eighth Karmapa was also a visionary artist, to whom we owe the Karma Gadri style—one of the major schools of thangka painting. He also composed many sadhanas, practice liturgies, and other devotional practices for the Karma Kagyu school.

Through many visions, including one of the Buddha Dipamkara, the eighth Karmapa realized that the manifestations of the Karmapa and of Guru Rinpoche are inseparable. Guru Rinpoche is considered one of the ways in which a buddha accomplishes enlightened activity. According to Buddhist cosmology, there will be one thousand buddhas in our universe; both the Karmapa and Guru Rinpoche are said to be the activity aspect of them all.

Foreseeing his imminent passing, Mikyö Dorje entrusted a letter of prediction to the Shamar Könchok Yenlak and entered parinirvana at the age of 47. Among his many disciples, the main ones were Shamar Könchok Yenlak and Pawo Tsuklak Trengwa. His prediction letter said, "In the life following this one, I will be born as the glorious, self-arisen lord (Wangchuk) of the world. In the upper regions of the snowy region of Treshö to the east, a place where there is the sound of water and the Dharma is heard. I have seen the signs that it will not be long before I am born there."

The Ninth Karmapa **Wangchuk Dorje** 1556–1603

A s predicted by the eighth Karmapa, the ninth was born in the Treshö region of eastern Tibet. He was heard reciting mantras in the womb during pregnancy, and he sat cross-legged for three days soon after birth and declared that he was the Karmapa.

In accordance with the prediction letter left by the eighth Karmapa, he was soon recognized by the Tai Situpa Chökyi Gocha, who was staying nearby, and by the Shamarpa Könchok Yenlak. A year later, Shamarpa enthroned him at the age of six and gave him extensive teachings.

Once Wangchuk Dorje had received the complete Kagyu transmission, he began to teach throughout Tibet, traveling in a monastic camp, which strictly emphasized meditation practice. Wangchuk Dorje did not visit China, but made important trips to Mongolia and Bhutan. He gave many teachings and restored monasteries and temples wherever he went.

The ninth Karmapa also received an invitation to visit Sikkim, and under his guidance, three monasteries were established there: Rumtek, Phodong, and Ralang. The Karmapa blessed and consecrated them from Tibet. Rumtek subsequently became the Karmapa's seat in India during the early 1960s.

Like the eighth Karmapa, Wangchuk Dorje was also a creative author and wrote many condensed commentaries on sutras and tantras, including three mahamudra treatises: *The Ocean of Definitive Meaning, Dispelling the Darkness of Ignorance,* and *Pointing Out the Dharmakaya.* These three works have played a major role in the teaching and transmission of mahamudra.

At the age of forty-eight, Wangchuk Dorje passed into parinirvana, leaving his prediction letter, along with instructions about the next incarnation, with the sixth Shamarpa, Chökyi Wangchuk.

The Tenth Karmapa Chöying Dorje 1604–1674

As PREDICTED, the tenth Karmapa was born in the Golok region, in the far northeast of Tibet. He was recognized and enthroned by Shamar Chökyi Wangchuk, from whom he received the full Kagyu transmission.

By the age of six, he was a better painter than his teachers, as well as a gifted sculptor. Chöying Dorje anticipated the wars and political strife that were soon to come, realizing that certain political interests in Tibet would enlist the Mongol armies in the Gelukpa cause. Knowing he would be forced out of central Tibet by the political strife, the tenth Karmapa gave away most of his wealth to the poor and appointed Goshir Gyaltsap his regent.

Gushri Khan's Mongol armies attacked Shigatse and then continued to attack much of Tibet, causing considerable destruction throughout the land and eventually overrunning the Karmapa's camp. Chöying Dorje was forced to leave the area. With an attendant, he traveled throughout Tibet and then spent more than three years living in the wilds of Bhutan. They later traveled to what is today northern Yunnan, Burma, and Nepal. As always, wherever the Karmapa went, he fostered the Dharma, and he was able to establish some monasteries along his route.

Some twenty years passed before he could return to his homeland. He recognized the next incarnations of Shamar Yeshe Nyingpo, Goshir Gyaltsap, and Pawo Rinpoche and gave the transmission of the Kagyu teachings. Shamarpa became his main spiritual heir. At the age of seventy-one, Chöying Dorje passed into parinirvana, leaving instructions and a prediction letter. Goshir Gyaltsap Norbu Sangpo became the regent at Tsurphu.

By this time, the political landscape in Tibet had changed for good. Ngawang Lobsang Gyatso, the fifth Dalai Lama, had become the official ruler of Tibet, and this role of the Dalai Lamas would continue to be filled by his successive incarnations.

The Eleventh Karmapa Yeshe Dorje 1676–1702

YESHE DORJE was born in the Mayshö region in east Tibet to a devoted Buddhist family. Shamar Yeshe Nyingpo and Gyaltsap Norbu Sangpo recognized him as the next Karmapa in accordance with the instructions of the tenth Karmapa. Yeshe Dorje went to central Tibet and was enthroned at Tsurphu Monastery.

Yeshe Dorje received teachings and the mahamudra lineage transmissions from Shamarpa. He also received the terma teachings, which are the hidden teachings of Padmasambhava, from Yong-ge Mingur Dorje and Taksham Nuden Dorje. This fulfilled a prophecy of Padmasambhava that the eleventh Karmapa would hold certain terma lineages. Yeshe Dorje was a great visionary who performed many miracles.

Yeshe Dorje also located and identified the eighth Shamarpa, Palchen Chökyi Döndrub, who became his close student and next lineage holder. However, he was to be the shortest lived of the Karmapas. During his precious but brief existence, he blended the Kagyu and Nyingma teachings. He passed into parinirvana after leaving a detailed letter with Shamar Palchen Chökyi Döndrub concerning his next incarnation.

The Twelfth Karmapa Changchub Dorje 1703–1732

AS PREDICTED BY HIS PREDECESSOR, the twelfth Karmapa was born at Kyile Tsaktor in Derge Province of east Tibet. Chökyi Döndrub sent a search party and his envoys brought the child to Karma Gön, where Shamarpa met with the young child and recognized him in accordance with the previous Karmapa's prediction and instructions.

The young Karmapa studied under many illustrious masters. He gave profound Kagyu teachings to a famous Nyingma master of Kathok Monastery, who in turn shared his Nyingma teachings.

Changchub Dorje left troubled Tibet on a pilgrimage to India and Nepal, accompanied by the Shamar, Situ, and Gyaltsap Rinpoches. He was particularly honored by the king of Nepal, who credited him with stopping a raging epidemic and making rain that ended a serious drought. In India, they visited the sacred places of Lord Buddha.

After the Karmapa returned to Tibet, he accepted an invitation to China and set out for that land accompanied by the Shamarpa. However, foreseeing difficult political times and realizing the need to leave his body, the Karmapa sent the eighth

Tai Situpa a letter with details of his next incarnation and then succumbed to smallpox, as did the Shamarpa two days later. Tai Situpa became his spiritual heir.

The Thirteenth Karmapa Dudul Dorje 1733–1797

IN ACCORDANCE with the prediction, the thirteenth Karmapa was born in Nyen Chawatrong in southern Tibet. Found by Tai Situpa Chökyi Jungne, the child was brought to Tsurphu. He was recognized at the age of four and enthroned by Goshir Gyaltsap Rinpoche.

From the age of eight, Karmapa received the full transmission and teachings of the Kagyu lineage from his main guru, Tai Situpa. He also studied with many great masters of the Nyingma and Kagyu lineages of the time, such as Kathok Rigdzin Tsewang Norbu, Kagyu Trinley Shingta, Pawo Tsuklak Gawa, and others. At one point, the famous Jokhang Temple, home of the Jowo statue, was threatened by rising floodwaters. A prophecy from Guru Rinpoche had foreseen this and predicted that only the Karmapa could do something to stop it. Aware of this prophecy, the Lhasa authorities requested him to come. Unable to leave Tsurphu immediately, he resolved the problem by writing a special letter of blessing and invoking the compassion of Chenrezig. Later, when he was able to come to Lhasa, the thirteenth Karmapa offered a khata to the Jowo image, and it is said that the arms of the statue changed their position to accept it and have remained that way ever since. Dudul Dorje was also asked to consecrate a distant monastery. Remaining at Tsurphu, he threw blessing grains in the air at the appropriate moment of the consecration ceremony. They were seen to shower down from the heavens at the monastery hundreds of kilometers away.

Dudul Dorje and Tai Situpa along with Kathok Rigdzin Tsewang Norbu recognized the Shamarpa's reincarnation, Chödrup Gyatso, the younger brother of the fourth Panchen Lama, Palden Yeshe. The thirteenth Karmapa passed into parinirvana, leaving behind a detailed prediction letter and instructions on his next incarnation. Situpa Pema Nyinche became his spiritual heir.

The Fourteenth Karmapa Thekchok Dorje 1798–1868

WHEN THEKCHOK DORJE was born in the village of Danang in the Kham region of eastern Tibet. it was midwinter, and the histories say that flowers spontaneously blossomed and many rainbows appeared. The baby recited the Sanskrit alphabet. He was recognized by Drukchen Kunzig Chökyi Nangwa, the holder of the thirteenth Karmapa's letter giving the details of his next reincarnation. The fourteenth Karmapa was enthroned and later ordained by the ninth Tai Situpa. He received teachings and the lineage transmissions from Situpa Pema Nyinche Wangpo and Drukchen Kunzig Chökyi Nangwa.

The fourteenth Karmapa lived very simply and exemplified the ideal monk. He was gifted in poetry and dialectics and participated in the *rime* (nonsectarian) movement, whereby many noted scholars showed great interest in each others' traditions and teachings. This exchange was particularly intense between the Kagyu and Nyingma traditions, with the Karmapa passing on teachings to Jamgön Kongtrul Rinpoche. Thekchok Dorje received some tantras from the Nyingma visionary treasure-revealer Chokyur Lingpa, and those rituals were subsequently introduced into the Tsurphu calendar.

Chokyur Lingpa had important visions of future Karmapas, up to the twenty-first, which were recorded and then memorialized in a thangka. The fourteenth Karmapa's spiritual heir was the great nonsectarian master and prolific author Jamgön Kongtrul Lodrö Thaye. Thekchok Dorje taught widely in Tibet and recognized the tenth Situpa, Pema Kunzang. Thekchok Dorje passed into parinirvana at the age of seventy-one, leaving detailed instructions regarding his next incarnation.

The Fifteenth Karmapa Khakhyab Dorje 1871–1922

BORN WITH the very auspicious circle of hair between the eyebrows (found on the young Shakyamuni and known as one of the thirty-two marks of an enlightened being), Khakhyab Dorje spoke the mantra of Chenrezik at his birth in Shekar village of Tsang Province in central Tibet. He was recognized and enthroned by the major leaders of the nonsectarian movement in nineteenth-century Tibet: Khyabgön Drukchen and Migyur Wanggi Gyalpo, along with Jamgön Kongtrul, Jamyang Khyentse Wangpo, Terchen Chokgyur Lingpa, and Pawo Tsuklak Nyinche.

He was given a very thorough education from great scholars and eventually received the Kagyu transmission from Jamgön Kongtrul Lodrö Thaye, who also passed on to him the essence of his hundred compositions embracing the profound teachings of all Tibetan Buddhist traditions as well as the fields of medicine, art, linguistics, and general Buddhist studies. The fifteenth Karmapa studied with many great masters, such as Khenchen Tashi Özer.

He continued his activities of teaching and giving empowerments through-out Tibet and preserved many rare texts by having them reprinted. Khakhyab Dorje was the first in the line of Karmapas to marry, and he had three sons, one of whom was recognized as the second Jamgön Kongtrul, Palden Khyentse Öser. He was a brilliant example of the bodhisattva with an insatiable desire for learn-ing in order to help other beings.

Among many disciples, his closest students were Tai Situ Pema Wangchuk Gyalpo, Jamgön Kongtrul Palden Khyentse Öser, and Beru Khyentse Lodrö Mize Jampe Gocha. Some years before his passing into parinirvana, he entrusted a pre-diction letter to his closest attendant.

The Sixteenth Karmapa Rangjung Rigpe Dorje 1924–1981

THE SIXTEENTH GYALWA KARMAPA, Rangjung Khyabdak Rigpe Dorje, was born in Denkhok in Derge Province of east Tibet, the son of a noble fam-ily called Athup. Having received instructions from different masters in Derge that she would bear a great bodhisattva son, his mother had gone to stay in a holy cave, once used by Guru Rinpoche, where she waited to give birth. She was accompanied by a khenpo, who instructed her on the cleansing ceremony. It is said that at one point toward the very end of the pregnancy, the future Karmapa disappeared entirely from his mother's womb for a whole day. The day of his birth, his mother returned to her normal pregnancy size and soon gave birth to this great bodhisattva. Those present heard him say to his mother that he would be leaving soon.

The details of the birth coincided with those in a prediction letter given by the fifteenth Karmapa to his attendant, Jampal Tsultrim, setting forth the cir-cumstances of his new incarnation. Jampal Tsultrim handed the letter to the authorities at Tsurphu Monastery, who then asked Tai Situpa, Beru Khyentse, and Jamgön Kongtrul to clarify certain points. A search party subsequently located the incarnation. The eleventh Tai Situpa soon recognized the child as being the new reincarnation of the Gyalwa Karmapa and sought confirmation from His Holiness the Dalai Lama.

The Karmapa received first ordination and then bodhisattva vows from Tai Situpa and Jamgön Kongtrul Rinpoche, the two foremost disciples of the fif-teenth Karmapa. Eventually, the Dalai Lama gave his acknowledgment.

When he was eight years old and still residing in Derge, he received the Black Crown and ceremonial robes of the Karmapa brought to him from Tsurphu. On the way to Palpung Monastery, he stopped to visit and bless the Derge monastic publishing house, foreshadowing his publication of the Buddhist canon in India. Tai Situpa enthroned him as the sixteenth Karmapa, Rangjung Khyabdak Rigpe Dorje, then accompanied him on the long journey to Tsurphu, where the new incarnation was greeted by Goshir Gyaltsap Rinpoche, Jamgön Kongtrul Rinpoche, and Nenang Pawo Rinpoche.

Soon after his arrival at Tsurphu, the sixteenth Karmapa was received by the thirteenth Dalai Lama, who performed the hair-cutting ceremony. While so doing, the Dalai Lama had a vision of the ever-present wisdom crown above the Karmapa's head.

After this ceremony, the Karmapa was officially enthroned at his main seat of Tsurphu by Tai Situpa and the Head of the Drukpa Kagyu school. He received the full Kagyu lineage transmissions from Tai Situpa Pema Wangchuk Gyalpo and Jamgön Kongtrul Palden Khyentse Öser. The sixteenth Karmapa then studied many sutrayana texts with Gangkar Rinpoche and tantric teachings with Khyentse Rinpoche. He received the mahamudra transmission (pointing out the nature of the mind) from Jamgön Kongtrul Palden Khyentse Öser and many other great masters of the time. Karmapa then visited Lithang Pangphuk Monastery, where, in the tradition of the Karmapas and their inconceivable activity, he is said to have left footprints in solid rock.

Between 1941 and 1944, the young Karmapa spent much time in retreat at Tsurphu Monastery, which underwent expansion during this period. Beginning in 1944, the Karmapa began to strengthen relationships with neighboring Buddhist states in the Himalayan region as well as with India. During a pilgrimage in southern Tibet, he accepted an invitation from Jigme Dorje Wangchuk, the king of Bhutan; the Karmapa and his party visited Bumthang and other areas in Bhutan, engaging in many spiritual activities.

In 1947, the Karmapa and his party continued their pilgrimage to Nepal, India, and Sikkim, visiting the major places of the Buddha's life: Lumbini, just inside Nepal, where the Buddha was born; Sarnath, where he first taught; and Bodh Gaya, the place of Buddha's enlightenment. The following year, after traveling through Kinnaur in northern India and Purang to visit Mount Kailash, the Karmapa returned to Tsurphu Monastery.

With the Dalai Lama, the Karmapa and other high lamas of Tibet visited China in 1954. Returning to Tibet, the Karmapa stopped at many monasteries along the way in eastern Tibet. Two years later, he and his party traveled to Sikkim and from there continued on pilgrimage. The Dalai Lama, the Panchen Lama, and the Karmapa visited India at the invitation of the Mahabodhi Society of India to join the celebration of the 2,500th anniversary of Buddhism. During this trip, the Karmapa and his party revisited the holy sites of India as pilgrims.

During this visit, the Karmapa strengthened his ties to his disciples Chögyal Tashi Namgyal, the king of Sikkim, and Ashi Wangmo, the Bhutanese Buddhist princess. The king of Sikkim invited him to visit Rumtek, the monastery in Sikkim that the ninth Karmapa had founded at the end of the sixteenth century. The Karmapa was unable to accept the invitation at that time but said that he would go there in the future when it would be needed.

Foreseeing the Communist Chinese invasion of Tibet and the inevitable destruction of Buddhist institutions there, the Karmapa informed the Dalai Lama of his intention to leave his homeland in the spring of 1959. Accompanied by a large entourage, the Karmapa left Tsurphu and fled Tibet. The escape was organized by Damchö Yongdu, the General Secretary for the Karmapa. The party brought with them sacred statues, paintings, reliquaries, and other precious items of the lineage of the Karmapas. The timing and organization of the departure made for a relatively easy journey to Bhutan. After three weeks, the party arrived safely in northern Bhutan, where the most senior Bhutanese government officials received them.

The king of Sikkim extended a formal invitation to the Karmapa to establish his seat there, and two months after entering Bhutan the party arrived in Gangtok, Sikkim. Of the several sites proposed by King Tashi Namgyal, the Karmapa chose to settle at Rumtek, stating that Rumtek would be his seat outside Tibet, although he hoped one day to return there. Shortly after the Chögyal extended his offer, the Karmapa and his party left Gangtok for Rumtek. Established many centuries earlier by the ninth Karmapa, by 1959 Rumtek Monastery was almost in ruins. The surrounding area was also undeveloped and had no facilities for supporting the Karmapa and his party. The Karmapa, the teachers, and the community lived in temporary quarters for many years while resources were gathered to begin the construction of new facilities to support the Karmapa's monastic seat and surrounding lay community.

Construction began in earnest three years later. The foundation stone of the new monastic center was laid by the new king of Sikkim, who had assumed responsibility for the kingdom after his predecessor had passed away. Construction was led by the Karmapa's General Secretary, Damchö Yongdu. It was funded primarily through the generosity of the Sikkimese royal family and that of the Indian government, the latter arising from the Karmapa's meeting with Pandit Nehru.

Construction of Rumtek was completed in four years, and the sacred items and relics brought from Tsurphu were installed there in 1966. On Tibetan New Year's Day, the sixteenth Karmapa officially inaugurated the new seat, called "The Dharmachakra Center, a place of erudition and spiritual accomplishment, the seat of the glorious Karmapa."

In 1974, the sixteenth Karmapa set out on his first world tour, visiting the United States, Canada, and Europe. Accompanied by other teachers, and a full entourage of monks and staff, he performed the Black Crown ceremony in the

Western hemisphere for the first time, gave empowerments, and bestowed Dharma advice. In January of the next year, the Karmapa flew to Rome and met with Pope John Paul the Sixth.

During 1976-77, the Karmapa again traveled to the West for a more extended visit, followed by a wide-ranging world tour. He visited religious centers on four continents and met heads of state, religious leaders, elders of many traditions, and people from the world of the arts.

On November 28, 1979, the Karmapa consecrated the ground for the construction of Karma Dharmachakra Centre southeast of New Delhi at a ceremony attended by the President and Prime Minister of India. The Centre was envisioned as a study, meditation, and translation center.

The Karmapa's last world tour began in May 1980 and took him to Greece, England, the United States, and Southeast Asia, where he gave teachings, Black Crown ceremonies, empowerments, interviews, and audiences, and engaged in many beneficial activities.

On November 5, 1981, the sixteenth Karmapa passed into parinirvana at the American International Clinic in Zion, Illinois. His *kudung* (body) was flown back to India and the cremation ceremony took place at Rumtek Monastery on Dec. 20. Indian dignitaries and thousands of his disciples from all over the world attended.

The following day, a general Karma Kagyu meeting was held in Rumtek at the request of the General Secretary, Damchö Yongdu. He requested Shamar Rinpoche, Tai Situ Rinpoche, Jamgön Kongtrul Rinpoche, and Goshir Gyaltsap Rinpoche to form a council of regents to take joint responsibility for the spiritual affairs of the Karma Kagyu lineage. He also asked them to locate Karmapa's instructions concerning his next rebirth and thus bring forward his next incarnation. The four rinpoches accepted the task and expressed their sincere desire to fulfill the wishes of the sixteenth Karmapa.

The Songs of the Sixteenth Karmapa

WITH THE SIMPLICITY of song and evocative images, these three texts not only reflect the poetic tradition of Tibet but also constitute important historical documents. They predict the flight of the Tibetans from the invading Chinese, commiserate with the ones left behind, and affirm the Karmapa's close connections with the Dalai Lama and Situ Rinpoche. Knowing of their significance, Thrangu Rinpoche suggested their translation and kindly provided guidance.

These poems also bring to mind the parallels between the lives of the sixteenth and seventeenth Karmapas: both were forced to flee Tibet and take refuge in India, both had close connections with the Dalai Lama and Situ Rinpoche, and both expressed their visions in poetry.

A Song

This song is ala thala thala,
Ala is the way it arose;
Thala is the way it is expressed in words.

In a pure land, rich with turquoise leaves,
On a throne of brilliant, white shell,
Is the deity of long life, the mother Lady Tara.
I pray to her from the depths of my heart.
May there be no obstacles to long life.

If you do not recognize this place,
It is the Retreat House of Palpung.
If you do not recognize a person like me,
Recall the upper valley of delightful Shukra
And the lower valley of delightful Shukra;

In the place between the two Shukras
Is a child who descends from Tshazhang Denma.
If you call him by name, it is Thubten Gelek.

Not now, but on a distant tomorrow, it will be decided.
Both the vulture and I know where to go.
The vulture soars into the depths of space;
We people do not stay but go to India.
In the springtime, a cuckoo comes as a guest.
In the fall when the harvest ripens, it knows where to go:
Its only thought is travel to the east of India.

In the lofty land of Tibet, the inhabitants, high and low,
And in particular, you, Tai Situ, the Lord and Protector Maitreya,
Who remains above the crown of our head,
May your activities, like the sun and moon set in space,
Be continuous, stable, and without hindrance.

I pray that we meet again and again.
May the three roots—the lamas, yidams, and dakinis—
Protect him from negative conditions and obstacles.
Keep the precise meaning recorded here in the depth of your heart.

In the sixteenth of sixty-year cycles, during the Year of the Iron Dragon [1940], the sixteenth incarnation of the Karmapas, Rangjung Rigpe Dorje, composed this song when he was seventeen years old at Palpung Chökhor Ling. May it be auspicious. (Transl. in 1994 and revised in 2000 and 2002.)

Notes

Composed when he was just seventeen, this famous song of the sixteenth Karmapa predicts the flight of Tibetans from the invading Chinese. In 1959, nineteen years later, his prophecy came true and the Chinese incursion dispersed the Tibetans throughout the world. Many of them know this plaintive song by heart. It opens with melodious sounds, *ala thala thala*, which signify the source for the arising of the poem. Its first words are a prayer to *White Tara*, asking her to remove obstacles to long life. Her realm is known as the one of *turquoise leaves*, and she is addressed as *mother* due to her close relationship to Prajnaparamita, the Perfection of Wisdom, she who gives birth to all the buddhas. *Palpung* is the name of Situ Rinpoche's monastery, located in the mountains south of Derge in eastern Tibet, where the Karmapa wrote this song. Using a favorite rhetorical device, *if you do not know*, the next lines describe the Karmapa himself: he was born between the upper and lower *Shukra* Rivers and *Thubten Gelek* is a name given to him before he was recognized as the Karmapa, by the fifth Dzogchen Rinpoche. The Karmapa's familial lineage comes from *Tshazhang Denma*, one of the chief ministers of Gesar of Ling, the great Tibetan warrior and emanation of Guru Rinpoche.

   The fifth verse foretells the Tibetans' escape, *on a distant tomorrow*. The flight of the *vulture*, known to soar highest in the sky and see what is far distant, symbolizes the flight of the Karmapa and the Tibetans to India. The sixteenth Karmapa loved birds, and the analogies of himself and birds continue with the cuckoo. Following its pattern of migration, the *cuckoo* comes in the spring and leaves in the fall; in this same natural way, the Karmapa knows when it is time to leave Tibet for *the east of India*, where he will eventually take up residence in Rumtek, Sikkim. The last two verses are a prayer for the Tibetan people in general and in particular for Tai Situ Rinpoche, whose previous incarnation gave the sixteenth Karmapa bodhisattva vows, ordination, and lineage transmission, and who enthroned the Karmapa at Palpung. The Karmapa prays *that we meet again and again*, alluding to his recognition of the next incarnation of Situ Rinpoche, who, in turn, will play an important role in the recognition of the seventeenth Karmapa, so they will meet again and again.

The Song Whose Time Has Come

THE MELODIOUS HUM OF THE BEE

This song is ala ala ala.
It is thala thala thala.
Ala means it is a song of the unborn;
Thala is a word that invokes.

If you do not recognize this place,
It is the place of Akanishtha's heart chakra.
In the mandala of glorious Chakrasamvara,
The main seat is Tsurphu in the Dowo Valley.

If you do not recognize a person like me,
I belong to the family lineage of *'den,* a good ancestry.
If you call me by name, I am known as Rigdröl Yeshe.

This victory banner of the teaching of glorious Dakpo's lineage
Is raised high on the summit of worldly existence, they say,
Planted at the end of a series, held high and never declining.
Nourished by the essence of the father lama's oral instructions,
It is the perfection of the great display of innate primordial wisdom.

From the land of high snows, this turquoise lion mane
Pervades the countries of the future, they say.
In the exquisite sandalwood forests, lives a huge tiger
With a powerful roar and the radiant color of clouds at dawn.
Insatiably he conquers the wild animals of wrong views.

What I have spoken is the truth, the Victorious One's power,
Resounding over the lake with its waters of eight qualities
Like the pleasant sound of hastening geese.

In the sky, vast and all-pervading,
Are set the sun and moon, luminous and natural.
The most famous one called Rigdröl
Does not remain, yet knows not where he will go.

The swan places its trust in the lake
And the lake, unreliable, turns to ice.
The white lion places its trust on the snow,
But the fine white snow attracts the sun.

May all the noble ones left behind in the snowy land of Tibet
Not come under the sway of the four elements.
From unmanifest space, the protector Padmasambhava looks after them,
Holding them always with his gentle hook of compassion.
May all sentient beings who have a connection with me
Bring to fruition the four supreme kayas.
I do not stay now, yet my place is uncertain;
I go to experience the fruition of previous lives' karma.

In springtime a cuckoo will come to Tibet.
Its lovely song will strike sadness in your heart.
Then you will wonder where the man Rigdröl is.
Will not you, who depend on me, know untold grief?

On the day the swan circles the edge of the lake
And leaves its fledglings in the darkening swamp,
The day the white vulture soars in the depths of the sky,
You will wonder where the man Rigdröl is.
O fledglings, I feel inexpressible sorrow for you.

Now I will not explain much; this is but a jest,
Yet unified with ultimate reality.
When the Lord of the Path is held by the king of birds,
In prayer I aspire that we gather in great joy.

For this life, take this as the essential point to be heard:
Speech is indestructible sound like an echo.
Mind is empty, free of material concerns.

On the path that does not take up the positive nor reject the negative,
The conduct of the king of birds is relaxed within itself.
Examine in detail this meaning in a hundred flavors.
Ki so so, gathering of wrathful Wermas.

In the sixteenth of sixty-year cycles, during the Year of the Wood Monkey
[1944], this was composed by the sixteenth incarnation of the Karmapas,

Rangjung Rigpe Dorje, in his residence Tashi Khangsar, located in the main temple of Tsurphu Dowolung. May it be auspicious. (Transl. in 1994, and revised 2000, 2002.)

Notes

Written in 1944, this song predicts the Tibetans' flight from their homeland, and it speaks more extensively than the previous song of their suffering and the Karmapa's anguish in being forced to leave them behind. Like the first, this song begins with mellifluous sounds to invoke the words from *unborn* space. The next two verses introduce the place and the author. The place is the *heart chakra*, the very center, of *Akanishtha*, (Tib. *'og min*), the Unexcelled, the Highest. Its many meanings include the dharmadhatu, the most excellent pure land, the highest of the form realms, and so forth. It is also a traditional epithet for Tsurphu, which is thought of as a pure land on the sambhogakaya level. Calling Tsurphu the place of the heart chakra also points to the enlightened mind, whose seed syllable is located in the heart. Traditionally, three of the main monasteries associated with the Karmapa are linked to the enlightened body, speech, and mind of the Buddha: in eastern Tibet, Kampo Gangra (Kam po gangs ra) represents the body and Karma Gön (Karma dgon), the speech, while in central Tibet, Tsurphu (mTshur phu) represents the mind. In this way, it is supreme as well. *Chakrasamvara* is one of the main yidam practices in the Kagyu lineage. *Dowo valley* (*mDo bo lung*) is the particular name of the valley where Tsurphu is situated. The Karmapa's familial lineage of *'den* is a shortened version of Tshazhang Denma, referred to in the previous poem as a chief minister of Gesar of Ling and an emanation of Guru Rinpoche. *Rigdröl Yeshe* is a name given to the Karmapa by the thirteenth Dalai Lama, when he performed the Karmapa's hair-cutting ceremony at Norbulingka, the Dalai Lama's summer palace.

The next three and a half verses speak of the Dharma lineage of the Karmapas. *Dakpo's lineage* refers to Dakpo Lhaje, or Gampopa, a student of Milarepa and the teacher of the first Karmapa. The *victory banner of the teaching* is a classic image for enlightenment and victory over the maras, and its coming *at the end of a series* refers to the unbroken lineage of the Kagyu teachings. Here, the *lama's oral instructions* lead to the realization of *primordial wisdom*. The snow *lion* with its *turquoise mane* is a magical creature, the presiding deity of Tibet's snowy ranges and known to leap playfully from peak to peak. Chosen as the animal symbol of Tibet, it is depicted on Tibet's national flag, government seal, money, and so forth. It is also associated with Shakyamuni Buddha and upholds the thrones of enlightened beings.[252] The snow lion's mane is vast and functions here as a metaphor for the teachings of Buddhism in Tibet. The *huge tiger* with its vivid saffron color, associated with the robes of the ordained sangha, is an analogy for the brilliance of the Dharma which overcomes wrong views, such as not accepting the pattern of cause and effect that comprises karma, or thinking that the self is permanent. The *eight qualities* of water are that it is cool, sweet, light, soft, clear, pleasant, wholesome, and soothing. The *lake* and the *geese* refer to the clear and pleasing quality of the Dharma and to its pervasive presence, filling space as the calls of migrating geese. The radiant *sun and moon* illustrate the naturally luminous and omnipresent qualities of the Dharma.

After giving the person, place, and teachings, the poem's next six stanzas describe the dark future the Karmapa sees for Tibet. Rigdröl, the Karmapa, is in a most difficult situation: he knows that he cannot stay but where to go? In the next lines, the Karmapa is the *swan* residing on the *lake* of his Tsurphu Monastery. When the Chinese would invade Tibet and take over the monastery, it would become uninhabitable, like a frozen lake. The *lion* of the next two lines is also the Karmapa, who relies on his monastery in the snowy land of Tibet; however, the heat of the sun melts the *snow*, symbolizing the destruction of Tsurphu during the Cultural Revolution. Both images—the swan and its lake, and the lion and its snow—indicate that although the Karmapa wished to remain at Tsurphu, it was not possible.

The next two verses are a prayer for the well-being of the Tibetan people. Not coming *under the sway of the four elements* is a prayer for those who could not escape, supplicating that they will be protected from the harm of the four elements, such as being burned by fire or drowned in water, and that they will be held in Guru Rinpoche's compassion. He prays that they ultimately realize the *four supreme kayas*, the three discussed earlier plus the *svabhavikakaya*, (the essential dimension or body), understood as the union of the other three.

The next eight lines speak of his departure and the sadness of those who will miss him. The *untold grief* refers to the immense suffering of the Tibetans since the Chinese invasion, imaged as the *darkening swamp* where the *swan* circling the lake must leave its fledglings. The white vulture (there is also a black one), like the swan, refers to the Karmapa and his flight to India. Saying that his words are *but a jest* may be a way of softening their blow, for in the next line he states that they are linked to the truth of ultimate reality.

The following two lines are quite remarkable as a vision of the future. The *Lord of the Path* refers to the astrological path or cycle of twelve years, each of which is related to a different animal. *King of the birds* refers to the Year of the Bird, when the Karmapa in his next incarnation as the seventeenth will be back at Tsurphu beginning his activity again and can *gather in great joy* with his disciples. Since the Karmapa knows that he will not be returning to Tsurphu until his next incarnation, he offers his people advice *for this life* and gives them a profound Dharma teaching. Appearance and emptiness are inseparable, and therefore *speech*, however negative it might be, is like an *echo*; the *mind is empty*, not caught in concern for the material world, or in the extremes of grasping at the positive and rejecting the negative. This spacious frame of mind knowing appearances to be emptiness and emptiness to be appearance would benefit a people under the sway of a repressive regime, helping them to keep a mental balance. Following these oral instructions, mind could rest relaxed in its own nature, like the *king of birds*, the vulture, who soars and glides at ease in space. This is the Karmapa's gift, which he counsels people to contemplate. The last line seals the poem with *Ki*, indicating courage and intelligence, and *so so*, which is like a loud whistle, calling "Wake up! Be aware! Pay attention!" *Wrathful Wermas* are protectors of the Dharma (dharmapalas) who have great dignity and courage. In sum, the movement of the poem is from invoking a pure land and the glory of the Dharma to describing a world of suffering, and, finally, the gift of profound advice on how the Tibetans can relate to the difficulties they will undergo.

The Blissful Roar of Melodious Experience

Glorious Tölung Tsurphu is Akanishtha, supreme region of the mind,
A place where oceans of dakinis gather like clouds.
The mountain behind is the richly arrayed pure realm of Chenrezik.
On the mountain in front is a vast, dense forest, a swirling ocean of
    fierce deities.

The mountain between is Tushita, the joyful mind and pure realm
    of great Maitreya.
Let us go to that pure realm where lamas, yidams, and dakinis gather
    like clouds.
Having planted the victory banner of the Buddha's teachings in the land
    of Dharma,
Let us raise in the country of snow mountains and Kailash, too, the sun
    of happiness and well-being for all people.

[Dalai Lama,] pillar of all the Buddha's teachings, you are a great wish-
    fulfilling jewel.
Pervading the world with myriad lights,
May you be permanent, stable, and unchanging as a diamond
In the Red Palace of Lhasa on the golden throne held high by lions.

Your melodious teachings pour forth in the tones of Brahma.
In this limitless universe, please turn the three wheels of Dharma.
Unconditioned primordial wisdom, the expanse of your mind,
Sees without hindrance into the three times.
You maintain the Buddha's teachings without prejudice
And they do not decline but flourish.

May you reign as the three Dharma kings, with Dharma and worldly
    power entwined in a silken knot.
How joyful, how happy are sentient beings: the teachings of the Buddha
    spread;
The Sangha holds its head high; the honeyed rain of Dharma falls,
And the world of living beings is brought into happiness.

Though they prize happiness, sentient beings in number as vast as space
   gather only suffering.
With the first moment of self-awareness comes freedom from the net of
   the three realms.
Let us bring the vast universe into joy—that is called true peace.
From the expanse of the inexpressible nada sprang this joyous song.
Let us join in a happy dance, graced with the melody of delight.

On the seventeenth day of the fifth Tibetan month in the Year of the Iron
Ox (1961-62), this was spoken by the sixteenth Gyalchok [Karmapa]. As
these words are filled with blessing, Damchö Yongdu earnestly and
respectfully requested permission to print them in letter press. Following
the Gyalwang Karmapa's kind granting of permission, this edition was
published by the Dharmachakra Center in Rumtek, Sikkim, on the
twenty-fifth day of the fifth Tibetan month in the Year of the Iron Ox
(July 7, 1961). May it be a cause for the accomplishment of what was
prayed for. (Transl. under the guidance of Khenchen Thrangu Rinpoche
and Ringu Tulku, 1992, 1994, and revised 2000, 2002.)

Notes

The first two stanzas of the poem are a praise of Tsurphu that evokes its qualities by describing Tsurphu's sacred landscape. Tölung means "upper valley" (*stod
lung*) and refers to the large area of many smaller districts in which Tsurphu is
located. The name is given from the perspective of people living in Lhasa, about
two hours' drive away, for whom this countryside of valleys and mountains is seen
as higher up. Here in this poem, *Akanishtha* has the ultimate meaning of the
supreme region of the mind.[253] Within this realm, the mountains that surround
Tsurphu are described as the residences of various deities—Chenrezik, the
embodiment of compassion; Maitreya, the future Buddha; and the wrathful
deities—plus lamas, yidams, and dakinis. From the sixth to the eighth lines, the
sixteenth Karmapa envisions returning to Tibet, *the land of Dharma*, to plant a
victory banner and spread the Buddhist teachings once again, illuminating this
land *with happiness and well-being*. Mount *Kailash*, Tibet's most sacred mountain, is considered the residence of Chakrasamvara, and since Milarepa stayed
there in the eleventh century, it is a place where many realized Kagyu masters
practiced. It is interesting to note that the sixteenth Karmapa speaks of a return
to Tibet to plant the Dharma and that this poem was written in the early 1960s.
Since the sixteenth Karmapa never returned to Tibet, passing away in Zion,

Illinois, in 1981, these lines would refer to the seventeenth Karmapa, who did return to Tibet, taking birth there and spreading the Dharma.

The next three stanzas praise the Dalai Lama, just as the seventeenth Karmapa's "A Joyful Aspiration" paid him tribute, indicating again the close connection between the sixteenth and seventeenth Karmapas and the Dalai Lama, all of whom are emanations of Chenrezik. The *wish-fulfilling jewel* is one of the possessions of the chakravartin (world ruler): it answers all his wishes and the wishes of those who come within its radiance. It is said to balance out the weather, heal physical and mental disease, and stave off untimely death.[254] The *Red Palace* of Lhasa refers to the red section of the Potala Palace where the Dalai Lamas from the fifth onward lived and worked. *Brahma* was known for his melodious voice, which had sixty different tones. The *three wheels of Dharma* refer to the three times the Buddha taught, first focusing on the Four Noble Truths, then on emptiness and compassion, and finally on the buddha nature present in all beings.

Unconditioned means not subject to temporary situations or external change. This vast wisdom mind is omniscient, knowing the past, present, and future. The *three Dharma kings*, active during the Yarlung period (629-842 C.E.) were responsible for introducing Buddhism to Tibet and causing it to flourish: Songtsen Gampo (617-649/650 C.E.), Trisong Deutsen (755/756-797 C.E.), and Tri Ralpachen (reigned 815-838 C.E.).[255] *A silken knot* is an image for the harmonious intertwining of religion and politics.

In contrast to the vision of the golden age that ends the fifth stanza, the beginning of the last stanza speaks of the *suffering* that afflicts sentient beings who do not recognize their true nature and so live a life of pain and deprivation. Release from this state comes through *the first moment of self-awareness*, the first realization of mind's nature, which cuts through *the net* of illusion, *the three realms* of desire, form and formlessness. This clear seeing of emptiness separates an ordinary life of suffering from that of a bodhisattva on the first of the ten levels leading to full awakening. The motivation of such bodhisattvas as the Karmapa is to bring living beings into the *joy that is true peace*. When all phenomena are dissolving into their empty and luminous ground, the *nada* is the last, most minute trace, so subtle it can be considered a synonym for emptiness whence comes the joy of the dance.

~

Naturally arising dharmakaya, unchanging and ever-present,
Karmapa, you appear as the form kaya's magical illusions.
May the vajras of your body, speech, and mind remain stable in all realms
And your infinite, spontaneous activity blaze in glory.

A long-life prayer for the seventeenth Karmapa Ogyen Trinley Dorje
by Goshir Gyaltsap Rinpoche

~

Appendix: Tibetan Names

Amdo Palden. A yogic master and head of Karlek Monastery, where the Karmapa visited as a young monk.

Dabzang Rinpoche. An important Kagyu lama of Dilyak Monastery who founded monasteries in Nepal. An emanation of Gampopa, his reincarnation was discovered by the Karmapa.

Dargye. A Tsurphu monk. He was a driver on the scouting trip and escape.

Drubngak. An older attendant of the Karmapa at Tsurphu, he escaped with the Karmapa.

Drupön Dechen Rinpoche. Responsible for rebuilding Tsurphu and giving guidance to its residents. He played a significant role in guiding the search for the Karmapa and other reincarnate lamas.

Drupön Rinpoche. One of the main tulkus from Dilyak Monastery, he was instrumental in discovering the reincarnation of Dabzang Rinpoche and now serves the Karmapa.

Gyaltsap Rinpoche (or Goshir Gyaltsap Rinpoche). One of the five main Kagyu incarnate lamas, whose main seat is in Ralang, Sikkim. Along with Situ Rinpoche, he is responsible for offering empowerments and reading transmissions to the Karmapa.

Jamgön Kongtrul Rinpoche. One of the five main Kagyu tulkus, whose reincarnation was discovered by the Karmapa. Still a young boy, he lives in Nepal, and Lava near Kalimpong in northern India.

Karma Döndrub Tashi. The Karmapa's father.

Khenpo Tsultrim Gyamtso. A teacher of the Karmapa, founder of Marpa Institute for Translators. He teaches widely and is renowned as a master of mahamudra and Milarepa's songs.

Lama Nyima. A master of Buddhist philosophy and poetics, he was the Karmapa's tutor at Tsurphu and helped to organize the escape from within the monastery. He also played an important role in finding the tulkus of Jamgön Kongtrul Rinpoche and Pawo Rinpoche.

Lama Tenam. An attendant of Situ Rinpoche, who helped the Karmapa travel in India from Lucknow to Dharamsala. Also known as Tenam-la.

Lama Tsultrim. A monk from Tsurphu who escaped with the Karmapa, he rebuilt the courtyard at Tsurphu and traveled in Tibet giving teachings and empowerments, before helping to organize the Karmapa's escape.

Loga. The Karmapa's mother.

Nenang Lama. The head lama of Nenang Monastery near Tsurphu who was instrumental in finding Pawo Rinpoche. He worked from Lhasa to organize the escape and accompanied the Karmapa through Tibet to Dharamsala.

Ngödrup Pelzom. An older sister of the Karmapa, who resides with him in India.

Pawo Rinpoche. One of the five main Kagyu tulkus. His Nenang Monastery is down the valley from Tsurphu, and his reincarnation was discovered by the Karmapa.

Situ Rinpoche (or Tai Situ Rinpoche). One of the five main Kagyu incarnate lamas, whose main monastery is Sherab Ling in northern India. He is close to the Karmapa and, along with Gyaltsap Rinpoche, responsible for offering empowerments and reading transmissions to him.

Thrangu Rinpoche. The Karmapa's tutor and an important tulku himself. He is the founder of educational institutions and monasteries and the teacher of many, both in the East and West.

Thubten. The Karmapa's cook at Tsurphu, who helped with the escape.

Tsewang Tashi. The driver of Nenang Lama in Lhasa, he escaped with the Karmapa

Yeshe Rabsel. The Karmapa's older brother.

Notes

1 Technically, "Tsurphu" should be transliterated as "Tshurphu" (*mtshur phu*), but since the former spelling has become commonplace through years of usage, it has been kept here.

2 Born in Tibet in 1924, Khenpo Karthar entered Thrangu Monastery at the age of twelve. The next eighteen years he spent deep in retreat or studying the advanced teachings of Buddhist philosophy, psychology, and logic. In 1958, due to the pressure of Chinese Communists in eastern Tibet, Khenpo Karthar and Thrangu Rinpoche, along with other monks, were forced to leave their monastery and departed for central Tibet to be with the Karmapa at Tsurphu. Through his wisdom, the Karmapa knew that problems would also reach central Tibet, and, giving them supplies for their journey, he advised the party to leave for Bhutan and India.

Khenpo Karthar stayed for eight years at Buxa, a community organized for escaping Tibetans in northern India. In 1967, he went to Rumtek Monastery to be with the Karmapa and stayed until 1975. After a year in Bhutan, the Karmapa asked him to serve as the abbot of the new Karma Kagyu monastery he planned to build in the United States. In early 1978, the Mead House in Woodstock, New York, was purchased and became the home of Karma Triyana Dharmachakra. Since its inception, Khenpo Karthar has overseen the building of the monastery, all the while giving teachings, guiding his many disciples, and building a new three-year retreat center where three successive groups of his students have entered the intensive retreat. His teachings have formed the basis of popular books, which have been translated into Chinese by his Taiwanese disciples. Khenpo Karthar has also returned to Tibet four times, one of them for the hair-cutting ceremony of the Karmapa in the Jokhang.

3 Khenpo Karthar Rinpoche, conversation with the author, Karma Triyana Dharmachakra, Woodstock, N. Y., December 2001. Lama Norlha from Kagyu Thubten Chöling in Wappingers Falls, N. Y., was also present.

4 Tai Situ Rinpoche is one of the main "heart sons" of the Karmapa and considered an emanation of the future Buddha, Maitreya. His previous incarnation was one of the main teachers of the sixteenth Karmapa. Born in 1954, the twelfth Situpa was enthroned at his monastery of Palpung in eastern Tibet at the age of eighteen months by the sixteenth Karmapa. Forced to leave Tibet at the age of five, he went to live with the sixteenth Karmapa and receive his formal religious training at the newly constructed Rumtek Monastery. In 1975, Situ Rinpoche left to establish his own monastery, Sherab Ling, in northern India. He has traveled extensively in the East and West giving teachings and empowerments. He is especially well-known for

his mahamudra courses. When he first returned to Tibet in 1984, Situ Rinpoche ordained more than two thousand men and women. In 1991, on another visit, he recognized over one hundred incarnate lamas. Situ Rinpoche played a pivotal role in the identification and enthronement of the present seventeenth Karmapa and has continued to give him empowerments and teachings in India. Sherab Ling has expanded, and in addition to three-year retreat centers and an impressive shrine hall for ceremonies, it is home to a new and flourishing institute of higher Buddhist studies.

5 Conversation with the author, Lhasa, Tibet, 2 August 1992. See also "A Talk by His Eminence Tai Situ Rinpoche and His Eminence Tsurphu Gyaltsap Rinpoche on Friday, June 12, 1992 in the Front Entrance Hall of Rumtek Monastery," *Densal* (published by Karma Triyana Dharmachakra, Woodstock, N.Y.) 12, nos. 1&2 (winter/spring 1993), 5-7.

6 Ibid.

7 Clemens Kuby, *Interview with Jamgön Kongtrul Rinpoche,* 30 min.(Munich: Kuby Film TV, March 23, 1992). This was conducted soon after the four Rinpoches met and Situ Rinpoche informed them about the letter he had found (personal communication from Clemens Kuby). This key section of the interview appeared in Clemens Kuby, *Living Buddha,* feature film, 108 min., (Munich: Kuby Film TV, 1994). See also Clemens Kuby and Ulli Olvedi, *Living Buddha: Die siebzehnte Wiedergeburt des Karmapa in Tibet* (Munich: Goldman Verlag, 1994), 81-88.

8 The "white one" refers to the conch shell, a traditional ritual instrument in Tibet, which is white in color.

9 Mainly Situ Rinpoche and Gyaltsap Rinpoche. For the latter's explanation, see Ken Holmes, *His Holiness the 17th Gyalwa Karmapa Urgyen Trinley Dorje* (Forres, Scotland: Altea Publishing, 1995), 49.

10 The poetic equivalent of divine thunder, "sky iron" (*gnam lchags*), is found in the letter. *Lha thog* is the name found on maps of Tibet.

11 In the letter, the cow is indicated by the term *dö jo* (*'dod 'jo*), which means "wish-fulfilling," a traditional epithet for the cow. It would naturally call up that image, for example, to the Tibetans who make the traditional and common mandala offerings, where the term "wish-fulfilling cow" (*'dod jo'i ba*) appears.

12 The name Pema (Lotus) connects him with Guru Rinpoche (Padmasambhava, the Lotus Born) and the name Dönyö relates him to the buddha Dönyö Drupa (Amoghasiddhi), who like the Karmapa is especially connected with enlightened activity.

13 Information about life in Lhathok comes mainly from the Karmapa's sister, Ngödrup Pelzom, who keeps clear and detailed memories of her homeland and family life there.

14 In order of their birth, the children's names are given with their ages as of 2003, according to Western-style counting. The Karmapa's father, Karma Döndrub Tashi, has the family (*rus pa*) name of Chödo (Chos rdo) and his mother, Loga, has the family name of Gazi (Ga zi).

1. Yeshe Rabsel (Ye shes Rab gsal) 38, married man with three girls.
2. Tendzin Chodron (brTan 'dzin Chos sgron) 35, a married woman with two boys and two girls.
3. Tashi Yangtso (bKra shi Yang mtsho) 33, a married woman with two boys and two girls.
4. Kalzang Paldzom (sKal bZang dPal 'dzom), to whom the Karmapa gave the name Trinley Wangmo (Phrin las dBang mo) 31, a nun.
5. Ngödrup Pelzom (dNgos sgrub dPal 'dzom) 26, a nun.
6 Dendzom (bDen 'dzom) 23, a young woman.
7. Namse Lhendzom (rNam sras Lhan 'dzom), to whom the Karmapa gave the name Monlam Yangsto (sMon lam gYang mtsho) 21, a nun.
8. The Gyalwa Karmapa (rGyal ba Ka rma pa) 17, a monk.
9. Tulku Tsewang Rigdzin (Tshe dbang Rig 'dzin) 14, a monk, recognized as an incarnate lama.

15 This information came from the Karmapa's father, Karma Döndrub. In part 4, following the histories of the Karmapa, there are two poems by the sixteenth Karmapa that refer to the minister Denma: in "A Song" he is mentioned under his full title, Tshazhang Denma, and under a shortened version of *'den*, he appears in "The Song Whose Time Has Come: The Melodious Hum of the Bee."

16 The eight auspicious symbols are (1) the auspicious parasol. Its round shape is like the shape of the Buddha's head. (2) the two auspicious fish. They represent the shape of the Buddha's eyes. (3) the auspicious vase. This represents the Buddha's throat, the vase resembling his neck, whence comes the genuine Dharma. Like a precious vase, it removes the suffering of samsara and brings happiness. (4) the auspicious conch. This represents the speech of the Buddha, as the conch is known for its resonant and far-reaching sound. The Buddha's speech is always of an appropriate volume and tone. (5) the auspicious victory banner. This represents the beautiful quality and perfect proportions of the Buddha's body. (6) the auspicious, glorious knot. This represents the Buddha's heart/mind and means that he knows everything completely and without limitation. (7) the auspicious lotus. This represents the tongue of the Buddha, which is supple, fine, and slender. His enunciation is perfect. (8) the auspicious wheel. This is the sign found on the Buddha's feet and symbolizes his turning the wheel of Dharma to liberate all sentient beings.

17 Probably during the Cultural Revolution, when many Tibetans were imprisoned for their religious beliefs or social positions.

18 "Accomplishments," usually divided into the mundane (flying, walking on water, etc.) and supramundane (realizing the nature of mind).

19 Conversation with the author, Gyutö Ramoche University, Sidhbari, Dharamsala, India, June 2000.

20 His name as a monk was Lama Tsewang Palden, but he was known to everyone as Amdo Palden.

21 Amdo Palden, conversation with the author, Tsurphu Monastery, Tibet, 24 September 1992. He was sixty-eight years old at the time and has since passed away.

22 Ngödrup Pelzom, conversation with the author, Gyutö Ramoche University, Sidhbari, Dharamsala, India, 10 July 2001.

23 Amdo Palden, conversation with the author, Tsurphu Monastery, Tibet, 24 September 1992.

24 He was later recognized as the reincarnation of Chölek Rinpoche, a famous Drugpa Kagyu lama.

25 In 1954, the twelfth Goshir Gyaltsap Rinpoche was born in Nyemo in central Tibet to a family of famous tantric practitioners known for their high level of realization. Gyaltsap Rinpoche escaped with the sixteenth Karmapa in 1959 and received many important initiations from him. Like the three other main heart sons of the Karmapa, he studied texts, rituals, and meditation practice. As the years passed, he founded his own monastery at Ralang not far from Rumtek. He is also head of the Karma Shri Nalanda Institute for Higher Buddhist Studies at Rumtek Monastery, Sikkim, India.

26 His full name was Drupön Karma Dechen Tsewang Rinpoche. He was the hereditary lineage holder of Tana Gönmar Monastery in Nangchen, eastern Tibet.

27 Loga is the common form of Lolaga, her name as it appeared in the Last Testament.

28 The refuge prayer is the most widespread Buddhist prayer. Its simplest form states: "I take refuge in the Buddha. I take refuge in the Dharma.I take refuge in the Sangha" (the community of practitioners). For a discussion of refuge, see the Karmapa's talk entitled "Taking Refuge" on p. 199. The Three Jewels is another name for the Buddha, Dharma, and Sangha. Repeating prayers or mantras many thousands of times is typical of Buddhist practice in Tibet.

29 Clemens Kuby, *Living Buddha*, Kuby Film TV, Munich, feature film, 108min., 1994.

30 "A Talk," *Densal*, 12, nos. 1&2, 5-7. Also, Situ Rinpoche, conversation with the author, Lhasa, Tibet, 2 August 1992.

31 The text of the letter, available at www.kagyuoffice.org under Karmapa /Biographical info/Reference, is as follows:

> June 17, 1992
> On March 19, 1992, Tai Situ Rinpoche, Jamgon Kongtrul Rinpoche, Gyaltsap Rinpoche and I held a meeting in which Tai Situ Rinpoche presented us with His

Holiness' handwritten letter of prophesy, the sacred testament, which was found in Situ Rinpoche's protection talisman. At that time, a little doubt arose in my mind, but now I have attained complete confidence in Situ Rinpoche, and the contents of this letter, according to which the reincarnation has definitely been discovered and further confirmed by His Holiness the Dalai Lama as the incarnation of His Holiness the Gyalwang Karmapa.

I offer my willing acceptance and henceforth, I will no longer pursue the matter of examining the sacred testament, etc.

Sharmapa
Witnessed by Orgyen Tulku Rinpoche
Translated by Michele Martin

Note: The above translation was made and distributed at Rumtek shortly after the letter was written on June 17th. Subsequently, on July 18, 1992, after consultation with his advisors, Shamar released the following revised translation:

On March 19th, 1992, at a meeting with Jamgon Rinpoche, Gyaltsab Rinpoche and myself, Situ Rinpoche presented a handwritten prediction letter from his protection pouch, claiming it was the written instructions of H. H. the 16th Karmapa (indicating his reincarnation). I had some doubts (about the letter's authenticity). At this point, I rely on Situ Rinpoche (giving me correct information about H. H. the Dalai Lama's decision). Relying on our confidential discussion, I go along with the decision made by H. H. the Dalai Lama that a reincarnation has certainly been found as reincarnation of H. H. the Gyalwa Karmapa.

Hence, I suspend my demands such as having the handwritten prediction letter being subjected to a (forensic) test.

June 17th, 1992
Shamar Chokyi Lodro witnessed by Tulku Urgyen
Translation of Anne Ekselius authorized by Kunzig Shamar Rinpoche

32 From a transcribed and translated tape recording, 30 June 1992. See www.kagyuoffice.org for the full transcript. Also in *Densal*, op. cit., 9 and Ken Holmes, *His Holiness the 17th Gyalwa Karmapa Urgyen Trinley Dorje*, 55.

33 The officers at the time were Senior Officer Sönam Norbu, Junior Officer Trinley, and their colleagues.

34 Two famous lamas from eastern Tibet, Kyabje Dulmo Chöje and Drubwang Sangye Tendzin Rinpoche, offered the young reincarnation the traditional cleansing and new robes.

35 *Gnyan chen thang lha*. The white bodhisattva wears a white cape and rides a white horse. He is considered instrumental in the preparation of the precious black pills, and is said to provide the snow lion milk that is one of their essential ingredients.

36 Also known as the Lhasa-Ziling Highway, it takes a northwest route from Lhasa,

following the Tölung River, spanned by the bridge on the road to Tsurphu. It continues up to Yangpachen, where the northern route to Shigatse turns off to the southwest. Gyurme Dorje, *Tibet Handbook* (Bath, England: Footprint Handbooks, 1999), 134-38.

37 Literally, "I went through space to Rumtek."

38 Conversation with the author, Tsurphu Monastery, Tibet, 28 July 1992.

39 For more details on Chokgyur Lingpa and his predictions, see the discussion in "A Traditional Narrative of the Karmapas," p. 271.

40 At this time in China, when connections with the Dalai Lama were purely religious, these gifts were not considered illegal. By 1994-95, this had changed.

41 Interview with the author, Lhasa, Tibet, September 1992.

42 Situ Rinpoche explained that one of the positive signs was that at 12 noon Beijing time, four planets with the nature of fire are aligned. This is very rare. Ibid.

43 These included the *hutuktus* (in Mongolian, "The Blessing One," an inherited title given to high tulkus along with an imperial seal) Phagpa Lha of Chamdo and Rigdzin Chenmo of Dodrak, and important members of the Gelukpa monasteries of Sera, Drepung, Ganden, and Tashi Lhunpo, plus the monasteries of Sakya, Samye, Mindroling, and Drikung; and also the Jowo Temple in Lhasa, Norbulingka, Yangchen Monastery, Gyume Monastic University, and Nenang Monastery.

44 Among those attending were Dölmo Chöje Rinpoche, Sangye Tendzin Rinpoche from Ja Monastery, Kyodrak Selje Rinpoche, Dzoji Jedrung Rinpoche, and Nangchen Ade Rinpoche.

45 He was also offered a copy of a prediction by the Nechung Oracle, which had been requested by some of his disciples in Sikkim, India but is not traditionally part of the ceremony. They offered it to Situ Rinpoche in June of 1992. It reads: "On the tenth day of the fourth month in the Water Monkey Year, this prophecy was bestowed while earnest prayers were being offered at the Nechung Monastery: 'It is certain that my master, Thongwa Dönden, the bodhisattvas, and sentient beings of Tibet, land of snow, will gather together and the sun of joy and delight will appear. The time is close when you will hear speech like nectar. Be at ease then and remain in a state harmonious with samaya. Palden Lhamo and I, Zugme, never deceive.' Seal of the Nechung Oracle. [Notes:] This was requested by Sikkim government, Tsechöling Rinpoche and Pasang Namgyal, the Chief Secretary of Ecclesiastical Affairs, Sikkim."

46 The eight auspicious substances are as follows: (1) the auspicious conch shell. After attaining full awakening, the Buddha remained in samadhi for forty-nine days, then the god Indra appeared and offered him a right-turning conch shell with the request to teach. (2) auspicious yogurt. After six years of practicing austerities to show that this was not the path to full awakening (which is realizing the nature of the mind), a woman offered him yogurt and he became resplendent. (3) auspicious

durva grass. A grass seller named Tashi gave the Buddha durva grass as he was on his way to Bodh Gaya. The Buddha used this grass to make a seat under the Bodhi tree where he attained full awakening. (4) auspicious vermilion. As the Buddha was about to attain full awakening, Mara appeared and challenged him, saying that it was not possible for him to attain enlightenment. As a witness, the Buddha called upon the earth goddess, who offered the Buddha vermilion, a bright red powder, and served as a witness to his attainment. (5) the auspicious bilva fruit. When the Buddha first left his father's palace, he went to practice meditation underneath a tree. As a sign of his having attained a perfect state of calm abiding (*shamatha*), the goddess of the tree offered him this fruit. (6) the auspicious mirror. Once the Buddha had partaken of the yogurt and his body became radiant, the goddess of form offered him a mirror so that he could witness his own majesty and splendor. (7) auspicious givam. A medicinal substance from the elephant, possibly the gall bladder. Devadatta, jealous of the Buddha, had tried to kill him by sending a mad elephant into his path. The Buddha pacified the elephant, and the elephant bowed to the Buddha, offering his body. (8) the auspicious mustard seed. On the eighth of the fifteen days when the Buddha was exhibiting miracles, he conquered six leaders from other religions, and Vajrapani appeared to offer him white mustard seed.

47 See note 16.

48 The seven royal articles are (1) the precious jewel. This corresponds to the virtue of faith, which serves as the ground for the development of all the other qualities. (2) the precious wheel. This corresponds to *prajna*, or deeper knowing. His special wheel enables the chakravartin to be victorious in battle; similarly, prajna allows the practitioner to be victorious in conquering the kleshas or afflictions. (3) the precious queen. She corresponds to meditative stabilization, or samadhi, which is the necessary ground for prajna, allowing it to be steady, tranquil, and effective. (4) the precious minister. He corresponds to joy, for example, the joy of attaining the first bodhisattva level, called Complete Joy. The minister gives wise counsel to the monarch and thus promotes joy. Sometimes, this is known as the precious householder, who brings his monarch good advice. (5) the precious horse. This corresponds to diligence. Just as the precious horse carries the monarch wherever he wishes to go, diligence enables the bodhisattva to cultivate the qualities of samadhi and prajna and thereby eliminate the afflictions and increase positive qualities. (6) the precious elephant. This corresponds to mindfulness, as this elephant is very peaceful and tame. Mindfulness allows one to tame one's mind by being aware of what is going on within. (7) the precious general. This corresponds to equanimity, a state in which one is free of attachment to one thing and aversion for another. Through equanimity one conquers the afflictions, just as the general conquers all warfare and aggression.

49 Another perspective is available in Robert Barnett, "The Karmapa's Journey to India, 1999–2000," unpublished: "The lamas reached a unique and unpublished arrangement with the Chinese (they insist that this arrangement was an informal understanding rather than a deal), whereby they agreed not to smuggle the recognized

child to India, and to allow the Chinese state to take part in the recognition process. . . . In return they expected the Chinese side to allow the child to visit the exile seat of the Karmapas which since 1959 had been at Rumtek Monastery in Sikkim in Northern India, where his most important ritual implements were kept. They also expected that they—Situ, Gyaltsap and Akong Rinpoches— would be allowed to visit the child regularly in Lhasa in order to give him advanced religious teachings." p. 44. See also, "Karmapa leaves Tibet:" "The Karmapa had not been allowed to leave Tibet to visit his teachers in India since his enthronement in 1992, despite assurances from the Chinese authorities at the time of his recognition that he would have access to his religious mentors, including the senior Kagyu lama, Situ Rinpoche, who played a central role in the discovery of the reincarnated Karmapa. These senior lamas, key figures in the religious education of a young Karmapa, had also been refused permission to visit the boy in Tsurphu monastery." *TIN News Update*, 7 January 2000.

50 Dzogchen Ponlop Rinpoche is one of the most active and creative of the younger generation of incarnate lamas. Holding the Kagyu and Nyingma lineages, he graduated from the monastic college in Rumtek, Sikkim, with high honors and has fostered educational, text preservation, and computer projects in the East and West, where he travels widely to teach in English. His numerous activities can be accessed through his website: www. nalandabodhi.org.

51 In 1950, Bardor Tulku Rinpoche was born in Tibet and recognized at a young age by the sixteenth Karmapa. With his family, he escaped from Tibet to India, but his family gradually passed away due to the difficult conditions. With a young friend, Bardor Rinpoche made his way to Sikkim, where he was formally trained at Rumtek Monastery under the tutelage of the sixteenth Karmapa. He accompanied the sixteenth Karmapa on his world tours in 1974 and 1976. In 1977 the Karmapa asked Bardor Rinpoche to stay in the United States, and since then he has played a very important role in establishing the monastery that is the seat of the Karmapa in the West. Now married, he lives with his wife, Sonam Chotso, and their three children in Woodstock, N.Y. Bardor Rinpoche teaches widely and is known for his warmth and openness.

52 Born in Tibet in 1948, Tenzin Chonyi was forced to flee the country at the age of eleven. He joined the sixteenth Karmapa in Rumtek and was his close student for many years. At the direction of the sixteenth Karmapa, Tenzin Chonyi came to the United States in 1975. For many years now, he has served as the president of Karma Triyana Dharmachakra, representing the Karmapa in the overall guidance, development, and administration of the Karmapa's monastery and affiliate centers in the West.

53 Bardor Rinpoche, conversation with the author, Woodstock, N.Y., 24 September 2002.

54 The media attention on this 1994 tour was noticed, for example, in Sudip Mazu-

madar and Melinda Liu, "Inside the Dramatic Escape of a Living Buddha," *Newsweek*, 27 February 2000.

55 Transcript of the press conference at Gyütö Ramoche University, Sidhbari, Dharamsala, India, 27 April 2001.

56 *bla gza'*

57 In particular, they came from Dechen Dzong, the Chögong office of Gyaltsap Rinpoche, the office of Nenang Monastery (Pawo Rinpoche), Drubde Samten Yiong Ling (Tsurphu's three-year retreat center), Galo Tharpa Ling, and Dorje Ling Tsungön.

58 Lo yag.

59 The texts included *Orthography: The Lamp of Speech* (covering the more advanced studies of different Tibetan scripts), *Grammar: The Beautiful Necklace of Pearls* (a famous text by a previous Situ Rinpoche), and *The Sutra of Melodious Language*. He also studied other texts on poetics, such as *The Mirror of Poetry, Imbued with Melodious Sound*, and *A Drop from the Ocean of Synonyms*.

60 One of his later explanations is in the second section of this book, "A Discussion with Foreign Students Studying in Dharamsala," on p.154.

61 For another translation of this or the whole text, see Shantideva, *The Way of the Bodhisattva*, trans. Padmakara Translation Group (Boston: Shambhala Publications, 1997); and Shantideva, *A Guide to the Bodhisattva Way of Life*, trans. Vesna A. Wallace and B. Alan Wallace (Ithaca, N.Y.: Snow Lion Publications, 1997).

62 For a translation and discussion of the text, see John W. Pettit, *Mipham's Beacon of Certainty: Illuminating the View of Dzogchen, the Great Perfection* (Boston: Wisdom Publications, 1999).

63 For a translation in progress, see Jamgön Mipham Rinpoche, *Gateway to Knowledge*, trans. Erik Pema Kunzang (Hong Kong: Rangjung Yeshe Publications), vol. 1, 1997 and vol 2, 2000.

64 For the root text, see Arya Maitreya and Acharya Asanga, *The Changeless Nature*, trans. Ken and Katia Holmes (Eskdalemuir, Scotland: Karma Drubgyu Darjya Ling, 1985). For commentary, see Khenchen Thrangu Rinpoche, *A Commentary on The Uttara Tantra Shastra* (Delhi: Sri Satguru Publications, 1989), and Maitreya, *Buddha Nature: The Mahayana Uttaratantra Shastra*, with commentary by Jamgön Kongtrul Lodrö Thaye (Ithaca: Snow Lion Publications, 2000). The Karmapa discusses this text and buddha nature in the talk entitled "All-Pervading Buddha Nature" on p. 160.

65 Maitreya through Asanga, *Byams chos sde lnga'i rtsa ba phyogs bsdebs* (Varanasi, India: Kagyud Relief and Protection Committee, 1984), 167.

66 In the Kagyu tradition, the main deity practices are Chakrasamvara, Vajrayogini, and Gyalwa Gyamtso, plus the rituals of the protector Mahakala and the special ceremonies related to Guru Rinpoche.

67 Known as *gos sku* or "cloth image," these scroll representations are a venerated tradition of Tibetan art.

68 For further discussion of Tibetan art and also the Gadri style, see David Jackson, *A History of Tibetan Painting* (Vienna: Verlag der Österreichischen Akademie der Wissenschaften, 1996), esp. chapters 5 and 11; and E. Gene Smith, *Among Tibetan Texts* (Boston: Wisdom Publications, 2001), 254-55.

69 From www.asianart.com/tsurphu. More information about and images of the thangka may be found at this site. For the unveiling of the thangka at Tsurphu, see Ward Holmes, *The Thangka Ceremony*, 25 min. (Honolulu: Tsurphu Foundation, 1994), videocassette.

70 Ri skor.

71 rTse skor.

72 Gangs sbal chu mgo.

73 They found 125 *tamkar* made of silver, 4 *sang sum gor*, also of silver, 14 *chu gor* made of copper, and 200 *zho nga* also of copper.

74 *phur pa dkar zhal.*

75 *sgrig zhal.*

76 Jean West, "The Boy Buddha," *The Herald Saturday Magazine* (Scotland), 24 July 2001.

77 Tendzin Namgyal, *"Dus gsum rgyal ba tham chad kyi phrin las (The Activity of All the Buddhas of the Three Times)."* Unpublished, 2001.

78 It was the eighth incarnation of Surmang Garwang Rinpoche of Retshang Monastery.

79 From Thubten Samdrub Chökhor Ling.

80 The Karmapa, conversation with the author, Gyutö Ramoche University, Sidhbari, Dharamsala, India, 8 June 2002.

81 This account, from here up to the section entitled "Rainbows," is based on an abridged version of *EMA HO! The Reincarnation of The Third Jamgon Kongtrul,* written by Michele Martin and approved by the Jamgön Kongtrul Labrang. Their assistance is greatly appreciated and copies of the book may be obtained from the Jamgon Kongtrul Labrang, PO Box 6956, Kathmandu, Nepal or from the Internet: pullahari@jamgonkongtrul.org.

For the remarkable life story of the first Jamgön Kongtrul, Lodrö Thaye, see *The*

Autobiography of Jamgön Kongtrul: A Gem of Many Colors, trans. Richard Barron (Chokyi Nyima) (Ithaca, N.Y.: Snow Lion Publications, 2003).

82 This is according to Western calculations. He was born in 1985. The Tibetans add another year, as they count from the Tibetan New Year and so consider him to be one year older.

83 *metok charpa.*

84 The father's name is Gonpo, which contains the letter *ga.*

85 The mother's name is Yangkyi, which has the letter *ka* belonging to the same phonetic group as *kha.*

86 Lineage holders maintain the continuity of practice and textual transmission through their personal realization of the wisdom contained therein. They are key to the unbroken transmission of the Vajrayana teachings, linking them back to their source.

87 Also attending were Phuntsok Tashi and Dhundul.

88 Jamgön Lodrö Chokyi Nyima Dronme Chok Thamced Le Nampar Gyalwe De.

89 *EMA HO!*, 72.

90 Along with Situ Rinpoche, Jamgön Kongtrul Rinpoche, Gyaltsap Rinpoche, and Treho Rinpoche from Tana Monastery in central Tibet.

91 Chos dbang lhun grub, "Master of Dharma Spontaneously Present."

92 Phreng ba, "garland."

93 *rus rigs tsang ma.*

94 *btsan mkhar.*

95 Nenang Lama, *dPal ldan dpa' bo sku phreng rnams dang gdan sa gnas nang gi lo rgyus mdor bsdus* (*A Brief History of the Garland of Incarnations of the Glorious Pawo and His Seat of Nenang*) (Nenang Monastery, Tibet, n.d.), 8-9.

96 Btsan mkhar dgon pa.

97 This was the eighteenth day of the eighth Tibetan month, an auspicious day according to Tibetan astrology.

98 Retranslated from an interview in Ward Holmes, *The Lion Begins to Roar*, 80 min. (Honolulu: Tsurphu Foundation, 2000), videocassette.

99 The festival celebrating the descent of the Buddha from a higher realm where he went to teach his mother.

100 See Tibet Information Network, "Child lama forced to leave monastery following Karmapa escape," *TIN News Update*, 2 July 2001.

101 Form body or rupakaya (Skt.) refers to the two form bodies or dimensions: sambhogakaya, the dimension of enjoyment, and nirmanakaya, the dimension of manifestation. Here it mainly refers to appearing as or taking birth in a physical form.

102 Dza tod.

103 'Bri tod.

104 Dabzang Rinpoche is considered an emanation of Gampopa.

105 Kar ma Nges don bsTan pa'i Nyi ma Phrin las mTshungs ma Med pa'i sDe.

106 In the shedra, Khenpo Lodrö was the main teacher for the seventy students who began their studies in October 1998. At the ceremony to consecrate and officially open the new shedra on May 25, 1999, the great Tsurphu thangka of Shakyamuni Buddha was displayed and the monks presented lama dances. The Karmapa performed ceremonies in the shrine hall and watched with Pawo Rinpoche at his side while the monks debated what they had learned. See Palmo Arzt-Januschke, "Report on Shedra Opening in Tsurphu," *The Himalayan Voice* (Kathmandu), no. 16 (October/November 1999).

107 "Investigation into Karmapa Escape; Parents Detained by Authorities," *TIN News Update*, 29 February 2000, 2.

108 This refers to the unbroken transmission of the teachings, practice, and realization of mind's nature that passes from teacher to disciple in the Kagyu lineage. Originally there were two lineages, the mahamudra lineage and the lineage of union (pointing to the union of sutra and tantra). The mahamudra lineage begins with Vajradhara and passes to the bodhisattva Ratnamati, Saraha, Nagarjuna, Shawaripa, Maitripa, and Marpa. The lineage of union also begins with Vajradhara but then passes to Tilopa, Naropa, and Marpa. It was Marpa who united the two lineages, and this unified lineage has come down through numerous teachers to the present seventeenth Karmapa. For a full description of the lineage and each master in it, go to www.kagyuoffice.org and select Kagyu Lineage.

1109 The one identified by the Dalai Lama has not been seen since May 1995. The Karmapa was also taken to Shigatse to meet the Chinese-appointed Panchen Lama in July of 1999.

110 These included Li Ruihuan, Chairman of the Chinese People's Political Consultative Conference (CPPCC), which is composed of traditional and religious leaders who discuss and approve party policies.

111 Taken from a video recording of CCTV (the Chinese official government television station) reporting on the Karmapa's visit to China in early 1999.

112 Isabel Hilton, "Flight of the Lama," *New York Times Magazine*, 12 March 2000, 52.

113 Conversation with the author, Sidhbari, Dharamsala, India, 8 June 2002.

114 Conversation with the author, 1 June 2002.

115 From "A Brief Introduction and Clarification," a public letter of Situ Rinpoche dated June 15, 2002.

116 For a discussion of this, see the talk entitled "A Spiritual Friend" on p. 184.

117 The Karmapa speaks about this in the talk entitled "Taking Refuge," on p. 199.

118 See the talks entitled, "Practicing Chenrezik and Developing Bodhichitta," p. 149; "Benefiting Others," p, 182; and "Giving Rise to Bodhichitta," p. 201.

119 *Drang nges legs bshad snying po*, translated by Robert Thurman as *The Central Philosophy of Tibet* (Princeton: Princeton University Press, 1984.)

120 Since he was so connected with Pawo Rinpoche's Nenang Monastery, Lama Tsewang Tashi received the name Nenang Lama. To make it easier to keep Tibetan names straight, he is referred to in the text as Nenang Lama.

121 Bod ljongs nang bstan slob grwa. Sponsored by the government, it offered a ten-year course covering the major treatises and sciences of Tibetan Buddhism, but was closed down in 1990. After three years, he left because Drupön Dechen had returned to Tsurphu from Ladakh and was rebuilding the monastery.

122 Conversation with the author, Dharamsala, India, 28 June 2002.

123 It is also known as Dranggo Monastery.

124 Conversation with the author, Sidhbari, Dharamsala, India, 14 June 2002.

125 gNas nang dbang sdus, also known as Lo Tulku. The Karmapa has recently given him a new name, Karma Mönlam Rabsay.

126 *gsang mchod*.

127 See "A Traditional Narrative of the Karmapas," on p. 273 for an explanation of the Black Crown.

128 Conversation with the author, Gyutö Ramoche University, Sidhbari, Dharamsala, India, 8 June 2002.

129 Ibid.

130 The transliterated names of the towns are: Lha rtse, Ngam ring, bZang bzang, and Sa dga'.

131 'Brang sgo.

132 Conversation with the author, Sidhbari, Dharamsala, India, 29 May 2002.

133 Chon rgya.

134 Paul Raffaele, *The Australian Weekend Magazine*, 6 April 2002. See also the *South China Morning Post*, 31 March 2002.

135 rDzong gsar pa. For the identification with Jomsom, see David Snellgrove,

Himalayan Pilgrimage (Boston: Shambhala Publications, 1989), 174 n.

136 Also known as Nyeshang, and famous for its Buddhist practitioners and expert traders.

137 Shangrila Maps, *Mustang, Trekking Map*, Kathmandu, 2000.

138 "It was an Ecureuil-type craft, which is a four seater... The helicopter made two one-hour journeys to transport the team to Kathmandu.... Chartering the helicopter is a normal commercial procedure in Nepal and would not have attracted undue attention or required any special permissions." Robert Barnett, "The Journey of the Karmapa to India 1999-2000." Unpublished manuscript, 2000, 33.

139 Lama Norbu was the *sölpön*, a special attendant of the Karmapa at Tsurphu.

140 Barnett, 45. See also *TIN News Update*, 29 February 2000.

141 *ring bsrel.*

142 *dam rdzas ril ngak.*

143 Lama Tenam, conversation with the author, 17 May 2002.

144 Ibid.

145 Ngödrup Pelzom, conversation with the author, 17 May 2002.

146 Conversation with the author, 1 June 2002.

147 Conversation with the author, 19 July 2002.

148 Ibid.

149 Conversation with the author, 1 June 2002.

150 For the outlines of this story, I am grateful to Michael Gregory, who was in Rumtek at the time.

151 Isabel Hilton, "Flight of the Lama," *New York Times Magazine*, 12 March 2000, 52.

152 *TIN News Update*, 29 February 2000.

153 Later, TIPA made a CD of the Karmapa's songs entitled "Melody of Truth." For a translation of the whole poem, see p. 226.

154 It seems that the Dalai Lama knew of the escape ahead of time: "Apparently he [the Dalai Lama] advised then that the escape should not be made. He says he was not informed in advance of the later, successful attempt (Isabel Hilton, personal communication following interview with Dalai Lama, April 2000)." Barnett, 77 n. 34.

155 Translated by Alexander Nariniani.

156 From a question and answer period at Karma Triyana Dharmachakra, Woodstock, N.Y., April 2000.

157 Translations based on commentary by Thrangu Rinpoche during the Namo Buddha Seminar, Baudha, Nepal, March 2000. See also Ken McLeod, *The Great Path of Awakening* (Boston: Shambhala Publications, 1987) and Chögyam Trungpa, *Training the Mind and Cultivating Loving-Kindness* (Boston: Shambhala Publications, 1993).

158 *Abhidharmakosha* by Vasubhandu.

159 *Chos mngon par mdzod gyi 'grel pa rgyas par spros pa grub bde dbyid 'jo (The Springtime Cow: An Extensive Commentary on the Abhidharmakosha Easily Accomplished).*

160 *bCig shes kun 'dro.*

161 *Bka' brgyud sngags mdzod,* mostly compiled by the great translator Marpa and transmitted to his disciple Ngogtön. The practices include the well-known Vajrayogini, Chakrasamvara, and Gyalwa Gyamtso, a form of red Chenrezik.

162 E. Gene Smith on the *gDams ngag mdzod* in *Among Tibetan Texts* (Boston: Wisdom Publications, 2001), 263-64. These two treasuries are part of the famous Five Treasuries compiled by the great nonsectarian master Jamgön Kongtrul Lodrö Thaye (whose fourth reincarnation was discovered by the Karmapa in 1996).

163 For a translation of this sixth chapter, see Geshe Rabten, *Echoes of Voidness*, trans. and ed. Stephen Batchelor (London: Wisdom Publications, 1986), 47-91. The whole text has been newly translated by the Padmakara Translation Group, *Introduction to the Middle Way: Chandrakirti's* Madhyamakavatara *with Commentary by Jamgön Mipham* (Boston: Shambhala Publications, 2002).

164 *The Clear Lamp of Reality* (*De nyid gsal sgron*) by Je Redawa Zhonu Lodrö (Je Red mda' ba gzhon nu blo dros).

165 The full text of the resolution is available at www.kagyu.org at releases/resolution.

166 Author's notes taken during the talk, and citing a report on Tibet Information Network, reporting on the 21 August 2000 talk. See www.tibetinfo.net.

167 Ibid.

168 In the *Telegraph* (London), 4 January 2001.

169 Luke Harding, in the *Observer* (London), 29 April 2001.

170 Conversation with the author, Dharamsala, India, 21 May 2001.

171 Pratibha Chuahan, "Karmapa Desires to Go to Rumtek," *The Tribune* (Chandigarh, India), 30 June 2000.

172 Conversation with the author, 21 May 2001.

173 Kalön Tashi Wangdi, Press Conference, cited on www.nalandabodhi.org for February 3, 2002.

174 The third stanza from "A Long-life Prayer for Tendzin Kunkhyab Wanggi Dorje: Spontaneous Accomplishment of the Aims We Seek," in *dPal rgyal dbang karmapa sku phreng bcu bdun pa chen po'i zhabs brtan khag phyogs gcig tu bkod pa bzungs so* (*A Collection of Long-life Prayers for the Gyalwang Karmapa*), (Rumtek, Sikkim: The Library of the Rumtek Shedra, n.d.). Tendzin Kunkhyab Wanggi Dorje is the name the Dalai Lama gave to the Karmapa.

175 For information on the Buddhist places of pilgrimage, see *Holy Places of the Buddha*, Crystal Mirror Series, vol. 9 (Berkeley: Dharma Publishing, 1994).

176 For the full story of Guru Rinpoche's life, see Yeshe Tsogyal, *The Lotus-Born: The Life Story of Padnasambhava*, trans. Erik Pema Kunsang (Boston: Shambhala Publications, 1993).

177 Urgyen Heruka Phodrang of Sahor Pemachen (another name for Tso Pema).

178 *bsang mchod.*

179 Press Statement, Gyütö Ramoche University, Sidhbari, Dharamsala, India, 27 April 2001.

180 Excerpted from the transcript of the conference, April 27, 2001.

181 Jean West, "The Boy Buddha," *The Herald Saturday Magazine* (Scotland), 24 July 2001.

182 Peter Popham, "The Most Powerful Teenager in the World Breaks His Long Silence," *The Independent* (London) 28 April 2001.

183 Rahul Bedi, "Tibet's Boy Tells the World of His Leap to Freedom," *The Independent* (London), 28 April 2001.

184 Mick Brown, from his interview with the Karmapa, for *The Independent* (London), 28 April 2001.

185 Swati Chopra, "New Body, Old Mind," *Tricycle: The Buddhist Review* (spring 2002), 96.

186 An epithet for the Buddha meaning "Victorious One" or "Transcendent Conqueror."

187 Conversation with the author, Sidhbari, Dharamsala, India, 8 June 2002.

188 Gampopa, *The Jewel Ornament of Liberation*, trans. Khenpo Konchog Gyaltsen Rinpoche (Ithaca: Snow Lion Publications, 1998); Gampopa, *Gems of Dharma, Jewels of Freedom*, trans. Ken and Katia Holmes (Forres, Scotland: Altea Publishing, 1994).

189 *Dbu ma la 'jug pa'i rnam bshad dpal ldan dus gsum mkhyan pa'i zhal lung dwags brgyud grub pa'i shing rta (The Chariot of the Dakpo Kagyu Siddhas: An Extended Commentary on the Madhyamakavatara, The Oral Instructions of the Glorious Dusum Khyenpa)*.

190 Chopra, "New Body, Old Mind," 97.

191 See the talk entitled "Milarepa's Song" on p. 174.

192 Conversation with the author, Sidhbari, Dharamsala, India, 8 June 2002.

193 Conversation with the author, Woodstock, N.Y., 9 August 2002.

194 From a talk at Karma Triyana Dharmachakra, Woodstock, N.Y., 11 August 2002.

195 Conversation with the author, Sidhbari, Dharamsala, India, 8 June 2002.

196 These refer to four different types of meditation practice in the tantric tradition, known as *kriya, charya, yoga,* and *anuttara yoga.*

197 Conversation with the author, Sidhbari, Dharamsala, India, 5 July 2002.

198 Tenzing Sönam, "Out of the Red," *Time* (Asian edition), 22 April 2002.

199 Chopra, "New Body, Old Mind," 93.

200 Talk (as in note 194), 11 August 2002.

201 Nagarjuna, *dBu ma rtsa ba'i shes rab* (*The Fundamental Wisdom of the Middle Way*) in *dBu ma rig tshogs lnga* (*The Five Collections on Reasoning*), (Sarnath, India: Sakya Student's Union, 1994), 1. For another translation of these verses and a useful discussion of the text, see Jay L. Garfield, *The Fundamental Wisdom of the Middle Way: Nagarjuna's Mūlamadhyamakakārikā* (New York: Oxford University Press, 1995).

202 Conversation with the author, Karma Triyana Dharmachakra, Woodstock, N.Y., 10 August 2002.

203 From Radio Free Asia's website, www.rfa.org, 21 August, 2002.

204 Ibid.

205 Formerly known as Calcutta.

206 *The Telegraph* (Calcutta), 16 September 2002.

207 The preliminary practices are 100,000 repetitions each of four practices: the refuge vow and generation of bodhichitta accompanied by prostrations, the Vajrasattva mantra, the mandala offering, and the guru yoga. They are preliminary to the more advanced practices related to the yidams and insight into the nature of mind.

208 "Zab don rgyan brgyad" in *rNal 'byor gyi dbang phyug chen po mi la ras pa'i rnam mgur* (*The Songs of the Great and Powerful Yogi Milarepa*), (Ziling: mTsho sngon mi rigs dpe skrun khang, 1981, 1989), 724-725.

209 Generosity, discipline, patience, diligence, stable contemplation, and deeper knowing (*prajna*).

210 The first way of gathering disciples is being generous with the Dharma and material

things. The second is conversing in an engaging manner. The third is acting in accordance with what disciples wish for. The fourth is that all Dharma activity is done in a way that is related to the disciples' way of acting.

211 The ten unvirtuous activities are divided into the three categories of body, speech, and mind. The three unvirtuous actions of the body are killing, stealing, and sexual misconduct. The four related to speech are lying, creating discord, using harsh words, and meaningless chatter. The three related to mind are envy, ill will, and wrong views. The ten virtuous activities are the opposite of the ten unvirtuous ones: in relation to the body, not killing, stealing, or engaging in sexual misconduct; in relation to speech, not lying, creating discord, using harsh words, or indulging in meaningless talk; and in relation to the mind, avoiding envy, ill will, and wrong views.

212 This prayer summarizes basic elements of the practice for gathering merit into seven stages: (1) prostration to all the buddhas and bodhisattvas; (2) actual and imagined offerings; (3) acknowledging one's faults; (4) rejoicing in the merit of others; (5) entreating those who are realized to teach; (6) beseeching them not to pass into nirvana; and (7) dedication of merit.

213 This posture involves seven key points: (1) legs are crossed in vajra posture (or however close we can come); (2) the hands rest relaxed on the knees or with the right hand on top of the left, thumbs touching at the level of the navel; (3) the elbows are slightly raised away from the rib cage; (4) the spine is lengthened; (5) the chin is slightly tucked in, which lengthens the back of the neck; (6) the mouth is closed and slightly relaxed with the tip of the tongue touching the palate; and (7) the eyes' gaze rests about eight finger-widths in front of the nose.

214 See the previous note.

215 The provisional meaning refers to a teaching that was given when disciples were not ready to hear a more profound explanation, and so it is open to another level of interpretation. The definitive meaning is directly stated and usually describes the ultimate.

216 Able to fly as soon as it is born, this mythical bird is a symbol for primordial wisdom.

217 There are four levels of stable contemplation, which correspond to four main areas in the form realm. Each of these has three levels, making twelve, and when the five pure places of the form realm are added on, all these seventeen levels constitute the totality of the form realm. The form realm is one of the three realms making up samsara, known as the realms of desire, form, and the formlessness. For more detail, see Lati Rinpochay and Denma Lochö Rinpochay, *Meditative States in Tibetan Buddhism*, trans. Leah Zahler and Jeffrey Hopkins (Boston: Wisdom Publications, 1983, 1997), 142-45.

218 For example, the second category, function, is applied to each of the Four Noble

Truths: in relation to the First Noble Truth, the function is to pacify suffering; in relation to the Second Noble Truth, the function is to remove the source of suffering; in relation to the Third Noble Truth, the function is to eliminate the manifestation of suffering; and in relation to the Fourth Noble Truth, the function is to rely on the path. See *The Treasury of Knowledge*, Palpung edition, vol. 1, 308 and 358.

219 The other eleven are: (2) karmic formations, or impulses; (3) consciousness; (4) name and form; (5) sense faculties; (6) contact; (7) feeling; (8) craving; (9) taking on, or indulgence; (10) becoming; (11) birth; and (12) aging and death.

220 From a talk at Gyütö Ramoche University, Sidhbari, Dharamsala, India, 22 February 2000.

221 Sarasvati has a special relation to the arts of poetry, dance, and song and also to wisdom.

222 Conversation with the author, Gyütö Ramoche University, Sidhbari, Dharamsala, India, June 2000.

223 Ibid.

224 Ibid.

225 "A Talk to Music Students from New Delhi," Sidhbari, Dharamsala, India, 22 March 2000.

226 Public Talk, Namgyal Monastery, Dharamsala, India, 21 August 2001.

227 See note 16 above.

228 Robert Beer, *Encyclopedia of Tibetan Symbols and Motifs* (Boston: Shambhala Publications, 1999), 48.

229 *Tsad ma legs par bshad pa thams cad kyi chu bo yongs su 'dus ba rigs pa'i gzhung lugs kyi rgya mtsho zhes bya ba bzhugs so* (*The Ocean of Reasoning That Completely Contains the River of All the Excellent Explanations of Pramana*), 2 vols. Input by Nitartha International, sponsored by Khenpo Tsultrim Gyamtso. (Sarnath, India: Kagyud Relief and Protection Committee, 1999).

230 For a discussion of the four maras, see the talk entitled, "The Source of Obstacles" on p. 170.

231 Conversation with Khenpo Karthar Rinpoche, Karma Triyana Dharmachakra, Woodstock, N.Y., 31 August 2002.

232 For an explanation of the kayas, see the poem entitled "The Three Kayas," p. 230, and the Glossary.

233 Tulku Thondup, *Masters of Meditation and Miracles* (Boston: Shambhala Publications, 1996), 82.

234 The three rituals or commitments kept by the sangha: (1) *so jong* (*gso sbyong*), a rit-

ual to mend broken vows; (2) *gag ye* (*dgag dbye*), a ritual for ending the summer retreat; and (3) *yarne* (*dbyar gnas*), abiding in retreat during the summer months.

235 Milarepa, *rNal 'byor gyi dbang phyug chen po mi la ras pa'i rnam mgur* (*The Songs of Milarepa, Lord of the Yogis*), (Ziling: mTsho sngon mi rigs par khang, 1981, 1989) 300.

236 From the Fourth Vajra Point, *Theg pa chen po rgyud blama* (*Mahayana Uttara Tantra*) in *Byams chos sde lnga'i rtsa ba phyogs bsdebs* (*The Collection of the Five Dharmas of Maitreya*), (Sarnath: Kagyud Relief and Protection Committee, 1984), 165.

237 According to Mipham Rinpoche's commentary on the fifth chapter of *Distinguishing the Middle from Extremes* by Maitreya, the ten Dharma activities are the following: (1) writing the letters, which is a support for maintaining the genuine Dharma of both the greater and lesser vehicles; (2) making offerings in homage to the Dharma and offerings to those who elucidate it; (3) giving generously to those who set forth the Dharma and helping them to fulfill their needs; (4) listening to the Dharma without distraction; (5) reading Dharma texts; (6) memorizing words that express the meaning of the Dharma; (7) explaining to others the meaning of these words; (8) reciting aloud what has been memorized; (9) considering deeply the meaning of the Dharma; (10) meditating correctly with a one-pointed mind.

238 When not otherwise noted, the quotations come from the first chapter of Tendzin Namgyal's text.

239 For other histories, see Karma Thinley, *The History of the Sixteen Karmapas* (Boulder: Prajna Press, 1980); Nik Douglas and Meryl White, *Karmapa the Black Hat Lama* (London: Luzac & Company Ltd, 1976); and www.kagyuoffice.org/Kagyu Lineage.

240 Rinchen Pelzang, *mTsurphu dgon gyi dkar chag kun gsel me long* (*The All-Illuminating Mirror: An Index of Tsurphu Monastery*), (Lhasa: Mirig Pedrun Khang, 1995), 340.

241 Ibid.

242 Ibid.

243 For more information on him, see Yeshe Tsogyal, *The Lotus-Born: The Life Story of Padmasambhava*, 271-2.

244 Gyalwa Gyamtso is a particular form of red Chenrezik that was favored by many of the Karmapas.

245 At the same time as a sugata named Drayang Kyi Gyalpo (King of Melody).

246 He was known in his youth as Chökyi Lodrö (Mind of the Dharma).

247 His father was called Ngakchang Dorje Gonpo and his mother, Gangcham Mingdren.

248 Thubten Jampel Tsultrim from Serrong Lhatse in Golok, located in northeastern Tibet.

249 Pema Wangchuk Gyalpo (1886-1952).

250 His full name is Chökyi Gyalpo Orgyen Chokgyur Dechen Lingpa.

251 For another and complete translation of Chokgyur Lingpa's prophecy and the paintings of his visions, see Kagyu Thubten Chöling, *Karmapa: The Sacred Prophecy*, (Wappingers Falls, N.Y.: Kagyu Thubten Chöling Publications Committee, 1999).

252 Robert Beer, *Encyclopedia of Tibetan Symbols and Motifs* (Boston: Shambhala Publications, 1999), 78-80.

253 See the previous poem for more on Akanishtha.

254 Beer, *Encyclopedia*, 162.

255 These three dates are from Matthew T. Kapstein, "A Brief Chronology of Tibetan Buddhism," in *The Tibetan Assimilation of Buddhism: Conversion, Contestation, and Memory* (Oxford: Oxford University Press, 2000), xvii.

abhidharma (Skt.): In the early compilation of the Buddha's teachings known as the tripitaka, the abhidharma ("higher teachings") is the third of three parts (along with the sutras and the vinaya). It sets forth a systematic structuring of experience whereby it is analyzed into numerous categories, thus training discriminating wisdom and providing objects of meditation.

accumulations, two: The merit of virtuous activity and the development of a deeper knowing or wisdom.

afflictions (kleshas, Skt.): Among the different mental events, the afflictions are detailed as the six root afflictions of ignorance, aversion, attachment, pride, doubt, and wrong view. They are also described as the five mental and emotional afflictions of ignorance, aversion, attachment, pride, and envy, which can be condensed into the three poisons of ignorance, aversion, and attachment.

aggregates (skandhas, Skt.): The five constituents of our mental and physical life: form, sensation, discrimination, mental formations, and consciousness.

Amitabha (Skt.): The red Buddha who presides over Sukhavati, the pure land in the west, which is uniquely accessible to humans due to his particular aspirations. He is the focus for the practice of transferring consciousness at death and of ceremonies for those who have died.

Amitayus (Skt.): The manifestation of Amitabha on the sambhogakaya level and one of the three main deities connected with long life along with White Tara and Ushnisha-Vijaya.

amrita (Skt.): A nectar that brings freedom from birth and death; it can also function as a purifying liquid to cleanse away defilements.

Atisha: Also known as *Jowoje* (982–1054), the great Indian master who brought the teachings of the Kadampa school to Tibet. The practice he taught of sending one's happiness to others and taking on their suffering is widely practiced in Tibetan Buddhism.

bardo (Tib.): An intermediate state or interval, of which six types are usually enumerated: birth, dream, meditation, the time of death, dharmata, and becoming. The common understanding of bardo encompasses the last three, from the process of dying, to the dharmata, the various appearances, and rebirth.

Barkhor (Tib.): The wide stone pathway that is a pilgrimage route encircling the Jokhang, the central temple of Lhasa, where the most sacred statue of the Buddha, the Jowo, is enshrined.

bindu (Skt.): A sphere or drop of light, which rides the prana (q.v.) in the nadi (q.v.) of the illusory or subtle body.

bodhichitta (Skt.): In general, the motivation to attain full awakening and bring others to that same liberation. It is divided into ultimate bodhichitta, which is the realization of mind's nature, and relative bodhichitta, which is again divided into the aspiration and the actual engagement in the practice of the six or ten perfections. *See also* perfections.

bodhisattva (Skt.): In Tibetan, *chang chub sems dpa'*, literally, "warrior of enlightenment." Bodhisattvas are those who have dedicated their lives to compassionate action and the realization of mind's nature in order to help others on the path to liberation. The term refers both to individuals on the Mahayana path and to those who have achieved a high level of realization and abide in other realms, such as Chenrezik and Manjushri.

bodhisattva levels (bhumi, Skt.): The ten successive grounds or stages of a bodhisattva's practice, beginning with the initial realization of emptiness on the first level and culminating with the vajralike samadhi at the end of the tenth level that opens into full realization. On each level, there are defects to be discarded and qualities to be manifested.

buddha nature: A synonym for the ultimate nature of mind, emphasizing its presence within all living beings.

calm abiding (shamatha, Skt.): Common to most Buddhist schools, this is a meditation practice of bringing one's mind into sustained tranquillity. Through repeated practice, distractions are stilled and the mind is able to abide wherever it is placed. Calm abiding is the basis for the practice of deep insight.

channels, winds, and spheres: *See* nadi; prana; bindu.

Chenrezik (Tib.): The embodiment of compassion and Tibet's special deity, usually depicted as white. The Dalai Lama and the Karmapa are considered incarnations of Chenrezik.

Chittamatra (Skt.): Known as the Mind Only school and belonging to the Mahayana, this philosophical school emphasizes the mental nature of all phenomena as they arise from the seeds of habitual patterns. An analogy for this mental nature is the dream, wherein both subject and object are mentally produced. Further, just as we wake up from a dream, so can we realize the illusory nature of perception divided into subject and object. The self-awareness that comes to know this reality beyond duality is posited as the ultimate.

chuba (Tib.): The traditional Tibetan dress worn by women and men. The woman's version is full length, with long or short sleeves, and usually wraps around the body closely. The man's version is belted, has long, wide sleeves, and wraps loosely around the body to fall below the knee.

completion stage: The second phase of visualization practice, following the generation stage. At this stage, all the images are dissolved back into the emptiness whence they came. More subtly, this stage can be divided into an aspect that has features, referring to the practice of nadi, prana, and bindu (q.v.), and an aspect without features, referring to the practice of mahamudra. *See also* generation stage.

dakini (Skt.): A feminine figure who ranges in meaning from a worldly deity with a variety of functions to an enlightened embodiment of wisdom.

deep insight (vipashyana, Skt.): Coming after the mind has been stabilized through the practice of calm abiding, deep insight involves seeing into the nature of mind itself.

deeper knowing (prajna, Skt.): A native intelligence that sees beyond the surface to a more profound reality, which can be seeing the impermanence of all phenomena, or more deeply, mind's nature itself. In dialectics, deeper knowing is traditionally defined as the faculty of the mind that is able to distinguish between the relative and the ultimate. *See also* truths, two.

definitive meaning: The definitive meaning is directly stated; it can be taken to mean what it says, and usually describes the ultimate. It is paired with the term "provisional meaning."

dharmadhatu (Skt.): The expanse of all phenomena, a synonym for ultimate reality. It points to what the master Tilopa states in *Mahamudra: The Ocean of Definitive Meaning*: "From time without beginning, the true nature of mind is like space./ There is no phenomenon that is not included therein."

dharmakaya (Skt.): *See* kaya.

dharmata (Skt.): Reality itself, another synonym for the ultimate, often used to indicate it in the context of its presence as the empty nature of all phenomena, that is, as embedded or enfolded within relative truth. *See also* truths, two.

doha (Skt.): A song of attainment or song of experience spontaneously sung by realized masters.

dralha (Tib.): Special beings who assist warriors in battle.

dzogchen (Tib.) (mahasandhi, Skt.): The Great Completion, the most advanced practice in the Nyingma tradition (also practiced by the Kagyu and others), involving a focus on the nature of mind as pristine awareness and the appearances that arise from it. Full awakening is understood as the realization of the primordial and spontaneous purity of mind. The core texts of dzogchen are usually numbered at seventeen, and the teachings are divided into three main sections: mind, space, and instruction.

empowerment (abhisheka, Skt.): An initiation, usually given in a formal ceremony by a lama to disciples, transferring the authority to engage in a particular practice. A simple form conveys the blessing of the body, speech, and mind of the deity to the disciple's body, speech, and mind with the instruction to regard all forms as the deity, all sounds as mantra, and all thoughts as wisdom.

form body: *See* kaya.

Foundational Vehicle (hinayana, Skt.): In the Tibetan context, it is understood as the part of the Buddhist heritage that focuses on the rules and regulations for the ordained sangha and on the practice of liberating oneself from the ocean of samsara. In general usage, the term often overlaps with Theravada, "the school of the elders," which is still practiced in Thailand, Burma, Sri Lanka, Laos, and Cambodia.

generation stage: The first phase of visualization practice, in which the deity, arising out of emptiness, is brought to mind in vivid detail as a central focus while the deity's mantra is recited. *See also* completion stage.

Great Completion: *See* dzogchen.

Great Seal: *See* mahamudra.

Guru Rinpoche: Venerated by the Tibetans as the Second Buddha, Guru Rinpoche ("Precious Master") was invited from India to Tibet in the ninth century. By subjugating negative forces, he established Vajrayana Buddhism in Tibet and hid numerous terma (q.v.) throughout the Himalayan region for the sake of future generations.

gyaling (Tib.): A reed horn, sounding a bit like an oboe, used in rituals and played to welcome important lamas in general and, in particular, to usher them into ceremonial events.

Gyalwa (Tib.): Usually translated as "the Victorious One." The Karmapa is referred to as the Gyalwa Karmapa or the Gyalwang (Victorious and Powerful) Karmapa. In a more general context, "Gyalwa" refers to a buddha.

Hinayana (Skt.): *See* Foundational Vehicle.

Jokhang (Tib.): The central temple in Lhasa and the most sacred in all of Tibet, the Jokhang was established by King Songtsen Gampo in the seventh century and enshrines the famous statue of the Buddha, the Jowo Rinpoche (q.v.).

Jowo Rinpoche (Tib.): Also called simply the Jowo, a statue of Shakyamuni Buddha at the age of twelve. The most revered statue in Tibet, it is believed to date back to the time of the Buddha.

kalön (Tib.): A minister in the government.

Kangyur (Tib.): The recorded words of Shakyamuni Buddha, the Kangyur is found in many editions and numbers about 100 volumes containing 700 to 800 texts. Along with the Tengyur (q.v.), it forms the central corpus of Buddhist texts in the Tibetan tradition.

kapse (Tib.): Fried biscuits in ornamental forms made for New Year's celebrations.

kaya (Skt.): In the Mahayana, full awakening is often described in terms of the kayas, meaning "bodies" or "dimensions of reality," which are numbered two, three, or four. When they are two, they are the dharmakaya (dimension or body of truth) and the rupakaya (body of form). The dharmakaya is the perfect realization of mind's nature and replete with enlightened qualities; it is nonconceptual and synonymous with emptiness or omniscience. When the kayas are three, the rupakaya is divided into the samb-hogakaya (body of bliss or enjoyment) and the nirmanakaya (body of manifestation or emanation). Expressing the nature of radiant clarity, the sambhogakaya is visible only to bodhisattvas on the ten levels and is adorned with the major and minor marks of a buddha. The nirmanakaya is the fully awakened mind that manifests without impedi-ment in a variety of forms and remains visible to ordinary beings; Shakyamuni Buddha is an example of a nirmanakaya. When the kayas are four, the svabhavikakaya (body of the essential nature) refers to the inseparability of the other three.

khata (Tib.): A long white scarf, usually of silk, that is offered to deities and to indi-viduals as a gesture of respect and devotion or simply as a welcoming greeting.

khenpo (Tib.): An especially accomplished teacher who has completed a long and rig-orous course of study covering the major treatises of Buddhist philosophy. Some are also masters of meditation.

kleshas (Skt.): *See* afflictions.

lama (Tib.) (guru, Skt.): In general, a teacher. There are many levels of lamas and dif-ferent ways of awarding the title.

Last Testament: The letter composed by the Karmapa to predict his next incarnation, indicating the place, the names of his parents, and other details about his rebirth.

Madhyamaka (Skt.): The Middle Way school of philosophy, which evolved from the thought of the great Indian scholar Nagarjuna (second century C.E.). Its view focuses on the empty nature of all phenomena that allows for their dependent origination. Its rea-sonings radically cut through any tendency to reify an object or a subject. Of its two main subschools, the Rangtong approach emphasizes the empty aspect of mind's nature, while the Shentong approach emphasizes its clear and radiant aspect. Ultimately, the two are inseparable.

Mahakala (Skt.): A fierce, blue-black protector deity central to the Kagyu lineage.

mahamudra (Skt.): The Great (maha) Seal (mudra) is the supreme practice in the Kagyu lineage. Its practices lead to a recognition of the nature of the mind, which is often defined as the union of bliss and emptiness. Describing this practice in *Mahamu-dra: The Ocean of Definitive Meaning*, the great Indian adept Maitripa (1012–1097) states, "All phenomena are empty of self-essence. / The mind grasping them as empty is purified into its ground. / Free of intellect, with no object for the mind, / This is the path of all Buddhas."

mahasandhi (Skt.): *See* dzogchen.

Mahayana (Skt.): The Great Vehicle, a further development of Buddhist thought and practice that focuses on compassion and emptiness, also known as the path of the bodhi-sattva. Within the system of Tibetan Buddhism, it is the second of three vehicles—the Hinayana, Mahayana, and Vajrayana—and is understood to function as the basis of the Vajrayana.

Maitreya (Skt.): The fifth and future buddha, now abiding in Tushita heaven as Shakyamuni did before taking birth. Also considered the author, through Asanga, of "The Five Texts of Maitreya," an important set of teachings of which one is *The Supreme Continuum.*

mani wheel: A prayer wheel, often carried by older Tibetans in the right hand, consisting of a handle serving as an axis for a spinning metal container filled with mantras. The metal is often embossed with Chenrezik's mantra, *Om mani padme hung,* and practitioners recite this mantra while turning the wheel, hence the name. The term can also refer to the larger drums filled with mantras, which can be lined up in walls, stood in a large room by themselves, or set in a stream to be turned by water or on a roof to be spun by the wind.

Manjushri (Skt.): A bodhisattva who embodies wisdom and holds a sword in one hand and a text in the other.

mantra (Skt.): Mantra is understood as "what can protect our mind" and refers to various sets of Sanskrit syllables, infused with meaning and power through practice and lineage transmission, and repeated during yidam deity practice.

Mantrayana, Secret (Skt.): A synonym for the Vajrayana.

maras, four (Skt.): The four maras are the afflictions, the five aggregates, the children of the gods (devaputra), and the Lord of Death (Yama). The Karmapa explains that in general, "The label 'mara' is given to what blocks a practitioner from attaining awakening or perfect liberation."

meditative stabilization: *See* samadhi.

Middle Way school: *See* Madhyamaka.

Mind Only school: *See* Chittamatra.

nadi (Skt.): The channels of the subtle body through which the winds, or prana, flow.

nirmanakaya (Skt.): *See* kaya.

obscurations, two: The afflictive and the cognitive. The first refers to the five or six afflictions, which are purified during the first seven bodhisattva levels. The second refers to obscurations that prevent realization of omniscience, which are purified on the last three bodhisattva levels.

Padmasambhava (Skt.): *See* Guru Rinpoche.

paramita (Skt.): *See* perfections.

parinirvana (Skt.): The final liberation of buddhas or, by extension, great masters, which is said to occur when they pass away.

perfections, six or **ten** (paramita, Skt.): Also translated as "transcendent perfection," or more literally, "gone to the other shore," since by practicing them, one is carried across to the far shore of samsara and into liberation. As six, they are: generosity, discipline, patience, joyful diligence, stable contemplation, and deeper knowing. As ten, four more are added: skillful means, aspiration, strength, and primordial wisdom. They constitute the bodhichitta of engagement and, along with meditation on the nature of the mind, form the path of a bodhisattva's practice. On each of the bodhisattva levels, the practice of one of the perfections is fully accomplished; for example, on the first level, generosity is brought to perfection.

Potala (Tib.): The pure land of Chenrezik and, by extension, the residence of the Dalai Lama in Lhasa.

prajna (Skt.): *See* deeper knowing.

pramana (Skt.): The term can refer to an instance of valid cognition or to the whole system of dialectics, which is a central part of the curriculum of higher Buddhist studies. It is considered a path to valid knowledge and is usually divided into three types: direct, inferential, and scriptural.

prana (Skt.): The winds or currents of energy that flow through the channels, or nadis, of the subtle body.

Prasangika Madhyamaka (Skt.): Sometimes translated as "the Consequentialist school," so named for its method of debate, which consists of drawing out unwanted consequences from another's argument while avoiding making assertions. This is the main Rangtong school and sometimes synonymous with it, although the Svantantrika school (q.v.) is also considered part of Rangtong.

pratimoksha vows (Skt.): Vows of individual liberation taken by the ordained sangha of the Foundational Vehicle.

pratyekabuddha (Skt.): Often translated as "self realizers" or "solitary buddhas," these practitioners of the Foundational Vehicle attain their realization without the help of a teacher and through the contemplation of the twelve links of dependent arising.

provisional meaning: This refers to a teaching that was given when disciples were not yet ready to hear a more profound explanation, and therefore it is open to other levels of interpretation. It is paired with the term "definitive meaning."

puja (Skt.): A ritual or ceremony.

pure land: A pure realm or the universe of a mandala, generated by a deity or a buddha and endowed with special characteristics related to the being at its center.

radung (Tib.): A long, deep-toned, telescoping horn that is played during ritual ceremonies.

Rangtong (Tib.): One of the two Madhyamaka schools, the Rangtong promotes a view that emphasizes the empty nature of all phenomena and their lack of inherent existence while focusing on the mind as free of mental constructs. The name translates as "empty in and of itself," reflecting the radical focus on emptiness. *See also* Shentong.

reading transmission: The recitation of a text aloud, which sustains the flow of the transmission. The resonant words bring the blessing of the practice and a connection with the masters of the past from the one who has heard to the one who is listening. Reading transmissions are given for specific practices, mantras, practice manuals, philosophical texts, and other treatises.

realms, three: First of the three is the desire realm, which has six divisions: hell beings, hungry ghosts, animals, humans, demigods, and gods. These are also modes of experience, created by our minds and then taken to be real. The form realm has seventeen levels and the formless realm, four. All three realms together constitute samsara.

rime (Tib.): Literally, "without bias" and usually translated as "nonsectarian," it often refers to the great renaissance of Buddhism in nineteenth-century Tibet.

ringsel (Tib.): Pearl-like relics left behind when the body of a highly realized lama is cremated.

rinpoche (Tib.): Literally, "precious one," an honorific given to all reincarnate lamas and also sometimes to exceptional teachers who have attained a high level of realization. When disciples use the term in relation to their lama, it conveys a sense of deep respect along with the warmth of a special connection.

Rumtek: The town in Sikkim, India, where the sixteenth Karmapa, Rangjung Rigpe Dorje, built the Dharma Chakra Center, also known as Rumtek Monastery, his main seat in exile, which is also home to the Karma Shri Nalanda Institute for Higher Buddhist Studies.

rupakaya (Skt.): *See* kaya.

sadhana (Skt.): A tantric practice for realizing the nature of a particular deity, who is the focus of the text. It usually begins with the preliminaries of taking refuge and generating bodhichitta, then moves to the main section of visualizing the deity and reciting its mantra, and closes with dissolution of the image and dedication.

samadhi (Skt.): A meditative stabilization that involves undistracted, deep concentration when one's attention is exceptionally clear and focused one-pointedly. Many different kinds of samadhis are described in the sutras.

sambhogakaya (Skt.): *See* kaya.

shamatha (Skt.): *See* calm abiding.

shedra (Tib.): An institute of higher learning focused on the in-depth study of the major Buddhist treatises.

Shentong (Tib.): One of the two Madhyamaka schools, the Shentong sees the fully awakened mind as resplendent with positive qualities and asserts that the buddha nature is present within all beings at the beginning of the path and becomes manifest at enlightenment through practices along the path that remove veils obscuring what was always there. Hence its name, which translates as "empty of what is other to it":

the nature of mind itself is free of and unaffected by temporary, adventitious stains. *See also* Rangtong.

shravaka (Skt.): A "hearer" or "listener," one who follows the practices of the Foundational Vehicle to move through four stages of realization and arrive at the stage of an arhat, the highest level in this tradition.

siddhi (Skt.): A special accomplishment stemming from authentic practice. There are two types: mundane siddhis, such as clairvoyance or walking through walls, which are not essential, and supramundane siddhi, which is the realization of mind's nature, the goal of meditation practice.

skandhas (Skt.): *See* aggregates.

stable contemplation (dhyana, Skt.): The fifth of the six perfections, this meditative stability involves a focused attention, undisturbed by the afflictions.

stupa (Skt.): A monument enshrining the relics of a buddha or realized master. There are many different kinds, but stupas usually have a square base with a round midsection topped by a spire. They symbolize the mind of the Buddha and are often major sites of pilgrimage, such as the Baudhanath Stupa outside Kathmandu, Nepal.

sugatagarbha (Skt.): Literally, "heart of the one gone to bliss," another synonym for full awakening used in the context of the Vajrayana.

sutra (Skt.): The second of the three sections (along with the vinaya and abhidharma) of the tripitaka, the early compilation of the Buddha's teachings. More generally, a sutra is a text containing the discourses of Shakyamuni Buddha or those inspired by him. Sutras are often in the form of a dialogue between the Buddha and a disciple on a particular topic. Within discussions of philosophical view, the sutra approach refers to a gradual path to enlightenment, as distinguished from the swift path of the Vajrayana.

Svatantrika (Skt.): Translated as "the Autonomy school," since it propounds the use of independent syllogisms to enable an individual to see that phenomena are not inherently existent and, further, that their true nature is emptiness. It belongs to the Rangtong school of the Madhyamaka tradition.

tantra (Skt.): Usually translated as "continuum" or "thread," tantra is synonymous with the Vajrayana or Secret Mantrayana and can also refer to a text that presents these teachings or practices. The translation "continuum" points to the continuity of mind's nature in the beginning as the ground, in the middle along the path, and at the end when it fully manifests as the fruition.

Tara: (Skt.) (Drölma, Tib.), "the Lady who Liberates," a female buddha much loved by the Tibetans. To protect beings from danger and assist them on life's path, she has twenty-one forms, the most popular being Green Tara and White Tara.

Tengyur (Tib.): Along with the Kangyur (q.v.), the Tengyur forms the central corpus of Buddhist texts in the Tibetan tradition. There are many editions, the Derge being the most popular, and they contain translations of over 3,500 Indian treatises in more than 200 volumes.

terma (Tib.): Treasures concealed by Guru Rinpoche and his consort Yeshe Tsogyal to be discovered at a later time when they would be needed. Of the many kinds, the most prevalent are mind terma, which are discovered in the depth of a tertön's mind, and earth terma, which take many forms, including texts, ritual and natural objects, and relics.

tertön (Tib.): A realized master who discovers or reveals terma.

thangka (Tib.): A Tibetan scroll image, usually of deities or mandalas, which is painted from ground precious stones (or, now, modern paints), stitched, or made of appliqué.

Three Jewels: The Buddha as the teacher, the Dharma as what he taught, and the Sangha as those who help one along the path. The Sangha is divided into three groups: the lay sangha, the ordained sangha, and the bodhisattvas.

truths, two: Relative truth involves the ordinary appearances of the everyday world and dualistic perception; whatever appears is interpreted in terms of subject and object. Ultimate truth is beyond the mundane world and its duality; a synonym for emptiness and free of all mental fabrications, it is also radiant and clear.

tsampa (Tib.): Roasted barley flour, a staple of the Tibetan diet.

Tseringma (Tib.): A special protectress of the Karmapa's lineage, and also known as a goddess whose dialogues with Milarepa are famous.

Tsurphu (Tib.): The main seat of the Karmapas in Tibet, located in the Tölung Valley about twenty miles west of Lhasa.

tulku (Tib.): An individual who reincarnates consciously with the motivation to take rebirth in order to benefit others.

Vairochana (Skt.): The central white buddha of the five buddha families, associated with the wisdom of the dharmadhatu.

Vajradhara (Skt.): "The One Holding a Vajra" and embodying the ultimate, the dharmakaya. Usually depicted as deep blue and holding a bell and dorje crossed over his heart.

Vajrapani (Skt.): The embodiment of enlightened power, shown holding a vajra; often mentioned together with Chenrezik and Manjushri. As Lord of the Secrets, he is the holder of the tantras.

Vajrayana (Skt.): It is said that like a diamond, a *vajra* is able to cut through everything, and this quality makes it a symbol of the realization of mind's nature that cuts through all delusions of duality. Vajrayana is translated as "diamond vehicle," a synonym for the tantric Buddhism that developed in India and came to Tibet, forming the core of its Buddhist practice.

vehicle (yana, Skt.): Refers to the three major systems of Buddhist teachings from the Tibetan perspective: the Hinayana, Mahayana, and Vajrayana. The term "vehicle" is used because these teachings carry one along the path of practice into ultimate realization.

vinaya (Skt.): The rules and regulations covering the practices of the ordained communities of monks and nuns. It is the first of the three divisions of the Tripitaka.

vipashyana (Skt.): *See* deep insight.

wheel of Dharma: Metaphorically, this refers to the three major teachings of the Buddha: in the first turning of the wheel of Dharma, he focused on the Four Noble Truths; in the second turning, he taught emptiness inseparable from compassion; and in the third turning he focused on the buddha nature pervading all living beings.

yangsi (Tib.): A term used to refer to reincarnate lamas before they have been enthroned or, more generally, while they are quite young.

yidam (Tib.): The fully awakened mind manifesting as the different forms of male and female deities who represent its myriad qualities. Often translated as "chosen deity," it refers to the specific deity selected as the focus of one's practice.

zi stone (Tib.): A white and black semiprecious stone having different numbers of "eyes" (circles), highly valued by Tibetans and thought to give protection. It is said to be a form of agate.

"A Talk by His Eminence Tai Situ Rinpoche and His Eminence Tsurphu Gyaltsap Rinpoche on Friday, June 12, 1992 in the Front Entrance Hall of Rumtek Monastery." *Densal* (Karma Triyana Dharmachakra, Woodstock, N.Y.) 12, nos. 1 and 2 (winter/spring 1993).

Ambun, Golok, comp. *Pod dang sa 'brel khag* (*A Map of Tibet and Adjacent Areas*). Dharamsala, India: Amnye Machen Institute, 1998.

Amdo Palden, Lama. Interview. Tsurphu, Tibet, 24 September 1992.

Arzt-Januschke, Palmo. "Report on Shedra Opening in Tsurphu." *The Himalayan Voice* (Kathmandu) no. 16 (October/November 1999).

Bardor Rinpoche. Interview. Woodstock, New York, 24 September 2002, and 7 November 2002.

Barnett, Robert. "The Journey of the Karmapa to India 1999-2000." Unpublished. 2000.

Bedi, Rahul. "Tibet's Boy Lama Tells the World of His Leap to Freedom." *The Independent* (London), 28 April 2001.

Beer, Robert. *The Encyclopedia of Tibetan Symbols and Motifs.* Boston: Shambhala Publications, 1999.

Brown, Mick. "Daunting Audience with a 900-Year-old Teenager." *The Independent* (London), 28 April 2001.

_____. "Dream of Freedom Fades for Boy Lama." *The Independent* (London), 4 January 2001.

_____. *Knower of the Three Times.* London: Bloomsbury, forthcoming.

Cabezón, José Ignacio, and Roger R. Jackson. *Tibetan Literature: Studies in Genre.* Ithaca, N.Y.: Snow Lion Publishers, 1996.

Chopra, Swati. "New Body, Old Mind." *Tricycle: The Buddhist Review* (spring 2002), 43-45, 93-97.

Chuahan, Pratibha. "Karmapa Desires to Go to Rumtek." *The Tribune* (Chandigarh, India), 30 June 2000.

"Child Lama forced to leave monastery following Karmapa escape." *TIN News Update* (Internet), 2 July 2001.

Dagyab Rinpoche. *Buddhist Symbols in Tibetan Culture.* Boston: Wisdom Publications, 1995.

Dalai Lama, His Holiness the. "Address at the Tibetan Institute of Performing Arts." Dharamsala, India, 7 March 2000. Translated by Alexander Nariniani, March 2000.

———. Public Talk. Namgyal Monastery, Dharamsala, India, 21 August 2001.

Dargye, Lama. Conversation. Sidhbari, Dharamsala, India, 14 June 2002.

Dorje, Gyurme. *Tibet Handbook.* Bath, England: Footprint Handbooks, 1999.

Douglas, Nik, and Meryl White. *Karmapa, The Black Hat Lama of Tibet.* London: Luzac, 1976.

Drupön Dechen Rinpoche. Interview. Tsurphu Monastery, Tibet, 23 July, 1992.

———. Interview. 9 and 10 June, 1992. Video recording by Richard Koch and Ward Holmes. Honolulu: Tsurphu Foundation, 1992.

Fan Kow, Jan trans. *His Holiness the XVIIth Gyalwa Karmapa.* Edited by Lee Chin Tee. Malaysia: 1993. In Chinese and English.

Gampopa. *The Jewel Ornament of Liberation.* Translated by Khenpo Konchog Gyaltsen Rinpoche. Ithaca, N.Y.: Snow Lion Publications, 1998.

———. *Gems of Dharma, Jewels of Freedom.* Translated by Ken and Katia Holmes. Forres, Scotland: Altea Publishing, 1994.

Garfield, Jay L. *The Fundamental Wisdom of the Middle Way: Nagarjuna's Mūlamadhyamakakārikā.* New York: Oxford University Press, 1995.

Gethin, Rupert. *The Foundations of Buddhism.* New York: Oxford University Press, 1998.

Hilton, Isabel. "Flight of the Lama." *New York Times Magazine,* 12 March 2000, 50-55.

Holmes, Ken. *His Holiness the 17th Gyalwa Karmapa Urgyen Trinley Dorje.* Forres, Scotland: Altea Publishing, 1995.

Holmes, Ward. *In the Footsteps of the Buddha.* 75 min. Honolulu: Tsurphu Foundation, 2001, videocassette.

———. *The Lion Begins to Roar.* 80 min. Honolulu: Tsurphu Foundation, 2000, videocassette.

———. *The XVII Karmapa Returns to Tsurphu.* 90 min. Honolulu: Tsurphu Foundation, 1993, videocassette.

———. *The Thangka Ceremony.* 25 min. Honolulu: Tsurphu Foundation, 1994, videocassette.

Holy Places of the Buddha. Crystal Mirror Series, vol.9. Berkeley: Dharma Publishing, 1994.

"Investigation into Karmapa Escape; Parents Detained by Authorities." *TIN News Update* (Internet), 29 February 2000.

Jackson, David. *A History of Tibetan Painting.* Vienna: Verlag der Österreichischen Akademie der Wissenschaften, 1996.

Jamgön Kongtrul. *The Torch of Certainty.* Translated by Judith Hanson. Boston: Shambhala Publications, 1977.

Jamgön Kongtrul Labrang. *EMA HO! The Reincarnation of The Third Jamgön Kongtrul.* Pullahari, Nepal, 1998.

Jamgön Kongtrul Lodrö Thaye. *The Autobiography of Jamgön Kongtrul: A Gem of Many Colors.* Translated by Richard Barron (Chökyi Nyima). Ithaca, N.Y.: Snow Lion Publications, 2003.

_____. *Shes bya mdzod (Treasury of Knowledge)*, Palpung edition. 4 vols. Kathmandu: Zhechen Publications. Kathmandu: Drugpa Kagyu Heritage Project, 2000 [Electronic version].

Kagyu Thubten Chöling. *Karmapa: The Sacred Prophecy.* Wappingers Falls, N.Y.: Kagyu Thubten Chöling Publications Committee, 1999.

Kapstein, Matthew T. *The Tibetan Assimilation of Buddhism: Conversion, Contestation, and Memory.* Oxford: Oxford University Press, 2000.

Karma Lekshey Ling. *His Holiness the XVIIth Gyalwang Karmapa.* Kathmandu: n.p., 1992.

Karma Thinley. *The History of the Sixteen Karmapas of Tibet.* Boulder, Colo: Prajna Press, 1980.

Karmapa, Gyalwa, the Ninth, Wangchuk Dorje. "Vajra Songs of the Masters" in *Phyag chen nges don rgya mtsho (Mahamudra: An Ocean of Certainty).* Translated by Michele Martin. Kathmandu: Marpa Institute, n.d.

Karmapa, Gyalwa, the Seventeenth, Ogyen Trinley Dorje. Conversation. Sidhbari, Dharamsala, India, 25 April 2001, 29 April 2001, 18 May 2002, 8 June 2002, 5 July 2002.

_____. Press Statement and Transcript of the Press Conference at Gyutö Ramoche University, Sidhbari, Dharamsala, India, 27 April 2001.

Karmapa, Gyalwa, the Seventh, Chodrak Gyamtso. *Tsad ma legs par bshad pa thams cad kyi chu bo yongs su 'dus ba rigs pa'i gzhung lugs kyi rgya mtsho zhes bya ba bzhugs so (An Ocean of Reasoning That Completely Contains the Rivers of All the Excellent Explanations of Pramana).* 2 vols. Sarnath, India: Kagyud Relief and Protection Committee, 1999.

Karmapa, Gyalwa, the Sixteenth, Rangjung Rigpe Dorje. *The Lion's Roar: The Life and Times of Tibetan Master His Holiness the 16th Karmapa.* Produced by James

Hoagland and Kenneth H. Green. Directed and edited by Mark Elliot. 50 min. Centre Productions, 1985, videocassette.

"Karmapa Leaves Tibet." *TIN News Update* (Internet), 7 January 2000.

Kuby, Clemens. *An Interview with Jamgön Kongtrul Rinpoche.* 30 min. Munich: Kuby Film TV, 23 March 1992.

_____. *Living Buddha.* Feature film, 108 min. Munich: Kuby Film TV, 1994.

_____ and Ulli Olvedi. *Living Buddha: Die siebzehnte Wiedergeburt des Karmapa in Tibet.* Munich: Goldman Verlag, 1994.

Lama Tenam. Conversation. Sidhbari, Dharamsala, India, 17 May 2002, 8 June 2002.

Lati Rinpochay and Denma Lochö Rinpochay. *Meditative States in Tibetan Buddhism.* Translated by Leah Zahler and Jeffrey Hopkins. Boston: Wisdom Publications, 1983, 1997.

Library of the Rumtek Shedra. *dPal rGyal dbang karmapa sku phreng bcu bdun pa chen po'i zhabs brtan khag phyogs gcig tu bkod pa bzungs so* (*A Collection of the Long Life Prayers for the Great Seventeenth Incarnation of the Gyalwang Karmapa*). n.d. Input by Lama Tashi Gawa.

Lodrö, Nyerpa. "An Account of the Search to Find the Reincarnation of the Gyalwa Karmapa." Tsurphu, Tibet. Unpublished. 1992.

_____. Interview. Tsurphu, Tibet, 14 July 1992.

Maitreya through Asanga. *Byams chos sde lnga'i rtsa ba phyogs bsdebs* (*The Collection of the Root Texts of the Five Texts of Maitreya*). Sarnath, India: Kagyud Relief and Protection Committee, 1984.

_____. *Buddha Nature: The Mahayana Uttaratantra Shastra.* Commentary by Jamgön Kongtrul Lodrö Thaye. Explanations by Khenpo Tsultrim Gyamtso Rinpoche. Translated by Rosemarie Fuchs. Ithaca, N.Y.: Snow Lion Publications, 2000.

_____. *The Changeless Nature.* Translated by Ken and Katia Holmes. Eskdalemuir, Scotland: Karma Drubgyu Darjay Ling, 1985.

Mandala Maps. *Mustang.* Kathmandu: Mandala Graphic Art, n.d.

Mazumdar, Sudip and Melinda Liu. "Inside the Dramatic Escape of a Living Buddha." *Newsweek.* 27 February 2000.

McLeod, Ken. *The Great Path of Awakening.* Boston: Shambhala Publications, 1987.

Milarepa. *rNal 'byor gyi dbang phyug chen po mi la ras pa'i rnam mgur* (*The Songs of the Great and Powerful Yogi Milarepa*). Ziling: mTsho sngon mi rigs par khang, 1981, 1989.

Mipham Rinpoche, Jamgön. *Gateway to Knowledge.* Translated by Erik Pema Kunzang. 2 vols. Hong Kong: Rangjung Yeshe Publications, 1997, 2000.

Nagarjuna. *dBu ma rtsa ba shes rab (The Fundamental Wisdom of the Middle Way). dBu ma rig tshogs lnga (The Five Collections of Reasoning).* Sarnath, India: Sakya Students' Union, 1994.

Namgyal, Tendzin. "Dus gsum rGyal ba thams chad kyi phrin las (*The Activity of All the Buddhas of the Three Times*)." Sidhbari, Dharamsala, India. Unpublished. 2001.

Nenang Lama. *dPal ldan dpa' bo sku phreng rnams dang gdan sa gnas nang gi lo rgyus mdor bsdus (A Brief History of the Garland of Incarnations of the Glorious Pawo and His Seat of Nenang).* Tölung Dechen, Tibet: Nenang Monastery, n. d.

_____. Conversation. Sidhbari, Dharamsala, India, 6 May 2001, 14 May 2002.

Padmakara Translation Group, *Introduction to the Middle Way: Chandrakirti's* Madhyamakavatara *with Commentary by Jamgön Mipham.* Boston: Shambhala Publications, 2002.

Peldzom, Ngodrup. Conversation. Sidhbari, Dharamsala, India, 10 July 2001, 19 July 2001, and 17 May 2002.

Pelzang, Rinchen. *mTsurphu dgon gyi dkar chag kun gsel me long (The All-Illuminating Mirror: An Index of Tsurphu Monastery).* Sichuan: Mirig Pedrun Khang, 1995.

Pettit, John W. *Mipham's Beacon of Certainty: Illuminating the View of Dzogchen, the Great Perfection.* Boston: Wisdom Publications, 1999.

Peissel, Michel. *Mustang, A Lost Kingdom.* Delhi: Book Faith India, 1992.

Popham, Peter. "The Most Powerful Teenager in the World Breaks His Long Silence." *The Independent* (London), 28 April 2001.

Rabten, Geshe. *Echoes of Voidness.* Translated and edited by Stephen Batchelor. London: Wisdom Publications, 1983, 1986.

Rigzin, Tsepak. *Tibetan-English Dictionary of Buddhist Terminology.* Dharamsala, India: Library of Tibetan Works and Archives, 1986, 1993.

Shangri-la Maps. *A Trekking Map of Mustang.* Kathmandu: Shangri-la Design, 2000.

Shantideva. *The Way of the Bodhisattva.* Translated by the Padmakara Translation Group. Boston: Shambhala Publications, 1997.

_____. *A Guide to the Bodhisattva Way of Life.* Translated by Vesna A. Wallace and B. Alan Wallace. Ithaca, N.Y.: Snow Lion Publications, 1997.

Situ Rinpoche. "A Brief Introduction and Clarification." Public letter, dated 15 June 2002.

_____. Interview. Lhasa, Tibet, 2 August 1992, 26 September 1992; Sidhbari, Dharamsala, India,1 June 2002.

Smith, E. Gene. *Among Tibetan Texts*. Boston: Wisdom Publications, 2001.

Snellgrove, David. *Himalayan Pilgrimage*. Boston: Shambhala Publications, 1989.

_____. *Buddhist Himalaya*. Kathmandu: Himalayan Booksellers, 1995.

Sonam, Tenzing. "Out of the Red: The Karmapa's Daring Escape from China Keeps Hope Alive for Tibetans." *Time* (Asian edition) 22 April 2002.

Tendzin Gyurme, Lama. Conversation. Tsurphu Monastery, Tibet, 28 July 1992.

Thondup, Tulku. *Masters of Meditation and Miracles*. Boston: Shambhala Publications, 1996.

Thrangu Rinpoche. *A Commentary on The Uttara Tantra Shastra*. Delhi: Sri Satguru Publications, 1989.

_____. Conversation. Sarnath, India, 2 March 2002; Woodstock. N.Y., 9 August 2002.

_____. Talk at Karma Triyana Dharmachakra, 11 August 2002.

Trungpa, Chögyam. *Training the Mind and Cultivating Loving-Kindness*. Boston: Shambhala Publications, 1993.

Tsewang Tashi. Conversation. Sidhbari, Dharamsala, India, July 2, 2002,

Tsogyal, Yeshe. *The Lotus-Born: The Life Story of Padmasambhava*. Translated by Erik Pema Kunsang. Boston: Shambhala Publications, 1993.

Tsong Khapa, Jey. *The Central Philosophy of Tibet*. Translated by Robert Thurman. Princeton: Princeton University Press, 1984.

Tsurphu Labrang. *The Life Story of His Holiness the Gyalwa Karmapa* from 1992 to 2000. Tsurphu Monastery, Tibet.

West, Jean. "The Boy Buddha." *The Herald Saturday Magazine* (Scotland) 24 July 2001.

Websites:

www.asianart.com/tsurphu/ relates the story of the large appliqué thangkas made for Tsurphu.

www.kagyu.org is the website of Karma Triyana Dharmachakra, the Karmapa's main seat in Woodstock, N.Y., providing current and background information on the Karmapa and Kagyu teachers plus links to sites of related centers and their teachers.

www.kagyuoffice.org is a website of the Karmapa with news of events related to him and background information on him and the Golden Rosary of the Kagyu lineage.

www.jamgonkongtrul.org is the official website of the fourth Jamgön Kongtrul Rinpoche, which lists his activities, retreat centers, and practice and study courses at his main seat of Pullahari in Nepal, plus many projects for social benefit.

www.ktgrinpoche.org is the website of Khenpo Tsultrim Gyamtso, who travels extensively to teach and is one of the Karmapa's teachers.

www.nalandabodhi.org. From Dzogchen Ponlop Rinpoche, this site provides references, excerpts, and analysis of current news about the Karmapa, plus photos, background analysis, and an extensive news archive dating from his arrival in India.

www.rinpoche.com is the website of Khenchen Thrangu Rinpoche, the Karmapa's tutor, who also travels worldwide to teach and fosters many educational and humanitarian projects.

www.rumtek.org is under the auspices of Rumtek Monastery and Bardor Tulku Rinpoche and provides information on the Karmapa.

www.shenpen-osel.org is the website of Kagyu Shenpen Ösel Chöling in Seattle, Washington. It provides a wealth of teachings from Kagyu teachers, including Situ Rinpoche, Thrangu Rinpoche, Khenpo Tsultrim Gyamtso, Tenga Rinpoche, and the late Kalu Rinpoche.

SITUATED ON Overlook Mountain in Woodstock, New York, the principal seat of the Karmapas in North America is known as Karma Triyana Dharmachakra (KTD). In 1976, at the request of his many new students, the sixteenth Gyalwa Karmapa founded the monastery and envisioned it as a center for the spreading of Buddhist study and practice in the West.

From its inception, KTD has sought to preserve the authentic teachings of Buddhism and to make available the tradition of the Kagyu lineage with its meditation practices, liturgy, and empowerments. Each year some of the most skilled and learned Kagyu masters visit from near and far to give teachings in the magnificent shrine room. Each day, the lamas and staff invite students and visitors to join in meditation and chanting pujas.

The two lamas in residence at KTD have dedicated their lives to carrying out the Karmapa's vision. Khenpo Karthar Rinpoche, abbot and senior teacher, is recognized around the world as an erudite scholar, monk, and meditation master. Bardor Tulku Rinpoche, the third in the Barway Dorje line of incarnations, lives with his family adjacent to the monastery, and in addition to teaching at KTD, guides and instructs at the many affiliate centers linked with the monastery. Under the auspices of the Karma Kagyu Institute, KTD has established an educational curriculum that includes a Tibetan language program, teachings on the traditional arts of painting (thangkas), making ritual offering sculptures (tormas), and playing the ceremonial instruments. The practices and seminars at KTD are open to all seeking to attain a mindful and compassionate way of life through meditation and the study of the Buddhism found in Tibet. All the many aspects of activity at KTD are dedicated for the benefit of every living being.